THE GUIDE FOR
JUNIOR GIRL SCOUT LEADERS

Girl Scouts of the U.S.A.

420 Fifth Avenue

New York, N.Y. 10018-2702

GIRL SCOUTS OF THE U.S.A.®

B. LaRae Orullian, *National President*

Mary Rose Main, *National Executive Director*

Inquiries related to *The Guide for Junior Girl Scout Leaders* should be directed to Membership and Program, Girl Scouts of the U.S.A., 420 Fifth Avenue, New York, N.Y. 10018-2702.

First Impression 1994

Printed in the United States of America

ISBN 0-88441-282-2

10   9   8   7   6   5   4   3

This book is printed on recyclable paper.

Credits

Authors
Judith Brucia
Rose Cryan
Sharon Woods Hussey
Harriet S. Mosatche, Ph.D.

Contributors
Chris Bergerson
Janice Cummings
Martha Jo Dennison
Toni Eubanks
Joan W. Fincutter
Karen Unger-Sparks

Editor
Janet Lombardi

Designer
Kaeser and Wilson Design Ltd.

Illustrators
Fanny Berry: *page 34*

Photographers
Cover: Ameen Howrani, Robert Foothorap
Fashion Shots: Anthony Edgeworth
Still Lifes: Fred Schenk Studios

CONTENTS

INTRODUCTION

Welcome to Junior Girl Scouts! Girls between the ages of eight and eleven are experiencing exciting changes in their lives. You, the Junior Girl Scout leader, play a vital role in helping Junior Girl Scouts explore their feelings, ideas, dreams, and the wonderful opportunities that await them. The purpose of *The Guide for Junior Girl Scout Leaders* is to help make this undertaking enjoyable and enriching for the girls and you!

How This Book is Organized

This leader's guide is really two books in one. Part I contains information about the Girl Scout program that cannot be found in the girls' handbook. Part II contains a complete edition of the *Junior Girl Scout Handbook.* Each page is reproduced exactly as it appears in the girls' handbook. Your version, however, contains additional program activities, safety tips, helpful hints, and program links. This information appears on the page next to each set of reproduced handbook pages.

To familiarize yourself with the book's organization, scan the contents pages and each chapter. Don't try to read this book in one sitting or memorize the contents. This guide is intended as a reference tool to use from time to time. You would use this guide to find out the answer to a question that came up in your troop or group meeting, for example. You might also use this book to get information about:

▲ Completing activities

▲ Religious recognitions

▲ Girl Scout resources

▲ Planning for troop or group meetings

▲ Managing troop or group money

▲ Creating and using a program trail

To help you organize and record ideas, this guide includes such tools as planning charts and activity checklists.

WHAT IS GIRL SCOUTING
CHAPTER 1

About Girl Scouting

Values in Girl Scouting

Girl Scouting is a values-based organization. When Juliette Gordon Low started the Girl Scout movement in the United States in 1912, she wanted to build an organization that would provide exciting opportunities for girls within the framework of a positive values-based movement. Today, these values, as expressed in the Girl Scout Promise and Law, continue to be the force that unites Girl Scouts nationwide.

Having a strong value system adds meaning and purpose to life. Girl Scouting promotes the development of values. Through program activities and events, Girl Scouting encourages girls to apply and strengthen values learned at home, school, and through religious instruction. Girl Scout activities and events also help girls appreciate the importance of values in their individual lives. Girl Scouting recognizes that the family is the primary educator when it comes to teaching values. The job of adults in Girl Scouting is to supplement and reinforce those values in an informal, educational setting.

THE GIRL SCOUT PROMISE

On my honor, I will try:

To serve God and my country,

To help people at all times,

And to live by the Girl Scout Law.

THE GIRL SCOUT LAW

I will do my best:

to be honest

to be fair

to help where I am needed

to be cheerful

to be friendly and considerate

to be a sister to every Girl Scout

to respect authority

to use resources wisely

to protect and improve the world around me

to show respect for myself and others through my words and actions

Religion in Girl Scouting

The motivating force in Girl Scouting is a spiritual one. Each girl pursues her own religious or spiritual beliefs and is expected to respect the beliefs and practices of others. Affiliation with an organized religion is not required.

When girls become Girl Scouts, they make the Girl Scout Promise and Law as part of their membership requirement. In the Girl Scout Promise, the word "God" is used to represent the spiritual foundation of the Girl Scout movement. "On my honor, I will try to serve God" is how the Promise appears in print, the same as it has been since the beginning of the movement over eighty years ago. Most girls when saying the Promise will use the word "God." For some girls, however, words other than "God" may be used to express their spiritual beliefs. Because Girl Scouting encourages respect for the beliefs of others, girls may substitute for the word "God" in the Girl Scout Promise the word that most closely expresses their personal spiritual beliefs.

For most girls in your troop or group, there will be no change in the way they make the Girl Scout Promise. If the word "God" is not the most relevant word for a girl and there is any question about which word is most appropriate, you can work with her, her family, and religious leaders to find a substitute word or phrase to say. You will not find a list of appropriate substitutions from which to choose. The way a girl fulfills her beliefs is an individual matter and is not defined by Girl Scouting. You are not expected to judge the suitability of the word she has chosen.

If you have questions or concerns, contact your Girl Scout council office for assistance.

See page 32 for information about religious recognitions available through Girl Scouting.

The Value in Diversity

As the United States grows more diverse, it is imperative that children learn acceptance and cooperation. Because Girl Scouting brings together girls from different racial, ethnic, religious, and socioeconomic backgrounds as well as girls with varying levels of physical and mental abilities, it offers an ideal environment for them to explore different cultures and better understand others. Girl Scouting is committed to promoting pluralism and to helping girls identify and eliminate prejudicial behavior in themselves and others.

The All-Girl Environment

Girl Scouting exists to serve girls. Girl Scouting's history shows that girls have unique needs and interests best met in a program designed specifically for them in an all-girl environment. Research studies have consistently demonstrated that girls often receive less attention and fewer leadership opportunities when in groups with boys. The all-girl setting allows girls to test their abilities without the pressure and competitiveness that frequently characterize co-educational situations. Furthermore, when girls first develop abilities in all-girl settings, they are more likely to use these skills in mixed groups.

In Girl Scouting, girls are the focus in an environment that aims to provide them with self-confidence and skills. In addition, in Girl Scouting girls routinely see women in positions of authority. This helps them understand that women can and do excel in leadership positions as well as in different careers and endeavors.

Girl Scouts of the United States of America is part of the World Association of Girl Guides and Girl Scouts (WAGGGS), the international organization dedicated to the development of girls. All national organizations that are members of WAGGGS share a common history. Robert Baden-Powell, First Baron Baden-Powell of Gilwell, England, founded the Scouting movement in 1908.

How Girl Scouting Began

In 1909, a Boy Scout rally was held in London at the Crystal Palace, a worldwide technological fair, where 6,000 girls turned up proclaiming themselves to be Girl Scouts. Recognizing that girls needed a program suited to their needs and interests, Lord Baden-Powell decided they should have an organization of their own. His sister, Agnes, assumed this undertaking, and by 1910, the Girl Guides Association in the United Kingdom was officially formed. As the movement spread, some countries used the term "Girl Guides" and others "Girl Scouts," but both names have come to represent those who embody the qualities of self-reliance, resourcefulness, common sense, and courage.

Juliette Gordon Low, a friend of the Baden-Powells, was enthralled with the idea of a youth organization for girls. In 1912, she founded Girl Scouting in the United States.

The World Association of Girl Guides and Girl Scouts

From these beginnings, WAGGGS has grown to 128 national Girl Guide/Girl Scout organizations with a total membership of approximately eight million members. National organizations must abide by the Constitution and bylaws of WAGGGS, have their own constitutions approved by the World Committee, adopt the methods of Girl Guiding and Girl Scouting, incorporate a trefoil in their badges, pay an annual quota (or dues), and send an annual report of their work to the World Bureau, the secretariat of WAGGGS.

Member organizations share common symbols. The trefoil is the unifying symbol of WAGGGS, and is used on the World Trefoil pin and the World Flag. Each national organization has a Promise, a motto, a left handshake, the sign or salute, and the World Song. These symbols remind all members that they belong to a worldwide organization.

Thinking Day is a celebration that all members of WAGGGS share annually on February 22, the joint birthday of Lord and Lady Baden-Powell. Girl Guides and Girl Scouts meet on this day to think of their sisters worldwide and to give voluntary contributions to the Thinking Day Fund. Contributions are used to promote Girl Guiding/Girl Scouting in underprivileged or isolated areas, to assist with training, or to support projects that deal with the problems of malnutrition, illiteracy, or the disabled.

The World Centers

The World Association of Girl Guides and Girl Scouts maintains four centers, each in a different part of the world. Girl Scouts who are 14 years or older may stay at these centers and experience the opportunities offered at each center.

Our Chalet, located in Adelboden, Switzerland, was founded in 1932. A gift to WAGGGS from Helen Storrow of Boston, Massachusetts, the center is high in the Swiss Alps and focuses on the out-of-doors, with hiking and climbing in the warm months, and skiing and other winter sports in the cold months.

Olave Centre, located in London, England, was founded in 1939 and serves as the home of the World Bureau and as a world center. The center includes a new facility called Pax Lodge where program and training events for Girl Guides and Girl Scouts take place.

Our Cabaña, located in Cuernavaca, Mexico, was founded in 1957. Girl Guides and Girl Scouts can learn about Mexican culture, customs, and crafts, and participate in special service and outdoor projects.

Sangam, located in Pune, India, was founded in 1966. At Sangam, which means "coming together," Girl Guides and Girl Scouts from all over the world have an opportunity to work together on activities and projects.

Girl Scout Membership

Membership in Girl Scouting entitles girls to participate in Girl Scout program activities and other Girl Scout-sponsored events, with adults serving in a leadership capacity. Both girls and adults are entitled (but not required) to wear the appropriate uniform and insignia, and to be covered by Girl Scout Activity Accident Insurance. In addition, adult members receive *Girl Scout Leader*, the official Girl Scouts of the U.S.A. magazine, and are entitled to receive training, consultation, and ongoing assistance.

Active membership as a Girl Scout is granted to any girl who:

▲ Has made the Girl Scout Promise and accepted the Girl Scout Law.

▲ Has paid annual membership dues.

▲ Meets the applicable membership standards.

The membership standards for Junior Girl Scouts are that girls must be ages eight, nine, ten, or eleven, or in grades three, four, five, or six. Any girl who meets or can meet these membership requirements shall not be denied active participation in Girl Scouting because of race, color, ethnicity, creed, disability, national origin, or socioeconomic status.

Active membership as a Girl Scout adult is granted to any person who:

▲ Accepts the principles and beliefs as stated in the Preamble of the Girl Scout Constitution (consult *Leader's Digest: Blue Book of Basic Documents*).

▲ Has paid annual membership dues.

▲ Is at least 18 years old.

Registration Procedures

The Girl Scout membership year is October 1st to September 30th. You or the coordinator of a Girl Scout troop or group are responsible for registering all girl and adult members in the troop or group, and collecting national membership dues each year. Your council supplies you with both registration forms and detailed instructions. If additional members join during the year, be sure to register them promptly so that they can receive the full benefit of Girl Scout membership.

The Girl Scout program is based on four goals. Each of these goals specifies how girls will grow and develop through the Girl Scout experience. The Girl Scout program goals serve as a useful tool in planning activities with girls. When you keep in mind these program goals, you help ensure that girls benefit from the complete Girl Scout experience.

Girl Scout Program

The Four Program Goals

The four program goals are:

1. Develop to her full individual potential.

Foster feelings of self-acceptance and unique self-worth.

Promote her perception as competent, responsible, and open to new experiences and challenges.

Offer opportunities to learn new skills.

Encourage personal growth.

Allow girls to utilize and practice talents and abilities.

2. Relate to others with increasing understanding, skill, and respect.

Help each girl develop sensitivity to others and respect for their needs, feelings, and rights.

Promote an understanding and appreciation of individual, cultural, religious, and racial differences.

Foster the ability to build friendships and working relationships.

3. Develop values to guide her actions and to provide the foundation for sound decision-making.

Help her develop a meaningful set of values and ethics that will guide her actions.

Foster an ability to make decisions that are consistent with her values and that reflect respect for the rights and needs of others.

Empower her to act upon her values and convictions.

Encourage her to reexamine her ideals as she matures.

4. Contribute to the improvement of society through the use of her abilities and leadership skills, working in cooperation with others.

Help her develop concern for the well-being of her community and its people.

Promote an understanding of how the quality of community life affects her own life and the whole of society.

Encourage her to use her skills to work with others for the benefit of all.

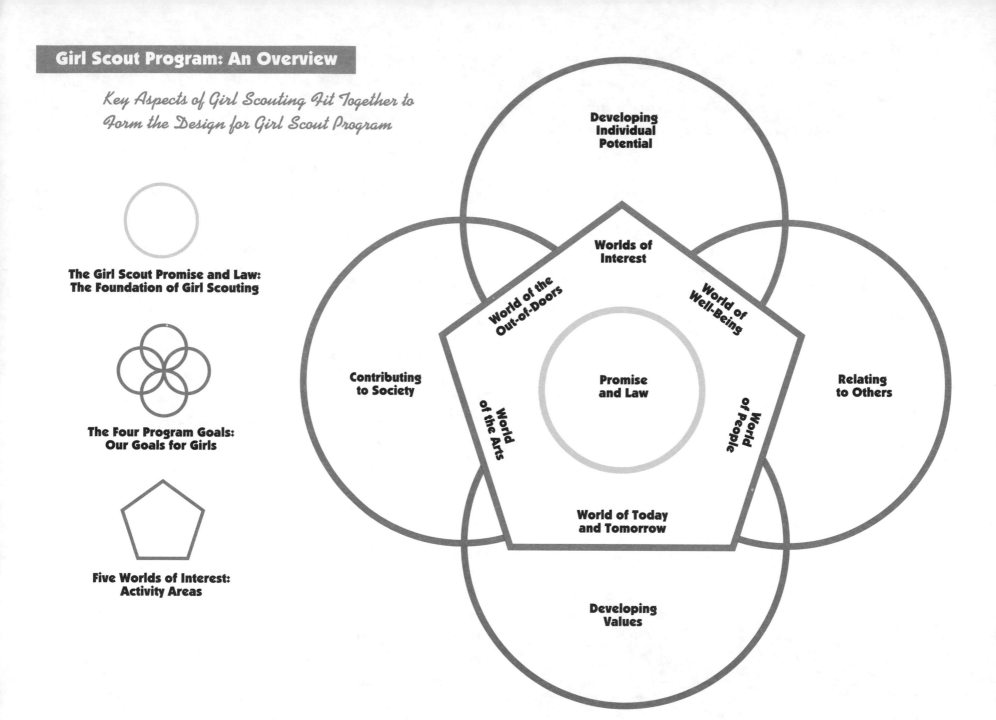

Key Aspects of Girl Scouting Fit Together to Form the Design for Girl Scout Program

The Girl Scout Promise and Law:
The Foundation of Girl Scouting

The Four Program Goals:
Our Goals for Girls

Five Worlds of Interest:
Activity Areas

Developing
Individual
Potential

Worlds of
Interest

World of the
Out-of-Doors

World of
Well-Being

Contributing
to Society

Promise
and Law

Relating
to Others

World
of the Arts

World
of People

World of Today
and Tomorrow

Developing
Values

The Worlds of Interest

Girl Scout program activities are divided into five worlds of interest: The World of Well-Being, the World of People, the World of Today and Tomorrow, the World of the Arts, and the World of the Out-of-Doors. It is useful to keep in mind the worlds of interest when planning activities with girls. This structure provides a framework for ensuring balance among troop activities and helps keep girls interested in Girl Scouting. Check from time to time that the activities your troop or group has completed, or is planning, cut across the five worlds of interest.

The World of Well-Being includes activities that focus on physical and emotional health: nutrition and exercise, feelings and self-awareness, personal relationships, sports, games, leisure-time activities, as well as home, safety, consumer awareness, and careers.

The World of People includes activities that focus on developing awareness of the various cultures in our society and around the world, and on building pride in one's heritage while appreciating and respecting the backgrounds of others.

The World of Today and Tomorrow includes activities that focus on discovering the how and why of things, exploring and experimenting with the many technologies encountered in daily life, dealing with change, looking to future events, roles, and responsibilities.

The World of the Arts includes activities that focus on enjoying and expressing oneself through art forms, appreciating the artistic talents and contributions of others, and learning more about the visual, performing, and literary arts.

The World of the Out-of-Doors includes activities that focus on enjoying and appreciating the out-of-doors, living in and caring for our natural environment, and understanding and respecting the interdependence of all living things.

Many of the activities in the *Junior Girl Scout Handbook* connect to more than one world of interest. For example, in Chapter Two of the handbook, girls will find an activity that suggests they observe how the media portray women, children, and men. This activity could fall into the World of People since it relates to portrayals of people and the World of Today and Tomorrow because it refers to technology in today's world. Although an activity may relate to more than one world of interest, it is still a good idea to make sure activities are not too concentrated in any one or two areas.

Delivery of Girl Scout Program

Girls and adults can participate in Girl Scout program in various ways, including:

Girl Scout Troops or Groups. A Girl Scout troop or group is a group of girls of similar age or grade who meet throughout the year under the guidance of trained, caring adults to explore new things, and to plan and carry out a wide variety of Girl Scout program activities.

Individually Registered Members. If becoming part of a Girl Scout troop or group is not possible for a girl, she may choose to register as an individual member. As an individual girl member, she can still choose to participate in councilwide and neighborhood events and trips. She also can use the Girl Scout handbook for her age level and earn Girl Scout recognitions.

Special-Interest Groups. Special-interest groups provide for more in-depth exploration of various topics (for example, outdoor survival skills or sports). They are usually organized as short-term Girl Scout program experiences. Adults serve as consultants and resource people.

Girl Scout Events. Girl Scout councils often sponsor special program activities for girls in their own councils and may also invite girls from other Girl Scout councils. These events include career days, trips and tours, and camping weekends. Adults serve in various roles, such as consultants, special resource people, and coordinators.

Activity Centers. Activity centers are neighborhood facilities serving as the sites for organized Girl Scout program activities. They operate at varying times during the year (after-school hours, on weekend days, etc.). In some cases, the centers accommodate a number of different age levels. An adult serves as director of the center and works with others to help girls carry out Girl Scout program activities.

Girl Scouting in the School Day. Girl Scout program activities can be carried out as a part of the regularly scheduled school day. Adult volunteers serve as group leaders, consultants, and coordinators.

For further information about any of these systems, their availability in your area, or ways to become involved, contact your local Girl Scout council office.

Being Safety-Wise

All Girl Scout program activities should meet the program standards and guidelines as stated in *Safety-Wise*. *Safety-Wise* aims to establish a safe and sound program experience that will protect and maintain the well-being of every Girl Scout. *Safety-Wise* provides general safety guidelines as well as specifics for some common Girl Scout activities.

Every Girl Scout leader receives a copy of *Safety-Wise*. One of your major responsibilities as a Girl Scout leader is to provide for the safety and security of girls. In addition to the program standards discussed here, you should carefully read the introduction to *Safety-Wise*, and the chapters "Basic Safety and Security Guidelines" and "Planning Trips with Girls." Once you are familiar with this content, turn to either the Table of Contents or the Index for page references that apply to a specific activity your troop or group is planning. Terms important to health and safety in Girl Scouting are defined in the glossary.

Girl Scout Program Standards

As a Girl Scout leader, you must be familiar with the 35 Girl Scout program standards in *Safety-Wise*. These standards describe how to put the principles of the Girl Scout program into practice and outline the necessary elements of a quality program experience. The standards also describe basic health, safety, and security practices that provide for the well-being of girls in your troop or group. Each standard is followed by specific guidelines that more fully illustrate what must be accomplished to meet each standard. Your Girl Scout council will provide assistance in interpreting and applying each of these standards.

1. Girl Scout Program—Foundation and Goals

Program experiences and activities should meet the needs and interests of girls, be based on the Girl Scout Promise and Law, and enable girls to grow and develop, as described in the four Girl Scout program goals.

2. General Activities

Program activities should include a balance of subject and interest areas. The types of activities should be determined in partnership by the girls and their leaders and reflect the girls' needs and interests, physical and emotional readiness, skill level, and preparation. The activities should provide for progressive learning experiences, both at the current age level and in preparation for the next one.

3. Health, Safety, and Security—Activity Planning Implementation

At all times, the health, safety, and security of girls should be paramount. All activities should be planned and carried out so as to safeguard the health, safety, and general well-being of girls and adults. Girls and adults should follow proper safety practices at all times.

4. International

Girl Scouting is part of a worldwide movement, and program activities should emphasize this international dimension.

5. Service

Service is inherent in the Promise and Law and is given without expectation of payment or reward. All girls should take part in service activities or projects.

6. Experiences Beyond the Troop/Group

Girls should have experiences that broaden their perspectives and enable them to interact with individuals beyond their immediate group. Program activities should provide girls with opportunities to have experiences beyond regular troop/group meetings.

7. Outdoor Education

Activities carried out in outdoor settings are an important part of Girl Scout program for each age level. The leader should receive the appropriate training from her council to help her guide preparation for and implementation of the outdoor activities.

8. Girl Scout Camping

Girl Scout camping should provide girls with a fun and educational group living experience that links Girl Scout program with the natural surroundings and contributes to each camper's mental, physical, social, and spiritual growth.

9. Girl Scout Recognitions

Girl Scout recognitions should acknowledge a girl's accomplishments and attainment of specified requirements. Leaders should work in partnership with girls to decide when recognitions, such as badges, patches, or awards, have been completed. At all times, adults should play a key role in stressing the quality of the program experience over quantity of recognitions.

10. Parental Permission

Written permission from a parent or legal guardian should be obtained for participation in Girl Scouting. Leaders and girls are responsible for informing parents or guardians of the purpose of Girl Scouting; of the date, time, and place of meetings; and of the type of activities included in troop plans. When activities take place outside of the scheduled meeting place, involve travel, or focus on sensitive or controversial topics, parents and guardians should be informed and asked to provide additional written consent.

11. Girl Scout Membership Pins and Uniforms

All Girl Scout members should wear the membership pin when participating in Girl Scout activities. Since Girl Scouting is a uniformed organization, girl and adult members should be informed, at the time they become members, that they are entitled to wear the Girl Scout uniform appropriate for their age level. Although the wearing of the uniform is encouraged, it should be clearly conveyed that the wearing of the uniform is not required for participation in Girl Scouting.

12. Girl/Adult Partnership

Girls and their leaders should work as partners in planning and decision-making. Tasks should be sensitive to girls' developmental maturity and commensurate with their abilities, with each girl encouraged to proceed at her own pace. With each age level, the girls' opportunity to act independently and handle responsibilities should increase.

13. Troops/Groups

Each troop or group should have at least one adult leader and one or more assistant leaders. Because the female role model is essential to fulfilling the purpose of Girl Scouting, at least one member of the leadership team must be an adult female.

The adult leaders must be at least 18 years of age or at the age of majority defined by the state if it is older than 18. Leaders should have training as specified by the council. In addition, an active troop committee of registered adult members should provide ongoing support to the troop.

14. Health, Safety, and Security—Adult Supervision and Preparation

Proper adult supervision and guidance for each activity are essential. Adults with requisite expertise are part of the adult leadership when implementing activities. Adequate training and preparation for girls and adults precede participation in any activity.

15. Council Support to Adult Leadership

All adults within the Girl Scout council work in concert to ensure the highest quality program experience for girls. Communication and cooperation are essential for providing training, giving ongoing support to troops and groups, and obtaining appropriate activity approvals.

16. Program Consultants

The regular adult leadership of any Girl Scout group should be complemented by program consultants who possess technical competence and the ability to share specialized skills.

17. Program Centers

All centers and facilities used for Girl Scout program activities should have present at least one adult with appropriate qualifications and competencies to guide girls in the type of program conducted at the facility. Additional adults trained for their particular roles should be present in numbers required to provide adequate adult guidance for the ages of the girls, the size of the group, and the nature of the activity.

18. Adult Leadership— Girl Scout Camps

All Girl Scout camps should be staffed by adults who possess the qualifications and necessary competencies for the positions held.

19. Pluralism and Diversity of Troops/Groups

Girl Scout troops and groups should reflect the diversity of socioeconomic, racial, ethnic, cultural, religious, and disability groups in the community. Whenever possible, troops and groups should include girls from different age and grade levels.

20. Size of Troops/Groups

Girls should be able to participate in groupings large enough to provide experience in self-government and in groupings small enough to allow for development of the individual girl.

21. Meeting and Activity Planning

Troops and groups should meet often enough to fulfill the needs and interests of girls and to maintain continuity of their program experience.

22. Meeting Places/Camps/Sites

All meeting places, camps, and other sites used for Girl Scout program activities should provide a safe, clean, and secure environment and allow for participation of all girls.

23. Girl Scout Camps

All Girl Scout camps should be operated in compliance with local and state laws for maximum protection of campers' health, safety, and security, and with regard to protection of the natural environment.

24. Overnight Trips, Camping

All sites and facilities used for overnight trips or camping should be approved by the Girl Scout council.

25. Private Transportation

Private passenger cars, station wagons, and vans may be used during Girl Scout activities. They must be properly registered, insured, and operated by adults with a valid license for the type and size of vehicle used. Any other form of private transportation may be used only after council approval has been obtained.

26. Public Transportation

Public transportation and regularly scheduled airlines, buses, trains, and vessels should be used whenever possible.

27. Travel Procedures

All travel procedures and preparations should make provision for adequate adult supervision and maximum safety.

28. Activities Involving Money

Troops/groups should be financed by troop/group dues, by troop money-earning activities, and by a share of money earned through council-sponsored product sales. Daisy Girl Scouts may not be involved in handling any money, including troop dues and proceeds from troop money-earning activities and product sales.

29. Troop Money-Earning Activities

Money-earning activities should be a valuable program activity for girls. Daisy Girl Scouts do not participate in troop money-earning activities.

30. Council-Sponsored Product Sales

Troops/groups may participate in no more than two council-sponsored product sales each year and only one of these may be a cookie sale. A percentage of the money earned through product sales should be allocated to participating troops and groups. Daisy Girl Scouts may not sell cookies or other products.

31. Product Sale Incentives

Participation in a council product sale incentive plan should be optional for troops and individuals. Incentives, if used, should be program-related and of a type that will provide opportunities for girls to participate in Girl Scout activities.

32. Council Fund Raising

Fund raising or fund development to support the Girl Scout council is the responsibility of adults and this responsibility should not be placed with girls. Girls may provide support to these efforts through voluntary service.

33. Fund Raising for Other Organizations

Girl Scouts, in their Girl Scout capacities, may not solicit money for other organizations. Girl members may support other organizations only through service projects. (See national policy on solicitation of contributions in the *Leader's Digest: Blue Book of Basic Documents*.)

34. Collaborations with Other Organizations

When collaborative relationships or cooperative projects are developed with other organizations, all Girl Scout program standards are followed.

35. Political Activity

Girl Scouts, in their Girl Scout capacities, may not participate directly or indirectly in any political campaigns or participate in partisan efforts on behalf of or in opposition to a candidate for public office.

You, the Girl Scout leader, play the most important role in helping girls derive the many benefits of Girl Scouting. You guide girls through the process of learning and planning, and encourage them to do things for themselves. You help girls with difficult tasks and applaud their accomplishments.

The Girl Scout Leader

Characteristics

A Girl Scout leader should:

▲ Be sensitive to the girls and their needs. You may have girls in your troop or group who have difficulty reading or speaking English, who have a disability, or who are experiencing a crisis at home. You need to be non-judgmental and tolerant of differences. You can help meet the needs of these girls by recognizing the issue and showing that you care about each girl as an individual.

▲ Share her skills and talents with other adults. A leader who has just begun working with girls may benefit from the knowledge and skills of experienced leaders.

▲ Be flexible. You may find that you need to make a change in the direction of troop or group activities to maintain interest.

▲ Be aware of health and safety factors in activities. Allow the girls freedom to explore and try new interests, but consult *Safety-Wise* to make sure the safety standards are being followed. In your planning with girls, always have them discuss necessary safety precautions.

▲ Most importantly, have a sense of humor! Encourage fun, spontaneity, and creativity. Relax and enjoy the girls—show a positive attitude!

Responsibilities

Some specific responsibilities of the Girl Scout leader are:

▲ To maintain a balanced set of program activities, keeping in mind the four program goals and five worlds of interest.

▲ To meet with the troop or group on a regular basis (i.e., weekly, biweekly, monthly).

▲ To help girls develop as leaders.

▲ To help girls take responsibility for the affairs of the troop or group. Learn how to implement girl/adult planning.

▲ To understand the basic developmental characteristics and needs of Junior Girl Scouts.

▲ To be familiar with the Girl Scout program resources available to both you and girls, especially those for Junior Girl Scouts.

▲ To become a registered Girl Scout member. Make sure that all girls and other adults in your troop or group are registered.

▲ To ensure that troop or group records are maintained.

▲ To communicate or meet with each girl's parent(s) or guardian(s).

▲ To encourage the participation of people who can enrich Girl Scouting by sharing their skills and knowledge.

▲ To participate in Girl Scout leader training sessions sponsored by your council.

▲ To keep up-to-date on what's happening in Girl Scouting/ Girl Guiding locally, nationally, and worldwide.

▲ To know whom to contact if an emergency occurs during Girl Scout activities.

▲ To use effective communication skills.

▲ To be adept at troop or group management including time, activity, and finance management.

▲ To be aware of Girl Scouting's goal to be pluralistic and act to foster pluralism. (See the Contemporary Issues booklet, *Valuing Differences: Promoting Pluralism*.)

▲ To know the Girl Scout policies and procedures as stated in the *Leader's Digest: Blue Book of Basic Documents* as well as your local Girl Scout council's policies and procedures.

▲ To be familiar with and follow the health and safety practices required in Girl Scouting. Know and follow the Girl Scout program standards (see this chapter) and all other regulations covered in *Safety-Wise.*

THE JUNIOR GIRL SCOUT AGE LEVEL
CHAPTER 2

Girl Scouting at the Five Age Levels

Junior Girl Scouts are one of the five age levels in Girl Scouting: Daisy Girl Scouts, Brownie Girl Scouts, Junior Girl Scouts, Cadette Girl Scouts, and Senior Girl Scouts. The Girl Scout program is designed to meet developmental, educational, emotional, and social needs of girls at these five age levels. Each age level has a unique form of troop government, a system of recognitions, and a variety of supplementary resources that complement the age level handbook.

	Daisy Girl Scouts	Brownie Girl Scouts	Junior Girl Scouts	Cadette Girl Scouts	Senior Girl Scouts
Age or Grade	5-6 years old or kindergarten or first grade	6-8 years old or first, second, or third grade	8-11 years old or third, fourth, fifth, or sixth grade	11-14 years old or sixth, seventh, eighth, or ninth grade	14-17 years old or ninth, tenth, eleventh, or twelfth grade
Form of Troop Government	Daisy Girl Scout circle	Brownie Girl Scout Ring or Brownie Girl Scout circle	Patrol system, town meeting, or executive board	Patrol system, town meeting, or executive board	Patrol system, town meeting, or executive board
Recognitions	Bridge to Brownie Girl Scouts patch	Brownie Girl Scout Try-Its Bridge to Junior Girl Scouts patch Badges earned as part of bridging activities Religious recognitions	Badges (Dabbler, white, green, tan) Signs (Rainbow, Sun, Satellite, World) Junior Aide patch Bridge to Cadette Girl Scouts patch Religious recognitions Junior Girl Scout Leadership Pin	Interest project patches Tan badges Leader-in-Training pin Counselor-in-Training pin From Dreams to Reality patch Religious recognitions American Indian Youth Certificate and Award Cadette Girl Scout Challenge pin Cadette Girl Scout Leadership Award Girl Scout Silver Award Bridge to Senior Girl Scouts patch	Interest project patches, Leader-in-Training pin, Counselor-in-Training pin, From Dreams to Reality patch, Religious Recognitions, American Indian Youth Certificate and Award Ten-Year Award Girl Scout Gold Award Bridge to Adult Girl Scouts pin Senior Girl Scout Challenge pin Apprentice Trainer's pin Career Exploration pin

	Daisy Girl Scouts	Brownie Girl Scouts	Junior Girl Scouts	Cadette Girl Scouts	Senior Girl Scouts
Basic Resources	The Guide for Daisy Girl Scout Leaders My Daisy Girl Scout Activity Scrapbook Who Is a Daisy Girl Scout? The Story of Juliette Low	Brownie Girl Scout Handbook The Guide for Brownie Girl Scout Leaders	Junior Girl Scout Handbook Girl Scout Badges and Signs Junior Girl Scout Activity Book The Guide for Junior Girl Scout Leaders	Cadette and Senior Girl Scout Handbook Cadette and Senior Girl Scout Interest Projects Cadette and Senior Girl Scouts Leaders' Guide	Cadette and Senior Girl Scout Handbook Cadette and Senior Girl Scout Interest Projects Girl Scout Gold Award Booklet Cadette and Senior Girl Scouts Leaders' Guide
Supplementary Resources	Sing-Along Songbook and Cassette Games for Girl Scouts Exploring Wildlife Communities with Children Contemporary Issues booklets	Sing-Along Songbook and Cassette Brownies' Own Songbook Sing Together—A Girl Scout Songbook The Wide World of Girl Guiding and Girl Scouting WAGGGS Brownie uniform and badge posters Games for Girl Scouts Exploring Wildlife Communities with Children Outdoor Education in Girl Scouting World Games and Recipes Trefoil Round the World Contemporary Issues booklets Here Come the Brownies series	Sing-Along Songbook and Cassette Sing Together—A Girl Scout Songbook The Wide World of Girl Guiding and Girl Scouting WAGGGS Girl Guide/Girl Scout uniform posters Games for Girl Scouts Exploring Wildlife Communities with Children Outdoor Education in Girl Scouting World Games and Recipes Trefoil Round the World Contemporary Issues booklets G*I*R*L* magazine	Sing Together—A Girl Scout Songbook The Wide World of Girl Guiding and Girl Scouting Games for Girl Scouts Outdoor Education in Girl Scouting World Games and Recipes Trefoil Round the World Contemporary Issues booklets	Sing Together—A Girl Scout Songbook The Wide World of Girl Guiding and Girl Scouting Games for Girl Scouts Outdoor Education in Girl Scouting World Games and Recipes Trefoil Round the World Contemporary Issues booklets

Special Traditions in Girl Scouting

Ceremonies, special days, and traditions are an important part of Girl Scouting. They make girls feel part of something very special. Chapter One, "Welcome to Girl Scouting," of the *Junior Girl Scout Handbook*, provides information about special days and traditions. Since many of these traditions and special days are celebrated worldwide, girls also gain a sense of belonging to the larger organization, the World Association of Girl Guides and Girl Scouts.

Girl Scout Ceremonies

Girl Scouts use ceremonies to celebrate special occasions, such as the welcoming of new members to the troop, the presentation of recognitions, or the Girl Scout birthday. Ceremonies can open or close a meeting, and can be short or long, formal or informal. You and the girls in your troop or group can decide which ceremonies to perform, and how they can make meetings special. Ceremonies can include girls from your troop or group, other Girl Scouts or Girl Scout leaders, and special guests like parents, relatives, or friends. Ceremonies can be performed by large groups or small groups, outdoors or indoors. *Ceremonies in Girl Scouting*, a publication available through the National Equipment Service (NES), contains details for planning a variety of ceremonies.

You will most likely need to assist girls in planning a flag ceremony, an investiture or rededication ceremony, and a recognition ceremony. The sample ceremonies on the following pages have been adapted from *Ceremonies in Girl Scouting*.

Types of Ceremonies

Investiture: A way to welcome someone into Girl Scouting for the first time.

Rededication: Girl Scouts who have already been invested renew their Girl Scout Promise and Law. Many girls do this at the beginning and end of the troop year.

Bridging: Girl Scouts move from one age level to another.

Court of Awards: A ceremony in which Girl Scouts receive recognitions (badges) and other insignia.

Girl Scouts' Own: A quiet ceremony designed by the girls in which the participants express their feelings about a particular theme.

Flag Ceremony: A ceremony that honors the flag of the United States of America.

Candle Lighting: A candle lighting (or flashlight) ceremony that helps remind people of the words and meaning of the Girl Scout Promise and Law.

Opening Ceremony: A short ceremony to start a meeting.

Closing Ceremony: A short ceremony to close a meeting.

Basic Flag Ceremony

Purpose: For opening/closing an activity or meeting.

Materials: American flag, troop flag (if available), and flag stands.

Procedure: The troop or group forms a horseshoe and stands at attention.

The Girl Scout-in-charge says: "Color guard, advance." The color guard advances to the flags, salutes the American flag, and picks up the flags. The American flag is always picked up first so it will remain higher than any other flag. Then they turn together and face the troop. The guards stand on either side of the flag bearers. They are silent throughout the ceremony.

The Girl Scout-in-charge says: "Color guard, present colors." The color guard walks forward carrying the flags to the standards at the open end of the horseshoe.

The Girl Scout-in-charge says: "Girl Scouts, honor the flag of your country." Each girl in the group salutes the American flag by placing her right hand over her heart.

The Girl Scout-in-charge says: "Girl Scouts, recite the Pledge of Allegiance." She may also lead them in a suitable song, poem, or the Girl Scout Promise.

The Girl Scout-in-charge says: "Color guard, post the colors." The color bearers place the flags in the stands. The American flag is placed last, and is always posted to the right of other flags. The color guard remains at attention next to the flags.

If the flag ceremony is part of a larger ceremony, the Girl Scout-in-charge dismisses the color guard and the main ceremony follows. Following the ceremony, the Girl Scout-in-charge says: "Color guard, retire the colors," and they carry the flags back to the place where they are stored. The ceremony is over when the Girl Scout-in-charge says: "Color guard, dismissed." All girls stand at attention during the closing. Usually, girls who are part of the horseshoe are silent during the ceremony.

Junior Girl Scout Rededication Ceremony

Purpose: For invested Junior Girl Scouts to reaffirm their belief in the Girl Scout Promise and Law.

Materials: Thirteen candles and candleholders, or a log with ten cut holes to serve as a candleholder.

Procedure: A three-candle grouping represents the three parts of the Girl Scout Promise. As each candle is lit, the girl who is being welcomed into Girl Scouting says a sentence or two about a part of the Promise: serving God and country, helping other people, and living by the Girl Scout Law. The total group of girls can then recite the Girl Scout Promise.

A ten-candle grouping represents the ten parts of the Girl Scout Law. As each candle is lit, each girl recites one part of the Girl Scout Law. Girls may also want to add personal comments explaining what the Girl Scout Law means to them.

Pledge of Allegiance

"I pledge allegiance to the flag of the United States of America and to the Republic for which it stands; one Nation under God, indivisible, with liberty and justice for all."

Recognition Ceremony

Purpose: To present recognitions to girls who have earned them. Can be similar to the rededication ceremony. May be held at any time during the year and can be combined with other special occasions.

Materials: Three tall and ten small candles arranged in candleholders on a table.

Procedure: Girls should stand in a horseshoe formation. The opening could include a flag ceremony, recitation of the Promise, and singing.

Leader #1 says: "The three tall, white tapers symbolize the threefold purpose of Girl Scouting as expressed in our Promise. The first part concerns service to God and our country (lights center candle). The second part refers to helping people at all times (lights end candle). The third part is our promise to live by the Girl Scout Law (lights remaining candle)."

Leader #2 says: "Each of the shorter candles represents one part of our Girl Scout Law."

Each of the ten girls lights one candle from the center candle and repeats her part of the Law. She may give her interpretation of that part.

Girls sing a song of their choice.

Leader #1 says: "Today the girls will receive the recognitions they've earned since (date) and each girl will tell something she did to earn one badge."

Girls take turns and, in their own words, state one thing they did or learned about to earn the badge.

Leader #2 says: "As you can see, our girls extended their knowledge in different directions. As a result, we hope they will be more helpful to their family, troop, and community."

Each girl is individually presented her recognitions. Recognitions might be taped to crepe-paper strips or stapled to construction paper cut in the shape of a trefoil.

Leader #1 says: "Remember that with each new badge a Junior Girl Scout takes on a new responsibility. A little more is expected at home, at troop meetings, and in your community. Strive always to be worthy of the symbols you wear and wear them with pride. Best wishes to each of you!"

Closing: Retire colors and sing a song of your choice while forming a friendship circle.

Singing

Singing is a tradition in Girl Scouting. Songs may begin a meeting, serve as a bridge to the next part of a meeting, or introduce new themes and topics to girls. The Annotated Resource List in Chapter Five includes the titles of Girl Scout songbooks.

Junior Girl Scout Uniform

The design of the Junior Girl Scout uniform components was based on the expressed needs and preferences of girls. Girls can choose from a variety of styles, and can mix and match pieces to suit their own tastes. T-shirts and sweatshirts are now official uniform options in recognition of the lifestyle of today's girls. While girls are encouraged to wear the uniform, it is not a requirement for membership, nor is it a requirement to own all the components (see Program Standard 11 in this chapter). Furthermore, girls do not need to purchase the uniform components shown here to have an official uniform. All uniform pieces from the past remain official uniform components.

The sash and vest show proper placement of Junior Girl Scout insignia.

Girl Scout recognitions—badges, signs, and patches—are symbols of something a girl has learned or accomplished. Whether she has developed a new interest or has expanded on something she already enjoys, a Girl Scout earns a recognition for completing activities to the best of her ability. Recognitions are only one part of the Girl Scout program, and should never serve as the main focus of a girl's experience in Girl Scouting.

Recognitions: Their Role in Girl Scouting

Junior Girl Scout Recognitions

Girls can learn about recognitions for Junior Girl Scouts from *Girl Scout Badges and Signs* and the *Junior Girl Scout Handbook.*

When you review the badges, you will notice that background colors for badges are either white, green, or tan. The badges in the *Junior Girl Scout Handbook* have a white background. Green and tan badges are found in *Girl Scout Badges and Signs.* The green background badges are simpler and can be completed by most Junior Girl Scouts. Tan badges are a bit more challenging, and can be worked on by both Junior and Cadette Girl Scouts. Girls can choose between green and tan badges based on their ability and degree of interest.

Keep in mind, when girls are working on badge activities, the importance of emphasizing the activities and not the symbolic reward. The number of recognitions earned should not be used as a determination of who is a good Girl Scout. Learning and service and just plain fun may come without the completion of a recognition. Girls are naturally motivated to work on activities if they are interested in them.

If the emphasis in your troop or group has become the acquisition of badges, rather than participation in a balance of program activities, it may be time for more creative planning. For example, you may have to encourage girls to use their handbooks more, or you may want to acquaint girls with other Girl Scout resources such as the Contemporary Issues series or *Outdoor Education in Girl Scouting.* Exposure to these and other Girl Scout publications can help keep girls excited about learning new things. Always remember: The quality of program should come first. Stress program over quantity of recognitions.

Girl Scout Badges and Signs: An Overview

Girl Scout Badges and Signs contains information about the many Junior Girl Scout badges and signs as well as tips to earn them. To ensure that girls participate in a balanced program, requirements for badge activities reflect a range of skills and experience. For example, within each badge are requirements that represent skill development, career awareness, and service.

Badge activities are designed to be flexible so all girls have an opportunity to participate, whether they are part of a troop or group or involved in another way. The activities are age-appropriate and reflect an informal rather than academic emphasis.

The format of the book encourages interactive use. The book is meant to be written in, marked on, colored in—in other words, used by girls. The format also provides girls with the opportunity to develop a written record of their badge activities and a chance to experiment with new topics. It's advisable to have your own copy of *Girl Scout Badges and Signs* to better work with the girls.

Girl Scout Badges and Signs is designed so girls can use the book as a tool while earning recognitions. The beginning of the book contains information that helps them choose a badge. As girls read through the book, they will find descriptions of specific badges and required activities. Reading through will allow them to try a variety of badge and sign activities. And finally, the "Helps and Resources" section helps girls identify badges and activities quickly.

Helping Girls Select Badges

In *Girl Scout Badges and Signs*, badges are grouped according to the five worlds of interest. Each badge is bordered by the same color used throughout Girl Scouting:

World of Well-Being	Red
World of People	Blue
World of Today and Tomorrow:	Orange
World of the Arts	Purple
World of the Out-of-Doors	Yellow

Each world of interest includes a Dabbler badge which is a sampler of activities contained in that world. A girl may earn the Dabbler badge or simply try some of the activities in it to guide her to other badges within that world.

Many times, a girl may choose only one or two activities in a badge, then move on to other activities in another badge. The book is designed to give her this flexibility. Girls should not feel that their efforts are wasted if they sample some of the activities, then decide not to continue to earn that badge. The value of the experience is rooted in the fun of learning and doing the activities.

Helping Girls Manage and Complete Badge Activities

The following are some questions you may have about helping girls with badge activities.

Q. Where Can Girls Find Help with Badge Activities?

A. Your community offers a storehouse of resources girls can use as they work on badges and signs. Libraries, museums, hospitals, colleges, universities, nature centers, and government offices offer a range of resource people and materials that can assist girls in completing badge activities. Civic, religious, volunteer, and other youth organizations can also prove invaluable. And don't forget your Girl Scout council which can provide information, resource people, and ideas.

Q. Can a Completed Activity Be Applied Toward More Than One Badge?

A. Girls may not complete a requirement for one badge and use it toward another badge. A girl should recognize that an activity fits a particular badge and that she must complete the requirements as stated for each badge she chooses to earn. Similarly, girls may not receive credit for activities they completed before working on a badge. For example, if a requirement asks that a girl perform in front of a group, she must participate in a new performance rather than try to satisfy the requirement with past dance or music recitals.

Q. How Can Girls Track Their Progress?

A. *Girl Scout Badges and Signs* is designed so girls can chart their progress in earning badges and signs. Girls can write their thoughts, plans, and ideas for earning badges. They can record badges they've earned in a badge chart or at the end of each badge description. They can also color and complete activities of their own design. As girls complete a requirement, they will ask you or another adult to initial the appropriate space in their books. This practice provides girls with a written record of their accomplishments and progress.

Q. What If It's Not Possible to Complete a Badge Requirement Exactly as Described?

A. The requirements in *Girl Scout Badges and Signs* are written to fit a framework for badge completion. There will be times when activities will need to be adapted to suit specific circumstances. For example, a requirement may be to visit a museum or a zoo. If your troop or group does not live near either of these, this does not mean the activity must be omitted. Instead, girls might have an expert come speak or invite someone with a related career to visit. Or, girls could view a video or film on the topic.

Another type of adaptation may relate to the amount of time spent on a badge or a particular activity. If girls do not meet every week, it could take months to complete some activities. You might suggest that girls divide up some of the responsibilities so they could each work on something different outside of the meeting, then teach the new skill to the other girls during the next meeting. The girls themselves will be able to come up with other suggestions for adapting activities to meet their needs and interests. Remember that adaptations do not mean watering down an activity. Adaptations merely increase accessibility and present another way of doing the activity. This is particularly relevant when working with girls with disabilities. Girls with disabilities should do the badge requirements to the best of their abilities. For more specific guidelines on adapting badge activities for girls with disabilities, see *Focus on Ability: Serving Girls with Special Needs*.

Receiving Recognitions

When it is time to present girls with the recognitions they have earned, you may want to use the recognition ceremony or another ceremony called the Court of Awards. The Court of Awards is a special ceremony used to recognize girls' achievements. It may be held periodically throughout the year as girls earn recognitions, or it may be held once, at the end of the troop year, so girls receive all their recognitions at the same time. The girls in your troop or group can decide the type of Court of Awards ceremony they would like to have. See *Ceremonies in Girl Scouting* for more about the Court of Awards.

Special Recognitions
Junior Girl Scout Leadership Pin

The Junior Girl Scout Leadership Pin is a new recognition designed to give girls the opportunity to strengthen and apply leadership skills. This recognition requires four steps which should be done in sequence. (See Chapter Eight in the *Junior Girl Scout Handbook*.)

Your role in this endeavor is to offer support and guidance, particularly for Step Four. For many Junior Girl Scouts, this may be the first time they have been charged with designing and implementing a service project by themselves. Therefore, you may need to help them identify what's needed in the community, locate printed materials or people to serve as consultants, calculate a budget, and design a project that is challenging but not so demanding that it becomes impossible to complete.

Junior Girl Scout Signs

Junior Girl Scout signs are another kind of recognition Junior Girl Scouts can earn. Signs include a wider range of activities than badges and are designed to recognize a girl's broad participation in Girl Scout activities. Activities may be completed by a girl over time during her Junior Girl Scout experience. The Sign of the World activities are included in the *Junior Girl Scout Handbook*. The Sign of the Rainbow, the Sign of the Sun, and the Sign of the Satellite all appear in *Girl Scout Badges and Signs*. The signs include a broad range of program activities, with sections on skill development, service, career exploration, Girl Scouting and Girl Guiding, and self-evaluation.

Sign of the Rainbow

This sign is designed to show that girls have completed activities from all five worlds of interest. They must also earn the Junior Aide patch. As girls complete each requirement, they color in a section of the rainbow in their book.

Sign of the Sun

When girls have completed this sign, they will have developed skills in both the World of Well-Being and the World of the Out-of-Doors. Badge activities from *Girl Scout Badges and Signs* are included; girls are also encouraged to complete activities from the Contemporary Issues booklets as well as their own ideas. As a girl follows the illustrated path in her book, she demonstrates health, fitness, and leisure skills.

Sign of the Satellite

The activities in this sign encourage girls to be aware of the world around them as they complete activities in the World of Today and Tomorrow, the World of People, and the World of the Out-of-Doors. As girls complete each requirement, they color in the star next to it.

Junior Aide Patch

By assisting Brownie Girl Scouts who are ready to bridge to Junior Girl Scouting, Junior Girl Scouts are eligible to receive the Junior Aide patch. *Girl Scout Badges and Signs* lists the requirements for completion of this patch.

Our Own Troop's Badge

Your troop or group may be interested in exploring something not addressed by any of the badges in *Girl Scout Badges and Signs* or the *Junior Girl Scout Handbook*. Or, they may want to continue working on a topic beyond the listed badge activities. The Our Own Troop's Badge was designed to accommodate these needs. *Girl Scout Badges and Signs* describes the guidelines girls must follow when developing their own badge. After a symbol and title have been chosen, submit copies to your local Girl Scout council along with a description of the badge activities. Girls may begin working on the activities they have created once the activities have received council approval.

Our Own Council's Badge

An Our Own Council's Badge reflects something unique to your area. Check with your local Girl Scout council to see if it has its own badge and, if so, what the requirements include.

Religious Recognitions

Through Girl Scouting, each girl is encouraged to become a stronger member of her own religion, and Girl Scouting recognizes that the responsibility of religious instruction rests with the girl's family and religious leaders. Religious recognition programs are always developed and administered by religious groups themselves. The following list of religious recognitions is periodically updated and revised. For more information, write to Religious Recognitions, Girl Scouts of the U.S.A., 420 Fifth Avenue, New York, New York 10018-2702.

	Brownie	Junior	Cadette
Baha'i	Unity of Mankind	Unity of Mankind	Unity of Mankind
Buddhist	Ages 6-8, Padma Award	Ages 9-10, Padma Award	Ages 12-14, Padma Award
Christian Science		Ages 9-10, Christian Science God and Country	Ages 11-14, Christian Science God and Country
Eastern Orthodox		Ages 9-10, Chi-Rho	Ages 11-14, Alpha Omega
Episcopal	Ages 6-8, Grades 1-3 God and Me	Ages 9-10, Grades 4-5 God and Family	Ages 11-14, Grades 6-9 God and Church
Hindu	Ages 6-8, Grades 1-3 Dharma Award	Ages 8-11, Grades 3-6 Dharma Award	
Islamic	Ages 5-9 Bismillah Award	Ages 9-11 In the Name of Allah Award	Ages 12-15 Quratula'in Award
Jewish	Ages 6-9 Lehavah Award	Ages 9-11 Bat Or Award	Ages 11-14 Menorah Award
Lutheran	Ages 6-8, Grades 1-3 God and Me	Ages 9-10, Grades 4-5 God and Family	Ages 11-13, Grades 6-8 God and Church
(Mormon) Church of Jesus Christ of Latter-Day Saints		Ages 10-11, Gospel in Action Award	Ages 12-13 Young Woman of Truth
Protestant and Independent Christian Churches	Ages 6-8, Grades 1-3 God and Me	Ages 9-10, Grades 4-5 God and Family	Ages 11-13, Grades 6-8 God and Church
(Quakers) Society of Friends	Ages 6-8, Grades 2-3 That of God	Ages 8-11, Grades 4-6 That of God	Ages 11-14, Grades 6-9 Spirit of Truth
Reorganized Church of Jesus Christ of Latter Day Saints	Age 8 Light of the World	Ages 9-10, Light of the World Age 11, Liahona	Ages 12-14, Liahona
Roman Catholic Church	Ages 7-9 Family of God	Ages 9-11 I Live My Faith	Ages 12-14 Marian Medal
Unitarian Universalist		Ages 9-11 Religion in Life	Ages 12-14 Religion in Life
Unity Church	Ages 6-8 God in Me	Ages 9-11 God in Me	Ages 11-13 Light of God

Senior	Adult	Where to Get Information
Unity of Mankind		Baha'i Committee on Scouting, Baha'i National Center, Wilmette, Ill. 60091, (708) 869-903
Ages 15-17, Padma Award		Buddhist Church of America , National Headquarters, 1710 Octavia Street, San Francisco, Calif. 94109, (415) 776-5600
		P.R.A.Y., P.O. Box 6900, St. Louis, Mo. 63123, (800) 933-PRAY (7729)
Ages 15-17, Alpha Omega	Prophet Elias	P.R.A.Y., P.O. Box 6900, St. Louis, Mo. 63123, (800) 933-PRAY (7729)
Ages 15-17, Grades 10-12, God and Life	St. George Award Adult mentor programs for each Girl Scout age level are available.	P.R.A.Y., P.O. Box 6900, St. Louis, Mo. 63123, (800) 933-PRAY (7729)
		North American Hindu Association, 46133 Amesbury Drive, Plymouth, Mich. 48170, (313) 459-5049 or 981-2323
Ages 15-17 Muslimeen Award		Islamic Committee on Girl Scouting, 31 Marian Street, Stamford, Conn. 06907, (203) 359-3593
Ages 15-17 Menorah Award	Ora Award	National Jewish Girl Scout Committee of the Synagogue Council of America, 327 Lexington Avenue, New York, N.Y. 10016, (212) 686-8670
Ages 14-17, Grades 9-12 Lutheran Living Faith	Lamb Award and Servant of Youth Adult mentor programs for Brownies, Juniors, and Cadettes are available.	P.R.A.Y., P.O. Box 6900, St. Louis, Mo. 63123, (800) 933-PRAY (7729)
Ages 14-15, Young Woman of Promise; Ages 16-17, Young Woman of Faith; Young Womanhood Recognition		Salt Lake District Center Church of Jesus Christ of Latter-day Saints, 1999 W. 1700 South, Salt Lake City, Utah 84104, (801) 240-2141
Ages 14-17, Grades 9-12 God and Life	God and Service Recognition Adult mentor programs for each Girl Scout age level are available.	P.R.A.Y., P.O. Box 6900, St. Louis, Mo. 63123, (800) 933-PRAY (7729)
Ages 14-17, Grades 10-12 Spirit of Truth	Friends Emblem	Friends Committee on Scouting, c/o Dennis Clarke, 85 Willowbrook Road Cromwell, Conn. 06416, (203) 635-1706
Ages 15-17 Exploring My Life and World	World Community International Youth Service Award	Youth Ministries Office, The Auditorium, P.O. Box 1059, Independence, Mo. 64051 (816) 833-1000
Age 15, Marian Medal Ages 15-17, Spirit Alive	St. Elizabeth Seton Medal and St. Anne Medal	National Federation for Catholic Youth Ministry, 3700-A Oakview Terrace, NE, Washington, D.C. 20017, Attn: Orders Clerk, (202) 636-3825
Ages 15-17 Religion in Life		Unitarian Universalist, 25 Beacon Street, Boston, Mass. 02108, (617) 742-2100
	Distinguished Youth Service Award Miniature Pin	Association of Unity Churches, P.O. Box 610, Lee's Summit, Mo. 64063, (816) 524-7414

International Pen Pals

Junior Girl Scouts who are ten years of age or older may request a pen pal from Girl Scouts of the U.S.A. Links cannot be made for girls younger than ten years old. Requests must be made using the "International Pen Pal" form available from your council office; otherwise, the request cannot be considered. The form must be filled out neatly. Many past requests have not been answered because they were illegible. The completed form should be sent to GSUSA (address is on form) with a self-addressed envelope. Until a link is made, girls should not send stamps, photographs, or letters about themselves since there is no one to whom they may be forwarded.

GSUSA will attempt to link the girl with a pen pal in one of the areas of the world she requested. If this is not possible, another area will be selected. The large number of requests for pen pals makes it impossible for the post-box secretary to notify those girls and adults for whom linkages cannot be found. If a request has not been filled within eight months, it is usually because a pen pal is not available. Girls should wait a few more months and reapply.

Pen pal links should not be used to complete badge requirements, bridging activities, or to provide input for a Thinking Day program due to the time required to establish linkages. Pen pal links should be requested by girls interested in long-term correspondence (two years minimum).

Contact your Girl Scout council to obtain proper forms and more detailed information.

WORKING WITH JUNIOR GIRL SCOUTS

CHAPTER 3

When you work with a group of Junior Girl Scouts, it's crucial to consider each girl as a unique individual with her own talents, gifts, personality, growth rate, intelligence, strengths, and weaknesses. At the same time, it's helpful to be aware of traits that generally characterize girls of this age level.

Junior Girl Scouts are in the late childhood years of eight to eleven. These years are filled with activity, intellectual growth, new friendships, deepening relationships, and discoveries of both the outside world and inner selves. While the family is still very important to the Junior Girl Scout, friends and outside interests and experiences are increasing in importance.

Studies have shown that at about age 11, many girls start to lose self-esteem and feel less confident about their abilities and ideas. Thus, they are less likely to say what is on their minds. This is a critical time for girls, a time when Girl Scouting can help girls maintain and strengthen their self-esteem.

A Girl Scout troop or group can influence a girl's behavior and development in many significant ways. Junior Girl Scouts have a strong need to learn to do things as well as a need to be accomplished and successful in their immediate world. They enjoy learning new skills, particularly ones they can demonstrate. They are also very capable of using their imaginations for both enjoyment and problem-solving. Their use of language is growing ever more complex. Girls of this age tend to enjoy codes, riddles, jokes, and puns.

The Junior Girl Scout is also more aware of herself as an individual. In turn, she may be more self-conscious and wonder how others see her. She strives for recognition, compares herself to others, reaches to achieve, develops her relationships, and deepens her sense of self-worth. It is important for her to learn that she is of value to her peer group, and is a skilled and unique person.

Games for Junior Girl Scouts can be both imaginative and complex. Games should help girls develop new and more demanding skills. These skills could relate to complicated physical activities like gymnastics or to intellectually challenging games like chess.

As the Junior Girl Scout reaches the age of 11, she is on the brink of adolescence. For many girls, the body's hormones have already set in motion the physical changes characteristic of adolescence. It is a time when girls are often looking forward with both excitement and apprehension to gaining greater freedom and responsibility, making new friends, and possibly attending a different school.

At this time, Junior Girl Scouts can benefit greatly from the support they receive in Girl Scouting. Unfortunately, many girls leave Girl Scouting at this age. You can help by making Junior Girl Scouting exciting, and by introducing them to Cadette Girl Scouting so they can learn more about the world filled with new surprises, joys, challenges, changes, and discoveries that awaits them!

Junior Girl Scouts with Special Needs

Many children have some kind of disability. Federal legislation gives all children with disabilities the legal right to a free and appropriate education designed to meet their individual needs. Disabilities are physical, psychological, cognitive, or health needs that affect a person's participation in daily activities.

Girl Scouting is an organization for all girls, and includes members with all kinds of abilities and disabilities. An atmosphere of understanding and acceptance can help children with disabilities discover their abilities, strengths, and gifts.

As the Girl Scout leader, the most important thing you can do is focus on the girl as an individual. Be sensitive to the special needs she has because of her disability, but involve her in all activities. Adapt activities only when absolutely necessary.

For further information on disabilities as well as specific tips for working with all girls, consult *Focus on Ability: Serving Girls with Special Needs*, available through the National Equipment Service, Girl Scouts of the U.S.A.

▲ Focus on the talents and skills of each girl rather than openly criticize her weaknesses or inabilities. For example, if a girl is knowledgeable about computers but is afraid to communicate that knowledge in a group, encourage her to share her expertise with one or two girls. This will slowly build her confidence and may lead to her speaking before the entire troop or group.

▲ Allow girls to learn by experience. Encourage girls to find out things for themselves. Offer help when you feel they may experience failure or discouragement.

▲ Encourage girls to solve their own problems, to go to each other for assistance, and to take turns leading the group. Intervene only if you are really needed. Try to foresee trouble. Step in immediately if anyone's safety is endangered.

▲ Help each girl develop positive feelings about herself. Help her feel she is important both as an individual and as a member of the group. Show respect for each girl's feelings and intelligence. Do not treat her as if she is "just a child."

▲ Rejoice with a girl when she achieves something important to her–no matter how small. Avoid making comparisons among girls.

▲ Give directions that girls of this age can understand. Phrase directions positively rather than negatively. For example, say "Please put your materials away," not "Don't leave your art materials all over the place."

▲ Set limits. Make them clear and consistent. Girls need and want clear and fair rules. Watch for opportunities where girls can participate in rule-setting. In many situations, they can help develop and implement rules, and change them when necessary.

▲ Encourage respect for differing cultural, ethnic, and racial backgrounds. Help each girl express pride in her heritage. Discover ways for girls to learn about and have positive experiences with girls and adults different from themselves.

▲ Allow and encourage girls to work on projects in pairs or in groups. Doing activities with friends is a critical part of the Girl Scout experience at the Junior Girl Scout age level. Because cliques form easily at this age, try changing groupings of girls. Make full use of the buddy system (pairing girls so they can watch out for each other). Rotate buddies so everyone gets a chance to know everyone else.

▲ Do not expect every girl to participate in all activities. Some girls will not be ready or willing to participate in large-group activities. Encourage participation, particularly for shy girls, but do not insist upon it. Suggest a quiet activity that will not disturb the group.

▲ Involve each girl's family as much as possible. Family support can lead to a more successful Girl Scout experience for you and the girls.

▲ Share your successes, problems, and resources with other leaders. Ask to observe their troops and groups, and see if you pick up some tips.

Working With Multi-Age Level Troops and Groups

As *Safety-Wise* Program Standard 19 states, Girl Scout troops and groups should include girls from different age and grade levels. A multi-age level Junior Girl Scout troop or group, which could include fourth through sixth graders as well as first-, second- and third-year Junior Girl Scouts, provides benefits to both girls and leaders. Younger girls can learn a variety of social, physical, and intellectual skills from older girls and look forward to progressing within Girl Scouting. Older girls strengthen their self-confidence and skills by sharing their expertise with younger girls and by being seen as role models. Leaders benefit because older girls can be paired with younger girls, providing the leader with time to focus on an individual girl or situation.

If you have a multi-age level troop or group, consider the following:

▲ Make sure your Junior Girl Scout patrols are mixed. In the beginning of the year, it may be appropriate for older girls to assume leadership positions but as the year progresses make sure younger girls are provided with the opportunity to fill these positions. Older girls can model the duties and responsibilities of troop or group government for younger girls.

▲ Capitalize on the strengths of the older girls. Involve them in delivering workshops, skits, lessons, or other activities that demonstrate their skills and abilities.

▲ Vary the format of your troop meeting. Some activities are best done in small groups while others may prove more successful in large groups. Or one or two girls may work on an activity while the rest of the group does something different. Work together in adapting activities when necessary.

▲ Be sure to emphasize to girls the positive aspects of a multi-age level troop or group. Make sure everyone feels welcome and do not divide girls into older and younger. Encourage girls to look actively for opportunities to assist one another.

▲ Give girls the opportunity to choose activities with which they feel most comfortable. For example, a girl may choose to read aloud her favorite published poem instead of an original piece. Even though you consider this to be the easier of the two options, the girl made her own decision. Engaging girls in the decision-making process is one of the most important things you can do as a Girl Scout leader.

Divorce, poverty, death, homelessness, substance abuse, child abuse, and teenage pregnancy are some of the issues that Junior Girl Scouts face directly or indirectly. Young people account for a large percentage of the nation's poor and, by the age of 18, nearly 50 percent will experience their parents' divorce. One in four girls has had a sexually abusive experience and more than one million teenage girls become pregnant each year. Approximately 12,000 children, ages five to fourteen, are referred to psychiatric hospitals annually for treatment of suicidal behavior.

Issues Confronting Today's Girl Scouts

Recognizing Signs of Distress

As a Girl Scout leader, you can help Junior Girl Scouts by recognizing signs of distress. Following is a list of signs that may indicate that a girl is troubled. Keep in mind, however, that these signs can be caused by many different emotional and physical problems. Use the relationship and trust you have developed with a girl to find out more about a particular problem she may be experiencing without being overly intrusive. Find out what procedures your Girl Scout council has established if you suspect that any girl in your troop or group is in trouble.

Be alert to the following signs:

▲ Giving up on goals or withdrawing from the Girl Scout group or from school and family activities

▲ A drop in the quality of her work

▲ Increased secretiveness

▲ Changes in behavior—more disruptive and delinquent, or more quiet and uncommunicative

▲ Erratic mood changes, or apathy and lethargy

▲ Neglect of personal appearance and hygiene

▲ Chronic lying

▲ Physical symptoms such as red eyes, sores, bruises, fatigue, drowsiness, and decreased or increased appetite

▲ Suddenly behaving in a more adult or sexually knowledgeable manner

Child Abuse

If you suspect that a child has been neglected or physically or sexually abused, follow your Girl Scout council's procedures for reporting this information. You will need to alert a council staff member, a child protection agency, or a law-enforcement agency. Since child abuse is a crime, an agency in every state is mandated by state law to receive and investigate reports of suspected child abuse.

Tips for Helping Girls Cope

The skills a girl learns and the experiences she has in her Girl Scout troop or group can help her handle difficult situations. To help girls strengthen their coping skills:

DO:

▲ Provide an atmosphere of openness, freedom, and trust so girls will feel comfortable when expressing themselves and seeking advice from you.

▲ Listen seriously to what girls have to say.

▲ Be sensitive to the girl's ethnic and cultural background, religious beliefs, family traditions, and social customs.

▲ Be in touch with your own attitudes and behavior related to these issues. Recognize when your own beliefs may affect your judgment.

▲ Take a preventative approach. Use creative methods like games and role-playing to learn what is on girls' minds.

▲ Help girls become assertive and let them know it is okay to say no in instances of negative peer pressure.

▲ Inform girls that they should always tell a trusted adult if they or someone they know is in distress. Know your council's guidelines and resources for girls who need help.

▲ Offer factual information in terms girls can understand.

▲ Help girls develop healthy ways to deal with stress. Have them make a list of relaxing activities they might enjoy or share with them the importance of discussing their feelings with a good friend or trusted adult. (See "Managing Stress" in Chapter Three of the *Junior Girl Scout Handbook*.)

▲ Foster the idea of peer support where girls help and reach out to each other. Encourage girls to listen to each other and accept one another.

▲ Be a positive role model of behaviors and attitudes.

DON'T:

▲ Impose your own values and opinions on girls.

▲ Promise to keep information confidential if it might affect the girl's safety.

▲ Leave a girl alone if the situation is immediately life-threatening.

▲ Be judgmental, regardless of what you are told.

▲ Provide information the girls do not want or need to know.

▲ Be afraid to seek help from others when you feel uncomfortable discussing certain topics.

Identifying and Locating Consultants

You are not expected to be an expert in providing information on the kinds of issues previously mentioned. In many instances, it may prove effective to invite a consultant to your troop or group meeting to discuss a particular topic. Depending upon the issue to be discussed, health educators, social workers, psychologists, psychiatrists, physicians, counselors, clergy, educators, historians, university personnel, attorneys, teachers, and community leaders could meet the needs of your troop or group.

When enlisting the services of a consultant, provide to that person a brief orientation to Girl Scouting. Also preview the consultant's presentation or materials to make sure they are consistent with Girl Scout program and philosophy. Consider the following criteria when selecting a consultant. The consultant:

▲ Should have a reputable background and references that can easily be verified.

▲ Should present facts and information, not opinions.

▲ Should provide new knowledge.

▲ Should not have a "hidden" agenda or motives beyond what she or he is asked to do.

▲ Should be sensitive to emotions and attitudes related to health and fitness issues.

▲ Should be nonjudgmental and supportive.

▲ Should be willing to adhere to both the Girl Scout council's and GSUSA's policies, standards, and procedures.

To find a consultant, contact volunteers or staff from your Girl Scout council, as well as parents, clergy, and teachers, who can help you locate resource people. You can also check the telephone directory under "Associations," "Organizations," "Clubs," "Universities," "Hospitals," and "Community Agencies."

Conflict Resolution

Conflicts will occur in your troop or group from time to time. Arguments may surface around minor issues such as whose turn it is to clean up after an activity, or major issues such as how to spend troop or group money. Girls might be more likely to argue if they are tired or bored, or have recently experienced a problem at home or

school. Sometimes, older girls might make fun of younger girls in mixed-age level troops or a clique may form that excludes some girls.

When disagreements arise over issues that affect values or goals, it becomes particularly important to come up with a solution in which both participants win. This is good conflict resolution. Aim at recognizing the problem and shifting the focus from the people to possible solutions.

Many of the activities in the *Junior Girl Scout Handbook,* the Contemporary Issues booklets, and other Girl Scout resources aim at strengthening girls' self-esteem and respect for others. Begin with the activities in these resources if you feel girls need more work in developing self-esteem and respect for others.

Techniques

Following are some conflict-resolution techniques. Always consider the situation and the girls before moving ahead.

Mediation: Each girl has a chance to tell her side of the story. Interruption is not permitted. The girl identifies the problem and what has happened. Each girl suggests some solutions. Together the girls try to choose one.

Active Listening: You or a member of your troop or group restates or paraphrases what each person involved in the conflict has said. You could use phrases such as "This is what I heard you say…" or "You are saying that…" or whatever sounds most natural to you. These phrases can help you discover the reason for the conflict. Then you can move ahead with a resolution.

Time to Work It Out: This technique is most suitable when you know the girls are capable of resolving the conflict on their own. You ask the girls to go off by themselves for a set period of time. When the time has expired, the girls return with their agreed-upon solution.

Role Reversal: Seeing another person's point of view is the focus

of this technique. Ask each person involved in the conflict to state the point of view of the other person.

Skillful Listening: The way in which you and the girls listen and speak to each other is important for resolving conflicts. Listening is a skill. Do you:

▲ Look at a girl when she is speaking to you?

▲ Listen actively so that a girl knows you have heard what she said?

▲ Wait to give a girl a chance to answer?

▲ Avoid interrupting her?

▲ Use body language and facial expressions that agree with what you are saying?

▲ Help girls understand that put-downs are not allowed in the troop or group meeting?

If you have established positive and open lines of communication, then you have already made tremendous strides toward avoiding conflicts in your Junior Girl Scout troop or group.

PLANNING WITH JUNIOR GIRL SCOUTS

CHAPTER 4

Girl/Adult Partnership and Planning

A key ingredient in Girl Scouting is the partnership of girls and adults who work together to plan and carry out Girl Scout program. Girl/adult planning is beneficial to girls in several ways. Girls feel involved and have more opportunities to become responsible and self-reliant. They learn how to plan and make decisions, and they develop leadership and interpersonal skills. Girls also are provided the opportunity to experience a variety of leadership roles in a non-threatening environment.

Girls need the experience of making choices and plans to mature and develop their competence and self-esteem. Research conducted by Girl Scouts of the U.S.A. has found that Junior Girl Scouts need to be encouraged to take the lead and be involved in troop decision-making. Girls who are encouraged to be actively involved, who develop leadership skills, and who accept responsibility also are more likely to enjoy their Girl Scout program activities and stay with them longer.

This girl/adult partnership should begin as soon as you meet the Junior Girl Scouts in your troop or group. At first, girls may wish to rely on you, their adult partner. With your guidance, however, they should quickly begin to take charge of the troop meeting, and make and carry out their own decisions.

Active listening is one of the most important skills you can use to foster an atmosphere where girl/adult partnership and planning thrive. In most troop or group meetings, girls should generate most of the conversation and ideas.

The level of planning and authority assumed by you and the girls is not always constant. You, as an adult, might take on a stronger leadership role when safety is a concern or when girls are trying an activity for the first time. However, when planning a troop camping trip, for example, girls with camping experience may take the lead in organizing the outing.

Troop or Group Government

Girl Scouting has a built-in structure to help leaders develop successful girl/adult planning and partnership. This structure is traditionally referred to as troop or group government. Chapter One of the *Junior Girl Scout Handbook* outlines three models of democratic troop or group government: the patrol system, the executive board system (also called the steering committee), and the town meeting system. The first two systems are representative as well as democratic forms of government, meaning that some girls represent others in meetings, though each girl gets a vote.

The Patrol System

In the patrol system, a popular form of troop or group government, the troop or group divides into small groups, with every troop or group member playing a role in structuring affairs. When the patrol system is new to troop or group members, patrols of four to six girls are recommended. In the patrol, each girl gets a chance to participate and express her opinions.

Patrols may be organized by interests, with different patrols working toward different goals. Patrols can also be organized as "work groups," performing activities that feed into a project. In this case, each patrol takes responsibility for some part of the total project. This approach works well in carrying out jobs at regular troop or group meetings–one patrol can be responsible for setup, another for cleanup, etc. The leader of each patrol represents her group at Court of Honor meetings.

The Executive Board System

In the executive board system, you do not have small group patrols. There is one leadership team for the whole troop or group called an executive board. (In some troops, this group is called the steering committee.) This system often works well with smaller troops and groups. The board's main responsibility is to help make plans and assign jobs for the entire troop or group based on interests and needs.

The executive board usually has a president, a vice president, a secretary, and a treasurer, and holds its own meetings to discuss troop or group matters. The length of time each girl can be on the executive board should be limited so that during the year all members of the troop or group can participate. All the girls in the troop or group decide on a way at the beginning of the year to pass their ideas and suggestions to the executive board. The number of officers on the executive board can vary. Some activities and projects may need more officers than others.

The Town Meeting System

In the town meeting system, there is no formal troop or group government. Business is discussed and decided at meetings attended by all the girls in the troop or group. And, as in the other systems, everyone in the troop gets the chance to participate in decision-making and leadership.

This system usually requires a moderator who makes sure that everyone gets a chance to talk and that all ideas are considered.

In all governing systems, girls need to consider which rules to have. Many rules can be adapted to fit the situation. Health and safety rules, however, must be strictly adhered to at all times. Keep *Safety-Wise* on hand to refer to regularly.

Evaluating the Troop's or Group's System of Government

At various times during the troop year, girls may want to evaluate how well their system of government is working. Perhaps they will find ways to improve the present system, or they may decide to try another system. Patrols and executive boards may also be reorganized to adapt to changing needs.

Be sure to give your troop's or group's system of government a fair trial. It takes time to learn how to work well together. The length of a trial will depend on how effective the system has been so far, and on how strongly the girls feel about keeping or changing it.

In deciding whether to keep or change a government system, ask yourself the following questions:

▲ Is the current system really working for us? Does this system help us make decisions easily? Does it help us do things in ways we want to do them?

▲ Is the system comfortable for us? Can we use it with a reasonable amount of effort and time? Is it fun or burdensome and confusing? Does it fit our style and the way we like to manage things?

▲ If we are not comfortable with the current system, does the problem lie with the system itself or something else? Has the trial been long enough? Are we sure we know how the system is supposed to work?

What are the problems as we see them? Might we have similar problems with whatever system we use?

▲ What would make the system work better? What would we need to do differently?

▲ What are the alternatives? How do other systems operate? What do we like and dislike about each?

Kaper Charts

A kaper chart is a method for organizing activities. Kaper charts serve as visual reminders of the kapers, or tasks, that need to be completed. Girls may volunteer for tasks or you may assign tasks. A sample kaper chart is pictured here.

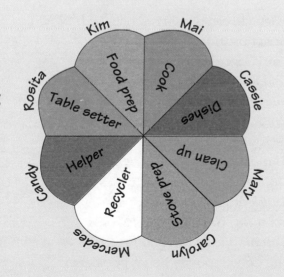

Planning Activities with Junior Girl Scouts

Activities found in the Girl Scout resources vary in terms of the time it takes to complete them, the amount of materials you will need, and complexity. This variety ensures that all Junior Girl Scouts can find activities that tap their skills and motivation. Help girls explore activities not only in the *Junior Girl Scout Handbook* and *Girl Scout Badges and Signs* but in the Contemporary Issues series, *Games for Girl Scouts, Outdoor Education in Girl Scouting*, and the *Junior Girl Scout Activity Book.* Girls need to know that these books contain activities for them. Your whole troop or group may opt to work together on one activity or tackle several activities in small groups. Encourage girls to sample activities they have not tried before. You may also need to explain exactly what the activity entails and what can be accomplished realistically.

Planning Tips

The following tips offer help in managing activities:

▲ Agree on what you as the troop or group leader will do and what the girls will do.

▲ Decide whether you need help from other adults or your Girl Scout council.

▲ Evaluate the activity. Ask why you and the girls are doing this particular activity.

▲ With the girls, set a realistic time frame for working on the activity. You may need to work with girls to simplify a project. At other times, you might need to show girls how to make the project more exciting or accessible.

▲ Consider your meeting facilities. Will the activity need to be adapted to ensure access for all girls?

▲ Break activities into steps. Allow plenty of time for planning and gathering resources.

▲ Consider practical points such as cost, permission slips, transportation, and supplies or equipment.

▲ Make a chart to display tasks or steps in the activity.

▲ Remember that abilities and development among Junior Girl Scouts vary significantly. For example, some girls may be physically coordinated while others may have better writing skills.

▲ Help girls handle frustration when it surfaces. Help them modify plans, if needed, or suggest they take a break. Sometimes it may be better to simply switch gears. Girls need to have fun and work at a comfortable pace.

▲ Be prepared for everything and anything! Be creative. Don't be thrown by unexpected outcomes. Always have something ready to do, such as a song or quick game, if the planned activities finish early.

Adapting Troop or Group Activities

Each Girl Scout troop or group personalizes the Girl Scout program in relation to its own needs, interests, abilities, and resources. Here are some ways to adapt activities:

▲ Change the method. For example, if an on-site visit is not possible, see a film or have a speaker come to the meeting.

▲ Modify the activity. If your troop or group is visiting a museum to view sculpture, for example, a girl who is blind might be given permission to touch the pieces.

▲ Substitute an activity that meets the same purpose. If part of an obstacle course requires girls to run from point A to point B, girls who are unable to run could be asked to do another type of physical activity for that part of the obstacle course.

In some instances, if adaptation is not possible, a decision may be made not to do the activity at all.

This can be appropriate since the needs and feelings of girls always come first.

Program Trails

A program trail is much like a flow chart for program activities and serves as a useful tool for planning. Here's how a program trail works: One idea sparks another and as the troop or group develops projects around these ideas (from such resources as the *Junior Girl Scout Handbook* and *Girl Scout Badges and Signs*), a program trail begins to take shape.

Each girl can design her own Girl Scout program trail or girls can work together on some activities and individually on others. You can suggest related activities girls might enjoy. Be sure to suggest activities beyond the *Junior Girl Scout Handbook* and *Girl Scout Badges and Signs*. (Consider activities in *Outdoor Education in Girl Scouting, Games for Girl Scouts, Ceremonies in Girl Scouting*, and the Contemporary Issues booklets.)

Program Trail

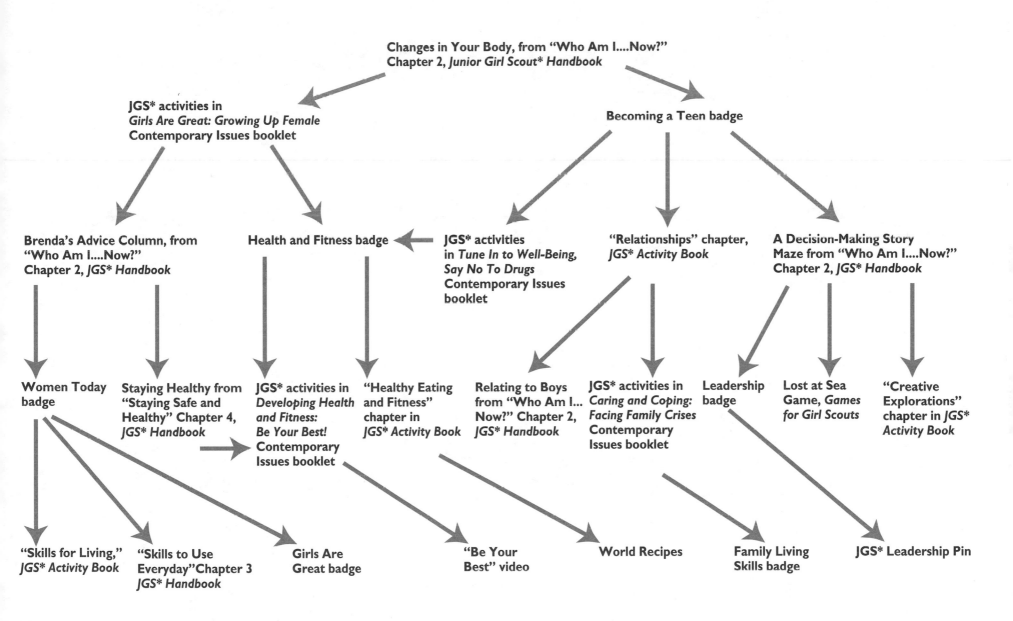

Changes in Your Body, from "Who Am I....Now?"
Chapter 2, *Junior Girl Scout* Handbook*

JGS* activities in
Girls Are Great: Growing Up Female
Contemporary Issues booklet

Becoming a Teen badge

Brenda's Advice Column, from
"Who Am I....Now?"
Chapter 2, *JGS* Handbook*

Health and Fitness badge

JGS* activities
in *Tune In to Well-Being,
Say No To Drugs*
Contemporary Issues
booklet

"Relationships" chapter,
JGS* Activity Book

A Decision-Making Story
Maze from "Who Am I....Now?"
Chapter 2, *JGS* Handbook*

Women Today
badge

Staying Healthy from
"Staying Safe and
Healthy" Chapter 4,
JGS* Handbook

JGS* activities in
*Developing Health
and Fitness:
Be Your Best!*
Contemporary
Issues booklet

"Healthy Eating
and Fitness"
chapter in
JGS* Activity Book

Relating to Boys
from "Who Am I...
Now?" Chapter 2,
JGS* Handbook

JGS* activities in
*Caring and Coping:
Facing Family Crises*
Contemporary
Issues booklet

Leadership
badge

Lost at Sea
Game, *Games
for Girl Scouts*

"Creative
Explorations"
chapter in *JGS**
Activity Book

"Skills for Living,"
JGS* Activity Book

"Skills to Use
Everyday" Chapter 3
JGS* Handbook

Girls Are
Great badge

"Be Your
Best" video

World Recipes

Family Living
Skills badge

JGS* Leadership Pin

*Junior Girl Scout (JGS)

Approximately once a month, use the following checklist to evaluate the effectiveness of your troop's activities. For each indicator, circle the number on the rating scale. Then look at the group of ratings for each statement for an overall indication of how effective troop or group activities are in delivering Girl Scout program.

Statement	Indicators of Effectiveness	Ratings (Circle number)		
1. Program activities of the troop or group are consistent with the beliefs and principles of Girl Scouting.	1. a. Girls show that they know and understand the Girl Scout Promise and Law.	1	2	3
	b. Girls have the opportunity to talk about the Girl Scout ethical code and what it means to them.	1	2	3
	c. Girls can apply the Girl Scout Promise and Law to their own behavior.	1	2	3
2. Program activities of the troop or group are based on the expressed needs and interests of the girls in the troop or group.	2. a. Girls freely express their needs, likes, and dislikes.	1	2	3
	b. The safety of each girl is ensured in all troop or group activities both away from and at the meeting place.	1	2	3
	c. The troop or group activities take into consideration the physical capabilities of each member so that no one is excluded.	1	2	3
	d. The costs of all troop or group activities are established so as not to exclude any member of the group.	1	2	3
	e. Troop or group events are planned at appropriate times to encourage family participation, and in consideration of cultural and religious holidays and customs.	1	2	3
	f. The activities at the troop or group meeting place are considered to be fun by the girls.	1	2	3
	g. At times when they seem bored, girls express how they feel.	1	2	3
	h. Girls actively participate in planning meetings and activities.	1	2	3
	i. The troop or group activities take into consideration the racial, ethnic, and cultural backgrounds of all girls and their families.	1	2	3

Statement	Indicators of Effectiveness	Ratings (Circle number)		
3. The activities of the troop or group reflect the unique benefits of belonging to the Girl Scout movement.	**3. a.** The girls have an opportunity to learn about and participate in Girl Scout ceremonies.	1	2	3
	b. The girls seem to understand the benefits of belonging to a Junior Girl Scout troop or group.	1	2	3
	c. Girls show pride in belonging to and making a contribution to the troop or group.	1	2	3
	d. Girls are aware of opportunities in Girl Scouting beyond the troop or group environment.	1	2	3
4. The Girl Scout program goals are in evidence in the troop or group activities.	**4. a.** Girls show interest in trying activities suggested by other girls.	1	2	3
	b. Girls seem to really listen to each other.	1	2	3
	c. Girls show a real interest in helping people in their community and in their families.	1	2	3
	d. When girls participate in group projects, they have good attention spans.	1	2	3
	e. Girls are getting along well with one another in their play and in other troop or group activities.	1	2	3
	f. Girls are choosing activities that introduce a wide range of interests.	1	2	3
	g. Girls feel accepted and positive about their individual contributions to the group.	1	2	3

Evaluating Troop or Group Dynamics

To help evaluate activities, here are additional questions to consider. Answers will help you determine how the troop or group year is going.

Statement	Yes	No

▲ Are girls prompt in arriving for meetings?

▲ Do a majority of the girls come to each meeting?

▲ Have you lost members over time? Do you know why?

▲ Do members of the group show respect for others?

▲ Do girls respect each other's racial, ethnic, and cultural backgrounds?

▲ Do girls work together to determine which activities they want to do?

▲ Do girls speak of "our" troop or group and say that "we" did it?

▲ Are conflicts frequent? Do they get resolved in a way that satisfies most everyone?

▲ Do girls seem to be growing in leadership abilities?

▲ Are girls working independently?

▲ Do girls take responsibility for leaving the meeting room in good condition?

Planning Troop Meetings

There is no such thing as a "typical" Junior Girl Scout meeting. The length and frequency of meetings depend on the needs and interests of the girls. In general, Junior Girl Scout troop or group meetings last 60–90 minutes and take place once a week or twice a month. But some Junior Girl Scout troops or groups meet once a month for three hours or, when engaged in a project, meet twice a week for two months.

What should you do? Ask the girls! Consider your availability and base your decision about meetings on the projects, ideas, and plans that girls have.

Although troop or group meetings can be run in a number of ways, the following is one suggestion. This design, however, should be discussed with the girls and modified, if necessary. Flexibility on your part is highly encouraged.

1. Start-Up Activity

The start-up activity can be something girls do alone or in pairs as they arrive. The activity should not require a great deal of time to complete or clean up. The start-up activity gives you time to greet each girl individually and talk to her parents if necessary. Some possibilities for activities are:

▲ A simple game. Have materials available for girls to create their own games or girls can teach each other a new game. You might suggest that they learn some of the games from *Games for Girl Scouts*. The chapter "Simple Games to Make and Play" offers many ideas for start-up activities.

"Egg Flat and Ball Game" is one game from this chapter.

You will need: an egg carton or egg flat, a Ping-Pong ball, scissors, and markers.

To make the egg carton: Cut the lid off the egg carton or cut the egg flat into nine to twelve compartments. Number each compartment consecutively.

To play: Each girl holds the egg carton in front of her body. She places the Ping-Pong ball in the #1 compartment. She must toss the ball in the air and attempt to catch it in the #2 compartment. Count the number of attempts that it takes to move the ball through the nine or twelve compartments.

▲ A group poster or mural. Invite girls to design a poster or mural, or write a group poem or song.

▲ Journal writing. Ask girls to record anything interesting that has happened to them since the last meeting. Or, they can write about a problem they're experiencing. Allow a few minutes for girls to share their thoughts with others.

▲ A review of Girl Scout program resources. Set out the materials available for Junior Girl Scouts. (See the Annotated Resource List in Chapter Five.) Encourage girls to try some of the activities.

▲ Reading magazines, books, or other materials. Display a collection of age-appropriate resources. Check with your local school or library to see if they will donate used books.

2. Opening

The opening should help girls focus on the meeting, and is the first activity that the girls do as a group. Allow girls to take turns planning the opening activity. Some possibilities for openings include:

▲ Conducting a flag ceremony.

▲ Asking each girl to share something exciting that has happened in school or with her family or friends.

▲ Singing a song or reciting a poem.

▲ Asking each girl to share one way she utilized a part of the Girl Scout Promise and Law since your last meeting.

3. Business

Troop or group business could include making special announcements, taking attendance, collecting troop dues or fees, planning for trips or activities, or revising the current kaper chart. Involve girls in conducting this part of the meeting.

4. Activities

Activities can be done alone, in pairs, or as a group. Choice of activities should be girl-directed and can cover a range of interests. See "Evaluating Troop or Group Activities" earlier in this chapter to assess the overall effectiveness of activities.

In addition to the *Junior Girl Scout Handbook*, there are many other resources full of activities appropriate for Junior Girl Scouts. See the Annotated Resource List at the end of Chapter Five.

5. Cleanup

Use the kaper chart to assign cleanup responsibility. Be sure to rotate cleanup duties among all members of your troop or group. Never use cleanup as a disciplinary tool. Cleanup should be viewed as a necessary component of a successful meeting, not as punishment.

6. Closing

The closing should focus on what the girls accomplished and what the girls can expect at the next meeting. Suggestions for closing activities are:

▲ Singing a song or reciting a poem, perhaps one written by a girl in your troop or group.

▲ Saying the Girl Scout Promise.

▲ Discussing the meaning of one part of the Girl Scout Law.

▲ Gathering for the friendship circle.

▲ Asking girls to state a personal goal they would like to accomplish.

▲ Highlighting something for the girls to look forward to at the next meeting.

It is important to be aware of each girl's arrangements for getting home. After the closing, be sure each girl is met by her parent, guardian, or other adult.

The Meeting Plan Worksheet

The "Meeting Plan Worksheet" will assist you in planning the troop meeting. Duplicate the page if necessary. Involve girls in filling in the planning page by soliciting their ideas. Sometimes it is easier to plan a meeting if you and the girls decide upon a specific goal or theme.

Keep the planning worksheets in a notebook or folder. During the year, read through the planning sheets to review plans and goals. Determine what was accomplished and what still needs to be done.

	What We Will Do	Who Will Do It	Resources Needed	Notes
Start-Up				
Opening				
Business				
Activities				
Cleanup				
Closing				

Managing Money

Troop or group dues are the amount of money the girls have decided each will add to the troop treasury. Keep in mind, however, that participation in Girl Scouting does not depend on, nor are girls required to pay, troop or group dues. Troop or group money-earning activities are activities planned and carried out by girls and adults in partnership to earn money for the treasury. Council-sponsored product sales are councilwide sales of authorized products, such as Girl Scout cookies and calendars, in which troops participate. *Safety-Wise* outlines broad standards and guidelines that must be followed. For example:

▲ Permission must be obtained in writing from a girl's parent or guardian before she participates in money-earning activities or council-sponsored product sales.

▲ Each girl's participation should be voluntary, and the number of money-earning projects should not exceed what is needed to support troop activities.

▲ Girl Scouts, in their Girl Scout capacities, may not solicit money for other organizations.

Girls need to play an active role in planning and carrying out all money-earning activities, including product sales. Product sales (e.g., cookies and calendars) should enhance a girl's experience in Girl Scouting. It is part of the Girl Scout program, and should be designed to increase decision-making, planning, and goal-setting skills. Chapter Four of the *Junior Girl Scout Handbook* outlines information on cookie sales for girls.

Before starting money-earning activities, read the relevant pages in *Safety-Wise*, obtain written permission from your Girl Scout council, and check with your Girl Scout council regarding any relevant laws, regulations, or insurance requirements.

Managing Troop or Group Money

Junior Girl Scouts are beginning to understand budgeting and group financing. They are capable of deciding whether to spend all their money on a party, to use it toward implementing a service project, or to save it for a future project. Experiences in Girl Scouting can help girls to learn to manage money wisely. Girls learn to understand and appreciate its value, and develop habits of thrift, honesty, and self-reliance.

Your troop or group should have a checking account with a council identification number. Check with your Girl Scout council for specific information on their policies for troop or group checking accounts. Troop or group money should be kept in this account. Balancing the account should be the responsibility of the girls either as part of the troop treasurer's job or as a shared duty among a treasury committee. However, all girls should be aware of the amount of money in the treasury. If your community does not have a bank in a convenient location, contact your council for assistance in investigating banking by mail.

At the outset, girls need to understand that this money is the troop's and Girl Scouts' money, not theirs or yours. Any money given or earned to support the Girl Scout troop is to be used by girls to support Girl Scout program activities. The same is true of any equipment or supplies given to or bought by your troop or group. All sports, camping, or arts and crafts equipment or musical instruments should be inventoried.

Keep accurate records of income and expenses, and save written invoices and sales slips. You should never mix your personal funds with Girl Scout money. If you use money from the treasury to buy supplies, be sure to show it as an expense and have receipts. If you add your own money, record that as income.

What happens to the money if your troop or group disbands? In some cases, leaders and girls plan a large party as a way to use up all of the money in the treasury. But, what message does this send to the girls? What they really may be learning is an attitude "this is our money and we don't want anyone else to get it."

If girls have not thought of the money as belonging to them individually, but as money given to them on behalf of Girl Scouting, then uses for this money other than a big party become more appropriate. Girls can brainstorm a list of equipment to purchase and donate to their council for other Girl Scouts to enjoy. Perhaps the money could benefit a council camp or program center. Or, girls may decide to donate money to a community project or other cause they select.

Raising money for trips or other major projects should not dominate your troop's or group's activities. You need to ensure that decisions about raising and spending money reflect the needs and interests of all girls. When planning trips and activities with girls, remind them to consider everyone's opinion and develop a plan agreeable to everyone. Girls don't join Girl Scouting to sell things. Spending an inordinate amount of time on raising money for one expensive trip or event can prevent girls from having other fun experiences.

Wider Opportunities

Planning a Wider Opportunity

Learning how to plan a trip should be a progressive experience for a Girl Scout, one that starts with an outing she is ready to handle. Girls do the planning themselves with guidance from adults. Thus, taking a Girl Scout trip is an important way for girls to learn many skills.

When planning a trip, you and the girls should answer the following questions:

▲ Why are we going?

▲ What do we hope to accomplish?

▲ What will we do when we get there?

▲ How long does it take to get there?

▲ Are facilities such as restaurants and restrooms easily accessible?

▲ Will special clothing or equipment be needed?

▲ What will the trip cost?

▲ What types of activities are suitable for the site and the girls?

▲ Will reservations be needed?

▲ Will council permission be required?

▲ How will members with disabilities experience the trip?

▲ What safety factors should be taken into consideration?

▲ What will we do when we get home?

The girls should do the planning in patrols or small groups, keeping the purpose of the trip in mind. Planning should include budgeting for the trip, learning skills that girls will need to know on the trip, and becoming aware of personal conduct and safety rules. As a leader, you will need to advise the girls and, when necessary, help scale their ideas into what is possible and fun.

Before going on any trip with girls, consult the *Safety-Wise* chapter "Basic Safety and Security Guidelines" as well as the section "Planning Trips with Girls" for specific guidelines on making the trip successful and safe. You must also check with your council support person regarding council procedures for trips. Keep in mind that parents and guardians must be informed and give written consent for activities scheduled outside the regular meeting place. For events, trips, and troop camping, there should be two adults to every 16 or fewer Junior Girl Scouts and one adult for each additional eight Junior Girl Scouts.

Progression of Trips

Trips should be planned progressively. Start with simple trips that are close to home, then slowly increase distance and duration. Junior Girl Scouts go on day trips in their own communities and to places of interest nearby. As they become experienced in planning and evaluating their adventures, their plans may include longer trips, with stays in hotels as well as program centers. Junior Girl Scout badge activities suggest trips to places in the community, as well as hikes, walks, and campouts.

The progression of trips in Girl Scouting is as follows:

1. Meeting-time trips are to points of interest in the neighborhood. A walk to a nearby garden or a short car or bus ride to an historic site could start the progression.

2. Day trips, away from the troop meeting place and outside the regular meeting time, are the next step. Girls might plan an all-day visit to a point of historic or natural interest and bring their lunches. Or they might visit a nearby city, have lunch, then return. Girls might also travel to a Girl Scout council-sponsored or Girl Scout neighborhood-sponsored event.

3. Simple overnight trips usually involve one or two nights away. The destination may be a nearby state or national park, an historic site, or a city. The group may stay in a hostel, hotel, or motel, or they may camp at a Girl Scout campsite or nearby campgrounds. Contact your council about training you may need for taking girls overnight camping.

4. Extended overnight trips can range from three or more nights camping to extensive travel within

the United States. The troop or group might use different accommodations and means of transportation throughout the trip. For information about planning this kind of trip, contact your Girl Scout council. Information about travel camping facilities at Girl Scout sites nationwide is compiled by Girl Scouts of the U.S.A. in the *Trekking Network Directory*, available through your Girl Scout council office.

5. International trips are taken by Cadette and Senior Girl Scouts who have progressed from overnight trips. Because of the special requirements of such trips, including regulations and procedures established by the World Association of Girl Guides and Girl Scouts, trips to other countries are dealt with in a special section of *Safety-Wise*.

On the following page, you will find a sample monthly planning calendar that you can duplicate and use to plan troop activities. At the beginning of the troop or group year, work with the girls to develop tentative plans for the year. Pencil in planning meetings, the names of possible resources and consultants, or any special events your Girl Scout council has planned. Perhaps the girls would find it interesting to focus on a different theme each month or may wish to devote two months to completing a service project. Whatever the case, the planning calendar helps ensure that experiences are varied and encompass the four Girl Scout program goals.

MONTHLY PLANNING CALENDAR

Monday	Tuesday	Wednesday	Thursday	Friday	Saturday	Sunday

WHERE TO FIND HELP
CHAPTER 5

Many volunteers throughout Girl Scouting can help make your responsibility as a leader easier and more enjoyable. These individuals also can add variety and freshness to troop or group projects and can help out with many "odd jobs." Take advantage of this help! The following diagram shows the different volunteers you can turn to for help.

```
                Program
               consultants

Troop/group                      Cadette
 committee                        and
                                 Senior
                    You          Girl Scouts

  Parents
   and                          Sponsors
 guardians

              Service team
```

Key Volunteers

Parents and Guardians

A leader can encourage parent and guardian involvement in many ways, some of which are listed below. Keep in mind the importance of maintaining open communication. Let parents know frequently about what's going on in the troop. If you keep parents and guardians informed, they are likely to want to participate and cooperate when asked.

Parents and guardians of Girl Scouts can help by:

▲ Sharing special skills and knowledge with you and your troop or group.

  ▲ Helping with phone calls, paperwork, and record-keeping.

  ▲ Providing transportation.

  ▲ Accompanying the troop or group on trips.

▲ Caring for younger children during meetings.

▲ Helping with money-earning projects.

▲ Coordinating, writing, or distributing a monthly troop newsletter for parents and guardians.

▲ Maintaining files of parents' and other adults' interests, hobbies, and careers that can be shared with girls.

Troop Committee

The troop committee, a group of three to six women and men who are registered Girl Scouts, is generally composed of parents and guardians. However, Campus Girl Scouts, young adults, senior citizens, professional and business people, and sponsors (see page 58) may be recruited to serve on the troop committee. Troop committee

members appoint a committee chair who works directly with you, finding out what kind of help you most need.

The troop committee can help by:

▲ Assisting with special projects.

▲ Substituting when you or your co-leader is absent.

▲ Recruiting consultants and other adults who can share their skills with girls.

▲ Helping with registration forms and other paperwork.

▲ Carrying out any of the duties listed under "Parents and Guardians."

To maintain good working relationships with troop committee members, many leaders arrange frequent meetings throughout the year. Others, however, find two or three meetings during the year sufficient.

Program Consultants

A member of the local geographic unit, a troop committee member, or a leader can recruit a program consultant to share her or his special interest and skills with the troop or group. This volunteer program consultant can offer help by:

▲ Participating in a service project.

▲ Consulting with girls or leaders about badge work.

▲ Organizing career exploration or field trips.

▲ Organizing interest groups.

A program consultant offers ideas, methods, and procedures for delivering Girl Scout program. She or he also can add variety and vitality. If you are specific about what your troop or group needs, when it is needed, and how much time it will take, a program consultant can be the right resource person with whom to work.

As are the members of the troop committee, program consultants can be parents, friends, neighbors, senior citizens, young adults, local business and professional people, or the sponsoring group. Sometimes members of the troop committee act as program consultants.

Cadette and Senior Girl Scouts

Cadette and Senior Girl Scouts can help you and your girls by:

▲ Teaching songs and games.

▲ Sharing special talents and skills.

▲ Planning and coordinating ceremonies.

▲ Helping with badge work and other activities.

▲ Accompanying the troop or group on field trips.

▲ Participating as Leaders-in-Training, Counselors-in-Training, or program aides.

▲ Assisting in the girl planning process.

▲ Serving as visible role models.

▲ Helping girls learn about the opportunities that await them in Cadette and Senior Girl Scouting.

Cadette and Senior Girl Scouts' first-hand knowledge and enthusiasm can often help turn reluctant group members into eager participants. By requesting the services of Cadette and Senior Girl Scouts, you will be helping both your own group of girls and the older girls.

Sponsors

A sponsor is a community organization or business that forms a voluntary association with a Girl Scout council on behalf of the girls and their adult leader. Sponsors, whose aims and objectives are compatible with the philosophy of Girl Scouting, may assist you by providing:

▲ Program consultants.

▲ Financial assistance.

▲ Supplies and materials.

▲ Transportation and equipment.

▲ A meeting place or a place for special events.

▲ A member to serve on the troop committee.

▲ Career exploration opportunities for girls.

If you have been approached by someone from a local business or agency about sponsorship, refer the person to the appropriate individual at your Girl Scout council.

Local Geographic Unit

The local geographic unit (also known as the service team, neighborhood association, support team, or other names) is a group of volunteers who provide direct service to Girl Scout troops or groups within a neighborhood or other geographic subdivision of the council. The unit is generally composed of a manager, one or more troop or group consultants, and one or more troop or group organizers and other specialists. It is important to become familiar with the members of your geographic unit because they serve as a great resource and provide another link with your Girl Scout council. This unit provides such services as:

Organizing groups of girls.
The service team helps with:

▲ Recruiting and placing girls and adults.

▲ Membership registration.

▲ Finding suitable meeting places.

▲ Obtaining parental support.

▲ Promoting of Girl Scout activities.

Guidance with program opportunities. The service team could:

▲ Suggest ideas for service projects and field trips.

▲ Provide information on program, camping, and council-sponsored events.

▲ Provide ideas and guidelines for money-earning projects.

Support to leaders. The service team can:

▲ Help with troop or group management.

▲ Supply information on educational opportunities.

▲ Help find consultants.

▲ Help in the use of program resources, such as the Contemporary Issues booklets.

▲ Provide feedback and act as a sounding board.

▲ Help interpret national and local policies, standards, and procedures.

Your Girl Scout Council

Your local Girl Scout council has been chartered by Girl Scouts of the U.S.A. to organize and maintain Girl Scouting in a specific geographic area. Your Girl Scout council has organized your local support team. Therefore, you may receive some services locally while others may be provided by your Girl Scout council.

Your council may provide:

▲ Program and outdoor resources and facilities.

▲ Councilwide activities and projects.

▲ Opportunities for adult learning and sharing.

▲ Access to Girl Scout books, audiovisual materials, and other resources.

▲ Information about council

organization and operation as well as national and local policies, standards, and procedures.

▲ Opportunities to express needs and make suggestions.

▲ Newsletters or other resources.

▲ Networking possibilities.

Whether you are new or experienced, keep in touch with your council office to find out about such events as educational opportunities for leaders. These events offer practical knowledge and skills through evening sessions or more in-depth day events or weekend workshops. Written modules also allow a leader to study independently.

In the space provided, record the name, address, telephone, and fax numbers of your Girl Scout council and geographic unit. Also include the names of people you may need to contact.

Council Resource List

Name of council _____

Address _____

_____

_____

_____

Telephone number _____

Fax number _____

Contact person _____

Contact person _____

Geographic Unit Resource List

Local geographic unit _____

Address _____

_____

_____

_____

Telephone number _____

Fax number _____

Contact person _____

Contact person _____

Girl Scouts of the U.S.A. (GSUSA), the national Girl Scout organization, conducts research, develops the Girl Scout program, and produces audiovisual materials and publications. GSUSA charters Girl Scout councils, provides them with criteria and standards for effectiveness, develops management resources, and offers consultative services.

Services Provided by Girl Scouts of the U.S.A.

GSUSA also offers services to adults and girls.

For adults, GSUSA:

▲ Provides national educational opportunities at Edith Macy Conference Center.

▲ Operates the National Equipment Service and publishes the Girl Scout catalog.

▲ Provides membership cards.

▲ Holds national meetings.

▲ Maintains the National Historic Preservation Center.

▲ Publishes *Girl Scout Leader* magazine.

For girls, GSUSA:

▲ Provides membership cards.

▲ Provides travelships for Cadette and Senior Girl Scouts to attend both national and international wider opportunities.

▲ Serves as a link for international pen pals.

▲ Provides travel assistance that includes cards of introduction for traveling troops, information for girls traveling across the border, information on the TREKKING network of camps and facilities, and information on and applications for grants and scholarships.

▲ Provides Girl Scout Gold Award certificates and lifesaving awards.

▲ Provides services to USA Girl Scouts Overseas.

▲ Provides activity accident insurance.

Furthermore, GSUSA:

▲ Serves as liaison to the World Association of Girl Guides and Girl Scouts.

▲ Provides consulting services to councils.

▲ Grants council charters.

▲ Maintains national centers.

GSUSA National Centers

GSUSA owns and operates two national centers: the Juliette Gordon Low Girl Scout National Center and Edith Macy Conference Center. These centers, partially supported by membership registration dues, provide opportunities for girl and adult members to meet other Girl Scouts from across the country, explore new places, and gain new knowledge and skills.

Juliette Gordon Low Girl Scout National Center

Located in Savannah, Georgia, the birthplace of Juliette Low is part of the largest National Historic Landmark District in the United States. The Juliette Gordon Low Girl Scout National Center is a program center and public museum where visitors can learn about her childhood and her life's work in Girl Scouting.

For further information, write to Juliette Gordon Low Girl Scout National Center, 142 Bull Street, Savannah, Georgia 31401.

Edith Macy Conference Center

Edith Macy Conference Center provides educational opportunities for adults and sometimes for girls. This site, located 35 miles from New York City, also contains the John J. Creedon Center, a smaller training facility. Edith Macy Conference Center offers courses on such subjects as the arts, serving girls with disabilities, leadership, science, and pluralism. Many courses are designed especially for adults who work with girls. These courses are open to any Girl Scout volunteer; you do not have to be selected. Some Girl Scout councils offer financial assistance for leaders to attend courses. The conference center can also accommodate day tours.

For additional information, write to the Training Registrar, Girl Scouts of the U.S.A., 420 Fifth Avenue, New York, New York 10018-2702. Your Girl Scout council should have the current educational opportunities catalog.

Annotated Resource List

In addition to *The Guide for Junior Scout Leaders*, GSUSA offers numerous resources for Junior Girl Scouts and Girl Scout leaders. The major resources include:

Junior Girl Scout Handbook. Serves as the basic book of activities for Junior Girl Scouts. Some recognitions, including the Junior Girl Scout Leadership Pin, are contained in this resource.

Girl Scout Badges and Signs. Details the recognitions available for Junior Girl Scouts.

Junior Girl Scout Activity Book. Contains hands-on activities that explore such themes as leadership, relationships, skills for living, and the natural world.

Safety-Wise. The basic guide of security and safety practices for Girl Scouts.

Leader's Digest: Blue Book of Basic Documents. Covers all the Girl Scout policies as well as excerpts from the Congressional Charter and the Girl Scout Constitution.

Contemporary Issues booklets. Contain information and statistics, tips for leaders, age-appropriate activities, and resource sections. Leaders can refer to the following booklets to find information and activities appropriate for Junior Girl Scouts.

▲ *Tune In to Well-Being, Say No to Drugs: Substance Abuse*

▲ *Staying Safe: Preventing Child Abuse*

▲ *Girls Are Great: Growing Up Female*

▲ *Into the World of Today and Tomorrow: Leading Girls to Mathematics, Science, and Technology*

▲ Reaching Out: Preventing Youth Suicide

▲ Caring and Coping: Facing Family Crises

▲ Earth Matters: A Challenge for Environmental Action

▲ Valuing Differences: Promoting Pluralism

▲ Decisions for Your Life: Preventing Teenage Pregnancy

▲ Right to Read: Literacy

▲ Developing Health and Fitness: Be Your Best!

Outdoor Education in Girl Scouting. Contains ways to introduce outdoor activities to girls. This book outlines information on camping, safety skills, and ways of evaluating the outdoor experience.

Exploring Wildlife Communities with Children. Helps adults explore the wonders of the environment with children.

Games for Girl Scouts. Includes a wide variety of old and new games: travel games, outdoor games, wide games, quiet games, and simple games to make and play.

Sing-Along Songbook and Cassette. Features old and new Girl Scout favorites.

Girl Scout Pocket Songbook. Contains 60 international and national Girl Scout songs.

Sing Together: A Girl Scout Songbook. Includes over 140 favorites. The Sing Together Sampler is a 40-minute audiocassette tape with helpful teaching tips.

Our Chalet Songbook. Contains songs compiled by the Our Chalet Committee of WAGGGS.

Canciones de Nuestra Cabaña. Includes 110 songs with lyrics in Spanish and English compiled by the Our Cabaña Committee of

WAGGGS. *Canciones de Nuestra Cabaña Cassette* has over 50 songs, most in Spanish.

The Wide World of Girl Guiding and Girl Scouting. Includes information on Girl Guiding/Girl Scouting activities in other countries.

Trefoil Round The World. Describes the history of Girl Guiding and Girl Scouting, including the basic facts of each member association.

World Games and Recipes. Offers games and food from around the world.

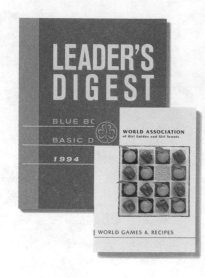

Girl Scout Uniforms, Insignia, and Recognitions. Includes photos and information on uniforms and insignia for all age levels and adults.

Focus on Ability: Serving Girls with Special Needs. Provides information on various disabilities and ways to work with girls with special needs.

Ceremonies in Girl Scouting. Offers a compilation of popular Girl Scout ceremonies.

Troop Records and Reports. Preprinted forms and a binder for recording dues, attendance, and activities.

The Girl Scout Catalog and the GSUSA Publications and Audiovisuals Catalog. Resources released annually listing merchandise for sale through the National Equipment Service.

All of the above-mentioned materials are available through the National Equipment Service, GSUSA, 420 Fifth Avenue, New York, New York 10018-2702. Check with your local Girl Scout council first or your local neighborhood Girl Scout group to find out which books are available. Many Girl Scout councils also have a Girl Scout council shop that sells books and many other NES items. You may want to set up a lending library with other Girl Scout leaders to offset some of the cost.

Increasing the number of resources that girls use can help maintain their interest in Girl Scouting. Many of the books, such as *The Wide World of Girl Guiding and Girl Scouting* and the Contemporary Issues series, can be used to supplement information and activities in the handbook. You may also want to try activities that you have used in other settings with children or that you have read about in an activity book. If you choose an activity that is not from a Girl Scout resource, be sure it is compatible with the Girl Scout Promise and Law, the four program goals, and safety standards.

Another important resource is *Girl Scout Leader.* This quarterly magazine covers news and articles about events and activities in Girl Scouting. All registered Girl Scout adult members receive this publication.

INTRODUCTION
PART 2

In Part II of this leaders' guide, you will find the entire *Junior Girl Scout Handbook* reproduced and accompanied by text that will take you through the handbook page by page. Each left-hand page in Part II contains two pages reproduced (and reduced in size) from the *Junior Girl Scout Handbook*. The adjacent right-hand pages of the guide offer "Tips," "Supporting Activities," and "Program Links." This information is given to help you provide a more enriching experience for Junior Girl Scouts.

The "Tips" category describes general behavioral, emotional, and social characteristics of girls at the Junior Girl Scout age level. "Tips" also include additional ideas related to each section in the handbook as well as safety suggestions to supplement those outlined in *Safety-Wise*. While the *Junior Girl Scout Handbook* offers numerous activities, those provided in "Supporting Activities" highlight additional skills and approaches. The "Program Links" section draws together Girl Scout resources and recognitions that correspond to the handbook pages.

The *Junior Girl Scout Handbook* includes eight chapters filled with timely topics and activities. The handbook is designed to be interactive, so girls should be encouraged to personalize their books by writing and drawing in them. You, as a leader, can enhance this process by offering your own expertise and practical knowledge.

An overview of the handbook is as follows:

▲ Chapter One, "Welcome to Girl Scouting," presents not only the traditional components of Girl Scouting such as the Girl Scout Promise and Law and the Junior Girl Scout uniform, but also includes a section on "Camping, Service, and Trips: Three Favorite Girl Scout Activities." Here girls will find steps for planning trips.

▲ Chapter Two, "Who Am I… Now?," discusses puberty, friends, family, peer pressure, and other topics related to growing up.

▲ Chapter Three, "Staying Safe and Healthy," focuses on health and safety and includes such topics as first aid, personal safety, fitness, and nutrition.

▲ Chapter Four, "Skills to Use Every Day," gives information about such skills as time and money management, clothing care, and home repair. A section called "Media Wise" encourages girls to examine the media and its influence. This chapter also educates girls about career choices.

▲ Chapter Five, "Everyone Is Different," discusses the issues of prejudice, discrimination, and stereotypes.

▲ Chapter Six, "Leadership in Action," aims to foster girls' confidence in their leadership abilities.

▲ Chapter Seven, "Exploring Interests, Skills, and Talents," details a range of activities in such areas as the arts, sports, science, and outdoor exploration. The activities and challenges can be tailored to fit group or individual interest.

▲ Chapter Eight, "Bridging and Recognitions," contains the requirements for earning the 13 handbook badges. This chapter details the steps girls will take when bridging from Junior to Cadette Girl Scouting. Chapter Eight also includes information about the new Junior Girl Scout Leadership Pin.

INTRODUCTION

Congratulations on becoming a Junior Girl Scout! Whether you've just joined or you've bridged from Brownie Girl Scouts, you're about to enter a world of fun, friends, and adventures.

This is your handbook filled with stories about girls like you, activities, games, and facts about growing up. In this book you'll learn about camping and the outdoors, staying safe and healthy, protecting the environment, enjoying time with friends and family, playing sports, enjoying the arts and sciences, and much more. You'll also learn about belonging to Girl Scouts of the U.S.A., the largest organization for girls in the country.

Some of your handbook activities you can plan and do with friends and some you will probably want to do on your own. The activities—things to make and do—help you learn more about yourself and what is important to you.

You can write in your handbook, take notes, draw pictures, or attach things to the pages. The chapters do not have to be read in any special order. Your Girl Scout leader can work with you to decide which chapters to read and activities to do. She can help find resources, too, that you might need when doing the activities. She can even suggest other ways of doing the activities.

As you read, you may notice symbols that appear more than once. You will see that some activities appear with a badge symbol that looks like this:

This means that those activities can be done as a badge requirement. In other words, if you finish the activity, you'd be working on earning a badge.

5

Handbook Page 5

Welcome to Girl Scouting

HANDBOOK CHAPTER 1

Tips

Introduction: The *Junior Girl Scout Handbook* has a new look and format designed to appeal to girls of this age level. In fact, the design of the *Junior Girl Scout Handbook* was based on research indicating what girls of this age wanted in their handbooks.

Give girls the opportunity to explore and get excited about their handbooks. Encourage girls to look at the Contents pages and scan the handbook's illustrations, charts, and photographs.

Point out that the handbook provides space to write, draw, and attach things, like photos, to the pages. In other words, space is available for them to personalize their books. For example, you might want to ask girls to write a journal entry somewhere in their books describing this first experience with their new handbooks. Their entries can be as brief or as long as they want, and remind them to date it.

The Introduction also lets girls know they can involve friends and relatives as well as other Girl Scouts in their activities. It is hoped this reminder will encourage them to use their handbooks during the week, not just during meetings.

Notes

Some other challenging activities are marked like this:

Some activities may require you to take safety precautions or be extra careful. These activities are marked by:

Also, to help you find things in this book quickly, there is an alphabetical index at the end.

Note:

Some badge activities are scattered throughout the chapters, but all badge activities are listed in Chapter Eight. Chapter Eight also has information about other recognitions such as Junior Girl Scout signs.

Why not explore the activities in your handbook? Try this activity treasure hunt.

You need: A *Junior Girl Scout Handbook* for every two girls, paper, and pencils.

With a partner, create a list of ten things that you both guess will be in the handbook. For example: a song, a ceremony, the Girl Scout Promise, a game, a badge, a safety tip, something that helps the environment.

Then, exchange your list for the list of another pair so that you will be working from a new list. Find each item in the handbook and write down the page number where it appears. Each pair then shares their list with the entire group and chooses one activity to do or learn more about.

6

WELCOME TO GIRL SCOUTING
CHAPTER 1

Who Can Be a Girl Scout?
page 13

The Junior Girl Scout Uniform
page 16

The Girl Scout Pyramid: Where Do You Fit In?
page 20

Camping, Service, and Trips
page 27

TAP

Now that you're a Junior Girl Scout, you follow in a long tradition of girls who've made the Girl Scout Promise. Since 1912, girls just like you have had fun making new friends, trying new activities, and helping in their communities.

In this chapter you'll learn how Girl Scouting began and about things like ceremonies, your uniform, and what Junior Girl Scouts do. You'll also learn about the woman who started Girl Scouts—Juliette Gordon Low or Daisy—who was curious and energetic as a child. She loved animals, the outdoors, and playing with her brothers, sisters, and cousins. Well, let her tell you herself…

7

The Introduction concludes by pointing out the symbols girls will encounter when reading their handbooks. As noted, activities throughout the handbook are accompanied by badge or handbook activity symbols. All badge activities are listed in Chapter Eight, though many badge activities are scattered throughout the text. Where extra care should be taken with an activity, a caution symbol will appear. Be sure to go over the meaning of these symbols.

Since some activities fulfill badge requirements, it might be a good idea to keep track of the activities completed by each girl. One of the girls can be responsible for this by creating a chart or you may use the one included in this chapter.

▲ **Activity Treasure Hunt:** This handbook activity encourages girls to look throughout the book for components of Girl Scout activities. When they finish, they will have a good idea about the topics or activities they'd like to pursue.

▲ **Chapter 1: Welcome to Girl Scouting:** Trends indicate that many girls leave Girl Scouting at the Junior Girl Scout age level. As a leader, you can enlighten girls to the benefits of remaining in this unique organization. Your approach and attitude towards Junior Girl Scout activities, ideas, and issues will strongly influence girls' attitudes about Girl Scouting. Be sensitive to the interests of girls and adapt material to your troop's or group's needs.

Appreciate the growing maturity of the girls throughout the year. As you and the girls progress, increase girls' accountabilities and responsibilities. Give girls ample opportunities to voice their opinions, ideas, and suggestions in all troop or group matters. Encourage girls to take on new challenges and be prepared to help them learn from their mistakes. Welcome diversity and present differences as a vehicle for learning about other cultures, religions, races, abilities, and economic levels.

The challenges and rewards of being a Girl Scout leader are immeasurable. Remember that you are part of a global network of volunteers all working toward the same goal—providing young women with memorable Girl Scout experiences. If, at any time, you need additional support or ideas, contact your service unit director, Girl Scout council office, or Girl Scouts of the U. S. A. Chapter Five in Part I of this guide lists individuals and units to contact for assistance.

So, "Be prepared" and have fun!

REMINDER!

Make a number of blank calendars (on 8 1/2" x 11" sheets) that girls can fill in with dates for regular meetings, field trips or overnights, service projects, etc. Girls can also write on the calendar dates they need to bring things, such as permission forms, snacks, or supplies, to the meeting. Suggest girls post these at home each month. These calendars will inform their families about the activities girls will be doing, and remind girls about troop or group commitments.

A Letter from Daisy Low

My darling Mama,

I rise at six, study an hour before breakfast which is at eight. During the morning I have nothing but French studies. At twelve we have lunch. Three times a week I go to my drawing. I wish you could see my teacher. He is a perfect character. On Saturday morning I go with five other girls from here to Dodsworth's dancing school where they are so swell, but I like it and know already lots of people there.

Daisy

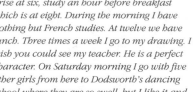

Most of you may know me as the founder of Girl Scouts of the U.S.A. But I imagine very few of you know much about me as a girl your age. I'm sure I wasn't much different from many of you.

I attended boarding school over 100 years ago in New York City, and that letter is one of hundreds I wrote throughout my life. In fact, before telephones, letter writing was the way people kept in touch.

MORE ABOUT DAISY LOW

My full name is Juliette Magill Kinzie Gordon Low. I was born on October 31, 1860, a few months before the Civil War began. My birthday fell on Halloween.

I was named after my grandmother Kinzie, but she was the only one who called me Juliette. When my father wrote to his family in Chicago about me, one of my uncles exclaimed, "I'll bet she'll be a Daisy!" And I remained "Daisy" to my family and to many of my close friends all my life.

I was part of a large family who played and had fun together. I loved animals of all kinds and had some pretty unusual ones. My pet parrot and mockingbird were two of my favorites.

Drawing was my favorite subject in school, and I was good at learning foreign languages. But spelling and arithmetic gave me problems. At times I was too active and fun-loving to sit still in school. My mother wrote: "I send a list of your words (spelled) wrong and the right way to spell them. Please study them hard, as you frequently, in fact, always, spell them wrongly."

Daisy's Spelling	Right Way
sleave	sleeve
idear	idea
disgrase	disgrace
suspence	suspense

I really enjoyed writing plays and acting them out with my brothers and sisters and cousins, and I also made paper dolls by drawing pictures of characters in storybooks and of famous actresses. You can see them today if you visit my home in Savannah.

I also enjoyed learning how to dance. If I were alive today, I would probably know all the latest dance steps. In the 1870s I went to dancing school to learn ballroom dancing. The polka was popular then. In those days, girls were taught more than how to dance. They had to learn how to enter a ballroom, how to curtsy, and most importantly, how to sit properly in a chair. Legs must never be crossed and both feet should rest on the floor. Our skirts had to be arranged in folds, just right. Boys had to learn how to make a formal bow and offer their arms to a partner.

8

9

▲ **A Letter from Daisy Low:** These pages contain biographical material about the founder of Girl Scouts in the United States, Juliette Gordon Low ("Daisy"). Her biography is presented in the form of actual letters written during her adolescence and a fictionalized narrative by Juliette Low herself. Readers get a chance to learn about Daisy when she was the age of Junior Girl Scouts.

Your troop or group might enjoy reading the letters together. After reading, girls can discuss what they have learned about Daisy, and how her life was different from and similar to theirs. Reading Daisy's letters could also prompt discussion about: favorite school subjects, teachers, hobbies, nicknames, family members, and pets.

Ask girls if they or anyone they know celebrates her birthday on a holiday. How does the holiday affect the way her birthday is celebrated? Daisy's birthday was on Halloween. Ask girls what they think it would be like to have a birthday on Halloween.

Daisy was named "Juliette" after her grandmother, but her uncle was the first to call her "Daisy. "From then on, that's what everyone called her. Ask the girls whether their names have special meanings. Suggest they create a drawing out of the letters of their names, or try a word game making words from the letters in their names.

Daisy's letter about the lost ring (see the next page) may bring to mind similar experiences girls may have had. Daisy's narrative about becoming deaf and her troubled marriage to Willy Low reveals that she too had problems in her life, but they did not prevent her from achieving her goals.

By reading Daisy's life story, girls get the opportunity to explore their own life stories and to learn about each other. Girls discover that, like them, Daisy had her favorite school subjects (drawing and languages) and those subjects that caused her difficulty (spelling and arithmetic). What are their favorite and not so favorite school subjects? What kind of dances do they do, and how different are they from Daisy's dances of the 1870s? If girls express interest, have them create a mural, scrapbook, time line, or collage about their families and interests.

▲ As Daisy states in her narrative, letter writing was the way people kept in touch before telephones. Ask girls to write a letter to someone they don't see everyday such as a friend, relative, or pen pal.

▲ Find out about languages the girls might know or are learning. They may enjoy teaching each other words and simple phrases from languages other than English. Some of them may want to write their letters in languages other than English.

▲ Girls can make their own stationery by decorating plain paper with cut-out pictures, dried flowers or leaves, drawings, or stickers.

▲ Girls can make recycled paper or Japanese rice paper. Check the library for craft books with instructions.

As Daisy Grew

*S*avannah, Georgia, is very hot during the summers, and people in those days were afraid of catching yellow fever, a dreadful disease. So Mama and Papa sent us children to spend the summer with our Aunt Eliza, my cousin Caroline's mother, in Etowah Cliffs, Georgia. This was further north and much cooler than Savannah.

There was plenty of room in the big house. Sometimes as many as 20 cousins were there at one time. The boys slept on mattresses on the floor, and we girls slept on beds in the bedrooms. During the day, we played in fruit orchards, rose gardens, woods, and the countryside full of wild flowers.

Etowah Cliffs
November 8, 1876

Oh Mama!

I feel perfectly miserable, because you're going to give me an awful scolding and I know I deserve it. I've lost my beautiful little ring with the blue forget-me-nots on it that Uncle Julian sent from Europe to me!!!

This is the way I lost it. Percy lent me his gold pencil to wear around my neck on ribbon, and I lent him my ring (I know you will say "the little fool" but I expect you lent your rings to boys when you were a girl) and of course I didn't know he would lose it, but he did and he felt awfully about it….

Your prodigal daughter,

Daisy

On December 21, 1886, when I was 26 years old, I married an Englishman named Willy Low. I carried lilies of the valley in my wedding bouquet, the favorite flower of my sister Alice who had died. I had already lost some hearing in one of my ears. As I was leaving the ceremony, a piece of rice landed in my good ear and the doctor who removed the grain of rice punctured my eardrum. Eventually, I became almost totally deaf.

*T*hough our marriage got off to a hopeful start, Willy and I became very unhappy. We had a good life in England with lots of friends, but our marriage was not successful and we separated. We had decided to divorce when Willy got very ill and died.

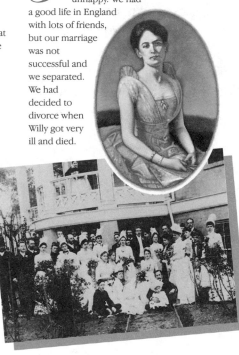

10

How Girl Scouting Came About

Scout in the United States. She loved to play basketball. In 1912, girls wore enormous pleated gymnasium bloomers to play basketball. They had to cover themselves with overcoats that reached their ankles to cross the street to reach the basketball lot. Before taking off their overcoats, they pulled together huge canvas curtains strung on wires which surrounded the basketball field. That way, nobody could see their bloomered legs from the street!

I was 52 years old and not in good physical health when I made the long boat trip home from England. I could have stayed in England. I had my sculpture and art and friends, but I had learned about an organization that was so exciting that I had to return home to share it with girls in the United States.

I had become friends with Lord Baden-Powell who founded the Boy Scouts. His sister Agnes was in charge of the girls who wanted to make their own Scout troops. They were called Girl Guides. Lord Baden-Powell told me that "there are little stars that guide us on, although we do not realize it." I thought about this saying while I was deciding what I should do next and the direction seemed clear: start Girl Scouts in the United States.

My niece, who was also named Daisy Gordon, was the first Girl

*T*oday, Girl Scouts continue many of the same traditions and activities we did when there were only 3,000 Girl Scouts in 1916. There are almost three million Girl Scouts from all parts of the United States, and there are many more Girl Scouts or Girl Guides in over 100 countries around the world and each has a Girl Scout Promise. Girl Scouts travel, go camping, and become leaders in their communities. They develop a set of values to help guide their actions and they plan many kinds of activities that are fun and different from what they might usually do. But most importantly, Girl Scouts learn how to work with and support each other and have a great time.

11

▲ Girls could practice folding paper in different ways, perhaps using simple origami designs. They could fold letters they've written into an origami design.

▲ Another activity Daisy enjoyed as a child was making her own paper dolls based on characters in storybooks. Why not have the girls make paper dolls of themselves by attaching photos of their faces onto bodies they draw or cut out from illustrations? Suggest they draw clothing or cut out pictures of fashions from teen magazines.

Program Links

▲ *Girl Scout Badges and Signs*: Art to Wear badge; Dance badge.

▲ **How Girl Scouting Came About:** This section begins with Juliette Low recounting the early days of Girl Scouting. It is important for girls to see that at age 52, she made what might be called today a "career change." Juliette Low had to make a decision: She could remain in England and develop her talent, perhaps becoming a highly accomplished artist, or she could change direction in life and start an organization for girls. Today's Girl Scouts are the beneficiaries of her important decision.

Also of note is that Juliette Low made several trips between the U. S. A. and England on Girl Scout business. Those trips, which would take a matter of hours by air today, took Juliette several days each way by boat. Juliette lived in the days before jets, computers, fax machines, VCRs, and television. Thomas Edison and Alexander Graham Bell were her contemporaries. It would be fascinating for girls to place Juliette Low and the story of Girl Scouting within the context of American (and world) history. She accomplished so much without the modern conveniences that we take for granted.

It might be of interest to know that Juliette Low's first experience working with girls in a troop was in Scotland. Seven girls met every Saturday; some had to walk as far as seven miles to get there. They learned about cooking, knitting, first aid, personal hygiene and knot tying—much of what girls in the first American troop would later learn.

The Scottish girls also became entrepreneurs. They raised chickens and spun wool to sell in London. This meant they did not have to leave home, as many other young people did, to work in city factories.

By sharing this information, you could help Junior Girl Scouts begin to see themselves as part of a worldwide organization of girls with similar goals and values.

Program Links

▲ *Girl Scout Badges and Signs:* Girl Scouting in the U. S. A. badge

Being a Junior Girl Scout

The Girl Scout Promise
On my honor, I will try:
To serve God and my country,
To help people at all times,
And to live by the Girl Scout Law.

The Girl Scout Promise and Law

All Girl Scouts, both girls and adults, make the Girl Scout Promise and agree to try to live by the Girl Scout Law.

Write down what each line of the Promise means to you and discuss what you've written in your troop or group.

On my honor, I will try:
(What does honor mean?)

To serve God
(To go along with their beliefs, some girls may choose to say a word or phrase other than God. What are some ways you can live by your beliefs?)

and my country,
(What are some ways you can serve your country?)

To help people at all times,
(What are some ways you can help people?)

And to live by the Girl Scout Law.
(What are some other words that mean "to live by"?)

 An important word or phrase is highlighted on each line of the Girl Scout Law. These words represent the personal characteristics of a Girl Scout. In pairs, choose one line of the Girl Scout Law and tell what the words mean to each of you.

Once the two of you have discussed your words, prepare a demonstration of the word or phrase for the rest of your troop or group. For example, perform a skit or pantomime, write a poem or a make-believe diary entry, draw a picture or make up a telephone conversation about your word. You could ask others to guess what your word or phrase is.

 Using the words from the Girl Scout Promise and Law, create a word search, crossword puzzle, or other word game. Exchange your word puzzles with each other and try them out. Put them together to form a word puzzle book. Exchange with other Junior Girl Scout troops or with troops of Brownie Girl Scouts.

The Girl Scout Law
I will do my best:
to be honest
to be fair
to help where I am needed
to be cheerful
to be friendly and considerate
to be a sister to every Girl Scout
to respect authority
to use resources wisely
to protect and improve the world around me
to show respect for myself and others through my words and actions.

Who Can Be a Girl Scout?

Any girl who is 5 through 17 years old or in kindergarten through the twelfth grade can become a Girl Scout in the United States. Girls of different races, cultures, and religious groups are welcome in Girl Scouting. Every Girl Scout is expected to make the Girl Scout Promise and try to live by the Girl Scout Law.

The five age levels in Girl Scouting are:

Daisy Girl Scouts
ages 5-6 or grades K, 1

Brownie Girl Scouts
ages 6, 7, 8 or grades 1, 2, 3

Junior Girl Scouts
ages 8, 9, 10, 11
or grades 3, 4, 5, 6

Cadette Girl Scouts
ages 11, 12, 13, 14
or grades 6, 7, 8, 9

Senior Girl Scouts
ages 14, 15, 16, 17
or grades 9, 10, 11, 12

Girl Scout Traditions

As a Junior Girl Scout not only do you get to try fun activities, but you get to be part of a group.

Juliette Low understood how special words and signs help girls feel they are members of a group. Girl Scouts and Girl Guides all

> The Girl Scout motto is "Be prepared."

around the world share special signs, a handshake, the friendship squeeze, a motto, and a slogan. These special signs overcome barriers of language and culture.

The Girl Scout sign is made by raising three fingers of the right hand. This sign stands for the three parts of the Promise. You give the sign when:

- You say the Promise.
- You are welcomed into Girl Scouting at an investiture ceremony (see page 14).
- You receive a patch or badge.
- You greet other Girl Scouts and Girl Guides.

The Girl Scout handshake is a formal way of greeting other Girl Scouts and Girl Guides. You shake hands with the left hand and give the Girl Scout sign with your right hand.

The quiet sign is used in meetings and other gatherings to let people know it is time to stop talking. The sign is made by raising your right hand high. As people in the group see the quiet sign, they stop talking and also raise their hands. Once everyone is silent, the meeting continues.

> The Girl Scout slogan is "Do a good turn daily."

12

13

▲ **The Girl Scout Promise and Law:** The Girl Scout Promise has not changed in its written form, and most girls will recite the Promise just as it is written. However, when reciting the Promise, some individuals may choose to use another word for God that more closely expresses their spiritual beliefs. This does not remove the word God from the Promise and the intent of supporting girls to learn about and act upon their spiritual beliefs remains. Girl Scouting's mission is to reach out to girls of every religious, cultural, racial, and ethnic background, and to help every girl be a better member of her own religious group.

For most girls, there will be no change in the way they make the Girl Scout Promise. If a girl is uncertain about how to make the Promise, the situation should be handled sensitively. For a girl hesitant about what to say, a discussion with the girl's family would be recommended.

Because of the importance of the Promise and Law to all Girl Scouts, you should spend some time discussing it with girls. Girls should be able to concretely apply the important words and concepts. If there is a problem with a girl using a word that is inappropriate, such as one chosen just to test boundaries, you might have a serious discussion within the troop or group.

Reserve time for girls to work on a variety of activities on the Girl Scout Promise and Law: word games, collages, skits, pantomimes, and discussions. One way to reinforce girls' understanding of these concepts is to encourage them to create activities for younger Girl Scouts. By helping others better understand the Promise and Law, they will understand it better themselves.

▲ **Girl Scout Traditions:** There are many Girl Scout traditions that are shared by girls all around the world. The special words and signs, including the handshake, motto, slogan, and friendship squeeze, give girls the feeling of being part of a special sisterhood.

It is often these traditions, practiced with each other, that girls remember in later years. Include some time in a troop or group meeting for one or more.

Supporting Activities

▲ Girls can create an activity around the Promise and Law to do at a Brownie Girl Scout bridging ceremony or at a Brownie Girl Scout troop or group meeting. This can be a presentation or an activity that involves the younger girls.

Program Links

▲ *Junior Girl Scout Activity Book:* Chapters One and Three

▲ *Ceremonies in Girl Scouting:* "Bridging Ceremonies"

▲ *Girl Scout Badges and Signs:* Girl Scouting in the U. S. A. badge

REMINDER!

When planning with girls, allow them to make mistakes, except of course, when safety is an issue. Sometimes the best lessons are learned from experience!

The **friendship circle** stands for an unbroken chain of friendship with Girl Scouts and Girl Guides all around the world. Girl Scouts and leaders stand in a circle. Each person crosses her right arm over her left and clasps hands with her friends on both sides. Everyone makes a silent wish as a **friendship squeeze** is passed from hand to hand. Form a friendship circle with the girls in your group and try the friendship squeeze.

Ceremonies in Girl Scouting

Many Girl Scouts at all age levels enjoy planning ceremonies. The best ones are created around a theme such as nature, heritage, friendship, or beauty. People express these themes in many ways: through music, songs, stories, poetry, dance, and light. And some ceremonies use common symbols such as a bridge for crossing over, a dove and olive branch for peace, and green plants for nature.

Important times for ceremonies in Girl Scouting are:

Bridging: welcomes girls into another level of Girl Scouts.

Rededication: helps girls think about the meaning of their Girl Scout Promise and Law.

Court of Awards: gives recognition to girls who have accomplished something (such as completing a service project, helping someone, or earning badges).

Flag Ceremonies: are part of any program that honors the American flag.

Fly-Up: a bridging ceremony for Brownie Girl Scouts who are bridging to Junior Girl Scouts.

Special Girl Scout Days: such as the Girl Scout Birthday or Thinking Day.

Investiture: girls welcome someone into Girl Scouting for the first time.

Girl Scouts' Own: an inspirational, girl-planned program to express girls' deepest feelings about something.

14

Ceremony Worksheet
USE THIS AS A GUIDE FOR PLANNING YOUR OWN CEREMONIES.

Name of Ceremony _____

Purpose or Theme _____

Date of Ceremony _____ Time _____

Place of Ceremony _____ Length _____

Who will attend? _____

How will the ceremony begin? _____
_____

What songs, poems, quotations will be included? _____
_____

What activities will be included in the main part of the ceremony? Will people speak? Will badges or other awards be given? _____
_____

How will the ceremony end? _____

Who will do each part? _____
_____

Who will record the ceremony for your troop's archives or records?_____

What decorations or props are needed? _____

Who will bring the items?

Item(s)	Who Will Bring Them?
_____	_____
_____	_____
_____	_____

What refreshments will be served? _____
_____

Who will bring them? _____

What will refreshments cost? _____

Who will pay for them? _____

When will a rehearsal be scheduled for the ceremony? _____

15

Tips

▲ **Ceremonies in Girl Scouting:** This section describes the most often-used Girl Scout ceremonies. Discuss ceremonies as a way of celebrating or commemorating events—and include ceremonies that can be joyful or sad. Ask girls to recount happy ceremonies they have attended such as weddings, birthdays, graduations, and holiday celebrations. A funeral is an example girls may give of a sad ceremony, but if the funeral celebrates one's life, it may not be considered sad. Aside from commemorating life transitions, other reasons to celebrate are: the closing of a meeting, friendship, or global awareness.

A ceremony may be simple and brief; it may include poetry, songs, props, and candles. To ensure that Girl Scout ceremonies are memorable, girls should plan and participate in partnership with adults.

▲ **Ceremony Worksheet:** The worksheet is a guide to help girls plan ceremonies. Girls could tailor the worksheet to meet their needs.

Supporting Activities

▲ After discussing ceremonies and special Girl Scout days, encourage girls to plan a ceremony of their own. They can start small by planning a ceremony to open or close the next Girl Scout meeting. They can then plan a more extensive ceremony to celebrate one of the special Girl Scout days.

▲ Using *Trefoil Round the World,* ask girls to select a few countries of interest and compare their Promises, Laws, and mottos with Girl Scouts of the U. S. A. Girls can take a look at the illustrations of each country's pin and compare the designs. If you have access to the WAGGGS Girl Guide/Girl Scout uniform poster, display it so girls can compare the different uniforms

Program Links

▲ *Ceremonies in Girl Scouting*

▲ *Trefoil Round the World*

▲ *The Wide World of Girl Guiding and Girl Scouting*

Notes

Girl Scouts' Special Days

Girl Scouts in the U.S.A. have four special days that are celebrated all across the nation. Girls often plan events or hold special ceremonies to celebrate these days:

October 31–Juliette Gordon Low's Birthday (also known as Founder's Day)

February 22–Thinking Day, the birthday of both Lord Baden-Powell and Lady Baden-Powell. Girl Scouts and Girl Guides all over the world celebrate this day in international friendship and world peace.

March 12–The birthday of Girl Scouting in the United States of America–celebrated on or as close to the day as possible.

April 22–Girl Scout Leader's Day, when girls show their leaders how much they appreciate them.

The Girl Scout Pin

Your Girl Scout pin shows others that you are a member of Girl Scouts of the U.S.A. Its shape is called a "trefoil," and represents the three parts of the Girl Scout Promise. There are two versions of the membership pin. The newer one has three profiles inside the trefoil. The dark and light profiles represent the ethnic diversity (all the different races and ethnic groups) of Girl Scout membership, and the equal value placed on all girls.

The older version of the pin has the initials "GS" inside the trefoil, along with the American eagle and shield that are part of the Great Seal of the United States of America.

Your World Trefoil Pin

Your blue and gold World Trefoil pin shows that you are part of a worldwide movement of Girl Guides and Girl Scouts. The blue stands for the sky and the gold stands for the sun. The trefoil stands for the three parts of the Girl Scout Promise. The base of the trefoil is shaped like a flame, which represents the love of humanity and the flame that burns in the hearts of Girl Guides and Girl Scouts around the world. The line in the middle of the trefoil stands for the compass needle that guides us, while the two stars stand for the Promise and Law.

16

The Junior Girl Scout Uniform

Just like wearing your Girl Scout pin, wearing a uniform is another way of showing that you belong to an organization. Your uniform was designed with the comments and suggestions of Junior Girl Scouts around the country. It is not a requirement that all Girl Scouts own a uniform. Girls who have one like to wear it to participate in ceremonies, attend an event as part of a Girl Scout group, attend an event on a special Girl Scout day, or attend regular meetings.

The Junior Girl Scout uniform has different pieces that you can mix or match. These pictures show the different styles of the Junior Girl Scout uniform.

17

Handbook Page 16

Handbook Page 17

▲ **The Junior Girl Scout Uniform:** When girls wear their Girl Scout uniform, pin, and insignia, they are identified as members of the national movement of Girl Scouts of the U. S. A. Being a Girl Scout member also makes you a member of WAGGGS and eligible to wear the WAGGGS pin. The WAGGGS pin (World Trefoil) is shared by Girl Scouts and Girl Guides all around the world. There are times when girls and leaders can wear their uniforms to help the public recognize the good efforts of Girl Scouts. This is especially true when giving service or doing money-earning projects or product sales.

The uniform also helps girls feel proud, and gives them a sense of being part of a large, important organization. Encourage girls to wear uniforms to school on troop/group meeting days.

Throughout the handbook, you'll see instances when wearing the uniform is encouraged.

Although wearing the Girl Scout uniform is not a requirement for membership, there are a variety of ways to help local troops/groups get uniforms. If an opportunity arises when a uniform is needed by a girl in your troop or group who is unable to get one, you could contact your Girl Scout council office to find out if they can help. Community organizations might be approached for help in purchasing uniforms for girls who cannot afford them. You might also discuss with your troop or group the possibility of using troop funds to purchase uniform components that can be lent to any girl when the need arises.

It is important for girls to understand the meaning and significance of their uniforms and insignia, and to wear them correctly.

The World Association of Girl Guides and Girl Scouts (WAGGGS) pin, illustrated here, is called the World Trefoil Pin.

Supporting Activities

▲ Have girls look at the various recognitions and insignia and discuss what the designs signify.

▲ Girls can select a troop crest to represent their troop. Or perhaps they want to design their own.

▲ Have girls design a uniform for the year 2000. Display the designs.

▲ Present a Junior Girl Scout uniform fashion show. Girls can demonstrate the many ways to mix and match the new uniform components.

Program Links

▲ *Girl Scout Uniforms, Insignia, and Recognitions*

REMINDER!

If parents or guardians pressure you to devote more time to working on badges or other recognitions, stress that the meetings are based on the expressed needs and interests of the girls. Girls need not earn a prescribed number of badges to benefit from Girl Scouting.

Wearing Your Girl Scout Insignia and Recognitions

Girl Scout insignia are the pins that identify you as a Girl Scout. Recognitions are what you earn by doing activities such as earning a badge from the book *Girl Scout Badges and Signs*. They stand for what you have accomplished and earned in Girl Scouting. See the illustrations below and on page 19 that show the correct placement of your insignia and recognitions on a sash or vest.

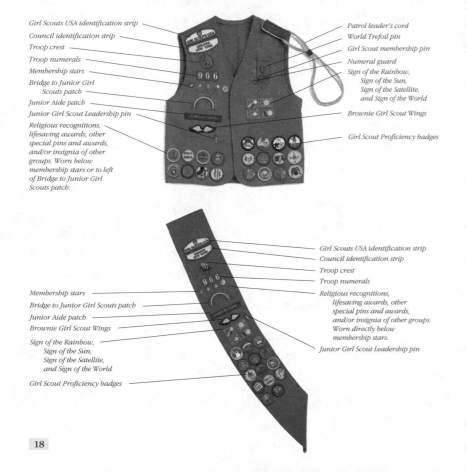

Girl Scouts USA identification strip
Council identification strip
Troop crest
Troop numerals
Membership stars
Bridge to Junior Girl Scouts patch
Junior Aide patch
Junior Girl Scout Leadership pin
Religious recognitions, lifesaving awards, other special pins and awards, and/or insignia of other groups. Worn below membership stars or to left of Bridge to Junior Girl Scouts patch.

Patrol leader's cord
World Trefoil pin
Girl Scout membership pin
Numeral guard
Sign of the Rainbow, Sign of the Sun, Sign of the Satellite, and Sign of the World
Brownie Girl Scout Wings
Girl Scout Proficiency badges

Girl Scouts USA identification strip
Council identification strip
Troop crest
Troop numerals
Membership stars
Bridge to Junior Girl Scouts patch
Junior Aide patch
Brownie Girl Scout Wings
Sign of the Rainbow, Sign of the Sun, Sign of the Satellite, and Sign of the World
Girl Scout Proficiency badges
Religious recognitions, lifesaving awards, other special pins and awards, and/or insignia of other groups. Worn directly below membership stars.
Junior Girl Scout Leadership pin

18

Insignia/Recognition Guide

  Girl Scout membership pin

 World Trefoil pin

  Insignia tab
Can be used to hold your World Trefoil and Girl Scout membership pins.

 Patrol leader's cord

 Girl Scouts USA identification strip

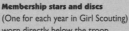 **Council identification strip**

 Troop crest

 Troop numerals

 Membership stars and discs
(One for each year in Girl Scouting) worn directly below the troop numerals, beginning with the Daisy Girl Scout star on a blue disc, Brownie Girl Scout stars on green discs, then Junior Girl Scout stars on yellow discs.

 Bridge to Junior Girl Scout's patch

 Junior Aide patch

  Brownie Girl Scout Wings

 Special awards
Religious recognitions, lifesaving awards and other special pins may be worn below the membership stars.

 Badges
On the sash, these are placed three in a row. On the vest, the first three are placed on the right side. Most badges will be worn on the left side because there is more space, but you can create additional rows on the right side.

 Sign of the Rainbow, Sign of the Sun, Sign of the Satellite, Sign of the World
Worn in two rows with Sign of the Rainbow and Sign of the Satellite on your right.

 Junior Girl Scout leadership pin

Note
Girl Scout patches from events, camp, or projects may be worn on the back of the sash beginning at the top. Badges that will not fit on the front of the sash may be placed on the back of the sash beginning on the bottom. Try-It patches earned as a Brownie Girl Scout may also be placed here.

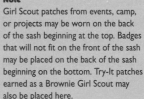 In your troop or group, divide into two teams. Each team should have the exact same set of insignia and recognitions. You could have a relay race to see which team can place its set of recognitions/insignia on a sash or vest correctly in the least amount of time. You could try this by yourself using a timer to see how quickly you can place the recognitions in the correct spots.

19

Handbook Page 19

80 *The Guide for Junior Girl Scout Leaders*

▲ **Other Girl Scout Insignia and Recognitions:** The chart below has been designed to help you track the *Junior Girl Scout* *Handbook* badges completed by girls in your troop or group. The "Steps Completed" column can be used to help girls keep track of the activities they have completed towards earning the badge. Photocopy a chart for each girl.

Girl's Name:_____

Badge	Steps Completed	Date Received	Comments
Arts and Media			
Careers			
Consumer Power			
Discovering Technology			
Girls Are Great			
Healthy Living			
Leadership			
Looking Your Best			
Science Discovery			
Talk!			
You and Your Community			
Your Outdoor Surroundings			
Wider Opportunities			

Working with Others in Girl Scouts

The Girl Scout Pyramid

Many people in Girl Scouting help make your Girl Scout experience successful. Look at the Girl Scout pyramid. You are at the top of the pyramid. Write your name. You and millions of other girls—around this nation and around the world—are the reasons that Girl Scouting exists.

One way to take part in Girl Scouting is to join a troop. If you are in a Girl Scout troop, put your troop number in the next part of the pyramid. If you are not part of a troop, write in the names of the friends with whom you do Girl Scout activities.

Adults in Girl Scouting

Adults help you carry out Girl Scout activities. They could be: Girl Scout leaders, volunteers who work with Girl Scout troops or groups, or other adults such as family members. Write in the names of the adults who work with your troop or group. If you are not part of a troop or group, write in the names of those special adults who help you with Girl Scout activities.

A Girl Scout council is a group of women and men who administer Girl Scouting in a specific area. These people have many different jobs. They may help start new troops, take care of camps, or sign up new members. There are more than 300 councils in the United States today. Find out the name of your Girl Scout council and write it on the pyramid. You can wear the name of your council on your uniform sash or vest. (See page 18.)

Next on the pyramid is Girl Scouts of the U.S.A. (GSUSA), the national organization. The membership dues that you pay to GSUSA each year provide services to members. GSUSA creates new program activities and books, like this handbook, and operates national centers (see page 22). GSUSA also coordinates national and international events, such as wider opportunities for Cadette and Senior Girl Scouts. Turn to page 27 to learn more about wider opportunities.

 Invite someone who knows about your council office to a Girl Scout meeting to talk about what she does and how the council operates.

Your First Name

Your Last Name

Your Troop Number

Adults Who Work with Your Troop/Group

Your Council

Girl Scouts of the U. S. A.

World Association of Girl Guides and Girl Scouts (WAGGGS)

20

21

Handbook Page 20

Handbook Page 21

▲ **The Girl Scout Pyramid:** The Girl Scout pyramid helps girls visualize the structure of Girl Scouting and lets them see where they fit in. The pyramid also helps girls see that they are part of a large national organization, which is part of a worldwide organization.

Offer help with filling in the pyramid. Since many girls may not know the name of their Girl Scout council, tell them the name and address and help them locate the council office on a map. Discuss how the council helps bring Girl Scouting to all girls in the community. Tell them how the council helped you prepare to become their leader. Talk about the careers one could pursue if she worked at a Girl Scout council, including outdoor specialist or computer technician. If possible, arrange a visit to your council office so girls can witness the "behind the scenes" work.

The national headquarters of Girl Scouts of the U. S. A. (GSUSA) is located in the heart of New York City. Help girls locate New York City on a map. National staff who work in this office facility develop and publish the *Junior Girl Scout Handbook* plus *Girl Scout Badges and Signs* and many other books. GSUSA also designs the Girl Scout uniform components and offers training to help adults keep Girl Scouting contemporary. Show girls any GSUSA publications you may have.

▲ Plan a party to help girls share the fun of Girl Scouting! Each girl can invite one friend or relative who is not currently a member of Girl Scouts.

▲ Girls play important roles at both the council and national levels. Help troop or group members investigate how they may become eligible to fill these roles.

▲ Your Girl Scout council and GSUSA are always interested in hearing suggestions about activities from the girl membership. Ask girls to look through their handbooks. Are there any topics or activities they would like to see included or feel need to be more clearly addressed? Are there any events they would like to see offered for the Junior Girl Scout age level? Encourage girls to select one or two ideas to send to their council or GSUSA.

▲ *Girl Scout Badges and Signs:* Girl Scouting in the U. S. A. badge; Girl Scouting Around the World badge

The National Centers

Girl Scouts of the U.S.A. owns two Girl Scout national centers, each with its own special activities.

Juliette Gordon Low Girl Scout National Center, in Savannah, Georgia, is the childhood home of the founder of Girl Scouting in the United States. Many troops visit each year. You can receive more information by writing to Juliette Gordon Low Girl Scout National Center, 142 Bull Street, Savannah, Georgia 31401.

Edith Macy Conference Center

At Edith Macy Conference Center, 35 miles from New York City, adults take classes to learn more about Girl Scouting. Camp Andree Clark, GSUSA's camp, is nearby.

Juliette Gordon Low Girl Scout National Center

The World Association of Girl Guides & Girl Scouts (WAGGGS)

At the base of the pyramid is the World Association of Girl Guides and Girl Scouts (WAGGGS). Your World Trefoil pin shows that you are a part of this growing worldwide movement.

Each of the national Girl Scout/Girl Guide organizations, including Girl Scouts of the U.S.A., belongs to the World Association of Girl Guides and Girl Scouts (WAGGGS). This means that because you are a Girl Scout, you are connected to eight million girls and women around the world.

WAGGGS owns four world centers. Our Cabaña is in Cuernavaca, Mexico; Our Chalet is in Adelboden, Switzerland; Pax Lodge is at the Olave Center in London, England; and Sangam is in Pune, India. Through international wider opportunities, Cadette and Senior Girl Scouts can visit these centers and take part in many activities. As a registered Girl Scout, you and your family can also stay at these centers on a visit to these countries if you have made arrangements ahead of time.

> For more information, write to
> Membership and Program
> Girl Scouts of the U.S.A.
> 420 Fifth Avenue
> New York, New York 10018-2702.

Tips

▲ **The National Centers:** Assist girls in locating the Juliette Gordon Low Girl Scout National Center and Edith Macy Conference Center on a map of the United States. If girls are interested in learning more about Edith Macy Conference Center, write to Membership and Program, Girl Scouts of the U. S. A. , 420 Fifth Avenue, New York, N. Y. 10018-2702

Supporting Activities

▲ The Juliette Gordon Low Girl Scout National Center offers girls the opportunity to step back to the late 1800s when Juliette was a young girl in the South. Have girls find out about the lifestyles of girls in their communities during this time period. What did girls like to wear? What did they do for fun? What was school like? Perhaps girls can design a brochure, write a play, or create a collage to share this information with others.

Program Links

▲ *Girl Scout Badges and Signs*: Girl Scouting in the U. S. A. badge; Women's Stories badge

Tips

▲ **The World Association of Girl Guides and Girl Scouts (WAGGGS):** Over 100 countries around the world maintain national organizations like GSUSA. A sample of these organizations includes: Association des Guides du Cameroun; Pakistan Girl Guides Association; Guías de Mexico, A. C. ; Persatuan Pandu Puteri, Malaysia; Girl Guides Association of Jamaica, and Soma Hellinidon Odigon, Greece. Most of these organizations refer to themselves as Girl Guides, the original name given to the movement by Lord Baden-Powell.

WAGGGS provides global education and organizes international meetings. A world conference for all member organizations is held every three years in different parts of the world. GSUSA has served as host for the fourth, twelfth, and twenty-fifth world conferences. *Trefoil Round the World* contains detailed information about WAGGGS and the member countries.

Supporting Activities

▲ Have girls find out more about Girl Guiding/Girl Scouting by looking through *The Wide World of Girl Guiding and Girl Scouting*, *World Games and Recipes*, and *Trefoil Round the World*. Suggest girls select a country they would like to visit. What would they tell girls in this country about Girl Scouting in the U. S. A. ?

Program Links

▲ *Girl Scout Badges and Signs:* Girl Scouting Around the World badge; Geography Fun badge; The World in My Community badge; World Neighbors badge

▲ *Trefoil Round the World*

▲ *Games for Girl Scouts:* International Kim's Game and New Zealand Game

▲ *Junior Girl Scout Activity Book:* Chapter Three

▲ *The Wide World of Girl Guiding and Girl Scouting*

Different Ways to Be a Girl Scout

Part of the fun of Girl Scouting is sharing experiences with girls your age. You can do this in many ways. You might be part of a group called the Girl Scout troop. A troop works together to make decisions, to choose activities to do together, and to make sure that everyone's feelings and interests are respected. You might also be part of an interest group, go to a program center, or even do Girl Scout activities by mail or computer.

1. The Patrol System

Troop and Group Leadership

Your Junior Girl Scout troop or group is the perfect place to practice and strengthen your leadership skills. (See Chapter Six for more about leadership.) Along with your Girl Scout leader, you and your troop or group members can set up a system for troop or group government. Within this system, you have different opportunities to take a leadership role.

Here are the three models of troop or group government most used by Junior Girl Scouts. Which system would work best in achieving your troop's or group's goals? What could be your role in troop or group government?

The troop or group is divided into small groups or patrols with five to eight girls in each. If you have 20 girls in your troop or group, how could you divide yourselves into patrols?

You can divide into patrols based on interests, by age, or at random. Because making friends and learning how to work well with others are a big part of Girl Scouting, you should not be in the same patrol an entire troop year.

How does a patrol work? Each patrol usually chooses a patrol leader, an assistant patrol leader, a patrol name, and a patrol symbol. The members of a patrol should rotate the patrol leader and assistant leader jobs so everyone has the opportunity to serve in a leadership role. The patrol name and logo can be

used on a patrol flag and on any special patrol materials.

During a special ceremony, the patrol leader is given the patrol leader cord, a recognition made up of two gold cord loops or circles, to wear on her left shoulder. The larger circle symbolizes the whole troop or group while the smaller circle represents the patrol.

The patrol leader is usually responsible for seeing that certain jobs are done. Some of these jobs can be organizing the patrol, helping new members, keeping patrol records, leading discussions, and representing the patrol at the Court of Honor meetings.

In Girl Scouting, a job is called a kaper and a list of jobs and who does them is a kaper chart. See the next page for an example.

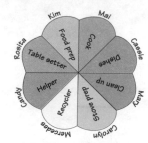

This kaper chart is one Girl Scouts might use for camping

The patrol leader wouldn't do all these jobs herself. She works with the girls in her patrol to get everything accomplished.

The assistant patrol leader is usually responsible for assisting the patrol leader during meetings and taking over patrol meetings in her absence.

Court of Honor

The Girl Scout leader, the patrol leaders, and the troop or group secretary and treasurer make up the Court of Honor. The secretary takes notes at troop or group meetings and keeps these notes as a record of what was discussed. The treasurer tracks troop or group dues and other Girl Scout money and supplies. In some large troops and groups, patrols might have secretaries and treasurers who do these jobs in the patrols. At Court of Honor meetings, held before or after regular troop or group meetings, the Court of Honor might come

up with plans or ideas for the patrols to discuss and vote on, ask for ideas and suggestions from patrols, and set up and maintain a troop kaper chart that outlines assignments for each patrol.

If you are not on the Court of Honor, attend a meeting when it is open to all members because it will give you an opportunity to see leadership in action.

2. The Executive Board System

In this type of troop government, you do not have small group patrols. There is one leadership team for the whole troop or group called an executive board. This system often works well with smaller troops and groups. (In some troops, this group is called the steering committee.) The board's main responsibility is to help make plans and assign jobs for the entire troop or group based on interests and needs.

The executive board usually has a president, a vice-president, a secretary, and a treasurer, and holds its own meetings to discuss troop or group matters. The length of time each girl can be on the executive board should be limited so that during the year all members of the

troop or group get an opportunity to participate. All of the girls in the troop or group decide on a way at the beginning of the year to pass their ideas and suggestions to the executive board. The number of officers on the executive board can vary.

3. The Town Meeting System

In this system, there is no formal group or troop government. Troop and group business is discussed and decided at meetings attended by all the girls in the troop or group. And as in the other systems, everyone in the troop gets the chance to participate in decision-making and leadership.

This system usually requires a moderator, a person who guides a discussion. She makes sure that everyone gets a chance to speak, that no one talks for too long, and that all ideas get considered. How do you choose a moderator? You could pick one girl at random, rotate the job, or select the person who knows the most about the topic. You also need to decide whether or not a secretary and a treasurer need to be elected and how long each would serve.

24

25

Tips

▲ **Different Ways to Be a Girl Scout:** This section begins by letting girls know that Girl Scout participation comes in many forms. For example, some girls will be part of a troop while others may belong to an interest group. Communicate to girls that all these forms of participation are legitimate ways to be a Girl Scout. See Chapter One in Part I of this guide for more about ways girls can participate in Girl Scouting.

Tips

▲ **Troop and Group Leadership:** By participating in troop or group government, Junior Girl Scouts get an opportunity to practice decision-making and learn leadership skills. However, effective troop or group government develops over time. Older Junior Girl Scouts can serve as excellent role models for demonstrating leadership abilities. Be sure, though, that older girls are

not the only ones in leadership positions. Responsibilities and accountabilities for other tasks should be routinely rotated among all girls in the troop or group.

Don't be discouraged if Junior Girl Scout self-government doesn't run smoothly from the start. It is possible that they may never function perfectly, but this imparts a lesson to girls as well. With your assistance, girls can still experience the benefits derived from designing, planning, and implementing their ideas.

You may find that some girls express hesitation at assuming any leadership responsibility at all. Some girls do not like to speak in front of groups but do take the lead with "behind the scenes" tasks. Do not push a girl into trying or doing something if she feels very uncomfortable. Instead, encourage her to share her ideas during brainstorming sessions or take

responsibility for small tasks (such as arranging the closing for a meeting). Ensure that her input is recognized in troop or group decision-making.

Chapter Four in Part I of this guide has more information about troop and group government.

Supporting Activities

▲ Ask the girls: What does a person have to do, say, or need to be a good leader? Have girls brainstorm a list of qualities that describes a good leader. Compare their lists to the checklist in Chapter Six. Discuss similarities and differences.

▲ Throughout the year, assist girls in evaluating their troop's or group's system of government. Be sure the current system is given a fair trial period. Read "Evaluating the Troop's or Group's System of Government" in Chapter Four of Part I of this guide.

Program Links

▲ *Girl Scout Badges and Signs:* Making Decisions badge; Junior Citizen badge; Active Citizen badge; Creative Solutions badge

▲ *Ceremonies in Girl Scouting*

▲ *Girls Are Great: Growing Up Female* and *Earth Matters: A Challenge for Environmental Action* Contemporary Issues booklets

Group Decision-Making

Sometimes it can be hard to make decisions as a group. How do you decide which service project to do or which trip to take? Here are some decision-making steps:

1. Brainstorm

Brainstorming is a way to get a group of people to talk about a lot of different ideas in a short time. For example, you can brainstorm a solution to a problem, ideas for activities, or suggestions for a trip. Here's how it works: a group usually sits in a circle; one person writes down everybody's ideas. A timer can be set to limit the brainstorming to two minutes, five minutes, or whatever is decided. Then, as people think of ideas, they say them. None of the ideas should be judged good, bad, possible, or impossible until the time is up. Everyone should feel free to say whatever pops into her mind. When the time is up, the group reviews the list of ideas to pick one or two possibilities.

2. Look at the Good and Bad Points of Each Idea

Have a group discussion about the ideas on your brainstormed list.

3. Make a Decision

If, after reviewing the good and bad points, one idea doesn't stand out as the best, the group may want to vote. Vote secretly by ballot or less formally by raising hands.

4. Evaluate

After a decision has been made, the troop or group should discuss their feelings about it at a later date. Is it time for a new decision?

Choosing Leaders

Whenever you choose girls as leaders, think about how you are making your choices. Think about being fair. Think about what it takes to be a leader. For more ideas, look at Chapter Six, which has lots of information about leadership styles.

26

Camping, Service, and Trips:
Three Favorite Girl Scout Activities

Camping

Camping is a favorite activity for many Girl Scouts, especially troop or group camping at council sites or at summer resident or day camps.

If you haven't gone before, you may be worried about your first camping experience. Bugs, no TV, no flush toilets, and cold showers might be just a few of your worries. "Roughing it is all very fine to talk about, but it's best to make your camp as comfortable as possible" was advice given the first Girl Scouts in their *Handbook for Girl Scouts*. Today, most girls new to camping stay in lodges, cabins, or four-walled tents with access to showers and flush toilets. Read pages 177–192 for more information on camping.

Community Service

Some of the activities you and your troop members discuss may involve providing service to others. Service means doing something helpful for others without expecting or asking for money or any other reward. Service is an important part of Girl Scouting. Read more about leadership and service in Chapter Six.

Wider Opportunities

A wider opportunity is any activity that you and your Girl Scout friends participate in outside of the troop meeting. Visiting a farm, camping, marching in a parade, or having

27

Tips

▲ **Group Decision-Making:** The decision-making steps encourage communication among girls. It may be a good idea to help girls establish some "rules" before the brainstorming session begins. Rules might be: only one person speaks at a time, no one is teased about any idea she puts forth, no name-calling, no labeling of ideas (e. g. , "That's stupid. Why would we want to do that? "). Remind girls about the rules before each session. Maintain flexibility so that rules can be changed.

Supporting Activities

▲ Another way of introducing brainstorming is to ask girls to complete the sentence: I would really like to

_____.

Have each girl write her answer on a slip of paper. One person collects the slips and reads the suggestions aloud. Girls continue with the decision-making steps using the suggestions.

▲ Here are some questions to consider when looking at the positive and negative aspects of each idea: (Let's say you are brainstorming about which activity to do.)

- Will everyone be able to participate in the activity?
- How much will the activity cost?
- Will girls be able to raise the money?
- Will the activity entail extra costs, such as transportation?
- Will doing the activity require extra adult chaperones?
- Will the activity require special equipment or clothing?
- Is it an activity mentioned in *Safety-Wise?* (If so, review the activity checkpoints.)

Program Links

▲ *Girl Scout Badges and Signs:* Making Decisions badge; Creative Solutions badge

▲ *Junior Girl Scout Activity Book:* Chapter Eight

Tips

▲ **Camping:** Before going camping overnight, the girls will need to have had previous outdoor experiences. In addition, they need to learn and practice outdoor skills, plan activities, and find out more about where they are going. Be sure to consult *Safety-Wise* prior to any troop or group camping experience. Consult Chapter Seven in the handbook for more information about outdoor living.

Program Links

▲ *Girl Scout Badges and Signs:* World of Well-Being Dabbler; Troop Camper badge

▲ *Outdoor Education in Girl Scouting*

▲ *Earth Matters: A Challenge for Environmental Action* Contemporary Issues booklet

Tips

▲ **Community Service:** Carrying out service projects is a very important part of Girl Scouting. Doing service is inherent in every member's Girl Scout Promise. Keep in mind that service projects can be big, like working with another community organization such as a voter registration league on election day, or small, like helping a younger girl cross the street, or in between, like planting flowers and pulling weeds at the entranceway to a town hall.

Supporting Activities

▲ Use the group decision-making steps to decide on a community service project for the coming year. Remind girls that a community service project should involve their interests and meet a need in their communities.

Program Links

▲ *Girl Scout Badges and Signs:* Making Decisions badge; My Community badge

▲ *Junior Girl Scout Handbook:* You and Your Community badge

▲ *Junior Girl Scout Activity Book:* Chapter Eight

a picnic away from where you usually meet are all examples of wider opportunities. Participating in wider opportunities as a Junior Girl Scout can help you grow and prepare for greater challenges.

Sometimes people think that wider opportunities refer only to those events that appear each year in the booklet *Wider Ops* and are open only to Cadette and Senior Girl Scouts. But, Junior Girl Scouts have lots of choices for wider opportunities. Brainstorm a list of wider opportunities for your group or troop.

 Invite a Cadette or Senior Girl Scout or someone from your Girl Scout council to talk to you and your friends about a wider opportunity. Find out which events and workshops you can attend as a Junior Girl Scout.

 Learn about wider opportunities now being offered by Girl Scout councils. Ask your Girl Scout leader to see if she can bring a copy of *Wider Ops* to a troop or group meeting. Look through it and find three wider opportunities you think you would enjoy when you are a Cadette or Senior Girl Scout. Make a list of the requirements, cost, location, and any special equipment you would need to bring.

Get Ready to TAP!

Before you board a bus or buckle your seatbelt, careful planning is essential to ensure the success of your wider opportunities. These steps would also be helpful in planning activities and service projects. (See Chapter Eight for Wider Opportunities badge activities.) What do you do first? Try following the Travel Action Plan (TAP) outlined below. You might need more than one meeting to do all the steps.

TAP Step 1

Listed below are some places you and your friends might like to visit or events you would like to attend. On the blank lines, record some other ideas.

- Library
- Park
- Zoo or wildlife center
- Government office
- Homeless shelter
- Science center
- Country fair

_____
_____
_____
_____
_____
_____

 Write a brief description of a real or an imaginary place you would love to visit!

TAP Step 2

When you have narrowed your list to two or three possible activities, you are now ready to hold a planning meeting. Consider and discuss:

1. What will you do once you arrive?

2. How much will it cost? How can you raise money or get help with the finances?

3. How will you get there?

4. What does each of you need to bring?

5. Will you travel in uniform?

6. How will you get your meals?

7. When is the best time to go? When will you leave? Get home?

8. Do you need to make reservations or get permission to visit the place?

9. Will the weather affect plans?

10. Do you need approval from your Girl Scout council?

11. What guidelines does your leader's copy of *Safety-Wise*, a Girl Scout book that outlines safety guidelines and standards, have for your plans?

12. How many adults need to go along?

Use the results of this meeting to help you make a final decision!

 You just finished your planning meeting for your fantasy trip. Summarize the decisions you made. Use the questions above to help you outline your thoughts.

TAP Step 3

Once you decide where you are going, find out as much as you can about the place you plan to visit. Write or telephone ahead to the place, or write to the visitors' bureau or Chamber of Commerce of the town or city you'll be visiting to obtain local maps or tourist brochures.

Design a travel brochure for your imaginary place. Include details about any special attractions, places to stay and eat, and weather conditions.

TAP Step 4

Calculate how much the trip will cost. Make a list of everything you expect to pay for and estimate how much each thing will cost. Include meals, transportation, equipment, materials, and admission and/or ticket fees.

Create a chart or graph that shows what it will cost to visit your fantasy place. Be sure to include the cost of meals, transportation, accommodations (hotels, for example), and fees to visit areas of special interest.

TAP! TAP!

Tips

▲ **Get Ready to TAP:** Wider opportunities are an important part of Girl Scouting at all age levels. Girls very often say that taking trips is one of the things they like most about Girl Scouting.

Careful planning is essential to ensuring a safe and successful trip. Before taking any trip, consult *Safety-Wise*, your council office, and Chapter Four in Part I of this guide.

The Travel Action Plan (TAP) steps can be used to "walk" girls through the stages in planning a trip. Each TAP step concludes with an activity to help reinforce the information outlined in the step. These TAP steps can also be useful for planning a community service project or other activities.

Suggest a brainstorming session to help girls complete TAP Step 1. Have girls review the brainstorming steps and remind them about any rules that have been established.

TAP Step 4 requires girls to calculate the cost of the trip. Consult Chapter Four in the handbook for ideas on raising and managing money. Also, make sure any trip being considered is one all girls can afford to take. It is important that no one be excluded because of her financial circumstances.

Supporting Activities

▲ Travel is often difficult for children, whether it be a long bus ride to camp or a field trip to another state. To keep girls occupied while traveling, try these travel games:

1. Use words from billboards or signs to create a story. The first girl picks a word and includes it in the beginning sentence of the story. The second girl chooses another word and uses it in the second sentence. The story ends when all girls have had at least one turn.

2. Prior to leaving on your trip, have each girl draw a grid of 20 squares on a blank index card. Girls then draw or write the name of an animal in a center square. During the trip, each girl places a check in a blank square each time her animal is seen, whether in a store window, on a billboard, or on a sign. The first girl to fill every square wins.

Instead of animals, you can use letters of the alphabet, car models, types of trees, etc.

3. While riding, have girls look for numbers and keep a running total until the sum of 100 is reached.

4. Divide girls into two teams. One team is designated "odd," the other "even." In a timed period, teams receive one point for each odd-numbered or even-numbered license plate they spot. Out-of-state plates count for two points.

Supporting Activities

▲ *Girl Scout Badges and Signs:* Safety Sense badge; Traveler badge; Geography Fun badge; Finding Your Way badge

▲ *Games for Girl Scouts*

▲ *Junior Girl Scout Handbook:* Wider Opportunities badge

TAP! TAP!

TAP Step 5

You must get written permission from your parent or guardian before going on any trip. You must also have enough adults to go with you. Your Girl Scout leader will consult *Safety-Wise*. Your leader will make sure there are permission slips from everyone and the right number of adults to accompany the group on a trip.

 Design a permission slip that girls would have to complete before visiting your fantasy place. Include any special information that you think their parents would need to know.

TAP Step 6

Determine ahead of time special clothing and equipment to bring. It is a good idea to sew name labels in your clothes so they don't get mixed up with other girls' clothes. Learn about rolling or packing clothes to fit into a suitcase, sleeping bag, or knapsack.

 Make a list of clothing, accessories, and special equipment a girl would need to bring to your fantasy place.

TAP Step 7

Review a map or a floor plan of the place you plan to visit to figure out exactly how to get there and where you will go once inside. Remember to bring the map with you on your trip!

 Draw a map of your fantasy place that shows major roads, large bodies of water, points of interest, names of towns, and anything else you think potential visitors might need to know!

TAP Step 8

Once you reach this step, you are ready to make your plans into reality! Have a great time!

 Put together all the pieces of your fantasy TAP package and make a presentation to the other members of your troop. How many girls would like to join you?

As you can see, Junior Girl Scouts get to enjoy all sorts of activities from camping and sports to computers to jewelry making. The choice is yours and so is the fun!

30

WHO AM I...NOW?
CHAPTER 2

Changes in Your Body
page 36

It's Party Time!
page 62

What's Important to You?
page 48

Values Check

A Fun-to-Read Story Maze
page 68

This is a truly exciting time in your life as each day brings new discoveries—about yourself, your family, your friends—and so many things in the world around you. This chapter is titled "Who Am I...Now?" because how you look and feel today may be different from how you looked and felt last year, and how you'll look and feel in a few months or next year. On the following pages, you will be asked to step back and look at yourself both inside and out. You will look at the ways your body is changing and the different feelings you are experiencing. You will explore how these changes shape what you value, including your relationships with your family and friends.

31

Who Am I ... Now?

HANDBOOK CHAPTER 2

Tips

▲ **Conclusion to Chapter One:** Chapter One contains quite a lot of information. To help girls digest this information, consider addressing sections of the chapter at different times or in conjunction with an activity. For example, if your troop or group is preparing to march in a parade, refer the girls to the section on uniforms and insignia.

Supporting Activities

▲ Use the following questions to make up a game about Girl Scouting:

1. Who is the founder of Girl Scouting?

2. Which book lists safety practices and guidelines?

3. Which sign is used to stop talking in a group?

4. What is special about February 22? March 12? April 22? October 31?

5. Which ceremony welcomes girls into another level of Girl Scouting?

6. What is the acronym for the World Association of Girl Guides and Girl Scouts?

7. Complete the following: Do a good turn _____.

   The Girl Scout motto is _____.

8. Which type of dancing did Daisy learn?

9. Which volunteers work with Girl Scout troops or groups?

Add some of your own questions to test the girls' knowledge of Girl Scout trivia!

Answers: **1.** Juliette Gordon Low; **2.** *Safety-Wise;* **3.** The quiet sign; **4.** Thinking Day, Girl Scout Birthday, Leader's Day, Juliette Gordon Low's Birthday; **5.** Bridging; **6.** WAGGGS; **7.** daily; Be Prepared; **8.** ballroom; **9.** leaders.

▲ **Chapter 2: Who Am I...Now?:** When girls enter Junior Girl Scouting, they are beginning to experience many emotional and physical changes. Their emotions are likened to a roller coaster ride, characterized by "highs and lows." The information in this chapter, coupled with your guidance and the troop or group's support, will help girls better understand themselves and feel comfortable with the changes they are experiencing.

Because some of the information is of a sensitive nature, some girls may feel uncomfortable, withdrawn, or giddy. Handle girls' reactions on an individual basis. Help the whole troop or group understand that some girls feel more comfortable talking about their bodies and feelings than do others. Don't force topics the girls do not wish to pursue.

Be sure to remember that religious beliefs, family situations, and cultural norms of your troop or group must be considered. Ideas, comments, and advice from parents also are of utmost importance when implementing these activities.

The Junior Girl Scout age level is a pivotal point for many girls. It is a time when girls' self-esteem often begins to diminish. Helping girls overcome negative feelings or confusion associated with any of the topics covered in "Who Am I ...Now?" will help them feel better about themselves and recognize that these changes are just a normal part of growing up.

WHO AM I NOW?

Use the chart below or write on a separate piece of paper the ways you have changed in the past year.

Topic	Ways I Have Changed
The Way I Look:	_____
	_____
	_____
	_____
Friends:	_____
	_____
	_____
	_____
Things I Like to Do:	_____
	_____
	_____
	_____
How I Feel About Myself:	_____
	_____
	_____
Things I Do with My Family:	_____
	_____
	_____
	_____
Other Changes I Have Noticed:	_____
	_____
	_____

32

THIS IS ME!

How would you fill in the blanks? You might want to use a separate piece of paper, as your answers could change during your time in Junior Girl Scouts. You might not be able to fill in all of the blanks. That's fine. Just skip ahead to the next one you can do.

My name is_____

and my parents called me this because_____

_____.

One thing I like about my name is_____.

My nickname is_____because_____

_____. I am_____

years old and am in_____grade at

_____School.

I am_____feet_____inches tall, have

_____hair,_____eyes, and weigh

_____pounds. One thing I do really

well is_____

_____.

I enjoy doing this because_____

_____.

To get even better at this, I could_____

_____

I also enjoy_____

and I hope to learn more about_____

_____.

Two things that I don't do as well as I

would like to are:_____

and_____.

Here is a picture of me:
(paste or draw)

33

Tips

These pages serve as "self-portraits" that can get girls thinking about themselves, their feelings, their families, their likes and dislikes, and their friends. Girls may choose to record answers on a separate piece of paper and do not have to fill in all the blanks.

These "self-portraits" can be used as an icebreaker, an activity that helps group members get to know each other. Girls may then feel more comfortable sharing their thoughts and suggestions. Because some of the information is personal, however, do not force any girl to share her answers. Some girls may be uncomfortable sharing their reflections, self-evaluations, or hopes. Chapter Three in Part I of this guide offers tips on handling sensitive issues.

Supporting Activities

▲ Girls can illustrate a section from these pages. For example, a girl can draw a picture of what she enjoys doing with her family. Display the illustrations and see if troop members can identify the "artist" and the message she has conveyed.

▲ Complete "Who Am I Now" or "This Is Me!" at the beginning and the end of the troop year. Discuss the differences in their self-portraits from the beginning to the end of the year. Help girls identify the factors that contributed to their revised perceptions of themselves.

Program Links

▲ *Girl Scout Badges and Signs:* My Self-Esteem badge; Family Living Skills badge; Healthy Relationships badge

▲ *Junior Girl Scout Handbook:* Girls Are Great badge

▲ *Girls Are Great: Growing Up Female* Contemporary Issues booklet

▲ *Junior Girl Scout Activity Book:* Chapters One and Two

REMINDER!

Let parents know about *Safety-Wise*. Encourage parents to review it and see that regard for safety is essential in Girl Scouting. Any limits on an activity are intended to safeguard their child.

Here are some of what I like and dislike:

	Like	Dislike
Food	_____	_____
	_____	_____
Clothes	_____	_____
	_____	_____
Music	_____	_____
	_____	_____
Book	_____	_____
	_____	_____
School subject	_____	_____
	_____	_____
Game/sports	_____	_____
	_____	_____

One thing that makes me feel really good inside is_____

_____. I am also very

happy when _____.

Families come in all shapes and sizes! I have _____ members of my family. _____ live with

me and _____ do not live with me. I have _____ pets. Their names are:_____

_____

I enjoy spending time with my friend, _____. One thing we often do

together is _____ and we love to talk about

_____. We haven't always agreed on everything, though. One time we had

a fight about _____. But we

eventually made up by _____,

And just one more thing I would like to share about myself is_____

_____.

GROWING UP FEMALE

Amy looked over at her sleeping sister. How did Ruthie manage to fall asleep so quickly? "Why am I so different from my sister?" wondered Amy, staring up at the ceiling of the room the two girls shared. Thirteen-year-old Ruthie knew just what she wanted to do when she grew up. She had her whole life planned. She was going to be a lawyer, marry Alex, and have two children. And she had known that since she was about eight. Eleven-year-old Amy, on the other hand, had no idea what she wanted to do or be. But Mom kept telling her she had lots of time to make up her mind.

Handbook Page 34

Handbook Page 35

Tips

▲ **Growing Up Female:** This section covers growing up today. It stresses that girls may feel challenged or, at times, not sure about who they are, where they fit in, and what their roles are "supposed to be." It might help girls when talking about these subjects to share some of your own "growing up" experiences.

When you talk with your troop or group, use language that does not encourage stereotypical roles for young women. For example, avoid saying "Girls shouldn't run and shout," or "Girls don't like to do that." Research has shown that gender-biased language and behavior have negative consequences for girls. Girl Scouting can be an environment for girls to develop to their full potential and strengthen and test their leadership and decision-making skills.

When completing the badge activity on the next page, have girls brainstorm a list of questions before interviewing the women. Discuss the issue of privacy and how it relates to the interview.

Supporting Activities

▲ Divide your troop or group into two groups. One group can create a collage that depicts contemporary careers for women and the other group can make a collage that shows traditional careers. Regroup and discuss the differences. Continue by talking about how careers for women have evolved over the past four decades.

▲ Have girls find out more about women who broke into traditionally male-dominated fields. Suggest they create a poster to highlight the achievements of these women. Girls can add their own aspirations to the poster.

Program Links

▲ *Girl Scout Badges and Signs:* My Self-Esteem badge; Careers badge; Women Today badge; Business-Wise badge

▲ *Junior Girl Scout Handbook:* Girls Are Great badge

▲ *Girls Are Great: Growing Up Female* Contemporary Issues booklet

It's not easy growing up. Your family, your teachers, and your friends expect you to act or look a certain way. You are faced with decisions about school, career, and family.

As a girl, you encounter particular challenges. Some people may think you should only be interested in certain jobs. Others may say that the most important thing is how you look. Or they may say it's not important for you to learn how to use a computer or do complicated math problems.

But being a girl today means that you can be smart and look any way you want. It means that you can be a caring friend and a math whiz. You can fix cars and have a stylish haircut. You can be a great baby-sitter and play a super game of basketball. You are an important person with talents and skills—some you may not have had the time to learn about yet! Opportunities are out there for you to grow up to be the best you can be!

 Interview women of different ages and backgrounds to find out what it was like when they were growing up. Talk to your mother, grandmother, aunt, neighbor, older sister, teacher, or Girl Scout leader. What challenges did they face when they were your age? What were their hopes and dreams? Collect their responses in a journal or on tape. What similar concerns do you have about growing up? What different concerns?

CHANGES IN YOUR BODY

Have you asked yourself: "Am I normal?" Are you quickly outgrowing your clothes? Do your arms and legs seem too long for your body? Do you feel happy one minute and sad the next? Would you rather spend more time with friends than with family members?

If you answered yes to one or more of these questions, you are sharing common feelings and experiences with girls and boys whose bodies are changing and becoming more adult. This period of change is called puberty.

Listen to a conversation between Megan, a ten-year-old Junior Girl Scout, who has been feeling confused about growing up, and her 15-year-old sister, Katrina, who has already experienced many of these changes.

Megan was listening, waiting for Katrina to come back from track practice. Boom! The front door slammed.

"I'm home!" Katrina yelled.

"Great—maybe now is the perfect time...." Megan thought, "I have to talk to her today!"

She stood by the open doorway of Katrina's room. "Can we talk?"

"Sure," Katrina said. "What's going on?" Katrina put her track clothes in her laundry bag and patted the bed. "Sit here. I could use a rest—practice was tough—but I made my fastest time this year!"

"Super—that's great.... I don't know what to ask you first. I was going to talk with Mom, but it's a lot easier to talk with you. Didn't you feel embarrassed talking about stuff when you were my age?"

"What kind of stuff?" Katrina asked.

"You know—getting your period and growing up stuff," Megan said.

"Yeah, sometimes, and I didn't have an older sister," Katrina said.

"All of my friends at school are talking about getting their periods and wearing bras and I feel like I don't know anything. How did you feel when you were ten?"

"Confused, unsure of myself, I didn't know at first what was going on...but, it's all a part of growing up. Talking about all of this is normal," Katrina said. "And, I found out most of my friends felt the same way. Your body goes through a lot of changes in puberty. And, puberty can start anywhere from 8 to 16 so everyone's going

through it at a different time. I remember in health class, we learned about the body—you know, about things like the pituitary gland and hormones and how they help your body grow and develop."

"What are glands? And what are hormones?" Megan asked.

"Let's see, if I remember, glands are parts of your body that make hormones for the body to use, and hormones are chemicals that travel through the bloodstream and help you to grow and develop. Wow—I can't believe I remembered that!"

"How come some girls have gotten their periods? And I haven't gotten mine yet?"

"Every girl is different. There is no right or

36

37

▲ **Changes in Your Body:** Girl Scouts of the U. S. A. respects the rights of parents to decide when and how to discuss human sexuality with their daughters. At the same time, some parents want and request support during the different stages of their daughters' development. For this reason, Girl Scouting has accepted a secondary role in providing information to girls about development and sexuality. The information in this section has been reviewed by various religious groups and educators. If you are planning to do activities with your troop or group that are more involved than the ones here, please see the sensitive issues section in *Safety-Wise* for guidelines.

Today, girls at the Junior Girl Scout age level are likely to be aware of a variety of issues related to the physical, emotional, and social aspects of sexuality. Unfortunately, much of the information available to girls through sources such as magazines, music, television, movies, and more "experienced" peers or older adolescents is misleading. This chapter and the accompanying discussions in your troop or group meeting can correct misinformation and help girls understand.

If some girls seem uncomfortable with a discussion, you may want to use the following techniques when reading the story:

● Before reading the story, write the word "puberty" on a large posterboard or on a chalkboard. Brainstorm with girls any associated words or ideas.

● Select volunteers to read the parts of Megan and Katrina.

● As they read, ask girls to circle words or phrases they would like clarified or explained.

● Have girls write questions about puberty on pieces of paper. After they finish reading the story, review the girls' questions to assess whether they have been satisfactorily answered.

Don't lead discussions if you do not feel comfortable talking about topics relating to puberty, even when using the ideas listed above. Look for help. Your council, parents, and troop committee members may all be able to recommend the right support.

wrong time to begin puberty. And, some of your friends will change really quickly and others more slowly. Some will have larger breasts and others smaller. Do you know when you'll see these changes in your body?"

"No, when?" Megan asked.

"When the time is right for you."

"When did you first notice that you were changing?" Megan asked.

"You have a lot of questions, don't you? Okay... I think I started to perspire more. I remember borrowing Mom's deodorant. I also noticed hair growing under my arms and near my vagina. My pants and skirts got tight and my breasts felt sore. So, Mom and I went bra shopping! I hated putting on one of those things. Would you believe some boys in class made fun of me? They were such jerks that I never let them bother me," Katrina said.

"I think getting my period will be a lot more embarrassing than wearing a bra," Megan said.

"Not if you know what to expect."

"Like what?"

Getting Your Period

One of the most important changes in your body will be the start of menstruation. An organ in your body called a uterus starts to make a lining that will build up and then shed and pass out of the body through the vagina. This tissue contains blood but you are not really bleeding when the tissue comes out. Menstruation usually begins between ages 9 and 16. It is okay to begin earlier or later.

You may have heard menstruation called "a period." That's because it is a periodic cycle that happens about every 28 days and usually lasts for a period of three to seven days. In the beginning it may be more irregular, though.

The first sign of menstruation is usually a small amount of blood, not a "gushing" of blood. Menstrual pads (sanitary napkins) or tampons can be used to absorb the menstrual flow. Menstrual pads are worn inside underwear. Tampons are worn inside the vagina. The use of pads or tampons is a personal choice that a parent or guardian can help you make.

"I still have a book called *Getting Your Period*. Why don't you read it?" Katrina reached to the shelf above her dresser. Tucked away to the side was a slim booklet, *Getting Your Period*. (See opposite page.)

"Katrina, can I ask just one more question? What about the weird feelings I get? I mean one minute I'm happy and then the next minute I feel like crying...."

"Well, how you feel changes as your body changes. I was so confused. Some days I felt great; other days I felt terrible. And when both happened in one day I thought something was really wrong with me. But my friends and I talked and we realized this was happening to everybody and these feelings were normal. It's really okay to feel embarrassed and concerned about all of these changes."

"Katrina, are the same things happening to boys?"

"Uh-huh, boys are changing too. Boys' voices become deeper. They get taller, grow body hair, and their muscles get larger."

"It's great to have a sister to talk to about these things—and of course, who'll be a famous track star someday, too! Thanks a lot, Sis!"

If you have questions or want information about menstruation and how your body changes during puberty, talk with an adult you trust, like a parent, older sister, teacher, school nurse, Girl Scout leader, or adult friend. Remember, menstruation is a normal, healthy function of the female body. It means you are becoming a young woman and that your body is able to produce a baby.

How much do you and your friends really know about puberty? Test your knowledge by taking this quiz. Some of the statements are facts and others are myths. Answers are on the next page.

Puberty Fact or Myth?

Answer TRUE if it is a fact and answer FALSE if it is a myth.

1. Girls shouldn't swim or bathe while they are menstruating.
2. It is common for girls beginning to menstruate to skip their period for a few months.
3. If a girl isn't menstruating by the time she's 15, there is something wrong with her.
4. Having oily skin and pimples is part of growing up for most teenagers.
5. Usually, both breasts are exactly the same size and shape.
6. A girl can become pregnant before she has her first period.
7. Girls usually begin puberty earlier than boys.
8. Boys can tell when a girl is having her period.
9. All girls have menstrual cramps during their period.
10. Young girls should not use tampons.

38

39

Supporting Activities

▲ Invite a health care professional to give a presentation about puberty. Provide time for a question and answer session. Be sure to keep parents/guardians informed and get written permission when appropriate. (See *Safety-Wise*.)

Program Links

▲ *Girl Scout Badges and Signs:* Becoming a Teen badge; My Self-Esteem badge; Looking Your Best badge; Health and Fitness badge

▲ *Junior Girl Scout Handbook:* Girls Are Great badge

▲ *Girls Are Great: Growing Up Female* and *Decisions for Your Life: Preventing Teenage Pregnancy* Contemporary Issues booklets

Tips

▲ **Get the Facts**: The facts listed in this activity are some of the key topics in understanding puberty. If you add your own facts, be sure they are accurate. You could consult with a health care professional or someone in a related field to lead a discussion.

When responding to girls' questions, provide information in a nonjudgmental, nonthreatening manner. Furthermore, make girls feel that all their questions are important, never silly.

Supporting Activities

▲ After completing "Get the Facts," help girls revise any statements incorrectly labeled as myths or facts.

▲ Invite a troop or group of older girls to talk about their experiences with boys, growing up, puberty, etc. Keeping in mind that Cadette and Senior Girl Scouts are not authorities on these issues, help your troop or group prepare questions that the older girls can answer or discuss.

Program Links

▲ *Girl Scout Badges and Signs:* Becoming a Teen badge; My Self-Esteem badge; Health and Fitness badge

▲ *Junior Girl Scout Handbook:* Girls Are Great badge; Looking Your Best badge

▲ *Girls Are Great: Growing Up Female* and *Decisions for Your Life: Preventing Teenage Pregnancy* Contemporary Issues booklets

Answer Key: Myth and Fact Quiz

1. MYTH. It is fine for girls to swim, and they should bathe or shower when they are having their periods. If a girl chooses to go swimming, she can use a tampon. A girl can also wash her hair. In fact, there is no reason to limit activity during your period.

2. FACT. When girls first start menstruating, they often have irregular cycles. They may skip a month or two at times.

3. MYTH. Absolutely not. A girl may begin her period as early as age eight or as late as sixteen.

4. FACT. Most teenagers will get pimples during adolescence and some into adulthood. There are some teenagers who do not get pimples.

5. MYTH. Most breasts are not the same shape and size. One breast may be a little larger or a little lower than the other.

6. FACT. A girl can become pregnant before she begins menstruating. An egg can leave the ovary before her menstrual cycle begins. It means her body is able to produce a baby, but does not mean that she is ready to handle the physical, emotional, and financial demands of caring for a baby.

7. FACT. Most girls begin puberty one to two years earlier than boys. However, boys do catch up with girls.

8. MYTH. No one will know you have your period unless you tell them. There is nothing to be ashamed of should a boy find out.

9. MYTH. Not everyone gets menstrual cramps. Some girls get cramps in their abdomen or lower back.

10. MYTH. With the help of their parents or guardians, girls can make their own decisions about which sanitary products to use. Young girls can use tampons; those who do will probably prefer to use the slender or junior size.

Why not try some of the activities in the badges Becoming a Teen and My Self-Esteem, or some of the activities in the Girls Are Great: Growing Up Female Contemporary Issues booklet?

40

Brenda's Advice Column

Brenda is a college student who spends a lot of time giving advice to young people. Below are some letters she has received from girls your age. Read the letters and discuss as a group what advice you would give each girl. Then, look at the answers to find out what advice Brenda gave. Keep in mind there is more than one way to handle each situation.

Dear Brenda:

I haven't gotten my period yet, but I am so nervous that it will happen when I'm at school. What will I do?

Nervous

Dear Brenda:

It seems like everybody else knows I'm growing up except my dad. He thinks he can come into my room anytime. I feel I should have some privacy. What should I do?

Growing Up

Dear Brenda:

Most of my friends are wearing bras. My mother doesn't think I need to wear one. How can I convince her that I'd feel better if I could wear a bra?

Anxious

Dear Brenda:

There is a boy in my class I really like. He always seems to ignore me. How can I let him know how I feel about him?

Confused

41

▲ **Brenda's Advice Column:** Just as with "Get the Facts," "Brenda's Advice Column" includes letters that represent the kinds of concerns or questions girls may have. You might want to point out that some girls may have these concerns and some girls may not.

Remind girls that Brenda's answers (see the next page) simply offer one way of handling each situation and that many advice columns are based on the opinions of the authors who are not always experts. Encourage girls to discuss other ways to deal with problems. "Critical thinking" skills (see Chapter Five in the handbook) should be stressed while reading the letters in the handbook. Discuss other advice columns girls may read.

▲ Have girls prepare a response to the following "Brenda" letter:

Dear Brenda,

I'm fourteen years old and all of my friends have started having periods, but I haven't. I'm really beginning to wonder if I am normal.

Different

Girls can compare their responses; discuss similarities and differences.

▲ Many children's magazines have advice columns written by young people. Have girls write a letter to a columnist about a problem they are having in school, a conflict with a friend, or a concern about growing up.

▲ *Girl Scout Badges and Signs:* Becoming a Teen badge; My Self-Esteem badge; Health and Fitness badge

▲ *Junior Girl Scout Handbook:* Girls Are Great badge; Looking Your Best badge

▲ *Girls Are Great: Growing Up Female* and *Decisions for Your Life: Preventing Teenage Pregnancy* Contemporary Issues booklets

Brenda's Answers

Dear Nervous:

One of the biggest concerns girls have about their period is where they'll be when they get it. To feel more comfortable about getting your period, consider keeping a sanitary pad or supply of tissues in your pocketbook, book bag, or locker so you can be prepared. Understanding ahead of time what will happen can help you feel more comfortable.

Brenda

Dear Anxious:

Wanting to be like your friends is quite normal. Let your mother know how important it is for you to wear a bra. Let her know that you think you are ready to wear a bra. You might even ask her to go shopping with you to buy one. If she still insists that you do not need one, wait a while and then talk with her again. No matter what happens, the most important thing is that you feel great about the way you look—with or without a bra.

Brenda

Dear Growing Up:

You are right. You should have some privacy. It seems like time for you to have a talk with your dad. He needs to be reminded that you are growing up. Let him know exactly how you feel. Let him know that you would prefer that he knock before coming into your room. If you feel uncomfortable talking to your dad or if he doesn't seem to understand, talk to your mom or another adult who can help you communicate your feelings to your dad.

Brenda

Dear Confused:

It is quite normal for boys to ignore girls at this age. If you really want him to know how you feel, you have to tell him. This may not be easy. You could tell him in person, call him on the telephone, give him a note, or have a friend tell him for you. You could even ask him questions to show that you are interested in him. You must decide which way makes you feel the most comfortable. Keep in mind that he may or may not like you. Good luck!

Brenda

42

BODY IMAGE

It's Monday morning and you stretch before you get out of bed. You feel rested after a good night's sleep. You brush your teeth, comb your hair, and pull on your leggings and an oversized T-shirt. As you turn to grab your books, you take a quick look in the mirror and think

_____ !

Some people look in a mirror and like what they see; others don't. Most people want to look their best, but many times girls believe that to be popular and appreciated by others, they must be beautiful.

What people think of as beautiful is greatly influenced by what they see in magazines, on television, in movies, and in books. (These are different kinds of media.) To find out what the media's definition of beauty is, try the following activities:

 With your troop or group members, gather different types of magazines; include magazines that have a particular focus such as gardening, sports, current events, or women's interests. Then, scan the pages, clipping out pictures of women and men. When you have at least a dozen pictures, spread them out on the floor. According to these pictures, how would you generally describe the following?

•Teeth	•Chest	•Hair
•Legs	•Lips	•Skin color
•Eyes	•Waist	•Arms

Now, separate the magazines by type or topic. Using the list above as a guideline, compare each magazine's definition of beauty. What differences do you notice?

 Keep a television log for one week. Tune in to different programs, including news shows, for approximately 15 minutes. Take notes on the appearances of men, women, and children. Look at hairstyle, clothing, age, skin color, weight, and facial features (eyes, nose, teeth, etc.). At the end of the week, look over your notes. What common characteristics do you notice?

Overall, how do the media define beauty for a female? a male? Do you feel this is realistic? Why or why not?

43

Tips

▲ **Body Image:** At the Junior Girl Scout age level, appearance can increasingly affect girls' self-esteem. As social relationships between boys and girls change, how one looks takes on a new, "exaggerated" importance. Furthermore, girls at this age begin to rely on images in the media for ideals of how they should look and on the opinions of their peer group as a measure of self-worth.

Although this is a natural, developmental stage, Girl Scouting can provide an arena where appearance does not play a significant part in a girl's feeling of acceptance. As a leader you can play an important role in highlighting each girl's strengths, talents, and skills—independent of physical appearance.

Supporting Activities

▲ Another way of doing the first handbook activity is to gather magazines from the 1960s, 1970s, 1980s. (See Chapter Eight, Girls Are Great badge, number 4.) Have girls compare the appearances with today's standards. What can girls conclude about the public perception of beauty and the current trends in beauty and health? For example, pictures from one time may portray women who were "super-thin," while another time period highlights an athletic look.

▲ If conflicts arise in your troop or group over clothing, hair, sneakers, or jewelry (e.g., arguments about whose is best, etc.), help girls recognize how alienating or hurtful this behavior can be. Review with the girls the section on cliques, later in this chapter, and the sections on discrimination and stereotypes in Chapter Five.

Program Links

▲ *Girl Scout Badges and Signs:* Health and Fitness badge; My Self-Esteem badge; Healthy Living badge

▲ *Girls Are Great: Growing Up Female* Contemporary Issues booklet

▲ *Junior Girl Scout Handbook:* Looking Your Best badge

REMINDER!

Give girls ample time to think before they respond to questions. Encourage them to express themselves completely and allow them to finish, without interruption.

Feeling Comfortable with Who You Are

Some girls believe that to be beautiful, they must be very thin. In fact, many girls think they weigh too much, and often they are wrong. When they look in the mirror, they see themselves as "fat" or "overweight." They go on diets to become even thinner or exercise excessively. Being very underweight or "too thin" can be dangerous to your health. On the other hand, some girls really are overweight and that is not healthy either. Always check with a doctor or nurse to find out what weight is right for your body type and what you can do to lose or gain weight if necessary.

Feeling good about yourself should not be based on just how you look. First, what is beautiful and attractive to one person may not be to another. Second, the real definition of beauty includes things that you can't always see in someone's face: intelligence, friendliness, kindness, and helpfulness are just a few things that can add to a person's beauty. What else do you feel adds to a person's beauty?

Remember, though, that wanting to change your looks can be healthy at times. If you are really overweight, you may want to lose some weight through exercise and a good diet. You may be wearing braces so that your teeth will be straight. Can you think of some other positive ways to change your looks?

 Prepare a short skit that uses not only words but also pictures, symbols, and body language to deliver one of the following messages: What's special about being a girl? What's exciting about growing up? What's your definition of beauty? Perform your skit for other members of your troop or group and for Daisy and Brownie Girl Scouts.

Tears filled Maria's eyes and she looked down, hoping no one would notice. "I can't believe I said 'no.' I do want to join their game. I don't know why I'm always saying 'no' when I really do want to play with them."

Sherry was about to burst. She couldn't wait until her mom got home so she could share the news—first place in the science fair!

Layla was doing her homework when her mom walked in the door. "Great! You made it home early today—can we go to the store and get those new sneakers I wanted?" Layla's mom said, "Honey, we have to have a serious talk. The reason I'm home early is I got fired from my job."

How do you think you would feel in each of these situations? Then, talk with your friends about some of the situations and describe the feelings: angry, happy, afraid, lonely, proud, worried, disappointed, loved, eager, frustrated, embarrassed, surprised, excited, jealous, sad. You'll probably find that your feelings in certain situations are different from those of your friends. There is no right or wrong way to feel.

"Did Abdul really say that?" Kayla asked her best friend Latifeh. "Yes, he really said that he liked you and that he thought you were pretty," Latifeh answered."

Chantal picked up the phone. "Hi, Dad. Are you leaving your office now? Carrie and I have been ready for ages." "Sorry, hon, maybe later this week. You know I've been working on this big case, and I just can't leave now."

People sometimes try to hide their feelings from others. But in many cases, letting your feelings show can help you feel better. And when people understand each others' feelings, they find it easier to get along. Think of caring, trusted adults you can approach when you are feeling upset. What qualities do they have that make you feel you can turn to them with personal concerns?

Georgia's mother had been ill with AIDS for many months. She would probably die within days, the doctor said. Georgia reached out to hold her mother's hand.

Migdalia hears her grandmother calling. "The movers have taken the last box. We have to go now." Migdalia takes one last look around the bedroom before heading out.

Ayako saved the most beautifully wrapped present—the one with the big yellow bow and yellow and white striped paper—to open last. She held the box on her lap for just a moment before starting to tear away the paper.

"Everyone said the new baby was so cute, so alert, so this, so that. I don't want to hear any more about the new baby," thought Song.

 Have you ever seen a public service program on television that offers advice or help to people who have family or emotional problems? Why not create and produce your own? Pick a topic and collect information. Some girls can be on a panel of "experts." Others can be the people with the problems, and one person could be the moderator. You might want to videotape your show for others to view or "take it on the road" for younger girls or other Junior Girl Scout troops or groups.

Feelings Feelings Feelings

▲ **Feeling Comfortable with Who You Are:** Anorexia nervosa and bulimia are eating disorders characterized by a preoccupation with food, an irrational fear of being fat, and a distorted body image. It is estimated that anorexia nervosa strikes about one in every 200 teenage girls and young women; the rate for bulimia is much higher.

Some of the characteristics of anorexia nervosa include extreme thinness (loss of 25 percent of body weight), preoccupation with food and diet, extreme fear of gaining weight, inability to respond to signals of hunger and fatigue, excessive exercise, and distorted body image. Characteristics of bulimia include a cycle of eating binges followed by rigid dieting, excessive exercising, forced vomiting, and/or laxative or diuretic abuse; dental problems; extreme fear of gaining weight; and frequent weight fluctuations.

Early detection and prompt professional treatment can increase the chances for recovery and cure. If you have reason to believe that a girl in your troop or group has bulimic or anorexic tendencies, it is important that measures are taken to help her. Her parents or guardians should be alerted. Contact your Girl Scout council, which may be able to provide sources of professional help.

The other side of the picture is obesity (at least 20 percent over normal weight). This is not only a health concern; it can also seriously impair a girl's self-esteem and her relationships with others.

▲ Some girls may express a desire to change their appearances in a positive way. If so, work with them to devise a realistic plan to help them reach their goals. Use the goal-setting plan in Chapter Four as a guide.

▲ *Girl Scout Badges and Signs:* Exploring Healthy Eating badge; Health and Fitness badge; My Self-Esteem badge; Sports badge; Sports Sampler badge

▲ *Junior Girl Scout Handbook:* Looking Your Best badge; Healthy Living badge

▲ *Girls Are Great: Growing Up Female* Contemporary Issues booklet

▲ *Junior Girl Scout Activity Book:* Chapter Four

▲ **Feelings:** Every day, girls face situations that test their feelings about friends, family, school, and themselves. In fact, some of the girls may have had experiences like those described in the introduction to the section "Feelings." After reading these anecdotes, girls may want to share how they felt.

Remind girls that feelings are personal and there is no right or wrong way to express emotion. Ridicule should not be tolerated. If a girl seems particularly disturbed by the troop's or group's discussion, you may want to talk privately with her.

Don't be surprised if girls' emotions run the gamut from happy to sad within the course of your troop meeting. At this age level, girls are prone to rapidly changing feelings. If a girl seems to experience periods of extreme highs and lows, it is advisable to alert her parent or guardian.

▲ *Girl Scout Badges and Signs:* Becoming a Teen badge; Healthy Relationships badge; My Self-Esteem badge

▲ *Junior Girl Scout Handbook:* Talk! badge; Girls Are Great badge

▲ *Junior Girl Scout Activity book:* Chapter Seven

Relating to Boys

Ten-year-old Sonia giggled. She told her best friend Sara about how she watched from the top of the stairs as her older sister and boyfriend kissed on Saturday night. "You know, those long, with-no-time-out-for-breathing kisses," Sonia said as the school bus took the girls home on Monday afternoon.

"Well, I really like Robert. I can imagine kissing him like that," Sara said quietly, thinking of the cute boy in her fifth-grade class. She watched Sonia's face for her reaction.

Sonia's eyebrows flew right up and her mouth turned into a giant "O." "You'd kiss Robert like that?!"

"S-h-h-h," Sara said. "You don't have to tell the entire bus!"

"I don't think I'm ready for kissing like that, even with Neil, and you know how much I like him."

"I bet Robert and Neil don't think about kissing and touching," Sara said. "Hey, this is my stop—see you tomorrow!"

• • • •

"How was school today, sweetie?" Mom asked Sara. Sara was putting the napkins on the table and started folding one of them into a dog shape—then a cat shape—then a boat. "Sara...?" "Okay, I guess," she answered. She was thinking about her conversation on the bus. She wanted to keep talking but she felt a little embarrassed.

"Is anything wrong, Sara? Did something happen at school?"

"Oh, no," Sara replied. "I was just thinking about something Sonia and I talked about today."

She described the conversation, including the part about the passionate kissing.

"Well, Sara, it's natural to be thinking about boys, but it's just as normal that some girls don't. Everyone develops at her own rate. Some girls your age feel attracted to boys. They want boys to notice them and they want to be close to boys. Other girls just aren't interested at all—and that's okay. Having a crush on a boy is exciting, but it can be kind of scary too. You keep thinking about what he thinks about you!"

"That's it!" Sara said. "You know exactly how I feel."

"When you start going out with a boy–Robert or anyone else–and, by the way, I don't think you're ready to date yet..."

"I knew you would say that..."

"Well, it's true...You learn," her mom continued, "what's it's like to have a special relationship with someone, to have one person to really care about and who really cares about you. Sonia's sister, Dolores, is going out with just one boy now. But last year, Dolores would hang around with a group of boys and girls. They'd go to the movies or to the mall. Group dating is a way to learn about relationships, too. And sometimes, being with a group is easier than being with just one person."

 Talk with friends about the following situations:

1. Sarit finds out the boy she has a crush on doesn't like her.

2. Kim likes Alex. And Alex likes her too. The trouble is Alex has been going with Kim's best friend Suzanne.

WHEN BOYS BOTHER YOU

While it's often nice for you to get attention from boys, sometimes boys say or do things that really bother you. Kwame may think it's cool when he snaps Kendra's bra. Joe may think Tonya should be flattered when he comments about her developing breasts.

Boys, and sometimes girls and grown-ups too, often think that "it's no big deal." But when it's your body someone is talking about or your bra that he is touching, it is a BIG DEAL! You don't have to put up with comments or actions that hurt you or make you feel uncomfortable. In a firm voice, tell anyone who says or does things you don't like to stop. Turn to page 72 to learn about acting in an assertive way.

If he continues to do things that bother you, or if it is too hard to tell him to stop, tell your parent, teacher, or another grown-up you trust.

46

47

Handbook Page 46

Handbook Page 47

▲ **Relating to Boys:** When discussing relationships, it is important to remember that girls may be at different maturational levels and some may have their parents' permission to socialize with boys on dates or at parties. It will be important to remind girls that such differences are to be expected.

Regardless of where a girl is socially, you can help her recognize that she should not feel pressured into doing anything that makes her uncomfortable. Family values are important considerations, too.

Reactions from the story may range from embarrassment to inquisitiveness to bragging about their own experiences. Provide an open, trusting atmosphere for girls. Try to give information in terms they can understand. If you do not feel comfortable talking about a particular issue, refer girls to their parents/guardians, teachers, or religious leaders.

Supporting Activities

▲ Have girls do one or both of the following and discuss their findings:

1. Ask parents or other family members to tell you about their early "crushes" and dating experiences.

2. Read a novel about a teenage dating situation. How do you think the characters handled conflicts, feelings of attraction, and family attitudes?

Program Links

▲ *Girl Scout Badges and Signs:* Becoming a Teen badge; Making Decisions badge; Creative Solutions badge

▲ *Decisions for Your Life: Preventing Teenage Pregnancy* and *Girls Are Great: Growing Up Female* Contemporary Issues booklets

Tips

▲ **When Boys Bother You:** Described in this section are behaviors that girls might encounter with boys. Girls may need to be reminded that they should not compromise their own self-respect to gain greater popularity. Sexual harassment is an issue that has received attention from both the legal community and the population at large. Awareness of inappropriate sexual comments

or actions at an early age will help young women recognize sexual harassment and empower them to not become victims.

Supporting Activities

▲ Invite an attorney or someone familiar with legal issues to discuss sexual harassment. Have her or him explain the issue in age-appropriate terms.

Program Links

▲ *Girl Scout Badges and Signs:* Healthy Relationships badge; My Self-Esteem badge

▲ *Girls Are Great: Growing Up Female* Contemporary Issues booklet

WHAT'S IMPORTANT TO YOU?

Was it tough answering any of the questions on this page? Your answers show some of your values. Values are those things in which you strongly believe.

Your values influence how you see something, as well as how you react to it. Your dreams, goals, and attitudes are all shaped by your values. If a girl values education, she might not mind having less spending money because she knows her family is saving money for college.

It's important to know what you really value, because those values can help you make decisions. You do this already on a daily basis—how you dress, what your room looks like, how you treat your mom or dad, or even how you relate to your friends—reflect your values.

Values help you use information and decide what you should do. Often, you will need to get more information before making a decision. Suppose you heard your friends arguing about vegetarianism—the belief that people should not eat meat. One of your friends doesn't eat meat because she thinks animals shouldn't be killed. Another friend completely disagrees. She thinks killing animals is okay for food, but she is against hunting as a sport. Another friend thinks killing animals is okay for food, but she is a vegetarian because she thinks it's a healthier way to eat. What do you believe?

How do you decide what to believe and how to act? You are influenced by your family and friends, the media, your community, your spiritual beliefs, and your education.

If you sometimes act in a way that is not in line with what you value, you may feel unhappy. Can you think of a time when you did something that went against what you valued? How did you feel?

•You are getting ready to blast off into outer space to explore the galaxy for one year. What five things would you take with you? Why?

•What do you like most about your best friend? Why?

•What family rule do you feel is most important to keep? Why?

•What if you could choose between having a lovely singing voice or an extremely beautiful face? Which would you pick? Why?

48

Values Check!

How important to you are each of these items in the chart below? In Column 1, place a "+" next to those that are very important to you, an "O" next to those that are a little important, and a "–" next to those that are not important.

Values	How I Feel Now	Six Months Later	One Year Later
	Date:	Date:	Date:
Being popular at school			
Doing well at school			
Making my own decisions			
Going out with a boy			
Spending time with my family			
Caring for the environment			
Helping others in need			
Standing up for myself			
Exercising and eating good foods			
Wearing expensive clothes			
Fighting prejudice			
Taking part in my religion			
Being with friends			
Other values			

Look at the items you marked as very important. Are you surprised by any of the items you marked? Of the items you marked as very important, which is #1? #2? #3? Place the numbers in the left-hand margin next to the item. Compare your ideas with other girls in your troop or group.

Changes in Values

As you get older, your experiences and the new people you meet may teach you a great deal about yourself and your world, and your values may change. In about six months, reread the values list again, recording your answers in Column 2. What changes in your values did you find? What are some experiences that caused you to change your values? Are those values that were important before just as important now? Sometime next year, record your answers in Column 3. What changed? What remained the same?

49

▲ **What's Important to You?** This section gives girls the opportunity to examine the values that help them make decisions. You can discuss the questions in the margins as a group after each girl answered.

Point out that values can be expressed as a thing or idea, such as respect, friendship, patriotism, or freedom of speech, or values can be thought of as an action, such as showing respect to your elders, being a good friend, or voting in an election. Have girls brainstorm things or actions that they think of as values and discuss how people act on their values.

▲ One technique for discussing the opening questions as a group is to put the questions on note cards, then have one girl draw a question, respond, and pass it on to the next girl for comment. Everyone should have an opportunity to speak to each question. This is also a good way to develop listening skills.

▲ The examples in the handbook illustrate how a similar action (being a vegetarian) has been chosen for different reasons by different people. The purpose is to spark discussion from different viewpoints, not to advocate a way of life. Ask the girls to examine the reasons they agree or disagree with the decision to eat or not eat meat. Be sure to point out that people with different opinions or views can co-exist. Discuss how you might go about planning a dinner for such a group. The discussion on vegetarianism might be a good introduction to a discussion of other values.

▲ In discussing the question that asks girls how they feel when they act in a way that is not in line with what they value (an example might be disobeying mom or cheating on a test), help girls identify values that are important to them personally. You might ask them to identify, if they can, what some of their values are based on. (For example: my family, my faith, my own feelings, what other people do.) Help girls identify actions that might make the right decision (i.e., identifying the problem, doing the "right thing" by acting on values, seeking help from someone whom they respect).

▲ **Values Check!:** This chart is not a test, but a way for girls to examine what is important to them today. Some items will change with time, while others will remain the same. Suggest girls add their own values to the list.

Ask them to think about why they marked each item the way they did. Which of the items are strongly influenced by family, peers, teachers, their faith, personal experiences, and media?

Values in Girl Scouting

Read the lines of both the Girl Scout Promise and Law. The Promise and Law are a set of values shared by all girls who belong to Girl Scouts of the U.S.A. and the World Association of Girl Guides and Girl Scouts.

 With a group of friends, discuss different examples of how you can act on each part of the Girl Scout Law. Discuss how the Girl Scout Promise and Law can be helpful when you are faced with making a tough decision or solving a difficult problem.

 Listed at the right are values that are an important part of Girl Scouting. Look through this book for examples of some of the values.

Keeping traditions

Recognizing the importance of being a girl and a woman

Respecting others

Being honest

Being a good citizen

Giving service to others

Learning about others

Celebrating cultural diversity

Practicing democracy

Recognizing the importance of family

Being a friend

Recognizing the power of an individual

Recognizing the power of group actions

Speaking up for human rights

Believing in yourself

Being a good role model

Working in girl/adult partnerships

Practicing good health and physical fitness

Taking responsibility

Values Dilemmas

Sometimes you are faced with a decision that has no right or wrong answer or you can see both sides of an argument. These choices are called values dilemmas. They can be the hardest decisions you have to make. You may think if you don't act, you are avoiding a choice, but you have made the choice not to act, and that can be worse than not acting at all.

 You have $25 to donate to a local charity. You have thought about making a contribution to a group that provides food to the homeless or to the local animal shelter that is in danger of closing. Who gets the money? Why?

Discuss this dilemma with your group or family. How would you act? Why? What are some of the reasons you decided to act as you did? What are some of the values you used to help make your decision?

Differences in Values

Every day, you will come into contact with people whose values differ from your own. No one should be teased or put down for having different values. And, you have the right to disagree with values different from your own.

To explore differences in values, try this activity with your friends or family. Think about each statement and decide if you agree, disagree, or are not sure. Explain your feelings and listen carefully to what others say.

- Money brings happiness.
- Women in the military should have combat duty.
- Everyone should have the right to carry a gun.
- Watching violence on television encourages a person to act violently.

Values That Conflict

Sometimes people's values conflict with the rights of others. People who practice racism or discriminate against others hold values that conflict with what our society and the laws of our country value. If you are asked to think seriously about what the United States really stands for, you might think about how the Pledge of Allegiance calls for "liberty and justice for all."

The rights of liberty, justice, and equality are human rights that many people in the United States and throughout the world believe. Although some people may take these rights for granted, the guarantee of these rights has attracted generations of people to the United States like a magnet.

In 1948, long before you were born, the United Nations wrote a Universal Declaration of Human Rights that listed 29 different human rights that were common to people throughout the world.

Some of these rights are listed below. Imagine life without them. Unfortunately, citizens of some countries live without many of these basic rights.

Included in the Universal Declaration of Human Rights are the right to:

- ✓ Equality
- ✓ Protection against cruel punishment, like torture
- ✓ Protection against racial, ethnic, sexual, and religious discrimination
- ✓ Privacy
- ✓ Freedom of movement in your country
- ✓ Seek safety in other countries
- ✓ Marry whom you want
- ✓ Own property
- ✓ Freedom of opinion and speech
- ✓ Participate in your government
- ✓ Work and choice of job
- ✓ Rest and leisure
- ✓ Education
- ✓ Know what your rights are

Tips

▲ **Values in Girl Scouting**: Girl Scouts and Girl Guides around the world of different nationalities, faiths, heritages, and skin colors share a common set of values through acceptance of the Promise and the Law. Therefore, as a leader, your guide for discussion on values can be the Girl Scout Promise and Law.

As an adult you are modeling your personal values for girls. Your role is that of facilitator and guide, giving girls opportunities to explore their feelings, concerns, and personal values in a safe and supportive atmosphere. If you have questions about your role as a leader in discussing values, refer to *Safety-Wise*, particularly the discussion on sensitive issues, or contact your local council.

Supporting Activities

▲ Discuss the Promise and Law with the girls and then look at the handbook activity at the bottom of the page. Have girls add their own examples of values that Girl Scouting exemplifies. They can look through the handbook or other Girl Scout resources. Discuss how each girl may have different values but that this does not make someone better or more right than another.

Tips

▲ **Values Dilemmas**: Dilemmas provide an opportunity for girls to look at all sides of an issue, using critical thinking skills.

This section might best be presented with a personal or troop-related dilemma. *Earth Matters: A Challenge for Environmental Action* Contemporary Issues booklet contains some excellent examples and includes these tips for developing dilemmas:

1. Build a dilemma so it contains realistic choices.

2. Use real-life problems whenever possible. Make the dilemma relevant to the girls by using Girl Scout situations when possible.

3. Focus on the choices to be made and not on the detailed evidence of the case. The dilemma should be written so that it is simple, interesting, and short. Extra details should be left out.

4. Construct a focus question that poses the choice to be made.

5. Provide a situation that presents a genuine conflict and choice of action. If the right answer or the answer that is accepted by the Girl Scout leader is obvious, then it is not a dilemma.

6. Ask questions about the choice, the reasons for the choice, and alternatives to the choice.

(The values section continues on the next page.)

With so many changes in the world, you may have a hard time recognizing when rights are being taken away. Is your mom's right to privacy being violated if someone reads all her computer mail at her place of business? How can you tell if the clothing you buy is being made by children your age being forced to work for pennies in dark, dirty workplaces? Can a boatload of people who claim they are fleeing unfair treatment be turned away? Questions such as these and the way individuals and governments react to them will be important issues in your lifetime.

 To learn more about human rights and the freedoms citizens share, do some activities from badges, such as Active Citizen, Celebrating People, Junior Citizen, World Neighbors, and The World in My Community.

 Interview a person who has lived in another country. What rights were guaranteed there? If possible, speak to someone who came to the United States for a better life.

What's Fair for Girls

Do you get called on in class as often as boys do? Do some adults expect you to have only certain careers when you grow up just because you're a girl? Are the girls and women characters you read about in books or see on television or in the movies strong, successful, and brave? Or are they shown as weak and unable to make decisions? Think about times when you have heard or seen things that did not seem fair to girls. Add your own unfair statements to the cactus on the opposite page.

 Read a newspaper. Look for possible violations of human rights both here and around the world. Share these findings with a group of friends through a discussion, poster, or debate.

 Here's a chance for you to see that words can be used to give messages that are fair or unfair. To the right are some examples of statements. With the girls in your troop or group, or on your own, place a "+" next to each statement that sounds fair and a "–" next to each statement that sounds unfair. If you want a real challenge, try changing the unfair statements into fair ones.

___ **1. Hakim Jamal is a smart lawyer and his sister Reza is a pretty redhead.**

___ **2. Scientists often become so involved in their work that they forget about their wives and children.**

___ **3. Twenty police officers were needed to control the crowd at the baseball stadium.**

___ **4. The teacher reminded her students to ask their mothers to send in snacks for the field trip.**

___ **5. The candidates were Brendan O'Malley, president of American Electronics, Inc., and Annamarie Piccione, a lively, blonde grandmother of four.**

___ **6. The girls took turns throwing the ball.**

"Ouch!"

52

53

▲ **Difference in Values:** The following points might come out in the course of a discussion. You may or may not decide to go further, depending on the level of understanding, interest, and your personal comfort. *Safety-Wise* provides information on discussing sensitive issues.

▲ Not all people have the same values.

▲ People express their values in different ways.

▲ People have the right to express their opinions.

▲ People have the right to act on their values if the action is not against the law or does not violate another's rights.

▲ **Values That Conflict:** Ask the girls to think of values that might be in conflict with society. They might be able to come up with examples from their own lives.

To make this section relevant, have the girls discuss the Universal Declaration of Human Rights list in terms of their own experiences. If possible, have someone who has immigrated to the United States (perhaps one of your troop members) for girls to interview. Human rights can also be discussed in the context of stories or books, such as *The Diary of a Young Girl* by Anne Frank.

(For "Values" Section)

▲ *Girl Scout Badges and Signs:* Active Citizen badge; Celebrating People badge; Junior Citizen badge; World in My Community badge; World Neighbors badge

▲ You can obtain additional information about the Universal Declaration of Human Rights from your library or the United Nations Educational, Scientific, and Cultural Organization (UNESCO), UNESCO Liaison Office, 2 United Nations Plaza, New York, N.Y. 10017.

▲ **What's Fair for Girls:** Discuss with girls the harm caused by any kind of stereotyping. Be certain your own attitudes and choice of language do not imply that there are things they should not say, do, or consider just because they are girls. Refer to the sections in Chapter Five for more on stereotypes.

▲ Have girls role-play the following situation:

The gym teacher is looking for a person to play first base. A girl raises her hand but the gym teacher ignores her. Instead, he selects a boy who has not even expressed any interest in playing the position. Encourage girls to discuss methods for handling situations where they feel they have not been considered fairly because they are girls.

▲ *Girl Scout Badges and Signs:* Becoming a Teen badge; Making Decisions badge; My Self-Esteem badge; Careers badge

▲ *Junior Girl Scout Handbook:* Leadership badge

▲ *Girls Are Great: Growing Up Female* Contemporary Issues booklet

WHAT IS A FAMILY?

Meet seven Junior Girl Scouts—each with a different kind of family*

Stephanie and her older brother live with their dad.

Tatyana is the youngest of five children and lives with her mom and stepdad.

Keisha's family includes her mom, her dad, her older sister, and herself.

Locita is the oldest of three children and lives with her dad, her mom, her twin sisters, and her dog.

Lily lives with her mom and her mom's cousin Betty and Betty's daughter.

Jennifer lives with her grandmother and pet cat.

Families come in different sizes and forms. You may live with two parents or with one, or you may be cared for and loved by people who are not your parents. You may have many sisters and brothers, two, one, or none. Great-grandparents, grandparents, stepparents, foster parents, guardians, aunts, uncles, and cousins may be part of your family. They may live with you, nearby, or far away. You may see them often or only on special occasions.

Alyssa lives with her mom and grandmother during the week and with her dad and stepmother on the weekend.

 Share stories about members of your family or your pets with the girls in your troop or group.

If you have a family photo album, look through it with older members of your family. Ask them to share stories about events that happened in your family when you were young or even before you were born.

Start your own family photo album or scrapbook.

What makes a family special? Family members give each other love and affection. They protect and keep each other safe. They provide food and clothing. You learn all kinds of lessons about growing up from your family. And your family gives you a feeling of belonging and helps you feel good about yourself. These three girls share special nighttime routines with their families.

Before ten-year-old Joanna goes to sleep, her mom always asks her about the best part of her day.

Mie's mom gives her a good-night kiss and a good-morning kiss at the same time—at night! That's because Mie's mom often has to leave for work before Mie is awake in the morning.

Dad used to read aloud to Rika at bedtime, but now that she's nine, Rika reads aloud to Dad— one chapter every night.

What special traditions and celebrations do your family share?

*The names of the girls and the descriptions of their families are made up. They are portrayed here to show the many different types of families girls live in today.

54

55

Tips

▲ **What Is a Family?**: Be sensitive to girls' home situations. A girl may have difficult circumstances to face and you can help her have Girl Scouting be a positive force in her life. However, respect the privacy of each girl and her family. Don't pry unnecessarily for details about her family situation. Also, recognize that a girl may be too embarrassed to tell you things directly. For example, she may not want to tell you she can't afford dues, recognitions, special fees, or a uniform.

Encourage girls going through a difficult time at home to continue to attend meetings and participate in troop or group activities. Your Girl Scout meeting can lend stability to a child's troubled world.

Be sensitive when planning activities. Requiring both parents to attend or specifying which parent is to attend—for example, a mother/daughter weekend or a dad/daughter dinner—can create problems for many girls. A change in the title of an event can make a world of difference. A proposed "dad/daughter" dinner can become "a special person and me" event.

Supporting Activities

▲ Ask girls to think about the things they enjoy doing with their families. These activities may include everyone in the family or only some family members. Some examples include playing board games, eating a special holiday dinner, or going to the park. Have girls plan an activity to do with their families. They can ask other family members for ideas and help in carrying out the activity.

▲ Suggest girls create a family tree on posterboard showing the names, dates of births, relationships, and any other interesting information about family members.

Program Links

▲ *Girl Scout Badges and Signs:* Family Living Skills badge; Across Generations badge; Healthy Relationships badge; My Heritage badge; Women's Stories badge

▲ *Junior Girl Scout Handbook:* Talk! badge

▲ *Caring and Coping: Facing Family Crises* Contemporary Issues booklet

▲ *Junior Girl Scout Activity Book:* Chapter Two

Responsibilities as a Family Member

Members of a family need to work together. Write the chores each member of your family does. Do you see a pattern in who does certain kinds of jobs?

Family Member   **Chores**

_____   _____
_____   _____
_____   _____
_____   _____
_____   _____

 Some mothers work outside the home for pay and others do not. Talk to at least two women in each group to find out how they manage their responsibilities. Then think about some of the things you juggle in your own life like school, family, and friends. Did you learn anything from talking to the group of mothers that will help you manage your own responsibilities? Discuss what you learned with other girls

 Make a list of some things that girls seem to be expected to do in the home and outside the home. For example, your list might include play with dolls, cook meals, or wear makeup. Make a second list of things that boys seem to be expected to do such as play with trucks, cut the grass, and play basketball. Share your list with others and discuss whether these expectations are unfair and what can be done to change them.

Family Problems

Family life does not always run smoothly. Big and little problems happen in every family. The families you see on television that solve their problems, even very serious ones, in one hour or less are not very realistic. It's important to remember that sometimes, no matter what you do, you have no control over a particular family situation. But, at other times, what you do may help to ease a sticky problem.

56

Sibling Rivalry

"Stop fighting!" Mrs. Martinez yelled for the third time in two minutes.

"He started it," Tanya explained.

"But she kicked over the building I was making," Eduardo quickly answered.

"It was an accident," Tanya responded.

"It was not. You did it on purpose."

"Did not."

"Yes, you did."

Eleven-year-old Tanya and nine-year-old Eduardo, the Martinez children, love each other, but often get into fights. "Sibling rivalry" is what their mother calls it. And she knows that sibling rivalry or arguments between sisters and brothers happen in every family. Whenever people live together, it's natural for arguments to occur.

What kinds of problems happen in families? You do not have to talk about specific examples in your own or another family, but about the types of conflicts that could happen in any family.

 Think of some things you might do to improve communication in your family. Try one of these ideas for at least one week.

Conflict Resolution

One way to solve conflicts (called conflict resolution) is to follow the steps below:

1. Figure out what the problem is. Every member of the Granger family wants to watch a different television program at 8 o'clock on Tuesday night (and there is only one television).

2. Suggest some solutions to the problem. Family members could take turns choosing shows. Or the names of the shows could go in a container, and the one selected is the one watched. Or the Grangers might save money to buy a second television.

3. Look at what would happen with each solution. Choosing a program from a container might result in the same show being watched two or three weeks in a row, and some family members might get angry. The Grangers can't afford to put much money aside right now for a new television. Saving could take more than a year.

4. Make a decision. After reviewing the suggestions made by all family members and the likely results, the Grangers make a choice. Taking turns selecting the 8 o'clock show on Tuesday night is seen as the best decision by the whole family.

5. Take action. The Granger family figures out who should make the first selection the following Tuesday night. The plan is put into action.

57

▲ **Responsibilities as a Family Member:** For the first badge activity, brainstorm with your troop or group a list of questions to ask. Help girls compare their own responsibilities with those of the mothers. Encourage them to apply one of the tips gained from the interviews.

▲ **Family Problems:** All families experience conflict in varying degrees at one time or another. If a girl shares a problem with you that you feel is beyond your scope, contact your council office to help her find a community agency better equipped to deal with the problem. Do not become involved in solving problems that require special expertise or training.

▲ **Sibling Rivalry:** Remind girls that each family member has qualities that make her or him special. Stress that they should think of themselves as individuals and not compare themselves or compete with their sisters and brothers. You also need to consider the feelings of a girl who is an only child. Similarly, you should avoid activities or discussions that foster comparisons among the girls in your troop or group. Don't single out any one girl and use her as the model for others.

▲ **Conflict Resolution:** Conflict resolution is a skill that can be used in many situations. When problems arise, help girls apply conflict-resolution skills by following the steps. For more information on conflict resolution, see Chapter Three in Part I of this guide.

▲ Ask girls to write a script that shows Tanya and Eduardo using conflict-resolution skills.

▲ Have girls scan the newspaper for an article that describes an incident where a conflict was resolved. Girls can describe, either verbally or in writing, how the parties used similar techniques to those outlined in the handbook.

▲ *Girl Scout Badges and Signs:* Making Decisions badge; Creative Solutions badge; Healthy Relationships badge

▲ *Junior Girl Scout Handbook:* Talk! badge

Notes

Teenage Pregnancy

Jessica heard sobs coming from her older sister Nikki's room. Ten-year-old Jessica wanted to share her news about making the soccer team. That would have to wait. "Nikki's probably broken up with her boyfriend–again," thought Jessica. "What's wrong?" Jessica asked. "I could hear you crying even before I got into the house."

"I can't tell you," Nikki answered.

"What do you mean, you can't tell me? You make me tell you everything," Jessica said. "Did something happen to Mom or Dad?" Jessica was really scared now.

"No, no, nothing like that." Nikki cleared her throat and wiped her eyes with a rumpled tissue. She looked down as she said, "I'm pregnant."

Jessica thought, "My intelligent, successful sister–the one who has an A-average, plays the violin in the school orchestra, is the editor of the student newspaper–pregnant. It can't be. She is just 16."

"What?" Jessica asked.

"I'm pregnant," Nikki repeated quietly.

Every year over one million teenage girls get pregnant in the United States. For each of these girls, this one event will forever change her life.

 Learn something about the 24-hour responsibility of motherhood by doing the following activity: Take care of a delicate seedling plant (representing a baby) for at least three days. You will have full responsibility for your "baby," making sure it is always safe, well-fed, and warm. Give your baby four feedings—one teaspoon of water and 1/8 teaspoon of sugar—during the day and night. If you need to leave your baby, even for a short time, you must find a baby-sitter. After the three days, share your experiences. Talk about how your baby changed your daily activities.

Separation & Divorce

Sometimes, conflict between parents is so strong that they divorce or separate. It can be very hard to get used to the idea of living with one parent instead of two. But sometimes it's a relief not to have to listen to the constant fighting between parents, or to be in a home that is very unhappy. Kids in a divorcing family often feel angry with one or both of their parents when divorce happens. Sometimes, they blame themselves, but a parent's leaving is NEVER a child's fault.

Sometimes, family situations change and you may start living with a new stepparent, or grandparent, aunt, or foster family or guardian. Remember that a family is made up of people who care for each other and that as you grow up you may be in more than one type of family situation. Always look for a role model—a strong person who has values you can learn and strengths you can share. A role model will help you get through difficult times—because she or he has taught you how to care for yourself.

A Family Member's Drug or Alcohol Problem

A parent, guardian, or older brother or sister who has a drinking or drug problem is a family problem because it affects every family member. Maybe the person acts very mean or even violently when he or she drinks too much. Maybe the person is so addicted to drugs that she or he doesn't pay attention to you. What can you do? You should talk about it with other people in your family, a teacher or other trusted adult at school, or a religious or community leader. Find an organization that helps kids from families where drugs and alcohol area problem. There are people who can help you cope with family problems.

A Pet's Death

Felice saw the look on her dad's face. "I have something to tell you, something sad," Dad said. Felice knew what her father was going to tell her, but she wasn't ready to hear the words.

"Spicy's dead." Dad spoke gently as he put his arm around Felice's shoulders.

Tears quickly came to Felice's eyes and spilled down her cheeks. "I know how hard this is for you," Dad said.

"No, you don't," Felice shouted. "Spicy was my dog." She ran to her room sobbing loudly.

Felice's dad knew that she was not really angry with him, but was very upset about the death of her dog. He understood that Felice was feeling sad, angry, even guilty, about Spicy's death, even though it was expected. Spicy had been sick for weeks.

Later on, he and Felice would talk about how Spicy would be buried, and how they would remember her. But right now, Felice just needed to cry.

Have you ever felt sad over the loss of something or someone dear? What helped you get through that sad time?

Perhaps you have a friend who has been touched deeply by a sad family event. You might feel uncomfortable or not know what to say, but a note or a phone call can make a person feel better.

 Look in the telephone book for names of agencies that can help people going through difficult times. Create a "Where to Find Help" brochure.

58

59

Handbook Page 58

Handbook Page 59

▲ **Teenage Pregnancy:** The problems of teenage pregnancy, teen sexual activity, and peer pressure exist even in your community. Ask yourself how you feel about these issues before discussing them with the girls. This way you will be clear and sensitive about the values you are communicating. If you do not feel comfortable talking about certain topics, ask someone to help facilitate the discussion. Contact your council or a community resource person if you need additional help.

Your troop or group may have questions surrounding the issues of teenage pregnancy. Your role as a leader should be to help girls acquire skills and knowledge in a supportive atmosphere, not to act as an advocate for a particular position. If girls have questions, provide information in terms girls this age can understand. Girls need correct information, especially when there are misconceptions and myths they may believe. Providing accurate information helps girls make responsible decisions. See *Safety-Wise* for information about handling sensitive issues.

Tips

▲ **Separation and Divorce:** Children respond differently to the divorce of their parents. For girls who perceived their parents as happy together, adjustment to divorce is much more difficult than for those who viewed the pre-separation period as an unhappy time for everyone.

If you are aware that a girl's parents are divorcing, choose carefully the activities the troop engages in during this period. For example, it may not be wise to host a family picnic or even a parent/ daughter event.

Supporting Activities

▲ Invite a social worker or family therapist to talk to your troop or group about sad things that may happen in families.

Tips

▲ **A Family Member's Drug or Alcohol Problem:** If you become aware that a girl's home life is affected by abuse of drugs or alcohol, you may need to give the girl special attention. Contact your Girl Scout council for advice and referrals to link her to a community resource person.

If you think a girl is suffering from physical neglect, contact your Girl Scout council to find out what assistance is available.

Tips

▲ **A Pet's Death:** While the death of a pet does not compare in severity to the death of a parent or other family member, the loss of a beloved pet is often a child's first experience with death and separation. Allow the girl to express her sadness in her own way. You also could encourage her to create a small memorial to her pet.

Program Links

▲ *Girl Scout Badges and Signs:* Becoming a Teen badge; Caring for Children badge; Family Living Skills badge; Healthy Relationships badge; My Self-Esteem badge

▲ *Junior Girl Scout Handbook:* Girls Are Great badge; Talk! badge

▲ *Caring and Coping: Facing Family Crises; Girls Are Great: Growing Up Female; Decisions for Your Life: Preventing Teenage Pregnancy;* and *Tune In to Well-Being, Say No to Drugs: Substance Abuse* Contemporary Issues booklets

▲ *Safety-Wise*

FRIENDS

One of the fun parts of growing up is having friends. Friends make life enjoyable. How would you describe a good friend?

What Kind of Friend Are You?

Think about the kind of friend you are to others. Think about one of your friends. Keep this person in mind as you answer "yes" or "no" to each question below.

	YES	NO
1. I listen carefully to my friend when she talks about something important to her.		
2. When I am upset with my friend I still speak to her.		
3. It doesn't bother me if my friend sometimes has other things to do.		
4. I let my friend know what I like about her.		
5. Sometimes my friend decides how we're going to spend our time together.		
6. My friend and I like to do things together.		
7. I do not try to make my friend be just like me.		
8. I stick up for my friend if I hear others put her down.		
9. I share what I have with my friend.		
10. My friend and I like to do many of the same things.		

Find out what your score means. Count the number of times you said "yes."

If your score is 8–10: You are a super friend!

6–7: You are a very good friend.

4–5: You are a good friend—sometimes.

3 or below: You need to work harder on being a friend.

 Make a "Friends" poster. Begin with a slogan that defines what a friend is. Cut out or draw pictures that illustrate friendship or make a list of words that describes a friend. Use these words to design a word puzzle. Have the girls in your troop or group complete the puzzle.

60

Making Friends

Everybody likes to have friends. But, friendships don't just happen. You have to work at them.

There are no rules about how many friends a person should have. Some girls have many, some a few, and others, only one. Some friends you have throughout life and others come and go as your interests and experiences change.

If you are happy with yourself, you usually find it easier to make and keep friends. Being friendly, upbeat, enthusiastic, and thoughtful are helpful, too. Your Girl Scout troop is a good place to make friends. You can also make friends by joining a club, sports team, or other group at school or in your neighborhood.

 Pretend you are meeting someone for the first time. Think about who that person might be. Tell how you would introduce yourself to her. Talk about what you would say and how you would keep the friendship going. Keep in mind that everyone may not want to be friends. Don't let that stop you from trying to make friends. Always remember that you have a lot to offer.

Make a plan to get to know two people in the next month. Complete the sentences below.

1. Two people I'd like to get to know.

_____   _____
(name of person)   (name of person)

2. Places where I will go to be with them.

_____   _____
_____   _____

3. Things we might talk about.

_____   _____
_____   _____

4. Things we might do together.

_____   _____
_____   _____

61

Tips

▲ **Friends:** Many girls state that one of the best aspects of Girl Scouting is making new friends. At the Junior Girl Scout age level, friends play an increasingly significant role in girls' daily lives. In fact, many times girls will try to emulate one another in terms of clothes, language, hairstyles, and attitudes toward boys. This handbook section strives to help girls understand their roles as friends.

The "What Kind of Friend Are You?" checklist is designed to help girls identify qualities that build solid friendships. To make sure no one feels threatened by this activity, consider having girls complete the checklist at home. If, however, you choose to do the activity during your troop or group meeting, avoid putting girls into "good friend" and "bad friend" categories.

Supporting Activities

▲ Encourage girls to add items that they feel are important in building friendships to the checklist. They can share their revised list with a friend.

▲ Many songs in Girl Scouting address the theme of friendships. (See the Annotated Resource List in Part I of this guide for songbook titles.) Girls can use the lyrics of these songs to make a list of words that describe friendships. Using this list, girls can create their own songs.

Tips

▲ **Making Friends:** Don't be surprised if the dynamics among the girls in your troop or group change from week to week. Girls at this age are "works in progress" in that they are still coming to terms with their own identities. It is, therefore, sometimes hard for them to maintain long-term commitment to one particular friend or a group of friends. If group dynamics become problematic, see Chapter Three in Part I for some tips on working with Junior Girl Scouts.

Supporting Activities

▲ In small groups, girls can discuss the situations below. One girl can pretend to be the girl in the situation and the other girls can each give her advice.

● Gerri has just moved to a new neighborhood. She doesn't know anyone and is a bit shy. She has noticed that a girl her age lives down the block.

● Juana likes to play basketball. Nobody likes to play with her because all she cares about is winning.

● Dana invited two of her friends over to play video games. They get tired of playing and want to do something else. Dana gets upset.

● Donovan is a new boy in your class. He does everything alone. No one seems to want to be friends with him.

Program Links

▲ *Girl Scout Badges and Signs:* Healthy Relationships badge; My Self-Esteem badge

▲ *Junior Girl Scout Handbook:* Talk! badge

It's Party Time!

Party Planning

Have you ever gone to a party that was a great success? What made it fun? In your Girl Scout troop or group, think of what makes a party fun for the people who are giving the party (hosts) and for people who are attending the party (guests). The chart below will help you plan.

Plan a party to celebrate your friendships. Having a party is a great way to get to know people better. You can have a party at home, in a park, in a backyard, at a skating rink, or some other place. A party can be small with just one or two friends, or large with many family members or your Girl Scout group or troop.

Party Theme _____

_____

Place _____

Guests _____

_____

_____

_____

_____

_____

Food, if any _____

_____

_____

_____

Activities _____

_____

_____

Other _____

_____

_____

62

Party Popcorn

Popcorn is an easy party food to make and almost everybody likes it. Here are some recipes to try:

Basic Popcorn
You could buy plain already-popped popcorn, or pop it on the stove following directions on the can, or pop some in the microwave. Make your plain popcorn into party popcorn with these additions:

Cheese Popcorn
Mix 1/2 cup of grated cheese into a large bowl of popcorn.

Cinnamon Sugar
Mix 1/2 cup of plain white sugar with 1 teaspoon of cinnamon and sprinkle over a large bowl of plain popcorn.

Party Activities

If you look through your Junior Girl Scout Handbook, you can find a lot of activities that are fun to do at a party. The activities for practicing your creativity on page 74 could be fun, as could many of the activities in Chapter Seven.

Chocolate Chip Popcorn
Mix 1 cup of small chocolate chips into a large bowl of plain popcorn.

Peanut Pop
Mix a can of roasted peanuts or flavored peanuts into a large bowl of plain popcorn.

63

Tips

▲ **It's Party Time!:** Party planning is not only fun and entertaining, but teaches girls valuable skills. Allow girls to participate in all aspects of planning, including budgeting, inviting guests, cooking, and decorating.

Avoid celebrating one girl's accomplishments without recognizing other troop or group members' achievements. Similarly, having a holiday party that celebrates a particular religious tradition can make some girls feel excluded. The needs of all girls should be acknowledged when planning any troop or group party.

Games and songs can create a festive atmosphere. Ask girls if anyone would like to play an instrument or teach a new game.

Supporting Activities

▲ Have girls discuss their favorite party activities or games. Girls can think about what makes a party fun for the guests and the hosts.

▲ Girls can create a party on almost any theme. At home, they could have a sleep-over or pajama party, a party to watch a sports event or movie, or a pot-luck party where each guest brings one part of the meal. Outdoors, they could hold a scavenger-hunt party where teams follow clues to end up at an outdoor picnic, a sports-day party, or a hiking party to a favorite nature spot.

▲ Have girls describe their favorite party foods. They may want to bring recipes to a subsequent meeting. For some ideas on inexpensive, healthy snacks, see Chapter Three in the handbook.

Program Links

▲ *Girl Scout Badges and Signs:* Making Hobbies badge; Exploring Healthy Eating badge; Art to Wear badge; Photography badge

▲ *Games for Girl Scouts*

▲ *Ceremonies in Girl Scouting*

Notes

Pen Pals

A pen pal is a friend you get to know through letters. She or he usually lives in another state or country, and will write about her or his hometown, school, family, pets, customs and traditions, special interests, or talents. Pen pals share things like games, recipes, solutions to problems, and photos.

Pen Pals Through Girl Scouts of the U.S.A.

Girl Scouts of the U.S.A. provides international pen pal links for Girl Scouts who are ten to seventeen years old. You can request a pen pal by getting a special form from your Girl Scout leader or council. You must use this form to have staff members at national headquarters try to link you with a pen pal in the part of the world you request. (Please send the completed form and a self-addressed stamped envelope; do not send stamps, photographs, or letters about yourself.) Sometimes it isn't possible to find pen pals for everyone. You may reapply after one year if a link is not made.

Peer Pressure

Peers are people in your age group. They may include the girls in your troop or group, your classmates, other friends, and even persons you do not know. Have you ever done or said something because your friends were doing it? Did you do it mainly to keep your friends or to stay a member of the group? That's peer pressure. In a peer pressure situation, everyone is expected to act a certain way, look a certain way, or to have only certain friends.

Peer pressure can be good or bad. It is good when it helps you feel good about yourself and you are learning new skills. Two friends pressured you into presenting your service project idea to your troop. Although you were nervous, your presentation went well and you felt good about all your hard work.

Peer pressure is not so good when it makes you feel uncomfortable, confused, or gets you in trouble. What if your friends convince you to take an unsafe route home?

Why do people pressure others? Some like to control other people. Some think it makes them more popular. Others do it so they can feel important. When faced with peer pressure:

• **Stand up for yourself!** Don't let others lead you to do something you would be ashamed of later.

• **Speak your mind.** Tell people how you really feel. They may learn something new from you.

• **Respect the feelings and decisions of others.** Let others follow their own decisions and you follow yours.

• **Find support from others.** If you feel pressured, talk to someone you trust.

• **Stay away from or ignore the group, if necessary.**

 Act out or discuss with a group of friends what you would do in these situations:

• A classmate asks you to cheat on a test.

• Your girlfriend's sister offers you a drink of beer.

• Everyone is wearing designer jeans and your father says it's silly to spend that amount of money on clothes.

• Your stepmother buys you a great outfit. You really like it, but your friends say it is ugly.

• Your parents always expect you to come home early. Your friends make fun of you and call you a baby.

 With some friends, put on a skit or play that shows both good and bad types of peer pressure. Write, practice, and perform the play. Invite parents and friends to see the play.

Cliques

Take a look at the top of this page. You might know someone like Stephanie and her friends who make fun of those who look or act differently. This type of group is called a clique. The members of a clique usually share something. For example, the members of a clique may be very good athletes and not friendly to anyone who is not. Some cliques make fun of anyone who is smart or likes school, or of kids who may not be popular.

Dear Diary:

I had the most awesome day until just a few minutes ago—Jennifer called! I almost dropped the phone when I heard her voice! I haven't talked to her in weeks because I've been so busy doing things with Mariah and Elizabeth. It's not that I don't like Jennifer anymore, but more like we don't enjoy doing the same things. And Mariah and Elizabeth are so cool—we go shopping together and they love to talk about boys! All Jennifer ever seems to want to do is play video games. Ugh! Now she calls to ask me if I would want to go to the soccer game with her after school tomorrow. I would kind of like to, but I know Elizabeth and Mariah think she's weird—then they'll make fun of me, too! I don't know what to do—maybe I should just make up some excuse to tell Jennifer or go to the game for only a few minutes and hope no one sees me or....

Members of a clique:

• Leave out kids different from themselves.

• Often tease or make fun of other kids.

• Are hurtful toward other clique members who want out of the clique.

• Aren't open to meeting new people or trying new things.

Read Stephanie's diary at the top of the page. What would you do if you were Stephanie? On the diary page (see next page), write what you would say to Jennifer. When you are finished, share your thoughts with others.

▲ **Pen Pals:** For more information on acquiring an international pen pal through GSUSA, see Chapter Two in Part I of this guide.

Program Links

▲ *Girl Scout Badges and Signs:* Communication Arts badge; Girl Scouting Around the World badge; Celebrating People badge; World Neighbors badge

Tips

▲ **Peer Pressure:** Coping with peer pressure is a daily struggle for some girls and the adults in their lives. Social problems such as cheating, shoplifting, disrespect for adults, and fighting often are the result of peer pressure. One way to help girls cope with peer pressure is to reinforce their self-respect, dignity, and values. Troop or group activities that center on leadership skills, decision-making, and conflict resolution are valuable learning experiences.

Offer support for the concept of "making up your own mind regardless of what everyone else is doing." Share anecdotes or information about people who listened to themselves when faced with a dilemma or difficult situation. Discuss the effects of immediate and long-term decisions in terms girls of this age can understand.

Supporting Activities

▲ Have girls think of a time when they gave in to peer pressure. Were there any consequences? If they could relive the situation, would they act differently?

▲ Girls can read the story maze in this chapter to identify examples of peer pressure. Ask the girls what advice they would give the story maze characters.

Program Links

▲ *Girl Scout Badges and Signs:* Becoming a Teen badge; Healthy Relationships badge; My Self-Esteem badge; Making Decisions badge; Creative Solutions badge

▲ *Decisions for Your Life:* Preventing Teenage Pregnancy; *Tune In to Well-Being: Say No to Drugs,* and *Girls Are Great: Growing Up Female* Contemporary Issues booklets

Tips

▲ **Cliques:** The sense of belonging to a group is an important feeling for girls at the Junior Girl Scout age level. Girls derive great benefits from group interaction. But when girls must deal with groups that are exclusionary or elitist problems arise. The desire to associate only with the "right" people often creates feelings of stress and anxiety. Some girls feel left out while others believe they have to conform to group norms or values. Thus, some girls change their

hairstyles or clothes, speak differently, smoke cigarettes, try new activities, and abandon friends.

If a clique forms within your troop or group, you can help by suggesting activities that create different mixes of girls. Select groups by:

● Counting off all the one's as a subgroup, two's as another, and so on.

● Using the alphabet—beginning or ending letters of names.

● Placing sets of colors, numbers, flowers, etc., into a grab bag for random drawing.

Program Links

▲ *Girl Scout Badges and Signs:* Healthy Relationships badge; My Self-Esteem badge

▲ *Valuing Differences: Promoting Pluralism* and *Girls Are Great: Growing Up Female* Contemporary Issues booklets

Gangs

The word "gang" can be used to describe a group of friends who enjoy spending time together. However, when activities that are illegal are involved, the word "gang" takes on a very different meaning. This kind of gang controls the kids who are its members, forcing them to do things that are often violent and criminal.

Gangs can be found in large cities, small towns, and suburban and rural areas. How do you know if a gang has formed in your community? Many gangs use or wear specific colors or symbols, and make all gang members agree to follow special rules. Many gangs use graffiti to mark an area as their own. Gangs also send out threats against other groups in the community, and, when a violent act has occurred, let others know they were responsible. Talk about gangs with members of your troop or group. Discuss the following:

• Why do kids join gangs? What do they get from gangs that they can't get from their families and communities?

• What are some things kids can do instead of joining gangs? How can a community help prevent kids from joining gangs?

• What are three things you would say to a kid who is in a gang?

Bullies

Every afternoon for the last two weeks, Damaris has followed Michelle home from school. Damaris calls her names, tries to get her to fight, and takes money from her. Michelle is afraid to tell her grandmother because she doesn't want Damaris to find out she told someone.

Damaris is a bully. If you have not already come into contact with a bully, sooner or later you will. Bullies usually shove, punch, steal from, make fun of, fight, or pick on others. Bullies are usually people who feel hurt, angry, afraid, or frustrated inside, and they take it out on others.

Write to Stephanie Here

With a group of friends talk about ways you have been bullied. Discuss ideas on how to handle a bully.

Have you ever bullied others? Do you know why you acted like a bully? Do you know how to stop?

To handle a bully you might: stand up for yourself, ignore her, walk away, refuse to fight, talk it out, scream or yell, or get help from an adult. Turn to pages 46–48 for ideas on handling conflicts and being assertive. Share this information with someone you know who is being bullied. Remember, a bully has no right to hurt you or anyone else.

Peer Support

Your peers can be a source of support for you. You can grow together, learn more about yourself and each other, and do activities. You can share skills, study hard, and achieve goals together. To help you decide whether a group of friends are right for you, ask yourself these questions:

• Do I feel comfortable?

• Do they accept me for who I am?

• Are their values the same as mine?

• What do they expect of me?

• Do they make me happy or angry most of the time?

• Do they make me feel good or bad about myself?

• Do I want others to know I'm part of this group?

If you have answered yes to most of these questions, this peer group is probably right for you.

Adults

You spend a lot of time with people your own age, but many adults are also part of your life. Your life is certainly influenced by the adults around you–family members, teachers, religious leaders, your Girl Scout leader, and your friends' parents. There may be some adults who understand you better than others. You may have a great time with some adults and not get along with others. That's a part of growing up.

 Make a list of the most important adults in your life. Write down their names and tell why they are important to you.

 Do or make something for a special adult. Write a letter, make a gift, or surprise her or him with a phone call.

Handbook Page 66

Handbook Page 67

▲ **Gangs:** The following fact-based skit could be acted out by girls and discussed.

Background: Cara, a Junior Girl Scout reporter, interviewed Joelle, a former gang member who now runs a leadership training program for ex-gang members.

Cara: When and how did you get involved with a gang?

Joelle: I was ten years old, in elementary school, when some of the rougher kids started bullying the weaker ones at school. Every day there was a fight before, during, or after school. As a kid, I felt as if I had to take sides, and I wasn't about to get caught in the middle, so I went for the so-called "tough" ones. I figured it would be a better way to be protected.

Cara: How much did gangs control life at school?

Joelle: When we were in elementary school, the "tough" kids were really just "the crowd" to be in—more like a clique, but by the time I was in junior high school, full-blown gangs were in control. They even controlled what colors and outfits you could wear. Gangs gave kids a false sense of security. For a long time they ran everything in my life, and in some ways I'm still paying for it now.

Cara: What do you mean?

Joelle: When I was running with the gang, I, like all the other girls who stayed in it, ended up doing things with the guys, just for initiation; to be a full-fledged member of the gang. I mean I wasn't even ready for anything serious and now I'm a carrier for HIV—the AIDS virus. My symptoms don't show, and I'm receiving medical treatment now, but there's still a chance that I'll end up with AIDS.

Cara: What are you doing now?

Joelle: One of the most important things I can do is give kids I meet a chance to do something positive. I helped organize a leadership group for kids—and the kids really run it! All of the kids were once gang members or about to get pulled into a gang. In this group, they've found the security they were looking for all along. They're developing a good outlook on life. And learning that education can help give them things like good jobs that can lead to a career, money to spend and save, and the know-how to have a happy family.

Cara: What advice could you give our readers?

Joelle: I know it can seem real hard to keep your mind on things like math and reading, but doing well in school is important! And if you're feeling pressured by anyone to do anything that makes you feel uncomfortable, don't do it. Tell an adult. What you really have to hold on to is knowing that you make a difference—and you do matter!

▲ *Girl Scout Badges and Signs:* Healthy Relationships badge; Making Decisions badge; My Self-Esteem badge

▲ *Junior Girl Scout Handbook:* Girls Are Great badge

▲ *Girls Are Great: Growing Up Female* Contemporary Issues booklet

(The section on Bullies is on the next page.)

A Decision-Making Story-Maze

Making Decisions and Solving Problems

Remember the section on values earlier in this chapter? It was mentioned that values influence decisions you make. In the following decision-making story maze, you get to be the main character. Follow the story wherever it leads you and see what choices you make. You might want to read the sections "Making Good Decisions," "Communication," and "Creative Solutions" when you're done with the story maze. Mark a ● where good decision-making is needed. Mark a ▲ where communication is needed. Mark a ■ where creative problem-solving is needed.

You and your best friend Monique are on your way home from school. Up ahead, you see the new girl in your class, Tina, walking alone. Monique tells Tina to wait; the three of you start walking together. Tina invites you and Monique to her house for a snack. Monique thinks it's a good idea and decides to go. You know that you have to go straight to your neighbor's house from school. Your mother doesn't think you are old enough to stay alone for an hour and a half. This makes you feel like a baby, and you always try to get her to change her mind. Now you have a chance to do something more grown up. What do you do? If you say "I can't, I have to go home right after school," go to **A.** If you say, "Sure, but only for a little while," go to **B.**

A. You cross the street and continue on your way. When you reach your neighbor's home, no one is there. You ring the doorbell several times. Still, there is no answer. You think this is very odd. Something very important must have happened for her to not be there. If you go into the backyard to do your homework and wait, go to **C.** If you try to catch up with Tina and Monique, go to **H.**

B. When you get to Tina's house, there are no adults at home, but her teenage brother and his two friends are there. You know your parents don't want you visiting a friend when there are no adults present. You tell Monique that you think you should leave. Just then Tina's brother offers to let you girls tag along with his friends to the mall. Everyone thinks it's a good idea. If you go to the mall with the others, go to **D.** If you say "Good-bye" and go on to your neighbor's home, go to **E.**

C. You've just finished your math assignment when your neighbor comes into the backyard. "I'm so glad you waited for me," she says. "I was stuck in the worst traffic jam. I knew you were responsible and would wait for me." **THE END.**

68

Communication

Communication is the ability to express your thoughts, feelings, and beliefs. Good communication skills are important in decision-making and problem-solving. Communicating well is a skill that takes practice. There are two types of communication—verbal and nonverbal. Using words to say what you mean is verbal communication. Using symbols, signs, or body language is nonverbal communication.

When people speak, they want others to hear and understand what they are saying. Here are tips for being a good listener.

- Pay attention to the person who is talking. Make eye contact.
- Concentrate on what the other person is saying.
- Try not to interrupt or think about how you will answer.
- Ask questions to help you understand what you heard.
- Repeat in your own words what you heard the person say when she or he is finished speaking.

How do you rate as a listener?

69

Handbook Page 68

Handbook Page 69

▲ **Bullies:** Usually, children who act aggressively toward others are acting on anger, resentment, rejection, or bitterness that they feel. If you discover that a girl in your troop or group bullies others, you may want to talk to her in private about any problems she may be having. If she is reluctant to talk about her behavior, you may need to contact her parent, guardian, or teacher. A group discussion on respect for others could help other girls be part of the solution.

Supporting Activities

▲ Have girls compose a song about how to handle a bully. They can get ideas for their song from concepts in this handbook (e.g., conflict resolution).

Program Links

▲ *Girl Scout Badges and Signs:* Healthy Relationships badge; Making Decisions badge; Creative Solutions badge

▲ **Peer Support:** You can help girls build better relationships. Although going on trips and doing activities together strengthen friendships, so, too, does sharing thoughts and feelings. Another way to build better relationships is by addressing problems when they arise and listening to others. To improve listening skills, a good listener:

- Pays attention to the person who is talking and makes eye contact with the person.
- Concentrates on what the other person is saying. She tries not to interrupt or think about how she will answer.
- Asks questions to better understand what she heard.

▲ **Adults:** Girl Scouting provides an opportunity for girls to interact with adults on a more personal level than they may at home or school. It is important, therefore, to nurture this relationship, to respect girls' privacy, and to honor the trust they place in you. If you sense that a girl is having a serious problem with an adult in her life, contact your council office for guidance.

Program Links

▲ *Girl Scout Badges and Signs:* Across Generations badge; Family Living Skills badge; Women Today badge

▲ **A Decision-Making Story Maze:** The story maze was created to help girls explore decision-making and its consequences. When reading or discussing the story maze with your troop or group, try not to impose your values or opinions. Rather, try to present an open atmosphere where girls can think about their decisions.

Opportunities for decision-making should be part of all troop or group activities. Girls will have the chance to see how their decisions go—both good and bad.

Making Good Decisions

When making a tough decision, it sometimes helps to follow a step-by-step process. Using the steps below may help you determine the best choice. You may not always need every step except to make big decisions.

1. Figure out the problem or issue.
2. Collect information about yourself and the situation—think about your values, goals, and interests.
3. Think of as many solutions to the problem as you possibly can.
4. Look at the good points and bad points (pros and cons) of each solution.
5. Make a decision.
6. Take action.
7. Evaluate: Are you happy with the decision you made?

Think about a tough decision you recently made. How might these steps have helped you? Try using these steps to help with your next decision.

D. You all pile into Tina's brother's car and go to the mall. When you get there the teenagers decide to go off by themselves. They will meet you in an hour. Tina, Monique, and you decide to look in a music store. Tina and Monique go down one aisle. You see a CD that you heard in a movie and go down that aisle. The next thing you know, Tina and Monique are gone. You think that maybe they are playing a trick on you and hiding. You look all over the store. You can't find them. You ask the cashier if she saw your friends. She says she thinks she saw them leave. If you go to the information booth and have them paged, go to **F.** If you call your father who works nearby to pick you up, go to **G.**

E. When you reach your neighbor's house, she says that she was just about to get worried. She expected you home sooner, and was just about to call the school. You apologize and start doing your homework. **THE END.**

F. Tina's brother and his friends meet you at the information booth. So do Tina and Monique. They apologize for playing that mean trick on you and decide to leave the mall. They drop you off at your neighbor's home. When you get there, she is very upset with you for being late. She promises to tell your parents when they get home. **THE END.**

G. Your father tells you to stay where you are and he'll be right there. On the way home, he tells you that you should have known better than to get in a car with strangers or people you don't know well. You tell him that you thought you would be safe. He continues to talk about all of the horrible things that could have happened to you, and now you will be grounded for a month. **THE END.**

H. You run to the corner where you left Monique and Tina. You see no sign of them. You don't know where Tina lives, so you head back to your neighbor's house. On your way, you decide to take a shortcut through the park. You see a group of older kids who are smoking. You recognize one of them. She calls you over and introduces you to her friends. They ask if you would like a cigarette. If you decide to take one, go to **I.** If you say "No thanks!" and walk away, go to **J.**

70

71

Handbook Page 70

Handbook Page 71

Tips

When reading the story maze, help girls evaluate the consequences of their decisions. For example, discuss the risks in choosing the option of going with the friend's brother to the mall. You could list abduction, theft, or driving with a person who is intoxicated as consequences.

Girls at this age often lack the maturity to see how present actions impact future events. In fact, girls may perceive themselves as invincible and adopt an attitude like "Oh, I know, but that won't happen to me." Keep this concept in mind when discussing long-term effects of decisions.

▲ **Sidebars in Story Maze:** The three sidebars, "Communication," "Making Good Decisions," and "Creative Solutions," are linked to the story in that the information offers a way for girls to handle some of the decisions they are asked to make. Girls are also asked to mark the story maze with a ●, ▲, and ■ where these sidebar skills apply. Since girls will mark the story maze differently, you can discuss these differences.

Supporting Activities

▲ Using the story maze as a model, have girls create a board game that requires the players to make choices and bear consequences.

▲ Challenge girls to create their own story mazes and share them with each other.

▲ To have girls learn about non-verbal communication, try a pantomime activity. Brainstorm a list of scenarios that express feelings (e.g., one person giving a present to another). Then have someone write the scenarios on pieces of paper for girls to select. Have girls work in pairs to communicate the scenarios in pantomime. Discuss with the girls the power of non-verbal communication.

Creative Solutions

To solve problems creatively, keep your mind open. If you do not solve a problem one way, try a different way. If that doesn't work, find a third way.

To get better at creative problem-solving:

- **Practice your creativity.** List different ways to use a piece of plain white paper (not just as a surface for writing). For example, you can make a paper airplane, wrap a present, make confetti, use as a mask, or crush into a ball. Do the same with a cup, a pencil, a sock. Think of other examples. The more you practice, the more creative you will become.
- **Brainstorm with a group.** You can often come up with creative solutions by listening to the ideas of others.
- **Take a break from problem-solving to solve problems!** When concentrating on a problem doesn't work, a change of scenery or activity may be helpful. You may find that when you are resting or playing with friends, an answer to a problem will suddenly appear.

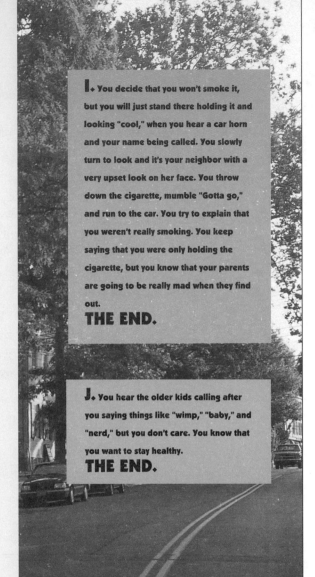

I. You decide that you won't smoke it, but you will just stand there holding it and looking "cool," when you hear a car horn and your name being called. You slowly turn to look and it's your neighbor with a very upset look on her face. You throw down the cigarette, mumble "Gotta go," and run to the car. You try to explain that you weren't really smoking. You keep saying that you were only holding the cigarette, but you know that your parents are going to be really mad when they find out.

THE END.

J. You hear the older kids calling after you saying things like "wimp," "baby," and "nerd," but you don't care. You know that you want to stay healthy.

THE END.

You respond to conflict or difficult situations in different ways. Your response may be different depending on whom you are talking to (friends, teachers, parents, sisters or brothers) or what the issue is.

Suppose you and your friends are trying to decide on a movie. One person suggests going to see a horror movie and the others all start agreeing. But, you hate horror movies. To respond **assertively**, you say, "I really hate horror movies. How about seeing *Jet Pilot III* with Tom News? He's great! Or, I heard *Superwoman* is really good—and it's playing right down the street." You've let your friends know that you would prefer to see another movie and you've given the group a couple of choices.

If you responded **aggressively**, you could have said, "I'm Not Going to THAT Movie and I'm Going to Just Sit Right Here until you all come up with a better idea!" You also have let people know that you want to see another movie, but you've made it difficult for them to respond to you in a positive way.

What if you just went along with the others and didn't say anything at all because you were afraid to speak up? That would be a **passive** response. A passive response means you have made the choice not to make a choice or a decision. You are letting others make choices for you.

Assertiveness involves expressing yourself honestly, standing up for yourself, and showing respect for the rights and feelings of others. When you communicate in an aggressive way, you use harsh words, maybe some hurtful ones, to express yourself. While an assertive way of speaking and acting is almost always better, sometimes an aggressive response may be appropriate. What if you have told someone twice already to stop tickling you so hard?

 Learn about body language by watching people. Observe three people (children or adults) at home, at play and at work or school. Watch how they sit, stand, gesture, and move. Discuss what you have observed at a troop or group meeting.

 Read the situations below and decide which would be the best way to respond. Maybe you could act them out showing different ways of responding.

- You have been waiting on line 30 minutes to purchase tickets to a movie. An announcement is made that there are only 20 tickets left. Suddenly, a boy your age jumps in line ahead of you. This may prevent you from getting a ticket.

- Your mom tells you to clean up your room. You are supposed to be at your friend's apartment in five minutes and your sister was the one who made the mess.

- One of the girls in your class—a really big bully—takes your pencil off your desk for the

▲ **Badge Activities:** Review personal safety tips with girls before they start the first badge activity. Discuss some common body language that they are familiar with and what feelings they signal. Some examples include folded arms, twisting or playing with hair, wringing hands, rolling eyes, etc.

For the second badge activity, once girls decide how they'll react, ask them to label their responses aggressive, passive, or assertive. To continue this discussion, ask girls if a particular situation could have been better or more easily solved with a different communication style.

▲ *Girl Scout Badges and Signs:* Making Decisions badge; Safety Sense badge; My Self-Esteem badge; Creative Solutions badge

▲ *Junior Girl Scout Handbook:* Leadership badge; Talk! badge

▲ *Junior Girl Scout Activity Book:* Chapters Two and Eight

▲ *Staying Safe: Preventing Child Abuse* and *Girls Are Great: Growing Up Female* Contemporary Issues booklets

fourth time today—chews the eraser and then throws it back to you.

• You are sleeping over at your friend's house and her grandmother has made dinner for you. You look at your plate—fish sticks—your worst nightmare food.

• Make up your own situations or share a time when you had to choose how to respond.

HANDBOOK ACTIVITY Look at items F, I, and J in the decision-making story maze and decide which responses are passive, assertive, and aggressive.

If you still have questions now that you have finished this chapter, ask your parent or guardian. Remember, no question is ever too silly or unimportant.

74

STAYING SAFE AND HEALTHY
CHAPTER 3

Safety Do's and Don'ts
page 76

Try a New Hairstyle
page 88

When Stress Becomes Unmanageable
page 91

Rules to Eat by
page 95

Taking care of yourself means guarding your safety, caring for your body, and eating right. Ahead in this chapter, you'll find lots of tips, facts, and activities on such things as first aid, personal safety, body care, and healthy food. See if you can come up with your own ideas for safety and health activities to share with your troop or group.

75

Staying Safe and Healthy

HANDBOOK CHAPTER 3

▲ **Chapter 3: Staying Safe and Healthy**: Girls at the Junior Girl Scout age level should begin to acquire good health habits and skills to help them live safely and responsibly. The activities and information in this chapter have been developed to help girls understand personal safety, first aid, health, and nutrition. While girls should have fun doing the activities, they need to be reminded of the value of these skills. Share with girls your copy of *Safety-Wise* so they can learn about the guidelines Girl Scouts of the U.S.A. provides for different activities.

To enhance the information in this chapter, go on field trips to community health and safety organizations or invite speakers to your troop or group meetings. Check with your Girl Scout council office for a list of resource people. If you decide to take a field trip, have girls check Chapter One in the handbook for tips on planning a trip.

▲ **Learning About Safety**: While many safety precautions are common knowledge to adults, Junior Girl Scouts are still in the process of internalizing safety rules. Use the following Do's and Don't's list to begin a conversation about safety. The list is not all-inclusive but is a good starting point to discuss important safety tips. Be prepared to talk about the reasons for these safety rules. You may also want to add more safety do's and don'ts to the list.

- Don't store items on tops of steps or staircases.
- Don't walk near or through a puddle after a big storm.
- Don't stand under a tree during a lightning storm because of possible downed electrical wires.
- Don't store old newspapers in a closet or other enclosed space.
- Don't go swimming alone.
- Don't leave an iron, coffee pot, or other plugged-in appliance unattended.
- Do wear a safety helmet when bicycling.
- Do carry some form of identification when you leave home.

Staying Safe

Whether you're home, at the park, at a friend's house, or walking down the street, you need to know safety skills.

CAUTION!

SAFETY DO'S AND DON'TS

SAFETY TIPS FOR TRAVEL

DO obey traffic signals and signs. Also, obey traffic police, crossing guards, and student safety patrols.

DO look both ways before you cross.

DO walk where you can see and be seen by other people.

DO follow the buddy system. When you are with someone else, you can look after each other.

DO go immediately to a police officer, an adult you know, or into a store if you think someone is following you.

DO wear seat belts when riding in a car, even if the trip is short.

DO wear light or white clothing when walking at dusk or night.

DO sit in a place on a bus or train where the conductor or driver can see you. If another passenger is bothering you or making you feel uncomfortable, tell the driver or conductor.

DO have your house key ready—but hidden from the sight of others—so you can go right into your house or apartment.

DO carry extra change in case you need to make an emergency call. **DO** keep your wallet or money in a front pocket. **DO** carry your purse under your arm (like a football) or wear it with the strap across your body.

DO know where to get help, how to do basic first aid, and what to do if you accidentally get separated from a group.

DON'T walk in the roadway, on the curb, or between parked cars.

DON'T take shortcuts through dark alleys, vacant lots, or abandoned buildings.

DON'T leave your buddy or your group.

DON'T take candy, gum, money, or other gifts from a stranger.

DON'T distract the driver, fool around, or stick your head or hands out a window when riding in a car or bus.

DON'T walk alone when it is dark.

DON'T enter your house or apartment if you think a stranger is inside. Go to a neighbor for help.

DON'T play on an elevator.

SAFETY DO'S AND DON'TS

SAFETY TIPS FOR PUBLIC SPACES

DO go immediately to a police officer, an adult you know, or into a store if you think someone is following you.

DO pick a meeting place beforehand in case you're separated from family or friends.

DO remain calm if you get lost.

DON'T be afraid to scream or yell if someone tries to get you to leave with him or her.

DON'T wander off alone.

DON'T play in deserted or out-of-the-way places, such as alleys and dead-end streets.

DON'T play around construction sites, abandoned buildings, or in vacant lots.

SAFETY TIPS FOR WEATHER

DO seek shelter during a storm. Stay away from tall objects like trees and poles. If you can't get inside, look for a low place and crouch down as low as you can. Lightning will often strike the highest point in an area. In a flat, open field that could be you.

DO be careful after a storm. Stay away from downed power lines (they may still be electrified and could shock you); loose tree branches (they could fall); deep puddles (they may be full of pollution, could carry an electric shock, or could be deeper than you think).

DO turn off the television and other electrical appliances if lightning occurs. Close windows. Try not to use the telephone. If you must use the telephone during a storm and you hear crackling noises on the line, hang up immediately. Lightning can travel along a phone line and shock you.

DO make sure you have emergency supplies at home. Make a regular check of your supplies. You should have a flashlight, extra batteries, a battery-powered radio, an emergency supply of candles, small cans of cooking fuel or a camp stove, a supply of water, and ingredients for making a meal that requires no cooking or water.

DO stay out of ditches and arroyos as flash floods could be heading your way.

DO go to the basement or the lowest point of a building if a tornado is heading your way.

DO dress properly. Being too hot or too cold can be harmful.

DO protect yourself against sunburn. Use sunscreen.

DON'T ignore your body's warning signals. Shivering is an early sign of hypothermia—too little body heat. Dizziness, weakness, and nausea are early warning signs of hyperthermia—too much body heat.

Handbook Page 76

Handbook Page 77

▲ **Safety Tips for Travel:**

Traveling with Girl Scouts can be fun and rewarding, and preparation will help prevent mishaps. Girls will be better able to conduct themselves in a safe manner if they know what to expect and are aware of safety rules.

Review the "TAP" steps in Chapter One of the handbook. If girls have planned an imaginary trip, have them brainstorm the safety precautions they would need to take.

Review the safety tips before any trip. Girls should come up with additional ideas, perhaps some particular to your geographic area. Here are some ideas to get you started:

- Know special safety rules for unexpected bad weather.

- Never stay in a vehicle while a tire is being changed.

- Arrange specific meeting points and times throughout the trip. This is especially important if the group splits into smaller groups.

- Don't display money in public places.

- Never leave belongings unattended.

- Wear a watch.

▲ **Safety Tips for Public Spaces:**

If your troop or group is planning to visit a recreation or amusement park (or similar public area), everyone should learn the rules and regulations particular to the area. Advise girls to:

- Stay away from groups that are roughhousing, drinking, or seemingly out of control.

- In public recreation areas, equipment should only be used for its intended purpose.

- Follow all posted safety instructions.

- Never carry a lot of cash when traveling. Make sure girls use travelers' checks or make arrangements to pre-pay for the group.

(The section on safety tips continues on the next page.)

First-Aid

First aid is the care you give someone who is hurt or ill before medical help arrives. Knowing first-aid skills and safety rules can help prevent accidents and prepare you for an emergency.

FIRST-AID KIT

Having a first-aid kit on hand and knowing how to use it can help you be prepared. With your troop or group or family, put together a first-aid kit. Here are some items to include:

- First-aid book
- Soap
- Safety pins
- Scissors
- Distilled water (in an unbreakable container)
- Tweezers
- Sewing needle to remove splinters
- Matches
- Adhesive tape and bandages
- Flashlight
- Paper drinking cups
- Sterile gauze
- Triangular bandage or clean cloth
- Cotton swabs
- Oral thermometer
- Latex gloves
- Instant chemical ice pack
- Pocket face-shield
- Plastic bag
- Emergency telephone numbers
- Change for telephone call

When an accident or emergency happens, stay calm and, if possible, get an adult to help you.

If the injury is serious, call a doctor right away. Do not move an injured person unless there is danger like a fire or exposed electrical wires. Always tell an adult afterwards if you have given someone first aid. Wear latex gloves to protect yourself from blood or other bodily fluids.

First-Aid Guide

Animal Bite

Wash the wound with soap and warm water. Apply a sterile bandage or cloth. Call a doctor or hospital. Try to identify the animal in case it needs to be tested for rabies.

Bleeding

Small cuts: If possible, use latex gloves or put your hands in plastic bags when caring for bleeding wounds. Clean the cut with soap and warm water, and cover with a bandage.

Large wounds that will not stop bleeding: Rest a clean cloth directly on the wound and press firmly. Apply pressure until the bleeding stops. Use adhesive tape to hold the cloth in place. Raise the bleeding part above the level of the person's heart if possible. Call a doctor.

Blisters

Wash the area with soap and warm water. Cover with a clean bandage. Do not break the blister.

Bumps and Bruises

Put a cold, damp cloth on the area. If there is a lot of swelling, call an adult for help.

Burns

If the burn has not broken or charred the skin, rest the burned area in cold (not ice) water, pat dry, and cover with a dry, sterile cloth. Do not use ointment, butter, or petroleum jelly. Have an adult check the burn. Call a doctor or the hospital if the skin is broken, blistered, or charred.

Choking

If the person can speak, cough, or breathe, do nothing. Otherwise, stand behind the person and grasp your hands around her, just under her rib cage. Press your hands into her stomach with four quick upward moves. Do this until the person spits out the stuck food or object.

Drowning

Someone should call the lifeguard or go for help immediately. It's important to get the person out of the water. Try to cover the mouth and nose with thin material or the face mask from your first-aid kit and find an adult to do CPR and rescue breathing. Then follow the directions for treating hypothermia.

Eye Injuries

When a person gets hit in the eye, put a cold, clean cloth over it. Have the eye checked by a doctor.

Foreign objects: If small objects (like an eyelash or piece of dirt) get into the eye, do not allow the person to rub her eye. Use a cup filled with cool water to rinse the eye. (Do this over a sink, if possible.) Have the person bend so that her head is sideways. Pour water over the opened eye, and tell the person to move her eyeball up and down. If an object is sticking into the eyeball, do not attempt to remove it. Call a doctor or hospital immediately.

Chemical burns: If bleach or some other cleaning chemical gets into the eye, immediately rinse it with cool water from a running faucet or cup for at least 15 minutes. To rinse, turn the person's head to the side so that the eye with the chemical burn is on the bottom. Let water run slowly across the eye starting from the part closest to the nose. Cover the eye with a clean, dry cloth. Call a doctor or hospital immediately.

Fainting

Help the person lie down or bend over with her head between her knees. Loosen tight clothing. Wipe her face with cool water. Call a doctor if the person doesn't open her eyes quickly.

Fractures, Sprains, Broken Bones

Do not move the injured person. Keep the person calm. Call a doctor or hospital.

Frostbite

Frostbite occurs when part of the body starts to freeze. The skin turns white, grayish yellow, or pale blue. As quickly as possible, warm the area. Put the frozen area into warm (not hot) water. Dry very gently (do not rub or press hard) and wrap in warm cloth, blankets, or both. Call a doctor.

78

79

Handbook Page 78

Handbook Page 79

Supporting Activities

▲ Using the safety tips mentioned, make up a true and false game to get the girls interested in health and safety.

▲ Find out about safety trainings that are available to girls in your troop or group, e.g., water safety, first aid, and baby-sitting.

▲ Have girls role-play or discuss the following situations:

1. You are walking down a street alone and you notice someone seems to be following you. What should you do?

2. You're in a large amusement park and you need to use the restroom. What should you do?

3. You're responsible for collecting your troop's or group's money for dinner at a restaurant. Where should you keep the money?

▲ Have girls write a variety of trip destinations on slips of paper: shopping mall, amusement park, zoo, fire station, museum, beach, community swimming pool, roller skating rink, corporate headquarters, airport, etc. Then, girls choose a slip of paper and list or discuss safety rules they would need to follow.

▲ Have girls discuss how to make a collect telephone call, a call to 911, and a credit-card telephone call.

▲ When visiting public areas such as amusement parks and movie theaters, ask girls to identify the nearest exits and explain how they would get out.

▲ Have girls discuss how they would get first aid at an amusement park, beach, or shopping mall.

▲ Try this memory game with your troop or group. Cut out pictures from magazines that show scenes full of people or action. Ask players to look at a picture for a set time. When time has expired, turn the picture over. Each girl then takes a turn recalling something from the picture. When a person can't remember something that hasn't already been said, she stops playing. The person remaining is the winner.

(The section on safety continues on the next page.)

Hyperthermia (too much body heat)

Heat exhaustion is mild; heat stroke is severe. Get the person out of the sun and cool her off. Have her slowly drink cool (not cold) water. Call a doctor if the person is very hot, not sweating, pale, nauseous, has trouble breathing, and seems dazed.

Hypothermia (too little body heat)

Get the person out of the cold, and warm her body slowly. Remove wet clothing and cover with dry clothing or blankets. If person is conscious and able to swallow, give warm liquids. Call a doctor or hospital.

Insect Stings and Tick Bites

Remove the stinger if you can. Don't use tweezers, as this may cause poison to be pumped into the bitten area. Instead, scrape across the top of the skin. Wash the area with soap and water, and apply ice to reduce the swelling. If there is a lot of swelling, or if the person seems to be getting sick or showing signs of shock, there may be an allergic reaction. In this case, call a doctor or hospital immediately.

• *Tick bite*: Use tweezers to pull the tick out directly. Put the tweezers as close to the tick's head as possible. Save the tick. (Tape it onto a white piece of paper.) Your doctor can test it for Lyme and other diseases.

Nosebleed

Have the person sit forward on a chair with her head bent slightly forward. Pinch the lower part of her nose for at least five minutes to stop the bleeding. Then place a cold, wet cloth on her nose and face.

Poisoning

Call your local poison control center or a doctor for help immediately. To prevent poisoning, look through your home for things that might be poisonous, such as medicines, cleaning fluids, plants, and cosmetics. With the help of an adult, label all poisons and store them in a safe place–out of the reach of young children.

Shock (can occur in any kind of emergency)

You may notice sweating, rapid breathing, nausea, and cold or clammy skin. Keep the person lying down. Elevate the feet. Place one cloth or blanket under the person and another cloth or blanket over her. Try to keep her comfortable and calm. Call a doctor.

Snakebite

If you cannot be sure that the snake was not poisonous, treat the snakebite like a poisonous one. Calm the person. Keeping a person calm makes her blood, and the poison, move more slowly. Get her to a doctor or hospital as soon as possible. If you can, carry her because you do not want the poison to circulate too quickly.

Splinter

Gently wash the area with clean water. Look for the edge of the splinter and try to pull it out using your fingertips or tweezers. Be careful not to push the splinter under the skin.

Sunburn

Prevent sunburn by using sunscreens. Look for lotions or creams with an SPF (Sun Protection Factor) number of 15 or higher. Limit your time in the sun and remember that sunburns can happen on hazy, cloudy days too. If a sunburn occurs, gently soak the burned area in cold water. Do not put ice on the area. If the person is in a great deal of pain, call a doctor.

Emergency Telephone Calling

Practice making some emergency telephone calls in your troop or group or with an adult. Learn how to give the most important information quickly and how to follow the directions given to you. Here are some practice situations. Try making up your own.

Keep an up-to-date emergency telephone number list near every phone in your home.

• You smell smoke in the hallway of your apartment building.

• Your friend accidentally drank some kerosene that was stored in a soda bottle.

• You are home alone and you hear glass breaking downstairs.

• The lights suddenly go out in the house.

EMERGENCY TELEPHONE LIST

Mom (or guardian) at work:_____

Dad (or guardian) at work:_____

Parents'/guardians' home phone numbers:_____

Other relatives:_____

Neighbors:_____

Emergency medical services:_____

Police:_____

Fire department:_____

Poison control center:_____

Doctor:_____

Dentist:_____

Utilities:_____

Taxi or car service:_____

Other important numbers:_____

_____

_____

Program Links

▲ *Girl Scout Badges and Signs:* Caring for Children badge; Creative Solutions badge; First Aid badge; Making Decisions badge; Safety Sense badge

▲ *Outdoor Education in Girl Scouting*

▲ *Safety-Wise*

Tips

▲ **First Aid:** Follow the procedures in *Safety-Wise* when you or someone in your troop or group administers first aid. Review the section "Being a Health and Safety Role Model" in *Safety-Wise* before starting work on this section.

Always wash hands with soap before (if possible) and after providing first aid. Latex gloves and a face mask should be worn when working with injuries involving blood.

Supporting Activities

▲ Have girls find out about careers that involve safety and first aid.

▲ Discuss how people can provide support to those who have experienced trauma, such as an earthquake, car accident, or flood.

▲ Girls can practice first-aid procedures or develop skits, stories, or posters about first aid.

▲ Suggest girls contact a school, community, or emergency medical service organization for field-trip ideas or to recruit speakers.

Program Links

▲ *Girl Scout Badges and Signs:* First Aid badge

▲ *Safety-Wise*

▲ *Tune In to Well-Being, Say No to Drugs: Substance Abuse* Contemporary Issues booklet

Fire Safety

One way to practice fire safety is to prevent fires from starting. Check your home, the place where you meet for Girl Scouts, or other places for fire hazards.

 Try to come up with a list of fire hazards. You can do this by yourself, with one or two friends, or in your Girl Scout troop or group. (Turn the page upside down to see a list. How many did you know?)

FIRE HAZARDS
- Electrical outlets with too many plugs
- Frayed electrical cords
- Portable heaters near curtains, fabric chairs and sofas, or beds
- Paint and cleaning supplies stored in places that can get hot
- Newspapers stacked in large piles
- Appliances plugged into extension cords for a long time
- Paint-stained, dirty, or oily rags piled together
- Curtains or towels hanging close to a stove or oven
- Full ashtrays
- Vases full of water placed on a television or other electrical appliance
- Matches or lighters left within the reach of young children
- Electrical appliances plugged in near sinks and bathtubs
- Pot handles sticking over stove tops
- Towels and other cloths used as pot holders

SOME FIRE-SAFETY RULES

If fire breaks out at home, remember these rules:

1. Get yourself and others out of the house quickly. Do not go back for anything or anyone.

2. Don't stay and try to put out the fire. Fires spread very quickly.

3. Call the fire department from outside. Give your name and address and the exact place of the fire. If you use a fire alarm box, stay near it so you can direct the fire truck once it arrives.

If smoke comes into a room and the door is closed:

1. Do not open the door.

2. Feel the door. If it is cool, open it a little and hold it with your foot. Feel the air outside with your hand. If the air is not hot, walk outside immediately. Use fire stairs, not elevators. If the door is warm, block the crack under the door with pillows, sheets, blankets, or a rug. Go to the window and call for help. Stay near the window until help arrives. Cover your nose and mouth with a wet cloth, if possible, and wet the materials you are using to block the door.

If you wake up and the room is full of smoke:

1. Roll out of the bed directly onto the floor.

2. Crawl to the nearest exit. Smoke rises, so the coolest, freshest air will be close to the floor. Remember not to open any door without first checking to see if it is warm.

If fire breaks out when you are in a public place:

1. Stay calm.

2. Walk quickly and quietly to the nearest exit.

An important fire-safety skill is to note the fire exits or the quickest way to leave whenever you are in a public space.

82

Stop, Drop, and Roll

Look at these illustrations. They demonstrate STOP–DROP–ROLL—the technique to use if your or another person's clothes catch on fire.

If your clothes catch on fire:

1. **STOP**–where you are.

2. **DROP**–to the floor or ground. Do not run. Running feeds more oxygen to the fire and makes it burn faster.

3. **ROLL**–back and forth making sure to cover your face with your hands. Or wrap a coat, blanket, or rug around you to smother the flames.

If another person's clothes are on fire:

1. Get the person to **STOP**.

2. Get the person to **DROP** to the ground.

3. **ROLL** the person over and over or wrap a blanket, coat, or rug around her to smother the flames.

 Find out how a smoke detector works and where to place one in an apartment, house, troop meeting place, or other location.

Plan and practice fire escape routes. Draw a fire escape plan for the place where you live, your troop or group meeting place, or school. Be sure to include at least two ways to escape.

Invite a firefighter to visit and speak to your troop or group.

Design a safety knowledge test for your group. Try to make it a game, a skit, or a relay race.

83

▲ **Fire Safety:** When discussing fire safety, stress the importance of preventive behavior. Girls should review the list of fire hazards to start a discussion.

Along the lines of preventive fire safety, suggest girls look at the tags sewn inside clothing to see which fabrics are not flammable. Children's sleepwear must be made from specially treated fabric to prevent it from burning.

Discuss with girls how to be safe around barbecue grills, stoves, fireplaces, and space heaters. Stress the danger of having plastic rain gear, long hair, and loose-fitting clothing around an open flame.

▲ With your troop or group, design and practice an evacuation plan for your meeting place. Decide where you will meet outside, who will make sure everyone is outside and safe, what to do in a real emergency.

▲ Help girls learn safety skills such as looking for exit signs when visiting public places. Practice emergency evacuation. Review safety procedures before going on a trip.

▲ Stop, drop, and roll is a valuable technique for girls to learn. Have each girl practice on a soft surface such as a grassy playing field or a padded floor. Each girl can also teach "Stop, Drop, and Roll" techniques to someone else. Discuss what to do with a small child who may not understand directions or someone who is not physically able to move in this way.

▲ Have girls discuss the following situations:

1. Someone's clothes catch on fire while she is sittings around a campfire. What do you do?

2. A grease fire breaks out in the kitchen. What do you do?

3. You are on the seventeenth floor of a high-rise building. An alarm signals and an announcement is made that there is a fire on the fifth floor and no one should leave floors 10 through 20. What do you do?

4. You are home alone and you smell gas. What do you do?

▲ Have girls invite a firefighter to speak to the group or plan a visit to a firehouse.

▲ *Girl Scout Badges and Signs:* Safety Sense badge

▲ *Safety-Wise*

Personal Safety

Personal safety means protecting yourself from physical harm caused by other people. People you know and people you don't know can hurt you. You can learn how to protect yourself from abuse–treatment that is injuring or harmful–and how to tell someone you trust if you have been abused.

Sexual harassment is a form of abuse in which someone says things or touches you in ways you do not want or in ways that make you uncomfortable. Sexual harassment is also when someone asks you to do sexual things you do not want to do. Usually the person who is doing the harassing feels that he or she can make the person being harassed feel afraid. Tell the person harassing you to stop it. Another way to stop sexual harassment is to tell someone you trust. If the person you tell doesn't believe you, tell someone else.

Sexual abuse is when an adult or child touches you in a way that makes you uncomfortable or that hurts you, and when the reason for the touching is to make the child or adult feel good. Sexual abuse can happen within a family or with someone you know well. This is a very difficult situation for kids because sometimes they believe that the abuse is their fault or they feel something terrible will happen if they tell. Abuse is wrong. If someone tries to abuse you, it is absolutely your right to say "NO!" You should tell

an adult you trust, and if this adult does not believe you, tell another trusted adult.

If you have been abused, tell someone. If you know someone who is being abused, get her to tell. Most communities have abuse hotlines to call, or you can call the police.

You can learn to protect yourself by avoiding potentially dangerous situations. However, if someone does harm you, try to remember: When did it happen? Where did it happen? What happened? Who was there? What did the person (or persons) look like? If the person was in a car, what did the car look like? Can you remember the license plate number?

Personal Safety Role-Playing

What would you do in these situations?

• You and your cousins are playing outside. Your older cousin starts tickling you so hard that it hurts.

• You wake up in the night when someone you know is sitting on your bed and touching you in places that make you feel uncomfortable.

• One of the older boys in the neighborhood asks if you want to play "special grown-up games" with him. He says you have to promise not to tell.

• You are at the shopping mall with your grandmother when you see this great pair of shoes in a store window. You run over to look. When you turn around, you can't see your grandmother.

• You are at the movies with friends. A man sits next to you and accidentally brushes your leg and says, "Sorry." When the movie starts, he does it again.

PERSONAL SAFETY DO'S AND DON'TS

When You're Out and About

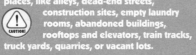

DON'T play in deserted areas or out-of-the-way places, like alleys, dead-end streets, construction sites, empty laundry rooms, abandoned buildings, rooftops and elevators, train tracks, truck yards, quarries, or vacant lots.

DO scream or yell if someone tries to get you to go with him or her. You can yell "Fire" or "Help–this person is not my parent," or "Help–I don't know this person."

DO go to a police station, store salesperson, or a uniformed official if you feel you are being followed or if something makes you nervous.

DON'T believe a message a stranger gives you like, "Your mother wants me to bring you home."

When You're Home Alone

DON'T open the door to a stranger, even if he or she is in uniform and has a package or flowers to deliver. Either tell the person to come back another time or just don't answer the door.

DO keep all doors and windows locked.

DO know how to answer the phone when you are home alone. Practice answering the phone in your Girl Scout troop or group or with family members.

DON'T give a person who calls the "wrong" number your telephone number, even if he or she insists. Just say, "You have the wrong number and hang up."

DO call the police or your emergency assistance number if you hear or see someone trying to break into your home.

84

85

 In your troop or group, brainstorm safety situations that fit into the categories of weather, water, personal safety, fire, and emergency preparedness. Role-play safe ways to act in these situations.

 Read the decision-making story maze on pages 68–71. A lot of the choices involve staying safe. Create your own safety story or safety skit that has different endings depending upon the path you choose.

 Create a game on safety using the information in this chapter. It could be a card game, board game, or a wide game (a game in which you move from station to station).

 Find out about bicycle safety and show that you know how to inspect and safely ride a bicycle.

 Pick a sport and create a safety checklist, poster, or booklet for that sport. (See pages 147–150 for sports ideas.)

▲ **Personal Safety:** Child abuse affects over 1.5 million children each year in the United States. Physical abuse, sexual abuse, emotional maltreatment, and physical neglect are four types of abuse.

Most abused children show one or more of the following symptoms: low self-esteem; anger; guilt; depression; aggressive, hyperactive, or disruptive behavior; poor school performance; and abuse of drugs and alcohol.

As a caring Girl Scout leader, you can play an important role in helping girls acquire knowledge and skills to protect themselves against abuse. You can also provide a supportive atmosphere to help them grow into healthy women. Here are some tips:

● Become familiar with information about child abuse, its symptoms, and reporting procedures.

● Be in touch with your own attitudes and feelings about child abuse before educating girls. Your council may have introduced this topic in your leader training, or you may wish to seek additional training and information. Be open to the fact that child abuse really happens— across all segments of our society. You may have a girl in your group who has been or is a victim of abuse.

● Take a preventive approach. Provide nonthreatening activities that will help girls feel positive about themselves. (See *Staying Safe: Preventing Child Abuse* Contemporary Issues booklet.)

● Provide an atmosphere of openness, freedom, and trust so girls will feel comfortable expressing themselves, asking questions, and seeking advice.

● Give factual information to girls in terms they can understand. Girls need information to counteract the myths they hear (for example, that strangers are most likely to abuse children), to help them avoid potentially dangerous situations, and to enable them to report cases of abuse.

● Give girls praise, recognition, and increased responsibility. Let them know you value and care about them. Girls who feel accepted are less likely to allow others to abuse them.

● Be sensitive to girls who feel pressured to be perfect. Encourage them to perform at a realistic level.

● Help girls become assertive and let them know that it is all right to say no to an adult if they need to protect themselves.

● Be sensitive to girls with disabilities who may be more vulnerable to abuse.

● Encourage parents/guardians to participate in group activities relating to child-abuse prevention.

● Listen seriously to what girls have to say. They seldom lie about being abused. Help girls with child-abuse problems by knowing how, when, and where to get professional help. If a girl tells you she has been abused:

■ Believe what she has told you.

■ Tell her it is not her fault.

■ Tell her you are glad she told you.

■ Tell her you are sorry about what happened.

■ Tell her you will do your best to protect and support her.

Remember that your primary role is that of a caring educator. If you suspect that a child has been abused, follow your council's procedures for reporting this information.

▲ *Safety-Wise*

▲ *Staying Safe: Preventing Child Abuse* Contemporary Issues booklet

STAYING HEALTHY

Taking Care of Your Body

Do you ever think about how you look? Do you wonder what other people think about how you look? Though people should judge others by what's on the inside–qualities like kindness and a good sense of humor, for example–lots of times a first impression is made by one's appearance. Keeping your body and clothing clean are some ways you show others that you care about yourself. The healthy habits you form now will help you be a healthy adult.

Your Skin

Sweat glands might make you perspire a lot during puberty. Sometimes, your skin gets oilier and, if you feel nervous or worried, you may start to sweat heavily. If this sweat is left on the body too long, bacteria will cause it to have an odor. You may need to use a deodorant or antiperspirant daily.

It is important to wash every day. Set a time to bathe or shower regularly and, if you exercise, you may want to bathe again.

Always wash your hands after you have used the bathroom, before you eat, and before and after you have handled food. Unclean hands can spread disease.

Cleanliness is especially important during menstruation because the hormones (chemicals made by glands in your body) that control your period also cause sweat glands to be more active. At that time of the month, your skin and hair may be oilier.

When You're in the Sun

Protecting your skin from the sun is important. Even on cloudy or cold days, ultraviolet rays from the sun can damage your skin. You won't see the damage right away, but you will when you are older–wrinkles, lines, and maybe even skin cancer. Sunscreens come in different degrees of protection. A rating of 15 or higher should protect your skin, but you need to apply it before you go out into the sun and after swimming or exercise.

Your Face

Washing your face not only keeps you looking clean, but rids your skin of extra oil, dirt, and bacteria that can cause pimples.

Almost everyone gets pimples at some time or another. When girls and boys enter puberty, they may find their skin becoming oily, and they may get pimples and blackheads. Acne is a skin disease in which the oil glands in your skin get swollen and blocked causing pimples and blackheads. A dermatologist has medicines and tips that can help control acne. Keep hair and hands off your face, and don't pick or squeeze pimples. You can scar your face!

Teeth

When you smile, you want people to notice your clean, healthy teeth.

To keep teeth healthy, remember these tips:

* Remove plaque (a combination of saliva, bacteria, and food particles) often. Plaque can cause cavities if it remains on your teeth, and it can cause bad breath.

* Brush after meals and use dental floss, because a toothbrush can't clean between your teeth.

* Eat raw fruits and vegetables, like apples, carrots, and celery.

Good dental habits are especially important if you wear braces as food can get stuck in the wires or bands.

Your Hair

Wash, shampoo, and condition your hair regularly. How often to wash depends on your hair type.

Some girls wash their hair once a week and some once a day. When it comes to hair care products–creams, mousses, curl activators, gels, sprays, relaxers, and permanents– choose those that are best for your hair type. Remember, all products have the potential to damage hair if misused or overused. This is also true of blow dryers, hot combs, and curling irons. So be careful and check with your parent or guardian.

▲ **Taking Care of Your Body:**
Talk about what girls need to do to care for their bodies and help them plan daily routines. Discuss managing time in the morning, before school. Help girls plan a smooth routine for getting up, getting dressed, and eating breakfast.

You might get some giggles when discussing personal hygiene. Girls may feel uncomfortable talking about sweating, deodorants, and menstruation. You may determine that the discussion of these subjects might be best handled by a consultant.

Besides discussing the importance of hand-washing to lessen the spread of bacteria, you could discuss nail-biting and nail care. Share ideas for breaking a nail-biting habit or invite a manicurist to demonstrate nail care. Likewise, invite a dermatologist or cosmetologist to discuss skin care, a dentist or dental hygienist to discuss dental care, or a hairstylist to discuss hair care. Remember, when doing hairstyling activities that girls should not share combs, brushes, or hair-care appliances.

▲ Bring in a variety of magazine photos of women. Look for athletes, models, actresses, businesswomen, etc., for ideas about different looks. Using the photos, girls can create a poster of the look that appeals to them. Have girls explain why they chose that style.

▲ Encourage girls to be knowledgeable consumers. Discuss advertisements for hair and skin-care products. How do advertisers get people to buy their products? What claims do they make? Compare the ingredients of higher- and lower-priced shampoos. What differences and similarities can the girls discover?

▲ Look at *Developing Health and Fitness: Be Your Best!* Contemporary Issues booklet for recipes for creating your own beauty products.

▲ *Developing Health and Fitness: Be Your Best!* and *Girls Are Great: Growing Up Female* Contemporary Issues booklets

▲ *Girl Scout Badges and Signs:* Becoming a Teen badge; Health and Fitness badge

▲ *Junior Girl Scout Handbook:* Looking Your Best badge

▲ GSUSA video *Be Your Best!*

HAIRSTYLES

Changing your hairstyle can give you a new look. Try bangs; part your hair differently; braid it; put ornaments in it. Below are different ways to braid hair. Remember, the best hairstyle for you is the one you like the most. You might feel pressured to have the same hairstyle as a friend or want to look like a performer you admire. But you have to decide if that hairstyle works with your type of hair and the shape of your face.

French Braids

❶ Divide the hair at the top of the head into three sections.

❷ Cross the right and then the left section over the center section.

❸ Take a small section of hair from the right side of the face. Add this hair to the right section of the braid.

❹ Pull the center section all the way to the right.

❺ Hold all of the braid in your right hand and then repeat the process on the left side.

❻ Continue moving from the right to the left until all the hair on either side has been caught up in the braid. Finish by braiding the bottom or turning the hair under into a roll.

Corn Row Braids

❶ Divide a section of hair into a straight row.

❷ Start making a tight braid adding hair from the right and the left and pulling to keep the braid neat and tight as you did with the French Braid, but using smaller amounts of hair within the two straight sides of the row.

❸ Once you have braided all the hair in the row, secure the ends, if needed, with a band, clip, or bead.

❹ You can make more intricate patterns by braiding in circles or swirls.

Why not hold a braid workshop or fashion show for other Girl Scout troops or groups?

Try these hairstyle activities

 Create your own party barrettes or fashion barrettes and bows to match different outfits. Braid into your hair beads and ribbons. Take a plain headband and wrap it with ribbons, fabric, or yarn. Sew or glue on beads or bows.

 Have a hairstyle party. Use the ideas here or look through magazines, talk with older girls or adults, or dream up some new hair creations! Try different hairstyles on each other. To keep things clean, it's best not to share brushes, combs, and other hair appliances that touch the hair. If you can, take some instant pictures or find another way to keep a record of your new looks!

 Create a "Looking Your Best" booklet, poster, video, or collage. Look through Chapter Two for some ideas about the images of beauty. These badges, in *Girl Scout Badges and Signs*, may also help: Becoming a Teen, Health and Fitness, and Walking for Fitness.

Harmful Substances

You can't look or feel your best if you are putting things in your body that are harmful. Taking drugs, like cocaine or marijuana, or sniffing glue, smoking cigarettes, and drinking alcohol affect your body in very negative ways.

Why You Should Say "No" to Harmful Substances

You might find that friends use harmful drugs and encourage you to join them. No matter what the reason for using drugs—to look more grown-up, to feel better, to be a part of the group, or to stop feeling bored—it's a mistake. You should say No! to harmful drugs, cigarettes, and alcohol because:

•You can become addicted. That means you need to take more and more or you can't stop when you want.

•Taking these substances can damage your body. For example, the chemicals in cigarettes can cause your blood flow to slow down and your heart to work harder. That's not good for your heart. And you can even get emphysema (a deadly disease that affects the lungs) or lung cancer. Women who smoke take another risk. If they smoke while pregnant, they can hurt their unborn baby.

•Taking these substances can affect the way you look, smell, and act. For example, smoking makes your hair, breath, and clothing smell and can cause you to get wrinkles around your mouth and on your face.

 Find out more reasons why taking drugs, smoking cigarettes, and drinking alcohol are not wise. Then with your troop or group create a poster, quiz, or booklet to share with others.

Tips

▲ **Harmful Substances:**
Substance abuse can affect girls in your troop or group. If they have not been affected directly, they may have a family member or know a classmate abusing alcohol, cigarettes, or drugs. Certainly, they will have seen television shows and movies that deal with this topic.

Help girls understand the effects of addiction from legal and illegal substances. Some girls may come from families where illegal drugs are used. If they share this information with you, speak with your Girl Scout council representative for guidance.

Some girls in your troop or group may have family members who smoke cigarettes. Discuss how girls can cope with second-hand smoke. You also can talk about strategies for helping family members to quit and how very hard this can be. If you smoke, you should read "Being a Health and Safety Role Model" in *Safety-Wise*.

Read the Contemporary Issues booklet *Tune In to Well-Being, Say No to Drugs: Substance Abuse* and "Tips for Handling Specific Sensitive Issues" in *Safety-Wise* before beginning substance-abuse activities. Find out from your Girl Scout council representative if an event or packet of activities on this theme has been developed. You also may want to familiarize yourself with any local substance-abuse programs.

If you are talking about drug abuse and the issue of AIDS comes up, consult with your Girl Scout council. The Girl Scout resource *AIDS Awareness Update* (available from your council) has information about AIDS awareness and prevention programs and activities. The number of women who are infected with the HIV virus is growing rapidly and is a major health issue for adolescents and young women today.

Supporting Activities

▲ Invite a police officer, substance-abuse counselor, or other health or law-enforcement professional to speak to your troop or group about substance abuse.

▲ Do the activities for Junior Girl Scouts in *Tune In to Well-Being, Say No to Drugs: Substance Abuse* Contemporary Issues booklet.

▲ Brainstorm a list of reasons why people abuse drugs and alcohol. Kids who have abused substances often say that they tried drugs because they had nothing better to do. In a group, discuss ways girls can say no to drugs and how they can help others to do the same.

▲ Find out how you might develop a service project to help babies with fetal-alcohol syndrome or babies born to mothers who were addicted to drugs.

Program Links

▲ *Tune In to Well-Being, Say No to Drugs: Substance Abuse* Contemporary Issues booklet

▲ *Girl Scout Badges and Signs:* Health and Fitness badge; My Self-Esteem badge

▲ *Junior Girl Scout Handbook:* Looking Your Best badge; Healthy Living badge

More About Alcohol

A lot of kids take their first drink because friends pressure them. The alcohol in beer, wine, wine coolers, and liquor is a very powerful. You can overdose and die from drinking too much alcohol! Some people who think they know exactly when to stop drinking fool themselves because alcohol is very sneaky. The part of the brain that would say "that's enough" or "time to stop" gets turned off by the alcohol. So you can easily drink too much and do some very foolish things.

Perhaps you've seen adults or even your parents drink alcohol from time to time. It's important to remember that many adults make responsible choices for themselves — which might include drinking in moderation — that children are not ready to make. It's never okay for a child or adolescent to make a decision for herself about drinking. For information about problems related to drinking, see page 59.

 It is very hard not to drink or smoke if your friends do. Read the section about "Peer Pressure" on pages 64–65. Practice some different ways you can let people know you don't want to drink or smoke cigarettes. If you want to know what to do about a family member's drug or alcohol problem, see page 59.

 Think of activities that you can do alone or with friends rather than just "hang out." Sometimes, you have to take a healthy risk and be the leader of your group by taking up a sport, hobby, or some other activity that would be a lot healthier than taking drugs. Look at Chapter Seven for ideas for different activities. Find three that look interesting, try them, and introduce them to your friends.

90

Stress

Stress is the way your body or mind reacts to people or situations that put demands on you physically, mentally, or emotionally. A fire alarm going off suddenly, an argument with your best friend, a piano recital—these are things that can cause stress. However, positive stress can help you do what you need to do every day, like work, play, and exercise. For example, positive stress is the feeling you may get before a test when you know you have studied. You feel a bit nervous but you are also more alert and ready for the test.

Everyone reacts in her own way to stress. Make note of what you do or how you feel when something stressful occurs. Do you have physical reactions: faster heartbeat, heavier and faster breathing, sweating, trembling, a dry mouth, weird feelings in your stomach, blushing or turning pale, a feeling of tightness or tension in your muscles? You and your troop can think about things that have been stressful to each of you and compare notes.

Managing Stress

When Stress Is Manageable
✔ You feel good, sometimes even great!
✔ Life can be hard sometimes, but you can handle it.
✔ You have more energy.
✔ You believe in yourself.
✔ You can learn new things.

When Stress Becomes Unmanageable
✔ You start to feel sick.
✔ Your stomach hurts.
✔ You get headaches.
✔ You feel tired.
✔ You don't feel like doing anything.
✔ You feel miserable.
✔ You feel like you can't take anymore!

Helpful Ways to Cope with Stress
✔ Face up to what's causing the stress.
✔ Express your feelings.
✔ Talk it over with someone you trust.
✔ Think about good things.

✔ Work with others to solve problems.
✔ Take a break!
✔ See if there's a way to reorganize things.
✔ See if there's another way to look at things that will help you accept them.
✔ Know that you can learn and grow from your mistakes.
✔ Treat your mind and body right: relax, exercise, sleep, eat well.

Responses That Don't Reduce Stress
✔ Ignore your feelings.
✔ Try to deal with it all by yourself.
✔ Just wish that it will go away by itself.
✔ Blame yourself.
✔ Think about only the bad things.
✔ Think that you're supposed to be perfect.
✔ Think that everything is wrong and needs to change.
✔ Treat your body badly with cigarettes, alcohol, drugs, undereating, or overeating.

 Here is a relaxation activity you can try with your Girl Scout friends.

Sit comfortably in a chair, on the sofa, or on the floor. Close your eyes.

Imagine a place or thing that makes you feel calm. It could be a sunset, a poem that you especially like, a beautiful painting, a piece of music, the sound of the ocean.

Listen to and feel the sounds around you.

Listen to and feel your breathing. Keep it slow and steady. Breathe in through your nose and out through your mouth.

Each time you breathe out, imagine all the stress and tension leaving your body.

After ten minutes or so, slowly get up. Keep your breathing slow and steady.

 Keep a journal to record events that cause stress. Note the ways you respond. Are they positive? Can you handle stress in more positive ways? Practice helpful ways to manage stress and find out what works for you.

 In your troop or group discuss the stressful things that can happen to kids and teens. Discuss how to deal with stressful situations.

91

Handbook Page 90

Handbook Page 91

Tips

▲ **Stress:** Many adults fail to realize that children are affected by stress. As do adults, children react to stress in different ways. The kinds of stress that affect children may be physical or emotional. By providing an atmosphere where girls can express their feelings freely, you are helping alleviate stress. Read the GSUSA resource *Focus on Ability: Serving Girls With Special Needs* for more about stress as it affects girls with disabilities.

Supporting Activities

▲ Have girls jot down a list of things that cause stress. Encourage them to think about ways (other than those mentioned) to manage stress. Suggest role-playing solutions to some stressful situations.

▲ Besides the relaxation activity in the handbook, try the following technique:

1. Have the girls lie on their backs on the floor in a circle, with each person's head facing the inside of the circle.

2. Say the following to the group:

- "Close your eyes."

- "Breathe deeply."

- "Each time you breathe in, take a longer breath. Then slowly exhale."

- "Tense your right foot (leg, arm, fingers, etc.)," working your way up the body.

- "Let it go and relax."

- When they're done: "Lie still for a few more minutes, then slowly get up."

3. Afterwards ask girls how they feel. Do they feel relaxed? When might they use an exercise like this?

Program Links

▲ *Developing Health and Fitness: Be Your Best!, Caring and Coping: Facing Family Crises, Reaching Out: Preventing Youth Suicide, and Girls Are Great: Growing Up Female* Contemporary Issues booklets

▲ *Focus on Ability: Serving Girls With Special Needs*

▲ *Girl Scout Badges and Signs:* Becoming a Teen badge; Dabbler—World of Well-Being; Making Decisions badge; My Self-Esteem badge; Sign of the Rainbow; Sign of the Sun

REMINDER!

Celebrate rather than tolerate. Tolerance sends the message that you are merely putting up with something you don't like. Celebration sends the message of appreciation and gratitude. Tolerance implies you *have* to do something whereas celebration implies you *get* to do something.

Exercise

One of the ways to care for your body is to exercise. Being fit helps improve physical and mental health and physical appearance. Make regular exercise a part of your life now—it's a good habit to keep as you get older.

Aerobic Exercise

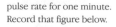

Dancing, skating, jumping rope, bicycling, walking, running, and swimming are all aerobic activities because they have continuous movements that keep the heart beating faster. Your heart is a muscle.

"To make yourself strong and healthy, it is necessary to begin with your inside, and to get the blood into good order and the heart to work well."
Juliette Gordon Low

By making the heart beat faster, you make it stronger. As your heart grows stronger, it takes less effort to do the same amount of physical work.

Discover how aerobic exercise helps your heart by doing some easy calculations. The illustration at the right shows how to measure your pulse rate. Take your pulse by placing your index and middle fingers on the inside of your wrist or on the carotid artery in your neck. Count the number of beats you feel for ten seconds. Multiply by six to get your pulse rate for one minute. Record that figure below.

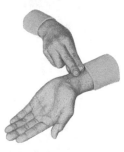

Number of beats you feel for 10 seconds = ____ x 6 = ____ (pulse rate for one minute)

Now suppose through regular aerobic exercise you lower your pulse rate by two beats per minute. How many beats have you saved for an hour? a week? a year? Do you do at least one aerobic activity three times a week? If you do, you are getting the exercise your body needs to stay in shape and keep your heart healthy. *Note*: Before you start a regular exercise program you should get a physical check-up.

 Do an aerobic activity at least three times a week, for at least 20 or 30 minutes, with a friend. Plan on doing different types of activities, so you won't be bored. Walking is a very good exercise. You can play a favorite sport, too, as long as you are moving for at least 20 minutes. Some sports are more aerobic than others. Find out which are the most aerobic.

 With the help of a trained adult, organize an exercise class for other girls your age. Demonstrate and teach activities that can be used to warm up, work out, and cool down.

 An exercise journal is a good place to record your progress. Here is a sample:

Exercise Journal

Date: _____

Time: _____

Type of Exercise: _____

Your Partner: _____

Comments: _____
_____

Date: _____

Time: _____

Type of Exercise: _____

Your Partner: _____

Comments: _____

Handbook Page 92

Handbook Page 93

Tips

▲ **Exercise:** Before doing any physical activity, review Girl Scout Program Standard 14 in *Safety-Wise* (also included in Chapter One in Part I of this guide). Be sure you have permission slips for all girls. Also, be aware of any girl's restrictions or limitations.

Exercise is a good method for helping girls release energy. Use exercise to vary the pace of meetings. For example, follow a group discussion with a brief exercise session or physical game.

Supporting Activities

▲ Ask girls about the kinds of exercise they do regularly. Encourage them to demonstrate their exercises and, if appropriate, let the rest of the girls join in.

▲ Girls can make a list of activities that will provide them with regular exercise throughout their lives. Suggest girls explore exercise options in their communities.

▲ Music enhances physical activity. Ask girls which kinds of music they would like to hear, and make a tape. You can also experiment with different types of music or sounds and have girls "interpret" what they hear. For instance, along with the more popular forms of music girls listen to, play a waltz, a folk song, a march, an opera, or sounds of the ocean so girls can move creatively. Girls might decide to include an exercise period at the beginning or end of each troop meeting.

Program Links

▲ *Developing Health and Fitness: Be Your Best!* Contemporary Issues booklet

▲ GSUSA's video *Be Your Best!*

▲ *Girl Scout Badges and Signs:* Dabbler—World of Well-Being; Dance badge; Health and Fitness badge; Hiker badge; Outdoor Fun in the City badge; Safety Sense badge; Sports badge; Sports Sampler badge; Walking for Fitness badge; Women Today badge; Sign of the Rainbow; Sign of the Sun

Notes

Nutrition

An important skill is choosing healthy foods. What you eat and drink affects your physical and mental health. Eating good foods and drinking enough water help your body grow, repair itself, and feel alert. How do you know what's nutritious?

The food pyramid, published by the United States Department of Agriculture, shows which proportion of foods to eat daily.

What do you learn about food groups by looking at the pyramid? Which foods should you eat the most? Less often? Think about the foods you eat. How would they fit in the food pyramid?

A Guide to Daily Food Choices

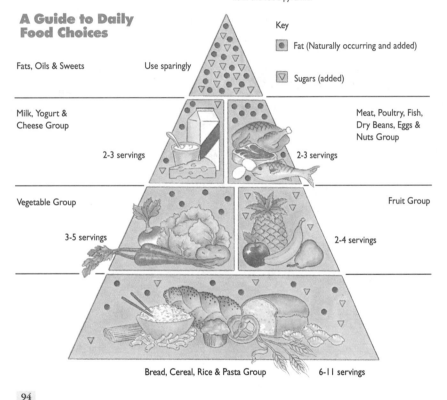

Key

 Fat (Naturally occurring and added)

▽ Sugars (added)

Fats, Oils & Sweets — Use sparingly

Milk, Yogurt & Cheese Group — 2-3 servings

Meat, Poultry, Fish, Dry Beans, Eggs & Nuts Group — 2-3 servings

Vegetable Group — 3-5 servings

Fruit Group — 2-4 servings

Bread, Cereal, Rice & Pasta Group — 6-11 servings

94

 Prepare a healthy meal using the food-pyramid categories as a guide. Serve an appetizer, salad, main dish, and dessert.

 Eat healthily by choosing snacks or lunches that are good for you. In your Girl Scout group or troop, sit in a circle. Each girl should write a snack or food that is not so healthy on a small slip of paper and put it into a bag or box. Take turns drawing a slip and brainstorming healthy substitutes. For example, if the snack was potato chips, you might suggest air-popped popcorn, rice cakes, or pita chips.

To make pita chips, separate pita-bread rounds into their two halves. Cut into sixths or eighths. Spray a cookie sheet with cooking oil and bake the pita slices at 350 degrees for 20 to 30 minutes—until crispy. You can sprinkle them with garlic powder, cinnamon-sugar, chili powder, or other flavorings. Use them as "dippers" for healthy, low-fat dips.

Food Labels

Foods that are processed—changed in some way or packaged or canned—may have chemicals added to make the foods taste fresher or to stay fresher longer. Many food products today are also artificially flavored to taste sweeter and artificially colored to look more attractive. Each American consumes about five pounds of chemical additives a year!

What can you do? You can learn how to read food labels and compare products. Labels provide a lot of information. Ingredients are listed in order from most to least. For example, if sugar is listed first, then that product contains more sugar than anything else.

Rules to Eat By

Follow these simple guidelines for nutritious eating. How could you share this information in an interesting way with younger girls or friends?

1. Eat a balanced diet with plenty of dark green, yellow, and orange-colored fruits, vegetables, and grains.

2. Eat food with fiber. Fiber comes from the cell walls in plants. Apples, beans, peas, oats, and barley are some foods that contain fiber.

3. Reduce sugar, fat, and cholesterol. Sugar doesn't do much to help your body. In fact, it can decay teeth, it might hurt your heart, and it can make you gain weight. Did you know that sugar is found in foods under the names fructose, sucrose, dextrose, molasses, corn syrup, or honey?

4. Maintain a healthy weight. If you eat right and get regular exercise, you can maintain a weight that is healthy for you.

5. Reduce salt. Many Americans eat too many salty foods. Instead of eating salt, try experimenting with herbs and spices. Check food labels for sodium or salt.

6. Drink lots of water—at least eight glasses of liquid a day, more if exercising. Remember soft drinks and some juices contain sugar and salt and may not be the best choices.

95

▲ **Nutrition:** Girls as young as those at the Junior Girl Scout age level have been known to suffer from eating disorders. Emphasize to girls that the way they treat their bodies now will affect their future health and well-being. See Chapter Two in Part II of this guide for more about eating disorders.

Supporting Activities

▲ Ask girls to jot down a list of favorite and least favorite foods (or refer girls to their answers about foods they like and dislike on the "This Is Me!" page in Chapter Two of the handbook). Then, ask them to consider the nutritional value of their foods and to decide where these foods appear on the food pyramid.

▲ Help each girl create a personal food pyramid to keep track of foods she eats. Girls can cut out pictures of foods and paste them on the food pyramid. Display the pyramids.

▲ Often, children like to ask "Why?" when given rules. Read "Rules to Eat By." Then ask girls "Why?" these rules are listed. Encourage them to think about, explore, and tell you the reasons for the rules.

▲ Girls can learn about each other by preparing and sharing food that represents their ethnicity. How do the ingredients in these recipes fit into the food pyramid?

▲ As a troop or group, shop for ingredients for recipes from *Developing Health and Fitness: Be Your Best!* Contemporary Issues booklet. Use the shopping trip as an opportunity to practice consumer skills. Girls can learn to think critically about such things as prices, product labels, and packaging. Then, try out the recipes.

▲ Girls can create a game, song, puzzle, or skit to help younger children learn about healthy eating.

▲ Girls can find out about community efforts to combat hunger. Suggest they start their own or participate in a community service project. For example, girls can help in a canned-food drive or volunteer at a soup kitchen.

Program Links

▲ *Girl Scout Badges and Signs:* Dabbler—World of Well-Being; Exploring Healthy Eating badge; Foods, Fibers, and Farming badge; Health and Fitness badge; Outdoor Cook badge; Sign of the Rainbow; Sign of the Sun

▲ *Junior Girl Scout Activity Book:* Chapter Four

REMINDER!

These days children and adolescents spend less time with adults—including their own family members—than years ago. Knowing this makes the girl/adult partnership in Girl Scouting of even greater value to today's girls. As a Girl Scout adult, you provide for girls a stable, reassuring presence and an example of the kind of caring adult they can become.

Tips

▲ **Careers in Health:** Trends indicate that jobs in the health-care industry will continue to grow rapidly throughout the next decade.

(The section on careers continues on the next page.)

Collect labels from cans and boxes of a variety of products. Bring them to your Girl Scout meeting. Copy down the following information from each label:

total calories _____	protein _____
calories from fat _____	Vitamin A _____
sodium _____	Vitamin C _____
dietary fiber _____	calcium _____
sugars _____	iron _____

Compare labels and suggested serving sizes and look for the products that have the healthiest ingredients. Which foods are highest in fiber? Which foods have certain vitamins and minerals such as calcium and potassium? Which foods are lowest in sodium and fat? How can this information help you?

 Plan a group health feast. Each person can prepare and bring one type of healthy food to share. Then, enjoy!

 Create a troop or group recipe for a delicious, nutritious snack food. Prepare your snack for your meetings, for trips, or create colorful wrappers or packages and sell your snack as a troop money-earning project.

Being able to take care of yourself—whether it's by practicing a first-aid skill, preparing a healthy lunch, or organizing an exercise group—can make you feel good about yourself. And sometimes, there's no better feeling than simply feeling proud!

96

Careers in Health

Health-related careers are some of the fastest growing areas of employment. Not only is the need for people growing, but the types of jobs keep expanding as medical technology becomes more sophisticated.

 Here is a list of some health careers. How can you find out what people who have these jobs do? You could also discover what education or training is required and what the average salaries are.

Dental hygienist	Food and drug inspector
Physician	Hospital administrator
Recreation therapist	Midwife
Acupuncturist	Biomedical engineer
Chiropractor	Nutritionist
Nurse	Optician
Orthopedic surgeon	Oncologist
Periodontist	Physical therapist
Psychologist	Veterinarian

SKILLS TO USE EVERY DAY
CHAPTER 4

Taking Care of Your Clothes and Home
page 98

Money: Should You Spend It or Save It?
page 105

What's It Going to Be Like Working in the Future?
page 110

Running Late? Try Time Management
page 117

As you become older, you make more decisions for yourself and have more independence in your daily life. In this chapter, you'll learn about important life skills such as taking care of your clothes and home, managing money, and setting personal goals. Can you think of why these skills might be good to learn? Read on to discover the everyday skills you'd like to explore!

97

Skills to Use Every Day

Although girls in your troop or group may not be thinking about a career yet, the more exposure and knowledge they acquire at this age, the better equipped they will be to make career decisions.

Supporting Activities

▲ Visit a hospital, laboratory, or other health-care facility so girls can understand health professions. Or, invite a health-care professional, preferably a woman, to speak to the troop or group.

▲ Ask girls why they think health-care careers are growing. (One reason is that technology has prolonged life.)

▲ Have girls play the following game:

1. Girls write the names of health-related careers on index cards.

When they're done, they place the cards face-down. Each girl chooses a card.

2. Each girl takes a turn acting out the career she has chosen.

3. After she is done, other girls ask her five "yes or no" questions to help guess the profession. The girl who guesses correctly goes next.

Program Links

▲ *Developing Health and Fitness: Be Your Best!* Contemporary Issues booklet

▲ *Girl Scout Badges and Signs:* Sign of the Satellite; Sign of the Sun; Sign of the Rainbow; Women Today badge

Tips

▲ **Chapter 4: Skills to Use Every Day:** This chapter focuses on teaching girls basic skills. Learning everyday skills can give girls a feeling of independence and self-reliance. Girls from all types of families would benefit from learning how to care for their clothes, do simple home repairs, manage money, be knowledgeable consumers, and strengthen study habits.

As a leader, encourage girls to do things on their own. Help a girl recognize when a job can be done better. For example, if a girl sews a button onto an article and the button is loose, help the girl decide whether she wants to redo the sewing. Though it's easier to redo the job yourself, a girl can learn a great deal by critiquing her own work. She will learn to set her own work standards with your guidance.

With regard to home repair, help dispel the notion that these skills are for boys only. Have girls think of situations where it would be important to know these skills. Invite women who have expertise in these areas to do demonstrations.

Taking Care of Your Clothes and Your Home

Besides learning skills to care for and protect your body, you also need to learn how to care for the place where you live, the things you own, and the clothes you wear. Learning how to repair your clothing, how to handle tools, and how to do simple repairs helps build your self-confidence. It feels good to know that you can do these things for yourself.

Clothes That Fit and Look Good

Whether buying or making clothes, it is important to know what looks good and what fits correctly. As you grow older, your measurements will vary. Remember there is no such thing as a perfect size. You might wear a Children's (6–14), Pre-teen's, Junior, Junior Petite, Misses, or Women's size.

No matter how much you spend on your clothing, consider whether the clothing is worth the cost. You can spend a little money or a lot of money, but you do want clothing that is well made. To help you make decisions while shopping, look at the clothing-buying checklist above.

Clothing-Buying Checklist

★ Is the clothing machine- or hand-washable or "dry clean only"? (Dry cleaning costs more than washing.)

★ Does the fabric wrinkle easily? (Squeeze it to find out.)

★ Is the clothing something you can wear often?

★ Does it go with other clothes you have?

★ Are there extra buttons?

★ If it needs to be altered, is it a simple alteration you can do yourself like sew a hem? (See pages 101–102 for sewing instructions.)

Washing and Drying Your Clothes

Whether you're washing your clothes by machine or hand, keep these instructions in mind:

★ Be sure to read clothing labels for care and cleaning instructions. Some will say "dry clean only," while others will say "hand-washable" or "machine-washable."

★ Follow the instructions on the inside label of the clothing to select water temperature, as well as the type of washing. (Some instructions may say "delicate cycle," "permanent press," or "regular wash." These apply to different types of machine washing.)

★ Close all zippers before washing.

★ Empty the contents of pockets before washing.

★ Check for stains and rub a small amount of laundry detergent or pre-washing liquid on those spots. It may be necessary to soak clothing if it has a heavy stain.

★ Follow the directions on the detergent box to determine how much detergent to use.

★ Follow directions on the washing machine to determine when and how to add the laundry detergent. (In some machines, you add detergent directly to the water; in others, you add detergent to a basket or opening.)

★ Some clothing can be washed in a machine but not dried in a clothes dryer. Read the label to see if you should lay the clothing flat to dry.

Clothing Care Symbols	
Symbol	**Meaning**
∪	Wash
△	Bleach
□	Tumble Dry
(iron)	Iron
(iron crossed out)	Do not iron
○	Dryclean
⊗	Do not dryclean

HANDBOOK ACTIVITY
Think of a way you can organize and care for your clothing so that your clothing stays neat and is easy to find in the morning. If you do not wash your own clothes, with an adult's permission, try machine washing or hand washing your clothing for a week.

98

99

▲ **Clothes That Fit and Look Good:** For most girls of this age, clothes are a means of self-expression. Some girls may already be identified by a "trademark," such as the way they decorate their jeans or tie their sneakers. Generally, some girls will show interest in experimenting with clothes, while others may show little interest in clothing or fashion trends.

The activities in this section encourage girls to be smart consumers when selecting clothing. The checklist is given to help girls judge the quality of clothing and other factors that go into buying clothing. Girls should know that clothing buying involves consumer skills and should not be based solely on what someone else says.

Many girls feel pressured to look and dress like models in magazines. Help girls think about how they can look their best, not look like someone else.

Fashion magazines can show girls how to expand their wardrobes, since many Junior Girl Scouts may not yet make clothing selections based on how well items coordinate. They can learn how to vary their wardrobes by adding articles of clothing that go with clothes they already have.

Also keep in mind that some girls may wear clothing, designs, or jewelry to make a cultural or ethnic statement. Be careful not to pass judgment. A girl's expression of her identity is important and may be tied to her self-concept.

Supporting Activities

▲ Using current magazines, girls can cut out pictures of outfits that they think coordinate well or they can design their own outfits. Fasten the pictures to posterboard and discuss mixing and matching of components and color coordination.

▲ Girls can find out which colors look best on them by holding different-colored scarves or other items against their skin and hair. If scarves or other clothing are not available, girls can use colored paper. Make large collars out of the paper by cutting a round hole and a slit in the middle for an opening. Girls can create a troop or group chart of which colors look best on each girl. Some will look better in "warm" colors like corals, browns, reds, and oranges. Others will look better in "cool" colors like violet, blue, blue-red, and gray.

▲ Throw an accessory party. Girls can create a troop or group accessory pool by collecting different sizes, shapes, colors, and types of scarves, belts, and jewelry. They can hold an accessory "grab-bag day" by wearing a plain outfit to their meeting and "accessorizing" after they arrive.

▲ **Washing and Drying Your Clothes:** Although doing laundry might not be anyone's idea of an exciting activity, it is a valuable skill. Having a brand-new sweater come out of the wash streaked, or a pair of pants shrink two sizes, can be costly mistakes.

The kinds of laundry tasks girls assume will probably vary considerably. Some girls may be responsible for washing their own clothes, some for washing the family's clothes, and some may not do any laundry at all.

Reading a clothing label to determine washing instructions might be difficult for some girls since labels contain a lot of information (clothing size, fabric, washing instructions, etc.). Discussing with girls such concepts as fabric type and water temperature can be helpful.

Quick and Easy Mend-Its

 Fashion designers can become very famous, but there are lots of other jobs in the fashion industry. Find out about careers in the fashion and cosmetic industries. Some suggestions are: clothing buyer, fashion consultant, personal shopper, cosmetologist, hairstylist, textile designer, salesperson. How can you find out about these careers? Maybe you can interview people who have these jobs or career shadow them for a day.

 Put on a fashion show with a theme. You might want to dress for different themes: Fashions for the Outdoors, Fashions for the Future, Fashions for Different Careers, Fashions for Parties. What other themes can you create?

100

Keep your clothes looking new and neat by sewing simple repairs. First you need sewing supplies.

 Choose a container (metal, like a cookie tin, or sturdy cardboard, like a shoe box) to make a sewing kit. Design and decorate with paper, paints, or fabric. These are some items you should have in your sewing kit:

★ **A package of sharp, assorted needles (the bigger the size number of the needle the smaller the eye of the needle, and the finer the point)**

★ **A thimble—to protect your finger**

★ **A small box of straight pins**

★ **A pair of scissors or shears**

★ **Spools of thread—of different colors and thicknesses (heavy-duty thread is great for sewing on buttons)**

★ **A pin cushion**

★ **A small ruler or measuring tape**

★ **Iron-on patches**

Sewing Stitches

Before stitching, thread your needle by carefully pushing the thread through the eye of the needle. Once it goes through, pull about four inches of thread through. Knot the longer end of the thread.

The diagrams on this page show the basic sewing stitches. Before sewing, pin your fabric in place with straight pins. Remember, the thimble makes it easy to push the needle through the fabric and protects the finger doing the pushing.

★ Hemming stitch—for hemming pants, dresses, skirts, tops. (See next page.)

★ Basting stitch—for holding the fabric in place before doing the final sewing by hand or machine.

★ Running stitch—for sewing straight seams.

★ Blanket stitch—to make a decorative edge that also prevents unraveling.

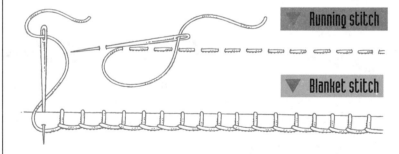

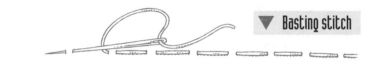

▼ Basting stitch

▼ Running stitch

▼ Blanket stitch

101

Handbook Page 100

Handbook Page 101

Supporting Activities

▲ Girls can experiment by washing and drying fabric swatches at different temperatures. For example, they will see what happens when an article of 100 percent cotton is placed in a hot dryer.

▲ Girls can bring in labels from discarded clothing, or take turns reading the labels in the clothes they are wearing. They can discover whether certain types of fabric, including velvet, corduroy, nylon, rayon, silk, and suede, have the same washing instructions.

▲ Girls can research the cost of dry cleaning dresses, jackets, pants, etc.

Tips

▲ **Quick and Easy Mend-Its:** Not everyone will be interested in learning even these basic sewing skills, but a group project such as a troop banner or a service project could bring everyone together.

To help girls practice sewing skills, have each girl bring in a sample piece of fabric, or you could purchase inexpensive remnants from a fabric store. Girls can practice different stitches or attach a button to their fabric. After a practice session or two, girls could start the project or mend pieces of clothing.

It might be a good idea for girls to think of situations where they would have to know these skills (for example, traveling, going away to camp, participating in a community service project, or helping themselves and other family members).

Supporting Activities

▲ As a service project idea, girls could use sewing skills to decorate plain baby bibs or other clothing. Girls can donate items to a women's shelter, hospital, or homeless shelter.

▲ Girls can create a new look on old clothes by sewing buttons, beads, or sequins onto used clothing from a second-hand store.

Program Links

▲ *Girl Scout Badges and Signs:* Family Living Skills badge; Textiles and Fibers badge

▲ *Junior Girl Scout Handbook:* Arts and Media badge; Careers badge; Looking Your Best badge

Make a Hem

Fold up the bottom of the skirt 1/4 inch (1/2 cm). Then fold the hem up to the length you want, usually one or two inches. A heavy fabric can take a bigger hem and a light fabric should have a smaller hem. Pin the hem and try the garment on to make sure the hem is even. Check the back and front in a mirror. Sew with the hemming stitch on the inside. Keep your stitches as tiny as possible so they don't show on the outside.

 Mend a piece of your own clothing or ask permission to mend a member of your family's clothing.

 Learn more about embroidery on page 157. Create a troop project that uses your sewing skills.

▲ Two-Holed Button

▲ Four-Holed Button

▲ Button on a Coat

Replace a Button

Mark the place for a button with two straight pins unless the original holes made by the thread are easy to see.

Start from underneath and pull your thread through the fabric and then through a hole in the button, then down through another hole and through the fabric.

Repeat this six to eight times—more if it is a coat or jacket—and tie off the thread on the wrong side.

The illustrations show the stitches for a two-holed button, a four-holed button, and a button on a coat.

Repair a Rip or Add a Fashion Patch

Cut a piece of fabric to a size about 1/2 inch (1 1/4 cm) wider than the rip or hole. Use the blanket stitch around the edges to attach to clothing. You can also use a ready-made iron-on patch. Just follow the directions on the package to attach this patch. Novelty stores sell different patches. Express your fashion style!

102

Simple Home Repairs ▲▲▲▲▲▲▲▲

 Caring for your home by making repairs is another important life skill. You can learn to make simple repairs with the right tools, an adult's help, and some practice. First become familiar with some tool-safety tips:

TIPS FOR TOOL SAFETY

- **Always make certain you have completely learned how to use a tool before you start working with it.**
- **Never use power tools unless an adult who knows how to use them is present.**
- **Make sure you have a clear and steady work surface.**
- **Keep tools out of reach of younger children.**
- **Make sure the tools you are using are in good condition.**
- **Wear goggles to protect your eyes, particularly if you are hammering, sawing, or drilling.**

Hammer–for pounding and removing nails. Make sure the hammer is the right weight for you. You should be able to hold it comfortably near the end of the handle. Raise the hammer with a backward flip of your wrist and then a forward flip.

Saw–for cutting wood or metal. You will probably use a common saw, or cross cut, for most projects. Use one that is about 16 inches long or slightly longer, depending on your reach.

Plane–for making wood smooth or for making wood just a bit smaller. Use a plane that fits comfortably in your hands. Be sure your board is in a vise (a tool that grips the wood) to make it steady. Use both hands and move the plane in one direction only.

Sandpaper–for smoothing rough surfaces. Sandpaper can be wrapped around and thumbtacked to a block of wood to make it steady. Coarse sandpaper should be used for your first sanding; then gradually move to finer grains for finishing.

Screwdriver–for turning screws that hold things together. In the illustration you can see two types of screwdrivers. Each type works with a particular kind of screw.

Awl–for making holes. An awl is good to mark the place where you want to put a nail or for starting the hole where you will put a screw.

Pliers–for gripping things. Pliers can help you make things tight or loosen things that are stuck.

Wrench–for turning nuts and bolts. A wrench makes nuts and bolts tight or loose.

Level–for making things straight. A level is used to keep angles and edges straight.

Drill–for making deep holes. The illustrations show a power drill and a hand drill. While all tools can hurt you when not used properly, drills can be extra dangerous, so make sure you follow the tool-safety tips before using one.

Standard

Phillips head

Hand Drill

Power Drill

103

▲ **Simple Home Repairs:** Not every girl will feel comfortable with hammers, saws, and other tools. Many girls have never had the opportunity to use them. Perhaps, they have never seen women using tools. Yet knowing how to use basic tools is an important skill for everyone.

▲ Give a demonstration or have another woman demonstrate how to use tools. With supervision let girls practice:

- Sawing wood
- Hammering nails
- Taking nails out of wood with pliers
- Screwing in a screw
- Drilling a hole
- Sanding wood.

Be sure to follow *Safety-Wise* guidelines.

If interest develops, girls can extend the activity by making simple items out of wood. They may decide on a group project or plan a service project using their skills. If you need help, consider asking high school students studying woodworking.

▲ **Doing Repairs and Maintaining Your Home** (see next handbook page): These sections outline some basic home-maintenance skills. Perhaps, girls can practice these skills at home with parental supervision.

As a group, you can plan a field trip to a carpentry shop, furniture or auto repair shop, or a crafts studio.

(The section on repairs continues on the next page.)

Handbook Page 104

▲▲▲▲▲▲▲▲▲▲▲▲▲▲▲▲▲▲▲▲▲

Maintaining Your Home

 Do you know how to:

✓ **Wash a window?**
✓ **Change the linens on a bed?**
✓ **Replace a vacuum cleaner bag?**
✓ **Program a VCR?**
✓ **Use a microwave oven?**
✓ **Turn off the water in an emergency?**
✓ **Install a shower head?**

✓ **Repot a plant?**
✓ **Shampoo carpeting?**
✓ **Use an extension cord properly?**
✓ **Clean a bathtub, toilet, or tile floors?**
✓ **Check a car's tires for air?**
✓ **Check the level of oil in a car?**
✓ **Remove stains from upholstery or carpeting?**

Choose three things from the list at the left and, in your Girl Scout group or troop or with an adult, demonstrate that you know how to do them.

Tool Kit

 Put together a home tool kit and practice using your tools:

➤ **Use a level and a hammer to hang a picture.**
➤ **Use sandpaper to fix a door or window that sticks.**
➤ **Use a screwdriver or wrench to tighten screws or bolts that have become loose.**
➤ **Use a wrench to replace a washer in a leaky faucet.**

Doing Repairs

 Find someone to show you how to do these home repairs:

➤ **Fix a hole in a window screen.**
➤ **Fix a loose chair or table leg.**
➤ **Install batteries in a flashlight or smoke detector.**
➤ **Caulk around a bathtub, shower, window, or door.**
➤ **Unclog a sink, bathtub, or toilet.**
➤ **Replace the cord on an electrical appliance.**
➤ **Repair a crack in a wall.**
➤ **Repair broken pottery.**
➤ **Repair a broken window shade or venetian blind.**

104

Handbook Page 105

Managing Money

Do you get an allowance? Do you earn money baby-sitting or delivering newspapers? Have you ever gotten money as a gift? How do you decide what to do with money–save it, spend it, or donate it to a worthy cause? As you grow older, you will make more decisions about money. One place to begin learning good money-management skills is in your Girl Scout troop or group.

Troop or Group Dues and Money-Earning Projects

As a Junior Girl Scout, you make decisions about how to earn and use the money in your Girl Scout troop or group. Money from dues or earned through special projects is money for you to spend on Girl Scout activities.

Girl Scout troops and groups need money for all kinds of things: project supplies, trips, games, books, equipment, donations. Girl Scout troops and groups often set up a troop treasury, depositing money from troop or group dues and money-earning projects.

Troop or Group Dues

The members of your troop or group agree to contribute an amount of money that everyone can afford. A troop's or group's dues may be $.10, $.25, $1.00; there is no one best amount. The troop or group also must decide: How often will dues be collected? Who will collect them? Where will the money be kept? How will the dues be used?

Often, this is decided in the beginning of the year when the troop or group sets its budget. You can also agree to raise the dues if you are saving for a special project, or lower the dues if you have enough money in the treasury. Remember the section about troop or group government on pages 24–25? How have you set up your troop or group government? How is your troop or group money collected and recorded?

105

Supporting Activities

▲ Using the list of simple home repairs and maintenance skills, have girls create a wide game where girls progress from station to station and demonstrate what they have learned.

▲ After girls have learned repair skills, suggest a community service project that involves repairing broken toys or household items. Girls can donate items to a community agency.

▲ Girls can find out what kinds of tools the following workers use: carpenter, plumber, electrician, welder, computer repair person, and telephone installer. Help girls research the education or training needed for these jobs. If possible, arrange for girls to career-shadow these workers.

▲ Girls can create a blueprint for the ideal bedroom. Ask girls to consider:

● What shape the room would be.

● Where the door and windows would go.

● Where the furniture would be placed.

● What special features the room would have.

Girls can design by pretending they are looking down into the room.

▲ Girls can investigate what an architect does. Ask girls to find out about education, salary, and skills. Suggest girls learn about one famous architect and display illustrations of her or his work.

▲ Help girls learn how to repair and care for a bicycle or a younger child's tricycle or wagon. They can learn how to put air in tires, change tires, lubricate joints, tighten handlebars and seats, make sure reflectors are working, test brakes, and attach a basket or carrying rack.

Program Links

▲ *Girl Scout Badges and Signs:* Art in the Home badge; Car Care badge; Do-It-Yourself badge; Family Living Skills badge; Ms. Fix-It badge

Tips

▲ **Managing Money:** Money management is an important skill for girls to learn before they set up a troop or group budget or participate in product sales. Read *Safety-Wise* for standards and guidelines for money-earning activities. Note that:

● You must obtain permission in writing from a girl's parent or guardian before she participates in money-earning activities or council-sponsored product sales.

● Each girl's participation should be voluntary, and the number of money-earning projects should not exceed what is needed to support troop activities.

● Girl Scouts, in their Girl Scout capacities, may not solicit money for other organizations.

See Chapter Four in Part I of this guide for additional tips on money-earning projects and managing troop or group dues.

Notes

Keeping Track of Troop or Group Dues

Your troop or group should have an easy and clear way of keeping track of money and equipment. You could use a budget like the one here or set up your own system. Every time money is collected or spent, it must be recorded and new totals must be figured out. This recording should be the responsibility of the troop treasurer. Whenever money is collected, it should be counted, recorded, and then put in a safe place. The best place to keep your troop or group money is in a checking account in a bank.

Your troop or group should set up a budget as soon as you have decided on the amount of troop or group dues. Make sure to include money left in your troop or group treasury from last year. Keep a special book or ledger for your budget. Your treasurer or troop or group leader can be responsible for bringing the ledger to each meeting. Part of your troop's or group's business at meetings will be a report from the treasurer on the amount of money in the account.

Troop or Group Budget

INCOME		EXPENSES	
Dues	_____	Supplies	_____
Product Sales	_____	Transportation	_____
Money-Earning Projects	_____	Fees (for example, for admissions)	_____
Contributions (from parents, sponsors, etc.)	_____	Refreshments	_____
Money from Last Year	_____	Recognitions	_____
Others	_____	Others	_____

Whenever your troop or group buys something with this money, it should save all receipts and sales slips. Deduct what has been spent from the total.

Money-Earning Projects

Girl Scout troops and groups often organize and carry out an activity to earn money for the treasury. Many troops participate in the annual Girl Scout cookie or calendar sales.

In your troop or group, practice your sales skills and your money manager skills. Think of different situations and what you could say. Figure out how much money you will earn and what you can do with it.

**Baby-sitting
Gift-wrapping
Car or bike wash**

Recycling drive

**Craft or baked-goods sale
Pet-sitting or plant-sitting**

**Neighborhood landscaping:
weeding, lawn mowing,
planting, etc.**

Selling Girl Scout Cookies

Junior Girl Scouts may decide to work on the Girl Scout cookie sale. As part of your troop or group, you want to contribute your talents and skills. Decide what you would like to learn about selling. There are many different jobs involved in a cookie sale. You can sell cookies. You can help organize cookie boxes and keep track of the money. Maybe you will be a part of a group that sells cookies at a shopping mall or in the lobby of an office building.

Decisions about what each person can do will be made in your troop or group.

If you decide to sell cookies, discuss and practice safety rules in your troop or group. Safety rules apply to any money-earning project. Be sure you follow the rules. You should also know some salesperson skills:

$ Learn about what you are selling so you can answer customers' questions.

$ Know what your Girl Scout troop or group is planning to do with the money it earns. What special things do Girl Scouts do?

$ Let the customer know how much money she owes you, when you will be collecting this money, and when she can expect to get the cookies and other products. Make sure you give customers the cookies and other products on the day promised.

$ Always say thank-you, even if someone doesn't buy anything. People will remember your good manners, which is important because you are representing Girl Scouts and yourself.

Other Money-Earning Projects

What are some other money-earning projects? Look at the column of ideas on this page. Do any ideas capture your interest? Add some of your own ideas.

Many of these activities can provide your troop or group with enough money to take a trip or carry out a service project. Before doing any money-earning activity though, you and your troop

Tips	Supporting Activities

Tips

▲ **Troop or Group Dues:** Girls should handle all troop or group money. They should participate fully in all financial decisions and be responsible for maintaining a troop or group budget. Other troop activities can involve money management (for example, planning trips), so all girls should get a chance to balance a checkbook or record financial data. Learning how to handle money wisely is one of the most important life skills you can share with the girls in your troop or group.

Supporting Activities

▲ Help girls get involved in family money management. Suggest they participate in food or other shopping trips to find out why their parents or guardians choose some products over others. Ask girls to talk to parents or guardians about household budgets and money management styles. Enlist the help of parents and guardians for more ideas.

▲ Girls can learn about the cost of living by studying classified advertisements to investigate salaries, the cost of renting an apartment, the expense of owning a car, and other expenses. Have girls devise a monthly budget for the lifestyle they would enjoy and decide on a job that would provide enough money.

▲ Invite a financial planner or credit counselor to visit your troop or group.

▲ Girls can survey classmates or friends to study spending habits. With that information, they can set up a financial workshop for Junior Girl Scouts.

▲ Girls can interview women business owners to ask about creating a business plan.

▲ Girls can create their own business plans for real or imaginary businesses. Some jobs that girls can do are: walking dogs, baby-sitting, repairing toys, selling printed cards or wrapping paper, delivering newspapers, washing cars, running errands, recycling, washing or sitting for pets, mowing lawns and gardening, selling lemonade, and sitting for plants. Girls should consider how much money and what kinds of materials or equipment they would need to start the business, how they would fit the business into their schedules, how they would keep track of money, how much they would charge for their product or service, and how they would know if their price was competitive.

Program Links

▲ *Girl Scout Badges and Signs:* Business-Wise badge; Money Sense badge

▲ *Junior Girl Scout Activity Book:* Chapter One

or group members must get permission from your parents or guardians. Your troop or group leader must get permission from the local Girl Scout council. Be sure also to find out about any safety rules, as well as local laws, or health department regulations, that could affect your activity.

Budgeting

Budgeting helps you decide where and how to spend money. Learning how to keep a budget is one of the most important money-management skills you can learn.

Look at the budget sheet below. Fixed expenses are those that hardly ever change.

Flexible expenses you can control. To use the budget sheet, fill in the amount of money you expect to have for each week (Week 1, Week 2, Week 3). Then record the amount you plan to spend in each category. At the end of the week, write in the amount you actually spent.

My Budget

Money I expect to have (total)	Week 1		Week 2		Week 3	
	Planned	Spent	Planned	Spent	Planned	Spent
Fixed Expenses						
School lunch						
Transportation						
Troop dues						
Flexible Expenses						
Snacks						
Tapes, CDs						
Video Games						
Magazines						
Other						
Savings						
Donations						

If you want to save money, decrease the amount you are spending on flexible expenses. How long can you stick to your budget? See if you can follow it for at least two months.

More About Money

Keeping money in a savings account is one way to keep your money safe. Once you have opened a savings account, the bank keeps a record of how much you deposit (put in), withdraw (take out), and the amount of interest earned (money the bank pays you for holding your money). Different banks give different amounts of interest.

Checking accounts are bank accounts from which you can sign a written order (a check) that tells the bank to pay a certain amount of money from your account to the person or company named on the check.

Here's your imaginary checking account. Imagine that for a month you have saved: two dollars out of your allowance ($2.00 per week), gift money ($20.00), and job money ($15.00). What is your total? _____

 How much do you know about credit cards? Learn about the interest charged by credit-card companies and stores.

 Visit a bank and find out how to open a savings and a checking account. Find out what other services are offered.

 Help your family with a household budget. What expenses are flexible? What expenses are fixed?

Invite someone who works in the financial industry, an accountant, a bank officer, a bank examiner, or a personal finance manager to visit your troop or group and explain what she does.

Now consider the amounts you would withdraw by writing checks. There's a special celebration coming up at school and the suggested donation is $4.00. You also want to pay your Girl Scout troop or group dues for the month (multiply your weekly troop dues by 4.3). What is your total? _____

Use your budget to help figure out the other expenses for which you would have to write checks. What is your balance (the amount left in your account)? _____

When you make another deposit, add it to your balance. Whenever you write a check to make a withdrawal, subtract it from your balance.

▲ **Selling Girl Scout Cookies:** The cookie sale has long been an important program activity in Girl Scouting. In 1923, Girl Scouts from Bridgeport, Connecticut, discussed in an issue of *American Girl* (a magazine once produced by Girl Scouts of the U.S.A.) how they baked and sold cookies to fund troop activities. By 1936, Girl Scout councils had their first nationally franchised Girl Scout cookie sale. At the end of World War II, the Girl Scout cookie sale became visible as interest in Girl Scout camps grew and profits helped girls everywhere enjoy the benefits of the Girl Scout camp experience.

You play an essential role in helping girls learn all the valuable skills that are part of participating in the Girl Scout cookie sale. Experience in goal-setting and the real-life opportunity to see how individual and group efforts count in reaching goals can provide life-long lessons. For many girls, this may be their first real experience in essential money management skills—budgeting, accounting, investing, and allocating funds.

The practice of interpersonal skills, as girls learn how to relate to new people in new ways, also are important. Involve girls in all aspects of the sale. Make sure they are part of all the decision-making. That will ensure the success at the end will be theirs. Encourage them to see how their efforts help beyond their immediate circumstances.

Today's cookie sale profits still build and maintain Girl Scout camps and much more—training and supporting leaders, underwriting the costs of special activities, financing travel scholarships, and making Girl Scouting accessible to all girls—girls in places like homeless shelters and migrant camps.

Cookie sales also help support the Girl Scout council office in the operation of council-sponsored program activities (including special workshops for leaders, day trips, and award ceremonies), in recruiting and organizing troops or groups, and in training Girl Scout leaders.

The annual Girl Scout cookie sale helps ensure that the Girl Scout program can continue to meet the needs and interests of girls.

▲ *Girl Scout Badges and Signs:* Business-Wise badge; Money Sense badge

▲ *Junior Girl Scout Handbook:* Careers badge; Consumer Power badge; Leadership badge

Notes

Exploring Careers

What's it going to be like working in the future?

There are a zillion jobs that were not around when your grandparents, or even your parents, were growing up. If you were to fast-forward into your future, you might be amazed at the jobs people will be doing and at the places people will be working.

The workplaces of tomorrow will link people through vast computer and communication networks across the country and around the world. You may need to work at night because the people with whom you do business are in a different time zone.

If you'd like to further investigate the work of the future...

 Interview three different women who work in companies with more than 100 people. Find out about work benefits. What changes would they like to see in the future? Interview several women who are self-employed and ask the same questions.

Whenever you think of possible careers or jobs, think about your skills and abilities, your characteristics, your goals, your values, and your interests. All help shape the ideal career for you.

Skills and Abilities

You probably do some things better than other things. Are you athletic? Are you artistic? Are you good at helping people get along? The special skills and abilities you have can help you find a career.

 Choose five activities from Chapter Seven and brainstorm a list of careers that could match those activities.

Someone who is athletic may do well as a coach, a physical therapist, or an aerobics instructor. Someone who is artistic may enjoy being an interior designer, architect, or film editor. Remember, while you seem to be born with some abilities, as you grow you add new skills.

Right now you may feel uncomfortable speaking in front of a group. Does that rule out a career as a teacher, corporate trainer, or broadcaster? No! Maybe you will become a patrol leader, run for student government, or become active in an environmental cause. You discover that it's not so difficult to speak to a group about something you believe. You might give a speech about Girl Scouting at a school assembly during Girl Scout Week. Each time you give a speech, it gets a little easier. Soon, you are able to add public speaking to your list of skills and abilities.

Your Characteristics

Are you quiet or outgoing? emotional or calm? a quick or slow decision-maker? Do you prefer to work alone or with a group? Your characteristics affect your career choice. A person who prefers to work alone might choose a job as a computer software designer or a truck driver rather than a police officer or a stockbroker. An air traffic controller needs to be a quick decision-maker. A counselor should be calm and reassuring. Just like your skills and abilities, your characteristics can change as you grow older.

My Skills and Abilities

_____
_____
_____
_____
_____
_____
_____
_____
_____
_____
_____
_____

Skills and Abilities I Wish I Had

_____
_____
_____
_____
_____
_____
_____
_____
_____
_____
_____
_____
_____
_____
_____

(What can you do to help your wishes come true?)

My Characteristics

_____
_____
_____
_____
_____
_____

Think of women you admire. What characteristics do they have that you would like to have?

Characteristics I Would Like to Have

_____
_____
_____
_____
_____
_____

Values

Read about values on pages 48–52. List those values that might influence your choice of career. Write them here.

_____
_____
_____
_____
_____

110

111

▲ **Exploring Careers:** This section encourages girls to reflect on their values, interests, characteristics, and abilities, and to imagine themselves in the world of work. Values, interests, and abilities are important components in career planning because they form the basis of career choice. By helping girls understand where their values, interests, and abilities lie, you are helping identify possible career paths.

Help girls recognize the variety of careers that exist and are likely to grow, or direct them to sources of career information. Encourage girls to keep their career goals open. Because predictions point to information and technology as an expanding field, encourage girls to take courses in math and science.

▲ Stimulate girls' imaginations by asking them to think about how the home and work environments of the future will differ from those of today. How will television, personal computers, and other forms of technology change their lives?

▲ Girls can envision jobs that may not exist today. Have girls think about how different a current job would be 20 years from now. (For example, girls might consider the role of technology in the fields of law enforcement, teaching, and farming.)

▲ Many jobs of tomorrow involve science and technology. Have girls investigate how companies in your communities are using new technologies. If possible, plan a field trip and help girls plan interviews with different workers. Girls could ask about the skills and education these people needed to get these jobs, and the skills and education they will need to further their careers. Girls can also ask the workers about how young people could prepare for careers in the field.

▲ Help girls learn about job families, i.e., jobs that revolve around a single career field. For example, a career field could be working with children. This job family might include: day-care center manager, teacher, school psychologist, children's book author, family therapist, dance instructor, toy designer, orthodontist, children's museum director, speech therapist, school bus driver, and children's librarian. Girls can interview people who have these jobs and find out about each job's benefits and drawbacks.

▲ *Girl Scout Badges and Signs:* Business-Wise badge

▲ *Junior Girl Scout Activity Book:* Chapter One

▲ *Junior Girl Scout Handbook:* Careers badge

For example, if one of your values is to be close to your family, you may not want a job that involves a lot of traveling. If you value independence or adventure, you may look for a job as a salesperson or consultant in which you'd travel a lot.

Your Interests

Lots of times your interests flow from your skills and abilities, your values, and your characteristics. A person who enjoys playing soccer may be athletic. A person who belongs to a choir may be a good singer. A person who goes white-water rafting may value adventure. Your interests may also reflect things you would like to do better. You might not be the greatest athlete, but you love to do things in a group and you love being outdoors, so you joined the after-school soccer league. Your interests should be things you enjoy doing.

Sometimes, you might feel pressured to go along with your friends' interests, even though you'd prefer to do something else. Read "Jamela the Future Scientist." Has this ever happened to you?

What would you tell Jamela? How can you finish her story? Why do other people make it hard for you to do what you want? What are some of the different things Jamela can do or say? Act them out; then, in your troop or group, vote on the best responses.

You might hear that girls can't have certain interests–like doing carpentry or playing football. Or you may be told that the most popular kids aren't on the swimming team, they're on the basketball team. It is hard, sometimes, to follow your own interests without pressure from others. But, you are a

unique and special person. And while you may share some interests with friends, you should feel good about doing things without friends' approval.

You might still hear people saying that some jobs are only for men and other jobs only for women. Some people are very old-fashioned! Women are doing lots of jobs today and will continue to be an important part of the workforce. Some jobs, such as secretary, teacher, or bank teller have traditionally been women's jobs. It is great if you want to be a bank teller. But, if you want to be a certified public accountant or bank examiner, you should not become a bank teller because

you believe only men can be bankers or accountants.

It is wrong to be discouraged from taking math courses because of the myth that girls don't do well in math. That's simply not true! Girls are great at math, science, and computers! It is important to believe this because jobs that require strong backgrounds in math, science, or

 Why not look in the classified advertisements of a newspaper or phone the professional associations or some businesses and find out how much a person makes who has one of these jobs? Compare these salaries with some of the more traditional "female" jobs. Is this fair?

computers almost always pay more than jobs that don't require that knowledge. Here is a list of some jobs that require college math or science courses.

- Accountant
- Economist
- Psychologist
- Statistician
- Computer Software Designer
- Architect
- Stock Broker

- Recycling Coordinator
- Physician
- Pilot
- Buyer
- Actuary
- Park Ranger
- Engineer

Jamela the Future Scientist

Tips

▲ **Your Interests:** As you get to know the girls in your troop or group and learn about their interests and personalities, you will be better able to support girls' pursuits.

You will notice that Junior Girl Scouts are often influenced by their peers. As a result, girls' interests change quickly and often reflect the interests of their current group of friends. Although this behavior is quite typical of girls this age, it is still important to continue to encourage girls to develop individual interests.

Supporting Activities

▲ Have girls create a troop or group mural that reflects their interests, skills, characteristics, and abilities.

▲ Hold a "Hobby Showdown." Have girls share their interests with the troop or group. For example, if a girl enjoys writing, she may want to read aloud a poem or story she has written.

Program Links

▲ *Girl Scout Badges and Signs:* "Collecting" Hobbies badge; "Doing" Hobbies badge; "Making" Hobbies badge; Sports badge; Sports Sampler badge

▲ *Junior Girl Scout Activity Book:* Chapters One and Seven

Tips

▲ **Jamela the Future Scientist:** This cartoon illustrates the dilemma of Jamela. She wants to pursue her interest but wants to conform and be popular as well. It also illustrates that girls are sometimes ridiculed for having an interest in science. You can use the cartoon to open a discussion about several topics including peer pressure, conformity, ridicule, and stereotyping.

Supporting Activities

▲ Ask girls to role-play the scenes with Jamela and the girls, and with Jamela and Dawn at the Science Club meeting with the boys. Girls in the troop or group can then give suggestions to Jamela and Dawn about how to handle this dilemma.

▲ Suggest that one group of girls role-play the situation from the boys' point of view, another group from the girls' point of view, and a third group from Jamela's point of view. Ask girls to think of ways they can challenge biased attitudes.

▲ After role-playing, encourage girls to share any similar experiences they may have had.

Program Links

▲ *Girl Scout Badges and Signs:* Creative Solutions badge; My Self-Esteem badge

▲ *Junior Girl Scout Activity Book:* Chapters Seven and Eight

Dorthea Brown:*

Expert Systems Specialist

Dorthea Brown is one woman combining a career in technology with the responsibilities of a family. She works as a specialist in expert systems–a kind of computer programming that copies how an expert makes decisions and solves problems.

As an expert systems specialist, Dorthea looks for tools to help people do their work better. A computer is programmed to copy the decision-making process of an expert. That helps people in a company do their job better because they can tap into the knowledge of experts who may not always be available.

Dorthea recommends that all students get a broad exposure to the sciences. She encourages taking courses in chemistry, biology, physics, and basic math even though their usefulness may not be clear at first. Dorthea offers these suggestions: "Take risks in subjects–don't just stick with what you already do well. Challenge yourself, and study things you can learn from."

After the birth of her son, T.J., Dorthea and her husband, Thomas, had to make some tough decisions about careers and family responsibilities. Some people choose day care or family providers, but the Browns felt that one of them should be home during the day with their son. So, for the time being, Thomas has put his career on hold and stays home with T.J., while Dorthea pursues her career. The Browns are fortunate that they can afford to live on one salary. Dorthea feels that her husband's support has been critical to her success. If Dorthea and Thomas decide to change roles, they will work together to do what is best for their family.

In the future, more women will be involved in the fields of science and technology, a growing job market because so much is changing. To be part of this change, seek out classes in science, computers, and math. Look for experiences that give you a taste of what science and technology are all about, like earning Girl Scout badges in the World of Today and Tomorrow, visiting science museums, and volunteering in places that can give you practical experience.

 Interview someone in the field of science and technology, such as a computer salesperson, a researcher, a futurist (someone who studies the future and makes predictions based upon current trends), a science reporter, or a telephone company employee. Find out what changes they are predicting for the next five years, ten years, twenty years.

 Find out about a career you might like to have. Find out about education, special training, and salary (beginning and after ten years). What clothes, tools, or equipment are used in this career? To what other careers does this career lead? If you and the other girls in your troop or group find out about different careers, think of ways to share or use this information

* Dorthea Brown is not a real person, but her story describes one kind of a choice a woman might make.

114

Your Goals

What are some of your goals? You might have a short-term goal–I want to finish my homework before 8 p.m.. You might have a long-term goal– I want to practice my violin so I can enter a special music high school. You need to think about your lifetime goals when you are thinking about a career. How can you combine a career and family life? Is it important to earn a lot of money? Some jobs pay more than others. Think about the kind of life you would like to have. Would you rather live in a city or in the country? Forestry might be a good field for someone who loves the country, and oceanography might be perfect for someone who loves the sea. Your goals may change as you get older and you may switch careers more than once during your lifetime.

Use this chart to help plan personal or troop or group goals.

Goal: _____

Steps to Reach This Goal:

1._____

2._____

3._____

Planned Date of Completion for Each Step:

1._____

2._____

3._____

People Who Can Help Me: _____

_____

I Will Reach This Goal by: _____

(date)

If you did not reach your goal by the date set, think about the following:

•Was my goal too hard for me to reach now? Do I need to spend more time on it?

•Do I need the help of others to reach this goal?

•Should I choose different steps that will help me?

•Am I still interested in this goal–or have my goals changed?

_____
_____
_____
_____
_____
_____
_____

Your Future

Here's some space to record your thoughts and dreams for the future. You might want to save this page and look back at it when you are older.

115

Tips	Tips	Supporting Activities	Program Links

▲ **Dorthea Brown:** This fictional account of Dorthea Brown illustrates some important issues for girls: combining work and family, pursuing a career in a traditionally male-dominated field, and the relevancy of math and science in today's job market. Help girls recognize that the choice made by Dorthea Brown is only one of many possible choices—all of which have benefits and drawbacks.

It is also possible that a girl in your troop or group might feel guilty that a parent or guardian has to manage many responsibilities. In this case, help the girl recognize that decisions that parents or guardians make often reflect factors beyond a child's scope (e.g., personal finances, rising cost of living, job market).

▲ **Your Goals:** Setting and accomplishing goals has many benefits. Not only is the task completed, but there is satisfaction in having reached a goal. Accomplishments foster a sense of self-worth and confidence in one's own abilities. In working towards a goal, girls can recognize their talents, strengths, and weaknesses.

Throughout Girl Scout program, opportunities exist for you to help girls set realistic goals. Allow girls to set their own goals and to progress at their own pace. If it appears that a girl is underestimating her potential, help her to set more challenging goals that you feel lie within her capabilities. Be careful, though, not to push girls to a level that is not attainable. This might "set them up for failure." If a girl resists your suggestions, allow her to pursue the goals that she feels are appropriate.

▲ Have girls draw pictures about their future. Challenge them by asking where they see themselves in 10 years? 20 years? Their pictures could be about careers, families, homes, animals, cars, or whatever they feel is important. Encourage girls to share their drawings or mount a display.

▲ *Girl Scout Badges and Signs:* Making Decisions badge; Women Today badge

▲ *Junior Girl Scout Activity Book:* Chapters One, Five, and Eight

▲ *Junior Girl Scout Handbook:* Discovering Technology badge; Leadership badge

Doing Your Best in School

Staying in school is one of the most important things you can do to reach your goals, but school does much more than prepare you for a career. School is a place where you learn to get along with different people. It gives you opportunities to win and lose, be a leader and a follower, try new experiences, and discover what you like and dislike.

School prepares you to be an adult. Skills such as writing a report or studying for a test will help you as a grown-up as you will need to read, write, and study information in your job or career. Your math and reading skills will help you find out which car gets the best gas mileage or which air conditioner uses the least electricity.

 ## Work and Study Habits

Some people get good marks very easily; others may have to work hard to get good grades. And wherever you fall in that range, you can feel good about schoolwork when you know you are doing your personal best. Here are some pointers to help you do your best.

 ## At School

If you find your schoolwork getting a bit rough, you can:

✔ Ask the teacher for extra help.
✔ Ask for a tutor.
✔ Set up a study group with your classmates or other friends. Compare and review each other's notes. A Girl Scout troop can be wonderful help in this way!

Don't be afraid to ask questions, especially when you don't understand something! Don't worry about what others might think–chances are they don't understand it either. The only silly question is the one that never gets asked!

Don't be afraid to make a mistake. School is a great place to learn from your mistakes.

At Home

Use a large wall or desk calendar to help track assignments, especially reports and tests. This will help you pace yourself and remind you to do some work each day. Use stickers to mark special days or days when assignments are due.

Perhaps one of the most important things you can do is develop a winning attitude. You may not be on the very top, but you should try to do your personal best. Knowing you've tried can really boost your self-esteem.

Managing Time

You will always have to make decisions about how to spend your time. Time management, like stress management and money management, is a skill you can learn. To manage time wisely you need to think about priorities (the things that are most important to you).

Make a list of all the things you did this week. What did you do at school? at home? Did you play sports? Spend time with friends? Make your list as complete as possible.

Now, examine your list and:

✔ Put an X next to all those things you had no choice about doing. For example, you had to sleep and get dressed.
✔ Put an H next to those things that made you feel happy or calm.
✔ Put an F next to those things that made you feel close to your family.
✔ Put a B next to those things that exercised your body.

Look over the list now. Circle those things you could spend less time doing.

What pattern can you see from your list? What kinds of activities are you doing the most? Are your activities balanced? What would you want to do more often? less often? Compare your list with other girls in your Girl Scout troop or group. How could a list like this (with different categories) be useful for planning Girl Scout meeting activities?

 Make a list of what you need to get done. Your list could be for an evening, a day, or a week. Once you have the list written, put a * next to those things that are most important. Do those things first. As you finish each thing on your list, cross it off. You'll feel good when you see how much you have accomplished.

Procrastination
—putting off doing what you have to do–is a bad habit many people share. For example, on Monday you learn that you have a social studies test on Thursday. That means you have to study your notes and read four chapters in your textbook. But, Thursday seems a long time away, so on Monday evening you chat on the phone with your girlfriend for an hour and watch television until 10:00 p.m. On Tuesday, your mom asks you to watch your younger brother after school. You feel you need a reward after doing that for three hours (he wasn't still for a second!), so once your mom gets home you go to your girlfriend's house to listen to music and practice some dance moves. Now it's Wednesday and the test is tomorrow. No more procrastinating! The problem is now you feel stressed because you have so much studying to do. What would have been a better way to prepare for the test?

There are lots of ways to manage time:

• You could have broken the work into sections and studied a little bit each day.

• You could have divided the work in half and studied Tuesday and Wednesday.

• You could have studied your notes while on the bus or standing on line somewhere.

▲ **Doing Your Best in School:**
Education that takes place in the classroom is paramount to a girl's success. Not only does she learn traditional subjects such as math, reading, and science at school, but she gains indispensable social skills. Girls learn to resolve conflicts, work as members of a team, make compromises, develop self-discipline, and respect others.

As a leader, you can stress the importance of education as it relates to careers. Girls need to know that the current workplace is highly competitive and that solid skills can help girls get the jobs they want.

Though some girls will excel more easily than others in academic areas, Girl Scouting is a place where success is not linked to academic achievement. Encourage girls to talk with their teachers about what they do in Girl Scouting. There may be opportunities for girls to earn "extra credit."

Girls at this age may comment that they "hate" school or dislike a particular teacher. You can help them deal with these negative feelings through troop or group activities. If you sense a deeper problem, engage the girl in a private discussion or contact her parent or guardian.

▲ **Managing Time:** Managing time is an ongoing life skill. How often have you said to yourself, "Oh, I wish there were eight days in the week!" or "If I only had another hour or two, then I could relax!" Many of the girls in your troop or group have similar feelings. In addition to schoolwork, girls might play on a sports team, attend religious instruction, take music or dance lessons, and socialize with relatives and friends.

Your troop or group meeting is an ideal environment for girls to learn time management. Have girls be aware of the meeting schedule so they know when it's time to clean up or finish their activities. Be flexible with scheduling parts of the meeting but encourage girls to see the importance of arriving or ending on time so as not to inconvenience other troop members.

▲ Have girls keep "To Do" lists for a week, then share, at the next meeting, the extent to which they accomplished their tasks. Ask girls how they managed to complete or why they did not complete the tasks on the list.

▲ Have girls debate the pros and cons of the following statements:

1. Staying in school is cool.

2. Only boys are good at math and science.

3. Teachers try to make things hard.

4. Homework is fun and challenging.

Program Links

▲ *Girl Scout Badges and Signs:* Health and Fitness badge; Healthy Relationships badge

▲ *Junior Girl Scout Activity Book:* Chapter Eight

▲ *Junior Girl Scout Handbook:* Girls Are Great badge; Healthy Living badge

Being Media Wise

Look back at your time management list. How much time was spent watching television? playing video games? watching movies? watching music videos? reading magazines or newspapers? Television, newspapers, and magazines are called media—sources of news and information.

Media Influences

No matter how much or how little you watch television or read magazines, you are influenced by media. Think of what you know about a major city. Besides the information in textbooks, your knowledge and opinions will be affected by what you see on the nightly news and by what you hear on the radio or read in a newspaper. Maybe you hear mostly about crime in that city or maybe you read about its money troubles. You might discover, though, that if you visit that city, it is very different from the way it has been shown in the media.

So much happens in any one day and the media can only report on a small amount of all that happens. What appears on the nightly news or on the front page of the newspaper is chosen by an editor or a group of editors or producers. By choosing one story or another, these people are influencing what you will know—and won't know. Also, the different

types of media are competitive. Everyone wants to be first with an exciting story. After it appears, other media will repeat the same story, perhaps adding information.

Besides wanting to give you information, the owners of newspapers and magazines want to sell more newspapers and magazines and the owners of television stations want you to watch their news programs. So you might see or read stories that are run more to get your attention than to give you information. Which story do you think a newspaper would put on its front page? A story about a T.V. star being hospitalized or a story that reprints a senator's speech to a local business group? The senator's speech could contain very important information on the local economy, new taxes, or new

jobs which the community needs to know, but often, the story about the T.V. star, a less important story, would be placed first.

 If you can get a copy of two or more newspapers printed on the same day, choose one story printed in both and compare. Where does the story appear? the front page? page 12? in a different section? How long is the story? Is the information the same? What is the tone—the overall impression—of the story? positive, negative, neutral, anxious, upbeat?

 Watch two news shows shown on television at the same time. Flip back and forth between the shows. Keep a log of what stories are reported, how much time is given to the story, who reports the story (the main newscaster or a reporter), and what differs in the report. Compare your log with other girls in your Girl Scout troop or group.

Television

In some families, the television is on most of the day. Other families may not own a television. If you watch television (and chances are you do since the average viewing time for an American family is about seven hours a day), you and your family have the power to choose what shows you will watch. Television shows can excite your imagination, give you new solutions to problems, teach you a new skill, or can bore you, have unbelievable characters, or contain a lot of violence. How do you decide which shows to watch?

 With your family or in your troop or group, create guidelines for television viewing. You could also develop similar guidelines for video games. Here are some points to consider:

- How much television can be watched on school nights and how much on the weekends?
- Do real people behave the way characters on the show behave? How does the behavior differ?
- Does the show contain violence? If it does, how does it fit into the story? Is it unnecessary?
- Does the show contain sexual situations? Does your family have rules about your watching these shows?
- Add your own ideas to the list.

118

119

Tips

▲ **Being Media Wise:** The media include such print and electronic forms of communication as newspapers, magazines, television, music videos, video games, and movies. Some girls may spend more time on media-related activities than others. Media can influence girls' opinions and values.

While some girls may find violence in the media distasteful, others may view it as characteristic of their home and school environments. Acknowledge that the media sometimes try to capitalize on violence as a way to increase viewership. Help girls understand that negotiation, cooperation, and compromise are more productive methods for resolving conflicts. See Chapter Two in the handbook for information on conflict resolution. (If you suspect family violence affects any girl in your troop or group, contact your council office for guidance.)

While many media messages are positive, some can be negative, especially those that degrade women, promote violence, or show stereotypes. You can counteract negative messages by encouraging girls to do the activities on these pages and those in handbook Chapters Two and Five. Be aware of what girls are reading, watching, and talking about and point out the importance of being "media wise."

Supporting Activities

▲ Have girls design and write their own newspaper, the "Troop Tribune," that details activities, events, ideas, and upcoming adventures. Girls can include stories, an advice column, artwork, photography, or other ideas. Girls can distribute the newspaper to other Girl Scout troops or groups, or to individuals at your Girl Scout council office.

▲ Girls can record how much time they spend watching TV. If they want to cut down, they can make a schedule and substitute more "active" things to do. Chapter Seven can provide ideas for activities.

▲ Girls can watch TV critically and chart the number of unrealistic things they view in one night.

▲ Girls can plan a family night that does not involve watching TV. They can decide to: read aloud, share family stories, play board games, listen to music, plan activities for the holidays, learn a new sport, or create something for their homes.

▲ Since advertising is often done through the media, help girls learn about consumer power. Discuss how girls can make choices that are healthy for the environment. Girls can think about pre-cycling (not buying products that use excess packaging) and look for the recycling symbol when they buy a product.

(The section on media continues on the next page.)

Try creating a Smart Music-Video Viewing Guide for you and your friends. Create your own awards or seal of approval for videos that meet your standards. What standards can you set? (A standard is a rule or model.) One standard could be not to allow violence. Other standards could be to limit bad language or to allow only positive portrayals of women and girls.

Advertisements

The media is also the means by which advertisers tell you about their products. Think about what makes you buy products, like clothes or CDs or tapes. You probably make buying decisions based on advertisements. Even if you feel you do not pay much attention to commercials or ads, they do surround you with jingles (songs in a commercial) and phrases that stick in your head: "Buy 'Hair So Beautiful' Shampoo—the One for a New and Exciting You."

Skills Log

Learning everyday skills such as doing repairs, setting career goals, and managing money can be a challenge. Which everyday skills did you enjoy learning most? Why not pick out five or six skills you've learned and include them in a "Skills Log."

Skills I've Learned	How I Did It
1. How to open a bank account	Read the section on managing money. Went to the bank with my Girl Scout leader. Talked to a bank officer. She helped me deposit money.
2. How to repot a plant	Watched and helped Uncle Charlie do gardening. Decided to work on "Plants and Animals" badge. Shared with my troop my observations about how plants grow; also showed everyone how to repot a plant.

Use this sample to create your own Skills Log. Why do you think it's important to learn new skills?

120

 Close your eyes for a moment. What advertisement pops into your head? Why do you remember it? How does this advertisement try to persuade you? In your troop or group, gather in small groups or pairs and pick an advertisement or commercial to analyze (study carefully). Think of three ways the advertisement is persuasive. Are there attractive people in the advertisement? Does the advertisement promise something new? What are some other messages the advertisement is sending? Pick one person in your group or pair to explain to the others what you discovered.

Advertisers try to convince you that a product is safe for the environment, good for your health, or fun to use, eat, or drink. They would like you to believe that you will be more popular, attractive, successful, happy, or rich if you buy the product. Unfortunately, it is a very unusual product that can do all those things! While advertising can be helpful when you are making buying decisions, you also have to think carefully about what the product can really do.

EVERYONE IS DIFFERENT
CHAPTER 5

SHAWN KRISTIN BETH ANNE
BERNADETTE ROBERTO YVONNE
ANDREA LIN DEBBIE MAILE

Prejudice-Busting
page 125

National Forum on Kids and Prejudice
page 122

Becoming a Critical Thinker
page 125

What Can You Do to Stop Stereotyping?
page 126

G I R L

Imagine if everyone looked the same, ate the same food, and had the same interests. Life would be pretty boring, wouldn't it? This chapter will be about differences in people—celebrating all groups and dealing with problems that come up when people don't respect each other. Do you have any ideas for helping people get along? If you do, start writing them down to use in some of the activities ahead.

121

Everyone Is Different

HANDBOOK CHAPTER 5

Program Links

▲ *Caring and Coping: Facing Family Crises* Contemporary Issues booklet

▲ *Girl Scout Badges and Signs:* Creative Solutions badge; Video Production badge; Visual Arts badge

▲ *Junior Girl Scout Activity Book:* Chapter Eight

▲ *Junior Girl Scout Handbook:* Consumer Power badge

REMINDER!

Research has shown that many girls experience a significant drop in their self-esteem during their pre-teen years. Girl Scout activities are designed to boost girls' self-worth by helping them tackle challenges, reach goals, and feel accepted and valued. Look for ways you can help girls feel great about their accomplishments.

Tips

▲ **Chapter 5: Everyone Is Different:** This chapter helps girls explore issues of identity, prejudice, discrimination, and stereotyping. Before working on the activities in this chapter, you might want to read *Valuing Differences: Promoting Pluralism* Contemporary Issues booklet. The information on how children develop prejudices and how prejudice can be counteracted will be helpful in your discussions with girls. Another helpful resource is *Promoting Positive Pluralistic Attitudes Among Girls*, a Council Service Publication, available through your Girl Scout council office.

Notes

National Forum on Kids and Prejudice

Imagine being chosen to attend a meeting of kids from across the United States interested in helping people get along better. Let's meet the participants at an imaginary National Forum on Kids and Prejudice. Find out how they tried to make a difference.

The whole group is meeting for the first time. Yvonne and Bernadette had been chosen as coordinators and had met the day before to do some planning. Everyone in the group was interested in helping people get along better, but no one was sure where to start.

YVONNE: Since I picked the card that said Facilitator, I guess I'll start facilitating…

SHAWN: Let's set some rules, first.

YVONNE: Like no interrupting! But, that's a good idea. We already thought about how to do this. Bernadette, you brought your notes with you?

BERNADETTE: I have them right here. Welcome everybody to our first National Forum on Kids and Prejudice. Some of you may feel uncomfortable talking about this subject, so we thought we should all discuss setting some ground rules—and everyone has to agree to them. No exceptions, right?

ROBERTO: She's tough!

ANDREA: What are you saying—girls can't be tough??? Maybe we have our first stereotype. And we haven't even been here a minute!!

ROBERTO: I was joking, okay?

LIN: That's part of the problem: jokes that make fun of people because of their race or because of anything—age, gender, abilities.

BERNADETTE: We're not saying you can't have a sense of humor; lots of times that helps a tense situation. But, ethnic jokes are wrong. Any joke that puts people down is not funny. Anyway, let's go over our rules. We're here to make a plan to fight prejudice—starting with ourselves and then working in our communities. We're hoping to leave with some practical steps we can all take. But, because we're starting with us—what's inside—we thought it was important that what we say in this room stays in this room. No going back and telling your crowd at school what so and so said at the forum. Everyone agree?

MAILE: That's really important. We have to trust each other enough to be able to share our feelings—and that's hard enough to do without thinking someone's going to be telling the whole world afterwards.

BERNADETTE: Great. Any problems? Okay, the next ground rule should be obvious: No name-calling, no disrespect, and no laughing at what other people say. What each person says is important, so give each other the chance to speak. And really listen to each other, too.

DEBBIE: Okay, where do you want to start?

KRISTIN: I'll start. In my neighborhood, well, I don't see many kids who are different from me. I mean, even at school—and the ones I do see always hang together. I don't think they really want to be friends with anyone else.

YVONNE: How do you know if you don't ask?

KRISTIN: But, I feel uncomfortable. I think people like to be with people who are like them—have something in common—including race.

ANDREA: That was what I was always taught by my parents and teachers—all people are basically the same. You know, it's a small world sort of thing. And, well, isn't that the way to stop people from hating each other—by talking about how people are really the same?

YVONNE: At the same time, when people emphasize the similarities, what happens to the differences?

ROBERTO: It's an easy way to ignore them!

YVONNE: Right! And how can we respect what makes people different and unique if we ignore those very things?

KRISTIN: Yeah, but, I still want to know how you can expect to value someone's differences if she doesn't want to hang around with you?

BETH ANNE: Well, no one is saying you have to like everybody. There are annoying people of all races—but, it's more of a respect thing.

DEBBIE: And taking the time to break down some stereotypes and find out what the person is really like—at the very least, not thinking that just because she is Asian, she is very smart. I get that stereotype all the time from my teachers and it is very hard. They expect me to be brilliant. And when I'm average, I almost think they're so disappointed because I don't match their expectations that I get even lower grades from them!

SHAWN: Wow—you know, I think I always kind of thought that too. And I'm embarrassed because I really know how it feels when people look at you and expect you to behave in a certain way. I'm sorry, Debbie.

DEBBIE: You're forgiven. But, I think it's harder when you're so visibly different. And, not only racially different. There's a girl in my apartment building. She's blind and has a guide dog, you know, and I always feel uncomfortable if she's leaving the building the same time as me—like, should I help her down the stairs? I open the door and then I start mumbling stuff.

YVONNE: I guess you should just ask her if she needs help and let her tell you.

BERNADETTE: Exactly! But, why do people feel so uncomfortable?

KRISTIN: Well, I think if I start by just talking to one person—one on one—maybe someone I sit next to in class or in band with me—and take it from there.

BEN: I don't know. I'm Jewish but people don't know that when they look at me. So the thing I find hard is when people start telling Jewish jokes in front of me. Then what do I do? Sometimes, I tell people, hey, I'm Jewish and then everyone gets really embarrassed and uncomfortable. And sometimes it's people I really want to get to know better and then I think I've put up a barrier. And so sometimes I just listen—but then I get so angry at myself.

BERNADETTE: You should never just listen. You have to speak up!

MAILE: That might be easy for you, Bernadette, but for some of us, it's not so easy.

LIN: You can let someone know his joke isn't funny—"Hey, putting people down isn't very funny," or "Let's be positive. Making fun of other people doesn't make me feel good."

▲ **National Forum on Kids and Prejudice:** This forum was developed to help girls see many of the ways prejudice develops and how it can be counteracted. Be certain to emphasize the following points:

● Ethnic jokes are wrong.

● Some people feel uncomfortable with those who are different.

● Getting to know people as individuals helps break down stereotypes.

● Some differences are very visible while others are less noticeable.

● Feeling pride in one's own heritage does not mean one is prejudiced.

● Diversity within groups should be recognized.

● People working together towards a common goal help reduce prejudice.

For more discussion ideas, see the questions at the end of the forum in the handbook. These questions are posed to help girls think about what they can do to fight prejudice.

If it seems like your community does not have people of different cultures and ethnic backgrounds, take a closer look. Many communities are becoming more multicultural and diverse. It is important for girls to recognize the strength in diversity. At school, at clubs or community organizations, and eventually at their workplaces, girls will be more comfortable and successful if they can understand differing points of view and help people work together.

Note: Planning a multicultural event in which everyone prepares food, sings songs, and does crafts projects from different countries may be fun in itself, but it is not a way to help reduce prejudice or really learn about other cultures. If the troop or group really wants to explore diversity and multiculturalism, invite people who have knowledge about or have spent time in other cultures. Perhaps you can ask someone who has emigrated from another country to share her or his experiences. These are ways to learn about global diversity.

▲ A service project that benefits a neighborhood or community is one type of cooperative effort Girl Scouts can participate in. Working together towards a common goal is one way that different ethnic, racial, cultural, and religious groups learn to respect each other's differences and strengths.

▲ Girls can explore their own heritages by researching their families' country of origin and finding out about traditions, folktales, family names, and ceremonies.

▲ Encourage girls to look for a role model who shares their race or ethnicity and find out about her accomplishments and strengths. Girls could also look at groups of famous people, such as athletes, musicians, authors, actors, and politicians, to find role models.

(The section on prejudice continues on the next page.)

ROBERTO: I think you have to feel comfortable about yourself—who you are—respect your own background—feel pride in it. Then it's easier to speak up.

YVONNE: My grandmother has told me stories since I was a baby about women in my family who were really strong. And I've read a couple of books. One was on queens and princesses in different African empires and another was on African-American women. Listening to my grandmother and reading those stories made me feel great inside. So, if I hear put-downs, I try hard to remember my great-great grandmother who supported her family with her own farm and managed to send two of her sons to college.

BETH ANNE: But some of us don't really identify with a particular group. My family is all mixed up, so I don't really think of myself as belonging to an ethnic group. If anyone asks me who I am, I say I'm a Southerner.

ANDREA: And really, though I have an Italian name and all, my Mom makes hamburgers more often than lasagna. And I hate when other kids think my father must be in the Mafia!

ROBERTO: That's why it's important not to stereotype people. Go back to what Debbie said. Don't expect

people to act a certain way because of how they look. Like, my grandmother gets so furious when she sees older people on TV shows or in commercials shown as being helpless. She runs her own graphic design company—and she's 78!

ANDREA: And don't think someone is poor or homeless because she is lazy. There are lots of reasons for poverty or homelessness, and they're complicated.

YVONNE: So, what are the important things that we are all saying here?

ANDREA: Respect the differences among us, but also celebrate what we all have in common—like, having the freedom to even hold a forum like this one. A lot of countries don't have our freedom of speech!

LIN: Respect your own heritage. Learn more about it. And respect yourself. Feel proud of who you are—your strengths and your talents.

SHAWN: And no put-downs. Ethnic jokes aren't funny.

KRISTIN: And look beyond the stereotypes that you might learn from TV or books and magazines—or even from adults. Try to see the person inside.

BETH ANNE: And make an effort. You have to work on your own attitudes—and then work on the attitudes of

others. Reach out to people.

DEBBIE: And have the courage to get beyond feeling self-conscious and make friends with people who are different. Learn more about them.

ROBERTO: Like in sports, or in debating groups, school and community clubs. Find places where different people can work together.

BERNADETTE: Like making the neighborhood better!

BEN: Exactly.

YVONNE: And when you start in your neighborhoods—well, then, you are making the world better, too. And that's a powerful feeling!

In your troop or group, discuss:

- **What ground rules did the group set? Why was this important?**

- **What problem did Kristin mention? What solution did the group develop?**

- **What advice did Lin have for dealing with put-down jokes?**

- **What were some steps the group thought would help fight prejudice?**

- **What can you do as an individual? as part of a community group?**

Prejudice & Discrimination

Prejudice means having a negative **feeling** or opinion about someone simply because of her race, ethnic background, religion, ability, or other difference. Sometimes, television, movies, and books show certain groups in an unfair way. People see these stereotypes over and over, and begin to believe them. Sometimes, people hear ethnic jokes (making fun of particular groups) or other negative remarks from their families or friends. It is hard sometimes to really keep an open mind; it is even harder to speak out or stand up for yourself or others.

Discrimination is the **action** of excluding people or treating them badly because they are seen as different. An individual, a group, an institution, or a government can practice discrimination. For example, suppose a landlord has an empty apartment he wants to rent. You call and make an appointment to go and see it. When you get there, the landlord decides that he doesn't want to rent you the apartment because of your racial, ethnic, or cultural background, or he thinks you are too old, or he thinks your disability will be a problem. So, he lies to you: "Sorry, too late, I just rented the apartment." That's discrimination. Have you ever felt discriminated against? If you haven't, can you imagine how you would feel if you really wanted to rent that apartment, and couldn't because of discrimination?

Prejudice-Busting

Remember what Roberto and Yvonne said? It is important to feel pride in yourself because studies have shown that people who have a lot of self-respect also have a lot of respect for others. Also, you might try becoming a prejudice-fighting activist. When you hear people using put-downs, tell them they are being unfair and that you don't want to listen. Also, find ways

to work with people from other cultures and backgrounds: Kristin mentioned starting small by speaking to the person sitting next to you in class, and Debbie suggested having the courage to make friends with people who are different.

Working together on a project or towards a common goal helps break down stereotypes. Even if your town might not seem to have a lot of people of different cultures and ethnic backgrounds, look around your school and your community. You will be more successful if you are able to understand differing points of view and if you can help people work together.

This week I promise to fight prejudice and discrimination by

_____

_____

Critical Thinking

Critical thinking means questioning things you read, see, and hear. Being able to think critically is a good skill to learn.

When you think critically you might question images, words, or other messages in the media. For example, if you used critical thinking while watching an old "western" television show and saw American Indians always shown as villains, never heroes, you might ask yourself if this is an accurate picture of American Indians. How could you find out? You could go to the library and find recent books that describe the wide variety in American Indian groups. Maybe your library or video store carries documentary videos that depict American Indian culture realistically. Perhaps you can

Handbook Page 124

Handbook Page 125

▲ Girls can learn about famous people who have fought injustice or look for people in the community who are peacemakers. The troop or group can hold a celebration to honor these people.

▲ Have girls create a display for a school or other public space that highlights the community's diversity in the past and present. The display can note benefits the community derives from that diversity.

▲ Girls can find out if their Girl Scout council office can set up an "exchange program" between the troop or group and a Junior Girl Scout troop or group from a different community. Girls can plan activities to do together throughout the year.

▲ Conflict resolution and peer mediation are skills being taught in schools and community organizations. Girls can investigate where these programs are being held and whether they can qualify to be trained as mediators. (See handbook Chapters Two and Three in Part I of this guide for more about conflict-resolution skills.)

▲ Girls can write their own play or create a videotape on the theme of strength in diversity. Encourage girls to share their work with people in your Girl Scout council.

Program Links

▲ *Girl Scout Badges and Signs:* Celebrating People badge; Creative Solutions badge; The World in My Community badge; World Neighbors badge

▲ *Junior Girl Scout Activity Book:* Chapter Three

▲ *Junior Girl Scout Handbook:* You and Your Community badge

▲ *Promoting Positive Pluralistic Attitudes Among Girls*

▲ *Valuing Differences: Promoting Pluralism* Contemporary Issues booklet

Tips

▲ **Critical Thinking:** Junior Girl Scouts spend a great deal of time talking with their friends about such topics as boys, things that happened at school, and music. Though trading information in this way is common and appropriate for girls of this age, it is important to point out that people cannot always believe everything they hear. As a leader, you should stress that sometimes stories become distorted as they travel from person to person. Remind them that this is often how rumors spread.

Critical thinking also applies to things girls see, read, and hear from other sources as well. Point out that girls should use critical thinking skills with media sources (e.g., magazines and television) and people outside their peers (e.g., adults and adolescents they don't know).

Supporting Activities

▲ To show how easily information can get distorted, have girls play "telephone": One girl begins by whispering a sentence to the person to her right. The game continues as each girl whispers what she thinks she heard to the next person. The last girl says the sentence aloud. The girl who started then reveals what she originally said. Are the sentences the same? Use this game to discuss how information gets distorted and rumors start.

Program Links

▲ *Girl Scout Badges and Signs:* Making Decisions badge

▲ *Junior Girl Scout Handbook:* Consumer Power badge

talk to American Indians and learn about their historical perspectives. (To read about being "Media Wise," see pages 118–119.

Remember, everyone is different in her own way. Every group has good people and bad, and people who are heroes.

Stereotypes Are Everywhere

A stereotype is the belief that all the people who belong to a certain group think, act, and look the same. Stereotyping can be found almost anywhere including on television, in magazines, in books, and in the classroom. One of the best ways to put an end to stereotyped thinking is to point it out when you hear it or see it. But, first, you must be able to recognize it and figure out why it is unfair. To help recognize stereotyping, try some of the following activities:

With a group or by yourself, complete the following sentences. Try to be as honest as you can with your answers.

Girls like to _____.

Boys like to _____.

Old people are _____.

People with disabilities are _____.

Rich people like to _____.

Poor people like to _____.

Fat people are _____.

Foreigners are _____.

Kids who get straight As are _____.

People who speak other languages are _____.

Think about your answers. Are they always true? Why or why not? Using the sentences above as a guide, talk about how stereotypes are harmful.

Page through books and magazines, or scan television programs to find stereotypes. An example might be an advertisement for a new computer game that shows a boy thinking about his next move with a girl looking over his shoulder. This may suggest that only boys are good at computer games or that girls don't enjoy working on a computer. Choose an example and show how you would break the stereotype.

Other Kinds of Prejudice and Discrimination

▲ Last night, Mr. Hawkins, the high school assistant principal, awoke in the middle of the night to the smell of smoke. The smoke was coming from the front of his home. He ran to the window and saw a cross burning on his front lawn.

▲ Melissa returned home from school in tears. Her mother gave her a big hug and asked her what was wrong. In a sobbing voice, Melissa told her mother that her friends said she was too fat to try out for the cheerleading squad.

▲ Alicia thought she was being punished. Why else would her teacher, Mr. Stevens, ask her to be science-project partners with Anthony? After all, Alicia was the most popular kid in the class and Anthony—well, Anthony had no friends, wore clothes two sizes too small, and smelled. She knew she would just die if anyone saw her talking to him.

Which of the above shows prejudice and discrimination?

That's right, all of them do. Prejudice doesn't always involve race, religion, or ethnic background. Some people may be prejudiced against others who don't dress like the popular group at school or against people who don't play sports well. Feelings of prejudice can be directed toward people who are homeless or are super-smart or wear hearing aids or use food stamps. Prejudice can be directed against a person's appearance, sexual orientation, class in society, age, or almost any part of the person that makes her different.

Have you ever been hurt by prejudice and discrimination? If so, how did it make you feel? What did you do about it?

Words Can Sometimes Hurt

"Is it okay if I sit here?" Maria asked quietly.

"Ummm, sure," said Allison without looking up.

Maria set her lunch tray down and slid in on the bench next to Kathy. She heard someone giggle at the other end of the table.

"Would anybody like to play baseball after school today?" asked Kathy.

"All right," said Allison. "Hey, Maria, would you like to come?"

Maria quickly looked up. "I would love..." Splat! The pizza slid right off the plate! Maria jumped up. "I'm sorry, Kathy...it was an accident...I didn't mean..."

Kathy started screaming before she could even finish. "Oh, Maria! You're such a jerk! How could you be so stupid? Forget it–you're not playing baseball with us today 'cause you're too big a loser!"

How would you feel if you were Maria? If you were Allison, what would you say to Maria? to Kathy?

Pretend you are sitting at the other end of this lunch table and had just witnessed this whole event. You are friends with both Maria and Kathy and are looking forward to the baseball game after school today. Continue the story telling how you would stop your friends from fighting. Go back to page 57 for tips on conflict-resolution skills.

Name-calling is very hurtful. Not only is it hurtful but it can lead others to form stereotypes. Some people tend to group others into categories because it is easier than really getting to know them. But this is an unfair way of looking at people because you never really get to know the individual.

For example, other kids who don't know Maria and heard what Kathy said may think Maria isn't smart or a good athlete and never ask her to be a part of a school project or sports team. And, if they believe Maria isn't a good athlete or student, they may put her close friends in the same categories. They, too, become "stupid" and "losers."

126

127

▲ **Stereotypes Are Everywhere:** Stereotypes can be damaging and hurtful. Helping girls identify their own biases is a challenging task because, in many instances, they are still formulating their own identities and ideas about the people around them. Furthermore, the media and family can reinforce misperceptions that lead to stereotypes. Therefore, you should always try to foster learning experiences that promote open-mindedness, equality, and critical thinking.

When girls do the You and Your Community badge activity in the left column ("With a group or by yourself...") remind them that although their answers should reflect their honest opinions, they should consider how their troop or group members may feel about a response. Becoming aware of how another person might react toward an attitude or perception about a group also teaches girls about the harm in using stereotypes.

When girls finish the badge activity in the right column ("Page through books and magazines..."), encourage girls to express their thoughts in a letter to the editor to the magazine or to the advertiser. Girls may even want to include their own sketches of how they think the advertisement should look.

Program Links

▲ *Girl Scout Badges and Signs:* The World in My Community badge

▲ *Junior Girl Scout Handbook:* Leadership badge; You and Your Community badge

▲ *Valuing Differences: Promoting Pluralism* Contemporary Issues booklet

Tips

▲ **Other Kinds of Prejudice and Discrimination:** Group discussions during meeting time can often be very productive. If you are discussing the examples under this heading, however, it is possible that a girl may feel uncomfortable revealing personal information about such a sensitive issue. In fact, prejudice is one area in which a girl or someone in her family may have had negative or frightening experiences. If a girl is reluctant to share her thoughts, it is generally advisable not to press her for details. Perhaps a private discussion at the conclusion of the meeting would be more appropriate.

Supporting Activities

▲ Challenge girls to create a public service announcement that sends an "anti-prejudice or anti-hate" message. If possible, videotape their productions and share them with your council office, other troops or groups, or other youth groups in your community.

Program Links

▲ *Girl Scout Badges and Signs:* Celebrating People badge; The World in My Community badge

▲ *Junior Girl Scout Handbook:* You and Your Community badge

▲ *Valuing Differences: Promoting Pluralism* Contemporary Issues booklet

Tips

▲ **Words Can Sometimes Hurt:** Most likely, you have witnessed girls calling each other names. This should not be surprising since television characters and pop singers often employ name-calling. Some girls may even be subjected to name-calling in their own homes.

(The section on name-calling continues on the next page.)

The Generation at the Top: Senior Citizens

"Hey, Miranda, where's Deborah? Is she coming to the movie with us?" asked Darcy.

"I called her to see if she wanted to go but she said she was going to her grandmother's house for dinner," replied Miranda. "I'm not really sure why."

"What d'ya mean?" asked Darcy.

"Well," said Miranda, "how much fun can that be? My grandfather never has much to say and goes to bed really early."

"Hmmm...you're kinda right. Now that I think about it, old people are pretty boring," Darcy said.

Senior citizens are another group of people hurt by stereotypes. Miranda's and Darcy's feelings show what many people have been led to believe about older people. Have you ever taken the time to get to know an older person? What did you discover?

Many older people have a great deal to share. In addition to talents and abilities, many senior citizens are involved in learning new skills and hobbies, earning a college degree, and beginning new careers. Older people are as diverse as young people in their talents, skills, and abilities. Try some of these activities to find out more about senior citizens:

 Invite senior citizens to be speakers, chaperones, and guests at your Girl Scout activities and events.

 Study how older people are portrayed on television programs, in movies, and in books. Are they represented as a diverse group of individuals or do they seem to be of the same type? What changes would you make to break the stereotypes?

 Find out more about the special joys and problems of growing old by talking to relatives or neighbors.

 Ask a senior citizen to share her knowledge of a subject or activity that interests you, such as a foreign language, gardening, art, travel, or local history.

People with Disabilities

Another group of people who have been hurt by stereotypes are people with disabilities. A person with a disability is not able to do certain things. A person who is blind cannot see and someone who is hearing impaired has less than perfect hearing. Although these individuals may have other abilities and talents, some people focus only on what people with disabilities can't do and not what they can do.

Sarah is blind and reads by using Braille, a special type of printing in which raised dots are felt by the fingers. Sarah can sing in a chorus, play games, solve math problems, and do all other things that do not require vision. Nancy uses special crutches to get around. She can write stories on her computer, cook a meal, and play video games with her friends.

Since 1912, many Girl Scouts with and without disabilities have worked together on learning and practicing camping skills, doing service projects, and completing badge requirements. Try some of the following activities:

 Do a survey of your meeting place to find out how accessible it is for people with disabilities. Measure the doorways and bathroom facilities to find out if they are accessible to someone in a wheelchair. Think of ways to get rid of any obstacles.

 Read more about people with disabilities like Ryan White, Stevie Wonder, Amelia Earhart, Agatha Christie, Marlee Matlin, Albert Einstein, or Juliette Gordon Low. Why are they famous?

 Experience the feelings and frustrations of having a disability. Put mittens on your hands or tape your fingers together and try to button your shirt or tie your shoe. Tune in to your favorite television program but turn the volume all the way down. How did you feel when you tried these activities? What reactions did you notice or receive from other people? Did you ask for or require assistance? Share your feelings with other members of your troop or family.

 Find out what services are available for people with disabilities in your neighborhood or community. Invite someone who works with people with disabilities to speak to your troop or group.

 Study the finger-spellling sign language alphabet on the next page. Learn to sign your name and say "hello," "I am a Girl Scout," "please," "thank you," and "goodbye."

Learning to Respect Differences

 Be a heritage investigator! What can you learn about people who share your heritage? Look for someone in your family's past who made a contribution or had qualities that you admire. Look for role models today in your community and beyond. Think of ways you can share what you have discovered with the girls in your troop or group or younger girls.

 Try to discover all you can about the contributions of groups different from your own. Look around your community, county, or state. What can you discover?

 To help stop stereotyping, try creating a "contract" that would make certain behaviors unacceptable. For example, "No ethnic jokes. If I hear an ethnic joke, I'll tell the person to stop." Try to get three people to sign the contract.

You can help girls realize the seriousness of name-calling by never tolerating it in your troop or group. Name-calling is frequently used as a defense against feelings of inferiority or as a way for an individual to be accepted by a particular group. "Name-callers" often act out of anger or frustration due to their own low self-esteem or feelings of insecurity. If you need to intervene when a girl is name-calling, focus on the inappropriate behavior and not the girl herself. For example, you might say: "Name-calling is not acceptable. It hurts people's feelings" instead of saying "You're really insensitive. How could you say something like that?" In this way, you will avoid diminishing her already poor self-image.

Supporting Activities

▲ Have girls discuss the effects of name-calling by asking someone to share a name that she would find the most hurtful or offensive. Ask her to explain why it's offensive. Girls can talk about how they would react if someone called them this name.

Program Links

▲ *Girl Scout Badges and Signs:* Celebrating People badge; The World in My Community badge

▲ *Junior Girl Scout Handbook:* You and Your Community badge

▲ *Valuing Differences: Promoting Pluralism* Contemporary Issues booklet

Tips

▲ **The Generation at the Top:** Due to medical advances and increasing attention to healthy living, the average life expectancy increases each year. As senior citizens make up a greater percentage of the population, they may play a significant role in delivering the Girl Scout program. Many senior citizens are Girl Scout leaders or assistant leaders. Because many older people are retired, they may have more time to devote to Girl Scout activities.

When senior citizens work with Girl Scouts, girls gain ideas, insights, and perspectives from individuals with a lifetime of experience. And, the older person gets an opportunity to share a young person's perspectives as well as stay active and involved in the community. Your council office, senior citizen organizations, or religious groups can help you locate older people interested in volunteering.

Program Links

▲ *Girl Scout Badges and Signs:* Across Generations badge

▲ *Junior Girl Scout Handbook:* You and Your Community badge

Tips

▲ **People with Disabilities**: Keep in mind that some disabilities are visible and some are not. Girls can learn that even though a disability cannot be "seen," they may have to consider the girl with the disability in planning activities. For example, if a girl with a learning disability is disruptive, girls may become angry with her. Help girls understand the source of the girl's frustration.

If your troop or group includes a girl with a disability, be sensitive to her capabilities and help her choose appropriate activities. At the same time, however, help her to feel challenged.

(The section on disabilities continues on the next page.)

Plan a "Prejudice-Free Day" in your community or school. Look at the action-plan steps on pages 141–142 for help in getting started. Why not try activities from Celebrating People, Creative Solutions, or The World in My Community badges.

 What does the Girl Scout Promise and Law state about the ways you should treat other people? How can you put what it says into action?

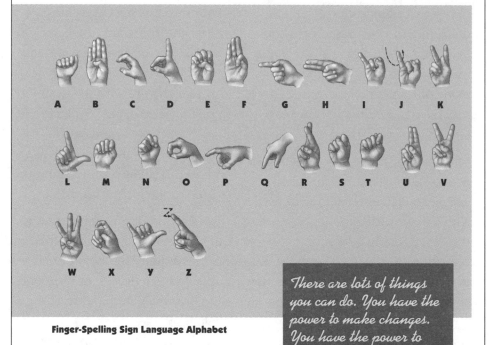

Finger-Spelling Sign Language Alphabet

There are lots of things you can do. You have the power to make changes. You have the power to help people learn to live and work together. It starts with you. What are your ideas?

130

LEADERSHIP IN ACTION
CHAPTER 6

What Skills Do Leaders Have?
page 132

Girls Can Do It
page 134

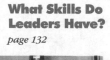

Your Own Leadership Action Project
page 141

Leadership Hall of Fame
page 135

Leadership, which can take many forms and styles, is an important part of Girl Scouting. This chapter will help you identify your own leadership style. Have you thought about how to channel your ideas into a neighborhood project? Why not use the information on leadership action projects to help you get started?

May Peace Prevail on Earth
Reine sólo la Paz en la Tierra

131

Leadership in Action

For more information on serving girls with special needs, read GSUSA's *Focus on Ability: Serving Girls With Special Needs.*

Program Links

▲ *Junior Girl Scout Handbook:* You and Your Community badge

Tips

▲ **Learning to Respect Differences:** In a discussion about respecting differences, ask girls:

- How do you think people from different groups are shown in the media? Are the images fair or unfair? What can you do to counteract unfair images?

- Are people from all races, cultures, ethnic groups, religious backgrounds, and economic levels welcome in your community? Why or why not?

- Do you think it is important to get to know people who are different from you? Why or why not?

- What is an American? What values and freedoms do Americans share?

- Do you believe boys are better at doing some things than girls, or that girls are better at doing some things than boys? Why or why not?

- Are you a member of a clique? How is a clique different from a group of friends? How can you move away from a clique?

- What are some things you can do to build respect for yourself and to increase your respect for others?

Tips

▲ **Chapter 6: Leadership in Action:** Experiences in leadership can provide girls with lifelong benefits. Girls can practice leadership skills by: joining school government, playing a team sport, directing a play, organizing religious youth activities, or joining a Girl Scout council committee. Girls can learn about the qualities a good leader has, such as responsibility, organization, communication, and the ability to be part of a team.

The troop or group meeting is an ideal environment for girls to practice taking charge and setting and accomplishing goals. Use this chapter as a resource for discussions on leadership as well as a guide to help girls complete requirements for the Junior Girl Scout Leadership Pin. This recognition was designed to help girls put their leadership skills into practice. (See Chapter Two in Part I of this guide and handbook Chapter Eight for more about the Junior Girl Scout Leadership Pin.)

The activities should be fun and educational. And you may find watching girls discover their leadership potential one of the most gratifying aspects of being a Girl Scout leader. Your words and actions can let girls know that girls and women have the power to be effective leaders.

What Is Leadership?

Leadership: to show the way; to guide or cause others to follow you; to direct; to be in charge.

Who are your leaders? Think of people you know and some you don't know. Did you think of the President of the U.S.A. or your Girl Scout leader? You can often identify a leader in a group by the way she acts, or the way others act towards her.

 List some leaders. Include leaders in school, community, state, nation, and the world. Pick your favorite leader from the list. Share with someone why you think that person is a leader.

_____

_____

_____

_____

_____

_____

_____

_____

Leadership Style

Juliette Gordon Low was a memorable leader. She loved what she was doing, and one reason that girls and adults followed her was because she communicated her enthusiasm. She also was known for her ability to begin something, then step back and let others take over, once she was sure they were on the right track.

Leadership doesn't depend on being Ms. Perfect or Ms. Right-All-the-Time. Most people who have leadership experience tell stories about things that have gone wrong when they were leading a group. But they will also tell you what they learned from their mistakes.

Part of being a good leader is helping others feel good about their work. That means choosing the right person for the right job and encouraging others when they are doing something new. People always like to feel that what they are doing is important to the group effort.

Here are some common leadership styles. Which ones best match your skills and abilities?

Director: Gives very good direction and makes sure everyone does her or his job. She will make certain that rules are clear and that everyone is expected to follow them.

Coach: Uses a style that provides both direction and supervision but encourages the involvement of everyone! She will explain the work that lies ahead, discuss decisions, and answer questions.

Supporter: Works with other members of a group to set goals and list steps to achieve those goals. She encourages everyone to make decisions and gives each member the help they need.

Delegator: Gives everyone a share of the work. She lets group members make decisions and take as much responsibility as they can handle. She is there to answer questions, but she wants them to take as much responsibility for their actions as possible.

 List all of the ways you are a leader. Decide on some skills or abilities that leaders have that you would like to develop in yourself. Come up with a plan for becoming a better leader and then do the following: Take on a leadership role for three months in your troop, school, or community. Be a leader for a sports team, an art project, a music group, or a computer network. Or, organize a neighborhood service club. Keep a journal of your time spent as a leader.

133

▲ **What Is Leadership?:** Help girls see that leadership can mean many things. By brainstorming a list of people they consider to be leaders, girls can see leadership qualities personified. Help them identify individuals of different ethnicities, races, ages, and genders. See the next handbook page, "Girls Can Do It," for information on women in leadership.

Once you know the girls in your troop or group well, you can help each girl identify personal strengths. Affirm qualities girls can easily identify with: "you are really good at…getting things organized, letting others participate, coming up with creative ideas, encouraging people, keeping a high level of energy, assigning work, etc."

Juliette Gordon Low is an example of a good leader. Discuss the ability she had to inspire others and to bring out the best in each person. Some called her exasperating because she would not accept "no" as an answer, using her deafness as an excuse not to understand. Some felt she was "bossy" when she wanted to get something done quickly. Those inspired by her enthusiasm and vision became hard workers. Everyone agreed she was a special and amazing person.

Help each girl see that through her own abilities and talents she can have many opportunities to be a leader. She might be president of a club at school, troop officer, or chair for a community event. Or maybe she will keep a group working towards its goal, even though she is not the designated leader. A leadership role can be broad, like directing a play, or it can be narrow, like directing cleanup after a troop meeting.

Point out that this section describes only some of the effective ways to lead. Girls might want to talk about other styles, some of which they may not want to copy, such as "bossy" or "know-it-all." Challenge girls to think of other effective leadership styles.

▲ Girls may need help in understanding and applying the concepts in the "Leadership Checklist." Offer examples from everyday experiences to explain how these concepts contribute to good leadership.

▲ Suggest girls play one of the games in the section "Challenge and Initiative Games" from the book *Games for Girl Scouts*. These games encourage team-building and give girls an opportunity to test leadership skills.

▲ *Games for Girl Scouts*

▲ *Girl Scout Badges and Signs:* Creative Solutions badge; My Self-Esteem badge; Women Today badge

Girls Can Do It

Quick, close your eyes and think of three people you consider to be leaders. Did you list any women leaders? Good for you if you did! A lot of people would not.

 Ask others to name some leaders. (Ask a variety of people.) Compare the answers that you get. Do answers vary from male to female? Does a person's age make a difference? Share your surveys in your group or troop.

When Juliette Gordon Low was a leader, it was not common for women to assume leadership beyond the family. Nor was it common for a deaf person to lead others.

Today, some people still believe that women and kids can't be leaders.

Here are some "Can't Do" statements you might encounter along your path to leadership:

- Girls take forever to decide on anything.
- Girls can't go camping—because they're afraid of bugs.
- Girls can't be leaders because they're not as strong as boys.
- You're just a kid; why should I listen to you?

What are some other "Can't Do" statements you have heard? Discuss how statements like these can put up "roadblocks" for girls. One way to leap over roadblocks is to use critical thinking skills. (See page 126).

Another way to achieve goals is to seek the help of a mentor, an older girl or woman in a leadership position who is willing to advise you. A mentor could be your troop or group leader, a teacher or a member of your family.

Note: There are certain things you cannot do while representing Girl Scouts because it is a nonprofit organization. Endorsing products or candidates, lobbying lawmakers, collecting money for other organizations, or asking for donations are some examples. Your leader will help you determine what can be done; you and your leader can use *Safety-Wise* as a guide.

You can learn how to do all of these things and put the leadership training you gain from Girl Scouts to use in community and school actions.

 Here are some situations that require leadership. Discuss which styles could be used with each situation. You might even want to practice each style with friends. Remember, there is no right or wrong answer.

- You have a large group. The job is to plan three activities for a Girl Scout camporee.
- You and five other girls have been asked to plan a flag ceremony for a councilwide event.
- You are leading a hike when you spot a tornado in the distance.

134

Leadership Hall of Fame

The girls in this fictional Leadership Hall of Fame represent leadership in action. One of them may remind you of someone you know, or may be you in a few years. Being a Girl Scout is a great place to learn and practice leadership. You can celebrate your successes with friends and learn from your mistakes. Listen to what the Hall of Famers have to say about their leadership projects. See if you can pick out some characteristics they share as leaders.

▼

Name: Maggie Rodriguez
From: California, U.S.A.
Claim to fame: Started a school recycling program with her Cadette Girl Scout troop. Received her Girl Scout Silver Award.
Highlights: After deciding that they wanted to do something about the waste at school, Maggie's troop got permission to start a trial recycling program. Each troop member was responsible for a different job: setting up the recycling in the cafeteria, and classroom, creating an education campaign, and organizing a recycling dance!

Maggie worked with the cafeteria manager to set up recycling of food, paper, and plastic utensils. The project was so successful that the school district adopted a full-time recycling program.
Comments about leadership: "This was definitely a team effort! Each of us was responsible for putting together our own committee. We rotated leadership of the meeting each week to make sure everyone had a chance to contribute. At one of our meetings, we had a woman, who is president of her company, come speak about working with groups. We had a lot of questions about the way some of our committees were working together and she really helped us."
Problems: "The hardest part was getting all of the students to cooperate at first. We ended up making some goofy awards for people who were not recycling. They were great sports, and when they decided to join us, their friends did, too."

135

▲ **Girls Can Do It:** There are women who have excelled in many fields. You might help girls find women leaders in your community. They might think about some of the fields in which women have moved to the forefront as leaders:

- politics
- medicine
- environment and conservation
- the law and the courts
- education
- civil rights
- the arts
- the rights of children
- peace
- humanitarian concerns
- science
- religion
- athletics

Girls should have no difficulty identifying "can't do" statements from their own experiences. Have them look for examples of girls and women assuming leadership and breaking stereotypes. Help girls recognize that they can set goals and excel.

Individual mentors or networks of women can be valuable sources of support for girls whether they are looking for advice on a leadership project or exploring a career path. Help girls by being a mentor yourself or by tapping into a network of Girl Scout women. Mentors can also come from women's service or professional organizations.

You can also find other resources through your local government's women's committee, the library, and woman's service organizations.

Note: If you have any questions regarding what you can or cannot do while representing Girl Scouts, refer to the *Blue Book of Basic Documents, Safety-Wise* program standards (particularly standards 28–35 involving fund raising and political involvement), and your council office. As a leader, you can help girls develop skills and encourage girls to participate in activities that would provide them with knowledge and a skill base for action. But, as Girl Scouts, you and your girls cannot be involved in fund raising for other organizations and cannot participate in partisan efforts to support or oppose a candidate for public office. If you have any questions about these policies, call your Girl Scout council representative.

▲ **Leadership Hall of Fame:** The girls depicted in the Leadership Hall of Fame are composites of Girl Scouts and Girl Guides around the world. These examples give ideas for projects, as well as techniques, problems, and characteristics of leadership. You might wish to invite older girls who are working on leadership projects (Girl Scout Silver Award, Girl Scout Gold Award, Leadership Institute projects, Leader-in-Training, Counselor-in-Training, or program aide) to discuss leadership with the girls. Your council office or service unit can help you identify Cadette or Senior Girl Scouts who can work with your troop or group.

(This section continues on the next page.)

Name: Sandi Baker

From: New York, U.S.A.

Claim to fame: Volunteer tutor at a homeless shelter.

Highlights: Sandi, a sixth-grader, was trained to tutor children through a program at her public library. After working on her Women Today badge, Sandi saw the need for tutoring kids at a community shelter. She worked with the shelter director to begin a program. Sandi involved her school, her community, and people at the shelter to create a children's recreation and study area.

Comments about leadership: "I didn't start out to be a leader. I just got tired of everybody talking about the homeless and not doing anything. I learned I could make things change by getting others to work with me on a goal. I also learned that it is important to involve the people you are helping. The residents now have a say in the running of their shelter. That's empowerment!"

Problems: "At first I thought that because people didn't do anything, they didn't want to get involved. I found that people needed to be asked. And I learned how to ask for help. There was no way I could build bookcases for the books we collected. So I asked some girls and boys in the shop class at school. Now they are building a playhouse for the kids."

Name: Emily Mabaya

From: Kenya

Claim to fame: A member of the Green Belt Movement, an organization that plants trees and gardens to fight soil erosion and deforestation in her country.

Highlights: After becoming a member of the Green Belt Movement, Emily saw the interest other women had whenever she talked about her efforts. So she started talking to others about the organization and showed them how to plant. Women from the next village came to see how they did it. Soon, she was talking to groups about the Green Belt Movement.

Comments about leadership: "I always thought of myself as a quiet person. But because I want my children to grow strong and healthy in this land and I feel strongly about what we're doing, I could talk easily to others. Bit by bit, I feel, we will make our country green."

Problems: "It was hard to make people understand how important trees and gardens are. I know many people thought I was foolish. But once women saw how much money they could make selling the vegetables in the market, they did not think I was so foolish. And I know how much these gardens help the environment."

136

Name: Sidshean O'Brien

From: Northern Ireland

Claim to fame: Meets once a week with children of Protestant and Catholic groups to play games and share friendship.

Highlights: Sidshean's mother began working with a movement to bring Protestant and Catholic women together to promote peace in Belfast. Sidshean organizes games and activities that she thinks the children will like. She's discovered that all children, despite their differences, like to have fun, laugh, and make friends.

Comments about leadership: "Sometimes leadership means taking a very small step. We can't stop the fighting that happens in our country, but we can bring groups of children together to learn about each other. If everyone took a small step, maybe the fighting and hatred would lessen."

Problems: "What we are doing with the children makes some people very angry. But I know there are other people who support the peace movement and that my mother and the other adults know what is right. They tell me it's important to act on one's beliefs."

It's up to you: What does it mean to be a peacemaker? What are the risks involved? What are the rewards? Design a way to express what the world would be like at peace. Or, make a peace pole, with the word "Peace," or the phrase "May Peace Prevail on Earth" written on four sides of a pole (See the next page for a sample peace pole.) Place the pole where people can reflect on what peace means, like in a public garden or at camp. Here are some ways of saying peace in different languages:

AMAMI	SWAHILI
FRIEDEN	GERMAN
HEIWA	JAPANESE
HEPING	MANDARIN
MIR	RUSSIAN
PAIX	FRENCH
SALAAM	ARABIC
SHALOM	HEBREW
WOKIYAPI	SIOUX
PAZ	SPANISH

137

Handbook Page 136

Handbook Page 137

Tips

▲ **Maggie Rodriguez:** (See previous page.) Maggie's project is very realistic for this age group, and is later profiled in a discussion of leadership action steps. In this group project, each girl had a task, other people were brought in, and everyone got behind it. Note the problems encountered. Ask the girls what other problems might be expected and let them spend time thinking up solutions. Maggie's project offers a framework for discussing the role of peers in contributing to a project's success. With the girls, talk about ways to solicit cooperation from others.

▲ **Sandi Baker:** Note that this project evolved from a badge activity that Sandi completed. Sandi had a vision of what she wanted (she saw the need for tutoring) and was able to get others involved.

Sandi says she didn't start out to be a leader. This is a good place to discuss why Sandi, not someone else, stepped into the leadership role. What leadership characteristics did she display? Note how she got things started, then motivated others to get behind the project.

Asking people to participate is key to community involvement. Ask girls if they have ever not done something simply because they were not asked.

▲ **Emily Mabaya:** Ask the girls to discuss the reasons Emily became a leader. Do people in our country do things for the same reasons? You might discuss the role of Girl Guiding and Girl Scouting throughout the world in empowering girls and women to become leaders in their communities. (See *The Wide World of Girl Guiding and Girl Scouting* and *Trefoil Round the World.*) If possible, ask an older girl who has traveled on an international wider opportunity to describe her experiences. You might challenge girls to become knowledgeable about a country outside the United States and then envision projects they could become involved in as Girl Scouts. Contact your council office for resources from WAGGGS. Or, ask your council representative if the council has developed material to commemorate Thinking Day.

▲ **Sidshean O'Brien:** This leadership project profiles a young woman who is acting on her beliefs, knowing that her "small step" is part of a solution towards peace. Stress to girls the importance of taking small steps to accomplish a goal.

Name: Kimberly Ting

From: Texas, U.S.A.

Claim to fame: Girl assistant troop leader. Helps lead a Brownie Girl Scout troop.

Highlights: Kim has always enjoyed working with younger children. This began when she earned her Caring for Children badge as a Junior Girl Scout and became a program aide at day camp. Last year, as a Senior Girl Scout, she completed her Leader-in-Training project under an experienced Brownie Girl Scout leader. This year she is paired with Mrs. Papadopolous, a new leader in her neighborhood, and together they lead a Brownie Girl Scout troop.

Comments about leadership: "I learned so much from my mentor leader last year! She let me try a lot of new things with the girls. And not everything worked...like the time a guest speaker didn't show and I didn't have a plan for what to do, or the time I led everyone down the wrong trail and had to ask directions from a ranger. But you know, I learned more from the mistakes than the things that went really well. And so did the girls. Probably the most important thing I learned was how to give others the chance to make decisions."

Problems: "It was hard at first working with Mrs. Papadopolous because she was so new to Girl Scouting. I knew more about the activities than she did. But I learned that Mrs. Papadopolous knew a lot about how to organize and get parents involved. Now, we're really working as a team."

May Peace Prevail on Earth

Reine sólo la Paz en la Tierra

Peace poles are four-sided wooden pillars inscribed with the words "May Peace Prevail on Earth" in at least four different languages. They have been placed all over the world to remind people to think about peace.

138

MAKING CHANGES IN YOUR COMMUNITY

You are a citizen of the world, your country, your state, and your community. As a citizen, you have rights and responsibilities. For example, you have the right to use a public park and the responsibility to let others enjoy it too by not littering or disturbing others with a loud radio. When you do things like recycle, conserve water, vote in a school election, or do a service project, you are acting as a responsible citizen.

Active Citizenship

Active citizens care for and improve the place they live. Sometimes it's easier not to act. For example, if the corner trash can is full, it is easier to throw a candy wrapper on the ground than walk another block to find an empty trash can, or write the sanitation department and ask them to empty the trash cans more often. But, if all your neighbors throw their trash on the ground, your community becomes dirty and unpleasant. This is why citizens need to act to identify and solve community problems. Take a look at the chart on the following page. It includes problems and actions to solve them. Do any of these problems look familiar?

139

Tips

▲ **Kimberly Ting:** Kimberly's leadership experiences mirror her progression through Girl Scouting. She discovered her interest in working with kids as a Junior Girl Scout and developed that interest as a Cadette and Senior Girl Scout. This profile also points out that mistakes can be used as opportunities to learn.

▲ **Peace Poles:** You can learn more about peace poles by writing to The Peace Pole Project, 800 Third Avenue, 31st Floor, New York, N.Y., 10022.

A variation of the peace pole is a colorful banner inscribed with different words for peace. The banner can be hung in a meeting place or school.

Supporting Activities

▲ Look through this handbook, *Girl Scout Badges and Signs*, and some of the Cadette and Senior Girl Scout resources for activities that can act as "springboards" to leadership.

▲ Plan a Girl Scout's Own ceremony with a leadership or peace theme.

Program Links

▲ *Girl Scout Badges and Signs:* Active Citizen badge; Girl Scouting Around the World badge; Girl Scouting in the U.S.A badge.; Junior Citizen badge; My Community badge; The World in My Community badge; World Neighbors badge

▲ *Junior Girl Scout Handbook:* Leadership badge; You and Your Community badge

▲ *Trefoil Round the World*

▲ *The Wide World of Girl Guiding and Girl Scouting*

▲ *Valuing Differences: Promoting*

Pluralism Contemporary Issues booklet

Tips

▲ **Making Changes in Your Community:** This section helps girls identify the steps needed to carry out a leadership action project. Point out that an action project is based on a series of steps that lead to an end.

Supporting Activities

▲ Discuss with girls why leadership skills are important in active citizenship. Spend time identifying "active citizens" in your community. Discuss ways to be an active citizen. (Voting is one way adults participate.) Have the girls interview someone leading or involved with a community or local government project.

Program Links

▲ *Girl Scout Badges and Signs:* Active Citizen badge; Making Decisions badge; My Community badge; Women Today badge

▲ *Junior Girl Scout Handbook:* Leadership badge; You and Your Community badge

▲ *Trefoil Round the World*

▲ *The Wide World of Girl Guiding and Girl Scouting*

Notes

Place	Issue	Action
School	The cafeteria is not set up for recycling	• Form a student/adult advisory committee. • Talk to a member of the parent/teacher's association. • Make a presentation to the school board.
Neighborhood	There is an increase in burglaries	• Form a group and talk to neighborhood residents. • Schedule a meeting with the police department. • Set up a "neighborhood watch" program and distribute stickers.
Larger Community	There is a lack of services for senior citizens and children	• Make a pamphlet of community services for senior citizens and children. • Ask your Girl Scout council for help with getting pamphlets printed. • Distribute pamphlets to senior citizens and parents at shopping centers.
Environment	A severe winter storm eroded the park's soil	• Contact county parks department about problem. • Organize volunteers for a "planting day" event. • Plant shrubs on hillside.

Where do you start when you want to be part of or begin a project? Each girl profiled in this chapter had a reason for starting or joining in a project. Most of the projects started as someone's vision of something that was needed, whether it was at school or in the community.

Although the projects were different, they shared some basic steps in becoming a finished project. If you have an idea for a project or want to come up with an idea for a project, consider these steps:

CREATING A LEADERSHIP ACTION PROJECT

1. Brainstorm possibilities with your troop or group.

Maggie's troop (see page 135) decided that waste was a problem at their school. They listed all the things they might do to make others aware of the problem:

• Make posters
• Have an art contest with recycled materials
• Recycle paper in class
• Circulate a petition
• Make recycling bins
• Talk to the cafeteria manager
• Talk to the recycling depot
• Talk to the principal
• Start recycling

2. Make decisions.

Maggie's troop members narrowed their list after discussion. They decided that talking to the principal was a friendlier approach than circulating a petition. They knew their project would take little money because they planned to use recycled materials. The big

Handbook Page 140

Handbook Page 141

▲ Chart That Lists Community Issues and Actions: This chart is offered as a way to help girls see what is meant by issues and actions. By reviewing this chart, perhaps girls can gain a sense of their own community's problems and ways to resolve them. You may want to concentrate on only one area as you focus your discussion.

▲ Creating a Leadership Action Project: Leadership is in action when you see what you want and work towards it until it happens. Your troop or group's goal might be to solve a problem, such as a lack of play equipment in a park, a neighbor's loss of household items due to fire, or a need for activities for younger girls at a special event. Creativity, determination, and a sense of responsibility will help

reach the goal of fulfilling these needs. Remind girls to remain flexible and offer ways to cope with changes that might affect their plans. For example, ask girls to consider what they would do if they plan an outdoor event and it rains. Or, ask them what they would do if someone doesn't show up to help.

Leadership in action in Girl Scouting often involves the active support of all members of a troop or group to reach a goal. The person fulfilling the role of leader can change when different skills are called for or it's time to give another person an opportunity to lead. Have girls think about times the troop or group set a goal. Were they acting as leaders or were they supporting the leader and the group?

It's hard to measure the rewards of leadership in action. Not everything girls do will earn them a badge or public recognition. Finishing their project can make girls feel good, but sometimes the process of working with a group towards a common goal is as important as getting the job done. Girls find out that they can work with others and really make a difference.

The steps under "Creating a Leadership Action Project" serves as the blueprint for action. Maggie's troop's recycling project is included here to illustrate how they proceeded through each step. When it comes time for your troop or group to create their own leadership action project have girls use the blank outline that follows. You can help girls move through the steps together by writing the action plan outline on a large piece of paper so all can follow.

You and the girls will want to refer to these steps for any action project you undertake. Girls will find these steps helpful for both group and individual projects. Action plan steps and additional examples also appear in the Contemporary Issues booklet *Earth Matters: A Challenge for Environmental Action*.

The following is a recap of the steps with additional points and considerations. You may also want to look at the section on group decision-making in handbook Chapter One.

1. Brainstorming: Brain-storming is when everyone thinks of as many ideas as they can. It is important to establish ground rules such as no criticism allowed, one person speaks at a time, and all ideas must be written down.

question was whether they could get the paper and plastics picked up by the recycling company or sanitation department. That was resolved when someone talked to the woman in charge.

3. Plan your calendar.

Several dates were chosen by Maggie's group. The dates needed to be checked out with the principal. The dance date needed to be cleared by the student activities group. Meetings were set up with the principal and the head of the recycling depot. It was decided that troop or group meeting dates would work for committee meetings.

4. Put your ideas into action.

Once the plans were outlined, Maggie's troop divided up the jobs. A committee was formed to complete each task. Committee heads met once a week to make sure they were on track before the big event.

5. Evaluate what was done.

One week after the event, Maggie's troop completed an evaluation. Each person told what she had learned, what she would change, and what she liked most about the project. The troop also wrote a report for their principal outlining what they had done and why. The principal used the report when it came time to describe the project to the school board.

6. Share your success.

After the successful project, the girls in Maggie's troop threw an ice cream party for committee members. Everyone got great buttons that came from the recycling depot. Maggie and her committee heads wrote thank-you notes to the cafeteria manager, principal, and the head of the recycling depot.

142

YOUR OWN ACTION PLAN

Create your own action plan for a community project. Use the following action plan outline.

1

Brainstorm ideas. These are the ideas that we brainstormed:

1._____

_____

2._____

_____

3._____

_____

4._____

_____

This is the idea we chose:

_____

_____

_____

2

Make decisions.

Information we need to get:

_____

_____

This is what the plan will cost:

_____

_____

We can get materials from:

_____

We can get help from:

_____

_____

Special permission will be obtained from:

_____

_____

Our troop or group voted that:

_____

_____

3

Plan your calendar.

We need to meet with:

_____

on _____
    (date)

We also need to meet with:

_____

on _____
    (date)

We need to meet on: _____
    (date)

Our date to finish is: _____
    (date)

4

Put your ideas into action.

_____
   (name of person or committee)

will work on _____

_____
   (name of person or committee)

will work on _____

_____
   (name of person or committee)

will work on _____

143

2. Making Decisions: Now it's time to narrow the list down to things or ideas that look possible. Girls may need to gather information about some items before making their decisions. Discuss the good and bad points of each idea. Have the girls determine the cost of the proposed idea. Is it too expensive? Will money have to be raised? Do the girls know people to ask to donate time or materials? Is the project practical in terms of time and effort? Is special permission required? The troop or group may have to vote to determine a course of action.

3. Planning Your Calendar: This step usually happens after the information has been gathered and the actions are determined. Here, girls schedule committee meetings with people in the community and determine dates for work or events. When planning your calendar, consider parents' and guardians' schedules as well. And, don't forget to ask parents and guardians to help out with such needs as transportation.

4. Putting Your Ideas into Action: Help the girls break the project into steps that can be handled by committees or individuals. Make sure everyone knows her job. Help girls build on each other's strengths when they are deciding who will do what. Be certain someone checks with committee heads or individuals to see how things are going. Let girls know they can evaluate how things are going at any point and make adjustments; they can even adjust their goals. Stress the importance of communicating.

5. Evaluation: This step helps everyone reflect on the process. Was the project fun? Did the project accomplish what the girls set out to do? Could the project have been done differently? Would the troop or group do it again? This step is an important part of the learning process. Help girls be honest in their evaluations, without being destructive. Discuss the lessons learned from mistakes.

6. Sharing Success: Celebrate success with those who have worked towards it. If your troop or group has relied on people in the community for help, be sure the girls thank them. Stress the importance of making people feel that their work, time, and energy are valued. Part of leadership is making people feel good about what they have accomplished. Discuss how to accept thank you's graciously, but how not to expect something in return for service.

5

Evaluate what was done.

What we liked about the project:

_____
_____
_____
_____
_____

What we would do differently:

_____
_____
_____
_____

We would do it/not do it again because:
(circle one)

_____
_____
_____
_____
_____

6

Share your success.

We need to send thank-you notes to:

_____
_____
_____

We will celebrate our success by:

_____
_____

on:_____
(date)

We will tell our Girl Scout council and
_____about our success.
(other people or groups)

 Now is the time to try your wings and fly with a leadership-in-action project. Focus on what you would like to do and work through the six steps of leadership in action while doing an actual project. Keep a journal to help you evaluate. If you do this as a troop or a group, make sure that each person has the opportunity to lead within the group.

As you can see, leadership can take many forms. And as a leader, you need to find your own style—one that feels comfortable and still helps you arrive at your goals. Remember that your troop or group members and Girl Scout leader are there to help you discover your unique way of leading.

144

EXPLORING INTERESTS, SKILLS, & TALENTS
CHAPTER 7

Playing and Watching Sports
page 147

Optical Illusions: What Do You See?
page 154

Study Bubbleology!
page 168

Skills for Outdoor Adventures
page 181

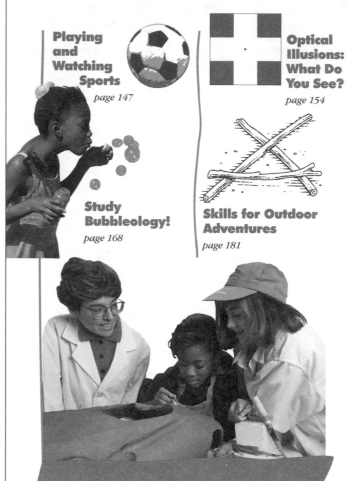

One of the best things about Girl Scouting is that it offers you lots of ideas for fun things to do. And, *you* get to decide the activities. In this chapter, you'll find many activities—for all interests, skills, and talents—to do alone or with your troop or group.

Some of the activities will have a safety symbol near them. This is to remind you to be extra careful in doing the activity or to ask an adult to assist you.

145

Interests, Skills, and Talents

Program Links

▲ *Earth Matters: A Challenge for Environmental Action* Contemporary Issues booklet

▲ *Girl Scout Badges and Signs:* Active Citizen badge; Making Decisions badge; My Community badge; The World in My Community badge

▲ *Junior Girl Scout Handbook*: Leadership badge; You and Your Community badge

REMINDER!

What was important to you when you were 9, 10, or 11 years old? While society has changed over the years, girls' concerns—about themselves, their families, their interests, and their friendships—may be very similar to the concerns you had. Review some old photos and letters or listen to music popular when you were the age of Junior Girl Scouts. Can you look at the world through a Junior Girl Scout's eyes?

Tips

▲ **Chapter 7: Interests, Skills, and Talents:** The activities in this chapter are designed to help girls learn more about their interests, develop their talents, and discover lifetime leisure pursuits. Encourage them to try new activities or expand on those with which they are already familiar. Some of these activities might lead to future career opportunities, but most will just present girls with the chance to try things in a comfortable environment. Make sure that all the girls in your troop or group are included in deciding which activities to pursue.

If a girl begins one activity, and then decides to move on to something new, that's okay. As long as she is enjoying the pursuit of new activities, she is successfully participating. If she never seems able to complete something, then encourage her to stay with the task to completion.

What do you do when you feel bored?

One of the great things about being a Girl Scout is that you have a group of friends with whom you can explore interests, skills, and talents! You don't have to worry about making a fool of yourself the first time you in-line skate because you have a friend cheering you on (or one who's fallen on the ground with you!).

Not everyone in your troop or group will be interested in exploring the same things. But you will probably find some girls who share your interest.

146

PLAYING SPORTS AND GAMES

Playing sports, either alone or with others, is a great way to have fun. No matter which sport you choose, you will need to learn certain skills and follow certain rules. Remember always to play fairly and do your best. To get started, you may want to try the Sports badge or the Sports Sampler badge in *Girl Scout Badges and Signs*.

TIPS FOR PLAYING SPORTS

☆ Always do warm-up exercises before taking part in a sports activity, and always do cool-down exercises afterwards.

☆ Wear clothing and shoes that are comfortable and suitable for the sport you are playing.

☆ Use equipment that is in good condition.

☆ Practice or play in an area that is safe and free of hazards.

☆ Drink water before you start and often during your exercise.

☆ Stop playing if you get hurt or feel tired.

TIPS FOR WATCHING SPORTS

Watching sports can also be fun. You can become an expert on a sport by learning all you can about it, even if you don't play. Here are some rules for being a good spectator or fan.

☆ Stay in the viewing area and away from the playing area at all times.

☆ Be quiet if players need to concentrate or listen, even if they are on the other team.

☆ Support players when they do well, but do not criticize when they make a mistake.

☆ Make sure you do not interfere with the enjoyment of other fans.

147

Handbook Page 146

Handbook Page 147

Tips

▲ **For Better or For Worse Cartoon:** You can use the cartoon to start a discussion about interests. Encourage girls to discuss their interests and how these interests have developed. Ask if they'd be willing to share their expertise with others.

Supporting Activities

▲ Girls might like to have a meeting where everyone exhibits or displays something. Or as a troop or group, have girls explore a topic through research or by visiting someone who is skilled in that area. Some girls may have collections of things such as postcards, dolls, or trading cards. Maybe the other girls in the group can help them discover ways to show off their collections. For example, a shell collection can be made into a mobile rather than put into an album. Buttons from a collection can be used to make jewelry or decorate clothing. A rock collection can promote discussions about travel, geography, and geology.

▲ Girls can share their knowledge about their interests. For example, a girl who is interested in cooking or baking can talk about the creativity and chemistry involved in what she does. Girls who have written stories or poetry can share their work. Or, a girl who has learned computer skills could teach others. Since many girls may be novices at these activities, don't plan too much for a meeting. Allow them plenty of time to share. In fact, you may want to schedule these activities over several meetings.

Program Links

▲ *Earth Matters: A Challenge for Environmental Action*, *Right to Read: Literacy*, and *Into the World of Today and Tomorrow: Leading Girls to Mathematics, Science, and Technology* Contemporary Issues booklets

▲ *Girl Scout Badges and Signs*: Any Dabbler badge; "Collecting" Hobbies badge; "Doing" Hobbies badge; "Making" Hobbies badge

▲ *Junior Girl Scout Activity Book*: Chapter One

REMINDER!

The Girl Scout program is rich in activities—many of which cannot be found in the handbook or this leader's guide. Talk to your local Girl Scout representative. What other program resources are available to Junior Girl Scouts? (See the Annotated Resource List in Chapter Five in Part One.) What wider opportunities has the Girl Scout council planned? What is available in your neighborhood, community, or city for girls to explore?

The sports described here are just a few you can try. See what others you can find out about.

SOFTBALL

Softball is like baseball in many ways, but there are a few differences. A softball is larger and weighs less, and the bat is also larger and lighter than the one used for baseball. Slow-pitch softball, which most people play, usually has two teams of ten players each.

Softball games may last either seven or nine innings, depending on the league rules. Each team gets three outs in their turn at-bat.

◆ Throwing

If you are right-handed, you will step forward with your left foot as you throw. If you are left-handed, you step with your right foot. Lean your body backwards as you use your arm.

◆ Pitching

In slow-pitch softball, all pitching is done underhanded. The ball should arc on its way to the plate.

◆ Catching

The most important thing to remember is always to keep your eyes on the ball. To "get under" the ball, keep your arms extended and your hands relaxed. When the ball hits your glove, let your arms and hands "give" a little.

◆ Batting

It sometimes takes practice to learn how to hit the ball, but once you learn how to stand comfortably, you will find hitting easier. If you are right-handed, you will stand with the plate to your right. If you are left-handed, it will be to your left.

BASKETBALL

Basketball is a team sport played with a ball and basket, usually on a court. It is a fast-paced game that involves running, dribbling, passing, and shooting.

◆ Playing the Game

Regulation basketball is played on a court with one basket at each end. The two teams are made up of five players each. Points are scored by shooting the ball into the basket the other team is defending. A team gets two points for every successful basket shot. But, if a player has violated a rule (such as tripping a player), the other team is given a foul shot. A foul shot is made from the free-throw line. One point is earned for a successful throw.

Players move the ball by dribbling it or passing it to members of their team. If a team member "travels," walks or runs with the ball without dribbling, she will lose possession of the ball to the other team.

You can learn a lot about the specific rules and strategies by watching a game.

◆ Techniques

Learn and practice these skills:

• Dribble (bounce) the ball while running and standing still.

• Pass a ball to another player in these three ways: a chest pass (with two hands), an overhead pass, and a bounce.

• Shoot a ball into a basket in these ways: a set shot, a jump shot, and a lay-up. For the set shot and the jump shot, use either one or two hands. Shoot the lay-up with two hands.

• Guard a player who has the ball.

◆ Variations of the Game

If you don't have ten players or a regulation court—or if you want to try something different—you can play variations of the game. For example, you can:

• Play a game with two, three, or four players on a team.

• Play with only one hoop.

• Change the rules so that only passing, no dribbling, is allowed.

148

149

Tips

▲ **Playing Sports and Games:** The sports included here can all be played as competitive team sports. If your troop or group is large enough, girls may want to divide into teams and play against each other. Or, they may want to set up games between themselves and other troops or groups. Some girls may be interested in activities that are more individualized or those that don't involve competition. Be sure to encourage these activities as well.

Supporting Activities

▲ The next column has two popular activities you may want to introduce. If you do not feel comfortable coaching girls in these activities, look for assistance from your local recreation center or school physical education program. Consult *Safety-Wise* before girls try these activities.

● **Gymnastics:** Girls of Junior Girl Scout age are particularly interested in tumbling. It is not at all uncommon to see girls trying out routines on their front lawn, a park, the schoolyard, or anywhere they can find the room! It is important, though, that girls use proper form and practice with a spotter. Invite an adult or high school student with gymnastics training to demonstrate such skills as forward and backward rolls, cartwheels, and headstands. Girls may want to make up a routine once they have learned to perform stunts safely.

● **In-line skating:** Instructors in many areas can teach girls the proper form for skating, stopping, and even falling. Check *Safety-Wise* for equipment and safety requirements.

Program Links

▲ *Games for Girl Scouts*

▲ *Girl Scout Badges and Signs*: Hiker badge; Horse Lover badge; Horseback Rider badge; Outdoor Fun in the City badge; Small Craft badge; Sports badge; Sports Sampler badge; Swimming badge; Walking for Fitness badge; Water Fun badge

▲ *Girls Are Great: Growing Up Female* and *Developing Health and Fitness: Be Your Best!* Contemporary Issues booklets

▲ *Junior Girl Scout Activity Book*: Chapter Four

Notes

SOCCER

 The object of soccer is to kick the soccer ball into your opponent's goal. It involves a lot of running, kicking, blocking, and dribbling. Soccer is played by two teams with a maximum of 11 players on each team. A soccer game has two periods. A good soccer player develops balance and timing, which come from practicing soccer skills.

◆ Kicking

To learn to kick well, practice from a standing position first. Keep your head down and your eyes on the ball. Put your non-kicking foot next to the ball. Use the instep (inside) of your foot to kick. After you kick the ball, keep moving your kicking leg forward (this is called follow-through). When you are comfortable with kicking this way, practice with others while the ball is rolling or bouncing.

◆ Blocking

There are three major kinds of blocks. In the "body block," bend your back slightly as the ball hits your body so the ball won't bounce wildly. "Heading" is a type of block where the player

controls the ball to clear, pass, or score by hitting it with the top of the forehead. In "trapping," you stop the ball with the inside or outside of your shoe or with the sole of your foot.

◆ Dribbling

Dribbling is one way to move the soccer ball forward. You do this by giving the ball short kicks with the inside or outside of your foot. At the same time, you try to keep your opponent from taking the ball.

MORE ABOUT SPORTS

There are other sports you and your friends in Girl Scouting may want to try. Swimming, field hockey, archery, tennis, and bicycling are just a few. Your school or local library may have some information about these sports, or a local recreation agency may be able to help you. You might also find ideas from such badges as Hiker, Horse Lover, Horseback Rider, Swimming, and Walking for Fitness in Girl Scout Badges and Signs. Remember, you don't have to be perfect at sports, you just have to find a sport you like and have fun!

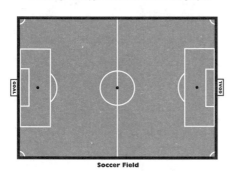

Soccer Field

150

Exploring the Arts

Arts activities help bring out your creativity. Don't be afraid to try something new. You might find you have a new talent just waiting to come out!

Music

Here are different kinds of music. Find out something about each of them and share your knowledge with your troop or group. If you play an instrument, you might want to play to demonstrate one of these styles of music.

- Swing
- Broadway show tunes
- Rock
- Symphonic
- Pop
- Country and Western
- Jazz
- Rap
- Cajun
- Salsa
- Reggae
- Bluegrass

Singing

Look at the music categories above and choose a song you want to sing or teach. Or, compose your own song using the blank music sheet. For more ideas, look at the Musician and Music Lover badges in *Girl Scout Badges and Signs*.

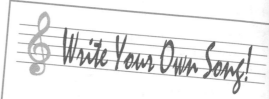

Write Your Own Song!

151

▲ **Exploring the Arts—Music:**
Some girls may be familiar with all the styles of music listed. Or they may prefer the music they hear most often. By introducing different kinds of music (not just those you personally enjoy), you may be offering them new avenues of expression.

Before girls complete the badge activities, encourage them to listen to different kinds of music. Bring to the meeting recordings of various types of music. Ask girls if different music evokes different feelings or if the music reminds them of a story, image, or culture. Music is not created in a void, but is an expression of some kind. Encourage girls to interpret what they hear. If possible, invite someone to visit who plays or sings a particular style of music.

After some experience with singing, dancing, and playing instruments, girls may want to put on a talent show. Or, you may want to combine talents with other troops or groups and perform.

Supporting Activities

Here are other expressive arts to share with the girls:

▲ **Dance** is physical expression through music. Some girls may already be taking dance classes. Ask a member of your troop or group or invite an older girl to demonstrate a particular dance style. Here are some styles girls may want to learn more about:

● Ballet

● Tap

● Modern

● Folk

● Line dancing (done to many different styles of music)

▲ **Creative dramatics** are another way girls can express themselves. They may want to combine music, dance, and drama to create their own plays. Or, they may want to find a familiar play and produce it themselves. Girls can even rewrite a new version of an old story. To help girls choose appropriate material, visit a library or local theater group. Girls might want to choose a play to perform for each other or an audience.

Besides acting, other jobs are important in the production of plays. Have girls try their hand at directing, costume or set design, or other behind-the-scenes responsibilities.

Girls may also want to try puppet-making, toy-making, and storytelling.

Program Links

▲ *Canciones de Nuestra Cabaña*

▲ *Ceremonies in Girl Scouting*

▲ *Girl Scout Badges and Signs*:
Dance badge; Folk Arts badge; Music Lover badge; Musician badge; Theater badge; Toymaker badge

▲ *Junior Girl Scout Activity Book*:
Chapter Seven

▲ *Sing-Along Songbook*

Drawing and Painting

Drawing

Some tools for drawing are pencil, pen, chalk, pastels, and charcoal. You can find out about each of these at an art-supply store. You can also learn about artists' supplies from an art teacher.

Painting

 Instead of painting with a brush, why not try painting with sponges, cotton swabs, bird feathers, or twigs? Choose one of these to paint a story or make your own design.

Scratchboard

Try this variation of a scratch board, a form of drawing in which, instead of pencil or ink lines being added to white paper, a covering of color is scratched away with a pin to form a design.

You Will Need:
- Heavy, smooth white paper
- Colored crayons
- Black crayons
- A large safety pin or metal nail file

1. Cover different areas of the paper with different colors of crayon.

2. Color over the entire paper with the black crayon, pressing hard.

3. When the entire paper is covered, scratch away your design. (It's best to do this over layers of newspaper, as the scraped crayon can make a mess.)

152

Decoupage

Decoupage is a means of decorating with paper cutouts. Originally, decoupage artists cut out paper designs and glued them to furniture. When the furniture was varnished or lacquered, it looked as if the designs has been painted on.

You can use pictures cut out from magazines, postcards, greeting cards, wrapping paper, or photographs for decorating with this technique.

Decoupage for a Planter

You Will Need:
- A clean soup can
- Paint
- A paintbrush
- A cup of water
- Paper towels
- Pictures or decal stickers
- Varnish
- Potting soil
- Gravel (or pebbles and seeds)

1. Peel the label off the empty can.

2. Paint all around the can and let it dry.

3. Wash the brush; then dry it.

4. Glue pictures on the can.

5. Varnish the entire can. Let it dry. Varnish again and allow it to dry completely.

6. Put gravel in the bottom of the can, and then add some soil. Carefully put your plant into the planter, and fill the sides and bottom of the planter with soil.

153

Tips

▲ **Drawing and Painting:** Most girls will have had experience with drawing and painting. They may not, however, be used to expressing themselves through art. Some girls have been limited to copying a pattern or drawing. Rather than developing creativity, such activities actually stifle girls' own ideas.

Creativity comes from children feeling free to produce their own artwork without others imposing ideas and limitations. Foster creative expression by offering assorted materials and supporting their efforts. Don't introduce "adult" models or projects for girls to copy. Children will often lead the way if you get them started and help them link their ideas for expression to other interests they may have.

Not everyone will display the same level of talent, just as with other activities in this chapter. If, however, girls develop an understanding of the processes of drawing and painting, they may acquire an appreciation for art.

Supporting Activities

▲ To help girls learn about artists and how they get their ideas, visit a museum, art gallery, art or poster store, or display an art book.

▲ Artists often use color as one means of expressing how they feel about their subjects. Have girls think about the different ways to use color in a picture. They may want to paint a city scene, the countryside, or another person. Encourage them to paint freely—they may want to make the sky orange or the ocean purple!

▲ Papier-mâché is another expressive art form that can be used to create three-dimensional objects, masks, and scenery. Here are two recipes.

You Will Need:

● Paper (newspaper, paper towels, paper egg cartons)

● Paste (flour and water or white glue mixed with water)

● A bowl

To make a flour paste, mix 1/4 cup (60 ml) of hot water with 1/2 cup (120 ml) of flour. To make white glue paste, mix 2 tablespoons (30 ml) of water to 1 tablespoon (15 ml) of white glue.

Paper Pulp Method

1. Shred the paper into very small pieces. Make at least 3 cups (.7 liters) of paper bits.

2. Put the paper bits in a mixing bowl.

3. Soak in about 3 cups (.7 liter) of hot water for at least one-half hour.

4. Drain water and then squeeze paper pulp so it is not dripping wet.

5. Mix with paste so that papier-mâché is moist but not dripping.

6. Use a hand or electric beater to make a smoother, less lumpy pulp.

Paper Strip Method

1. Tear newspaper into strips about 1" (2.5 cm) wide.

2. Dip strips into paste.

Forming with Papier-Mâché

Mold like clay, or shape pulp or wrap strips over other forms: wire frames, bottles, cardboard containers, wads of newspaper, blown-up balloons. You can make sculptures, drama props, masks, toys, decorative items for your room. After the papier-mâché has dried, it can be painted and varnished.

Program Links

▲ *Exploring the Hand Arts*

▲ *Girl Scout Badges and Signs*: Drawing and Painting badge

Optical Illusions

Hidden Picture

A picture mysteriously appears on a sheet of blank paper. You won't believe your eyes!

You Will Need:
- **White construction paper**
- **Colored paints or crayons**

Draw anything you like on a sheet of paper following these three rules:

1. The colors must be strong and solid with no shading.

2. The design must be no bigger than 3"– 6" (8 –15 cm) across (see example below).

3. Avoid small, intricate color patterns.

Put a dot in the center of your design to control the movement of your eyes. Stare at the center dot for 30 seconds. Don't move your eyes around. Keep them open wide. After 30 seconds, quickly stare at a blank sheet of white paper. Wait several seconds. What do you see?

The design you see is called an after-image. Did you notice that the colors in the after-image were different from the colors in your original design? You are seeing each color's complementary color. The basic complementary colors are:

Red–green   yellow-**purple**

blue–orange   **black**–white

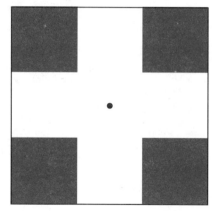

Printmaking

Mathematical Moiré

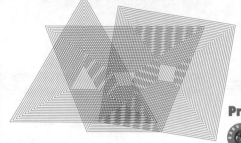

Can you draw straight lines that appear to be curvy?

You Will Need:
- **A pen**
- **A ruler**
- **A compass for making circles**
- **Sheets of tracing paper**

1. In the center of a piece of tracing paper, construct a small (1/2" or 13 mm) triangle, circle, square, or other geometric figure. Use a ruler for straight-line figures and a compass for circles.

2. Carefully draw the same figure outside the original, keeping lines parallel and as close as possible without touching. A space of 1/8" or 1/4 cm is good, 1/16" or 1/8 cm is even better.

3. Draw larger figures until half the page is full.

4. Repeat the same process on a different sheet of paper. You can make the same design or a different one.

5. Place one design over the other and move the sheets around. What happens to the straight lines?

For a variation, try making patterns with string art. Tap small nails into a wooden board. (Read about tools on page 103.) Then lace fine string or thread around the nails to make patterns that seem to curve and wave.

Printmaking

You can make prints in many ways. The Prints and Graphics badge in *Girl Scout Badges and Signs* has several ideas you can try. Here is one for stenciling:

You Will Need:
- **Wax paper or other nonabsorbent paper**
- **A scissors**
- **A piece of sponge**
- **Water-based paint or ink**
- **A bowl**
- **Blank cards or paper**

1. Cover your work surface with newspapers.

2. Draw your design on the wax paper.

3. Cut out the stencil design. You will use what remains on the paper as your stencil.

4. Pour the ink into the bowl.

5. Dip the sponge into the ink.

6. Press the stencil over the card or paper. Dab the sponge over the stencil to make a print. Be careful not to have too much ink or paint on the sponge. Tap off the excess onto newspaper. You may want to make your own greeting cards or wrapping paper.

Handbook Page 154

Handbook Page 155

▲ **Optical Illusions:** Have girls look in the library or bookstore for resources on optical illusions. Girls might also enjoy books of puzzles and brainteasers.

▲ *Girl Scout Badges and Signs*: Puzzlers badge; Visual Arts badge

▲ *Junior Girl Scout Activity Book*: Chapter Five

▲ **Printmaking**: There are different ways to make prints. For example, intaglio is a design that is depressed; relief is a design that is raised. Certain paints and inks work better for each type of print. You should be able to find water-based paints and inks, which are easy and safe to use as well as to clean up. Water- or oil-based printing inks can be used with block prints but are also good to use with stencils or silk-screens.

Have girls use textile or fabric paints when making prints on anything that will be washed or worn. Be sure to follow the directions that come with these paints.

To find out more about other printing processes, such as silk-screening, consult the Girl Scout publication *Exploring the Hand Arts*.

▲ Girls can make block prints by carving designs on a block of wood, wax, or soap. The design is raised above the rest of the wood (relief print). Girls put ink or paints on the raised design and stamp it onto paper or cloth.

▲ Girls can make stencils by first sketching and then cutting a simple design. Girls will use what remains on the paper as their stencils. For good results, make sure girls cut the lines sharply and cleanly. Tack the paper or fabric that will receive the design onto a flat surface. Then tack the stencil onto the spot where the design is desired. Each color of the design will require a different stencil and should be lined up exactly. A desk blotter may help position stencils and the surface material, and also may prevent paint from leaking through.

▲ Photography is another activity girls may want to try. A professional photographer can give them advice on taking good photographs. Here are some general tips to share with girls:

1. Use the viewfinder to find the best angle for the picture.

2. Have your eye scan around the edge of the viewfinder to make sure the background is not interfering with the view of the subject.

3. When photographing people, stand so that the light is not directly behind you, but behind you and just slightly to the side. This may keep your subjects from squinting and appearing to have red eyes.

4. The best pictures show people doing their everyday activities, rather than posing. Just make sure they are not moving around too much, so the picture is not blurred.

▲ *Exploring the Hand Arts*

▲ *Girl Scout Badges and Signs*: Photography badge; Prints and Graphics badge; Video Production badge

Sculpture

Plaster, clay, wood, paper, and even ice are some of the things used to make sculpture. By carving, modeling, or gluing things together, you can make sculptures. One type of sculpture is given here; you can find more activities in the Ceramics and Clay badge in *Girl Scout Badges and Signs*.

Carving

 A way to make sculpture is to mix plaster of paris and vermiculite. This mixture makes an easy-to-carve soft material, but looks like stone when you finish.

 You Will Need:
- **Plaster of paris**
- **Vermiculite (available in hardware stores or garden centers)**
- **A bucket with water for mixing**
- **Rags for cleaning**
- **Newspapers for a work surface**
- **A stick for stirring**
- **Cardboard milk containers**
- **A small kitchen knife**

1. Fill the bucket about half-full of water to make several sculpture forms. Mix the plaster of paris in the bucket by tossing handfuls of plaster into the water until small mounds form. Stir. The mixture should be slightly thick.

2. Add about as much vermiculite as you did plaster of paris, and stir until everything is well mixed. Be careful not to pour this mixture down a drain, as it can cause clogging.

3. Pour the mixture into the milk containers. Stir once to get rid of bubbles.

4. Let the containers set either several hours in bright sunlight or overnight. When the mixture has hardened, peel off the cardboard container.

5. Use the knife to chip or carve away pieces to make a figure or design.

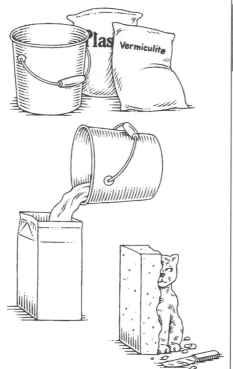

156

Embroidery

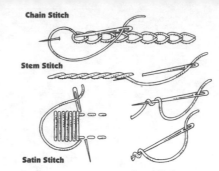

Chain Stitch

Stem Stitch

Satin Stitch

French Knot

You can use embroidery thread and needles to decorate your jeans, a jacket, a cloth purse, or a wall hanging. The basic stitches you will need are the chain stitch, the stem stitch, the satin stitch, and the French knot. Why not combine different stitches to decorate an item you choose?

Jewelry Making

You can use many different materials–clay, papier-mâché, bread dough, metal, wire, wood, paper–to make your own jewelry. Here are two jewelry-making ideas.

Beadwork

Use beads to make jewelry. Collect beads from craft stores, or you can make your own from clay, papier-mâché, or even paper. You might also want to try gluing beads onto T-shirts, hats, or fabric purses to make one-of-a-kind designs. Here is one type of beadwork to make necklaces, bracelets, or rings. Be sure to use a strong thread, like nylon.

Beaded Bracelet

1. Push two threaded needles (one at a time) through the first three beads.

2. Then use one needle to thread one more bead and the other needle to thread the other bead.

3. Push the two needles through one more bead.

4. Then use one needle to thread three beads and the other needle to thread three other beads.

5. Push one needle up through six beads and the other needle down through six beads.

6. Thread the number of beads you want in your design.

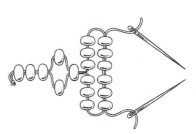

157

▲ **Sculpture:** A sculptor uses specific tools to achieve certain results. Consult an art teacher, artist, or someone in an artist's supply store for information about a sculptor's tools, techniques, and materials.

If girls carve jewelry, offer help gluing or fastening the piece onto pin backs or posts. As an alternative to using a glue gun, look for pin backs and other supplies with adhesive backings. These are often available at fabric and craft stores.

▲ In addition to carving, girls may want to make things from clay or similar substances. Some substances come in different colors, while others may be painted. With a little practice, girls can shape their materials into many designs.

▲ *Girl Scout Badges and Signs*: Ceramics and Clay badge; Jeweler badge

▲ **Jewelry Making:** After girls have learned to work with beads and know how to make knotted bracelets (see next handbook page), they may want to combine the two techniques. Have them plan their designs, and add beads as they weave the thread or cord into a necklace, bracelet, or other creation.

Besides beads, girls can also use buttons to make jewelry. Elastic thread works best when making button bracelets. Buttons also can be used to decorate jeans, vests, and other clothing

▲ **Embroidery:** Girls may want to use a thimble when they are first learning embroidery stitches. If a thimble seems awkward, a slip, such as the one quilters use, might be easier for girls to work with.

Instead of embroidery, girls might want to use fabric paint to decorate cloth. Make sure girls use paint specifically designed for fabric.

▲ *Exploring the Hand Arts*

▲ *Girl Scout Badges and Signs*: Art to Wear badge; Jeweler badge; "Making" Hobbies badge; Popular Arts badge; Textiles and Fibers badge

Knotted Necklaces and Bracelets

You can make necklaces with lightweight cord or friendship bracelets with embroidery thread. (See the section on knots, pages 185–186.) Experiment with different patterns and colors. Here's how you make a knotted bracelet.

You Will Need:
- Lightweight cord or embroidery thread

1. Pick four strands of cord or embroidery thread whose length is three times the circumference of your wrist.

2. Tie the cord at the loop tops.

3. Bring the right two cords over the left two cords.

4. Form a loop on the right side.

5. Bring the right cords behind the left cords and then through the loop on the right.

6. Then bring the left cords over the right cords.

7. Form a loop on the left side.

8. Bring the left cords behind the right cords and then through the loop on the left side.

9. Continue to tie knots from right to left.

10. Finish your bracelet with a bead a little larger than your beginning loop and use the bead to fasten the bracelet on your wrist.

Variations: You can insert beads at steps 5 and 8.

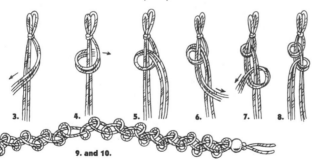

1.   2.   3.   4.   5.   6.   7.   8.

9. and 10.

158

Scrimshaw Pin

Try a modern-day variation of scrimshaw, the art of carving a pattern or drawing on ivory or whalebone, to make a pin. Because of environmental concerns, ivory and whalebone are no longer used, but you can create the same results on hard plastic.

You Will Need:
- A white candle or piece of white wax
- A piece of flat white or light-colored plastic
- A large-size sewing needle
- Black crayon
- Soft cloth
- Glue
- Pin back

1. Rub the surface of the plastic with the candle or wax to fill in any nicks or rough surfaces. Wipe the surface.

2. With the needle, scratch a design on the plastic.

3. Rub the crayon over the scratches so the crayon wax fills in the marks you have made.

4. Use the cloth to wipe away the crayon. The crayon should remain in the lines of the design. (To see your design develop, do a few scratch marks, use your crayon, then wipe. Repeat these three steps until your design is finished.)

5. Seal your design with varnish or clear nail polish.

6. Glue on a pin back and you're ready to wear your new jewelry.

Woodworking

Catch Board

This board can be used to hang keys, memo pads, eyeglasses, or jewelry.

You Will Need:
- A flat, wooden board
- At least 12 nails (each about 2" or 5 cm long)
- A hammer
- Medium-grain sandpaper
- A small block of wood (about the size of a bar of soap)
- A paintbrush
- Pliers
- A rag
- Heavy cord or string
- A saw
- Paint or clear varnish
- A drill (or 2 ring-topped screws)

1. Saw the board to measure 12" by 18" (30 cm by 46 cm).

2. Wrap the sandpaper around the small wood block, and smooth the edges and surface of the board.

3. Rub the board with a rag to remove any dust.

4. Paint or varnish the board. You can: paint designs; paste on pictures, drawings, or decorative pieces of paper and then coat with a clear varnish; draw with a permanent ink marker and then coat with a clear varnish.

5. Let your decorated board dry for at least 24 hours.

6. Hammer the nails 1/2" to 1" (1 1/4 cm to 2 1/2 cm) deep in assorted places on the board. The nails can coordinate with your design. Whatever you want to keep on the board will hang from these nails.

7. Grip the nail heads with the pliers and bend each nail upward.

8. You can prepare the board for hanging in two different ways. Use method A if you have a drill for making holes; use method B if you do not.

A. Drill holes in the top corners of the board.

B. You will need two ring-topped screws for this hanging method. These screws will go on the top corners of the board. Start holes for the screws by using an awl or by gently hammering nails into the spots for the screws. Pull the nails out and put the screws into place. Turn them until they fit tightly. If turning becomes difficult, insert a screwdriver through the opening and turn.

9. Thread the cord through the holes (or rings) and then knot the ends so that the cord will not pull through.

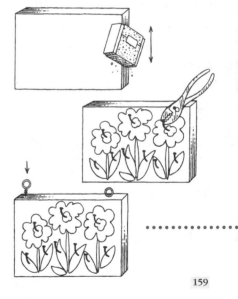

159

▲ **Weaving:** Here is a traditional arts activity that allows girls to design something useful. Start girls with simple hand-weaving projects made on a homemade cardboard loom. The following description of hand weaving can be found in the GSUSA resource *Exploring the Hand Arts*.

Purses, bookmarks, book covers are only a few of the possibilities girls can make on a cardboard loom. The principle is simple enough for the beginner yet it is still possible to carry out elaborate ideas and designs. The method of setting up the loom and weaving described below is specifically for a purse.

You Will Need:

● Woolen, silk, cotton, or linen yarns

● Cellophane tape

● Cardboard loom

● Heavy needle

● Comb

● Push pins

Setting Up the Loom. Cut two pieces of cardboard the exact size you wish to make a purse and paste them together. This double thickness will make your loom stronger. Paste cellophane tape over the top where the pins are to go. Place an even number of pins about 1/8"-1/4" (4–8 mm) apart, according to the thickness of the yarn. Use a pencil and ruler to make sure the pins are evenly spaced. The warp threads are the tight lengthwise threads that are the foundation of the work. The woof threads (also called "weft") are the crosswise threads that weave over and under the foundation. With a pin, fasten one end of the warp thread 1" (2.5 cm) from the top on the left side. Then take the thread up and around the first pin, going from the left to the right; carry it to the bottom of the loom and up again on the other side, hooking it over the same pin again from left to right. Bring the thread down the back, and up the front around the

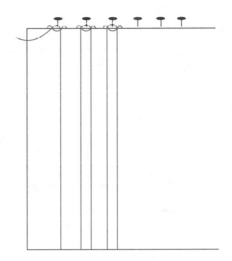

second pin; down the front, up the back around the same pin. Continue until all the pins are wound. End by pinning the warp to the right side of the loom, placing the pin about 1" (2.5 cm) from the top as on the other side.

Weaving the Fabric. Thread your woof thread into a very long needle and begin weaving at the lower right-hand corner of your loom and continue until you are all the way

across. Then turn your loom over and weave again until you are back where you started. Continue weaving around and around until the project is completed. Keep the warp threads straight with your needle and beat down the woof threads with a comb. You can join a new piece of thread by just leaving a long enough end in the center of the cardboard and weaving it in when the work is completed.

If you wish to make a book cover, bookmark, or place mat, you weave on only one side of the loom. The warp threads are wound on pins placed at top and bottom of the loom. Be careful not to pull the woof too tight to create a "pinched-in look." If you want to make a pattern or do more intricate weaving, see *Exploring the Hand Arts* for instructions.

Discovering Science and Technology

Science is the search for the what, how, and why of things, and the knowledge that comes from that search.

Technology is the application of science. It is using what people have learned about the why and how of the world to create practical things–things that help people live.

For example, a bird can fluff its feathers to create air spaces, which insulate the bird from the cold. So the warm, lightweight jacket you wear may use material that imitates bird feathers, or it can be made out of the real thing!

Have you ever wondered:
▲ How ducks stay warm in cold water?
▲ Why bubbles are round?
▲ How a computer works?

What Can You Live Without?

Try this game with friends. List 15 items made possible by technology, or the application of science. The items should be things that are important to you. Then cut the list down to ten items that everyone agrees she can live without. Then cut it down to five items. Talk about why particular things were chosen.

_____   _____   _____
_____   _____   _____
_____   _____   _____
_____   _____   _____
_____   _____   _____

160

Sharpening Your Observational and Investigative Skills

Observation is an important part of doing science. Here are activities to help sharpen your skills in observation.

Science and Technology Hunt

Find examples of science at work for each of the following and ask yourself why and how it works.

▲ A chemical reaction
▲ A liquid turning to a solid
▲ Something conducting heat
▲ Something stopping and going
▲ An action that causes a reaction
▲ A gear or a pulley at work
▲ Light traveling
▲ Sound traveling
▲ Colors mixing
▲ Water changing to gas
▲ Electricity traveling
▲ A magnet attracting
▲ Crystals being used

Artist and Scientist

Here are some words used to describe the way an object looks:

▲ Shape–circular, square, oval, trapezoidal
▲ Size–inches, centimeters, feet, meters
▲ Texture–rough, smooth, slick, gritty
▲ Directions–right, left, up, down
▲ In relation to–at a right angle to, parallel to, horizontal to, vertical to, smaller than, larger than
▲ Color–hue, shaded, intense

You Will Need:

▲ An assortment of objects that can be held easily (for example, a bird feather, a pine cone, a coffee cup, macaroni, a stamp) and that are not immediately recognized by description
▲ A pad of paper and a pencil for each set of partners

1. With a partner, sit back to back. One person is the artist and the other is the scientist.

2. The scientist holds an object that the artist has not seen. She must describe the object to the artist, who draws what is described.

3. When the artist is done, compare the drawing with the actual item.

You can see why it is important to use as many descriptive terms as possible! Change places and repeat the process with a different item.

161

Tips

▲ **Discovering Science and Technology:** As a leader, you can encourage girls to explore science, math and technology. How you feel about these areas greatly influences the girls' attitudes and choices. The activities included in this section are fun and hands-on, and link girls to everyday science and technology. Here are some tips if you are hesitant:

- Don't let personal fears interfere. You don't have to be an expert to do science.

- Stick with hands-on activities and ask questions of the girls.

- Don't worry about knowing the answer—part of the scientific process is asking questions and then discovering answers.

- Ask for help if you need it. Look for someone, preferably a woman, working in a scientific or technical field to act as your resource person.

Program Links

▲ *Into the World of Today and Tomorrow: Leading Girls to Mathematics, Science, and Technology* Contemporary Issues booklet

Supporting Activities

▲ Play the game of categories. Break girls into teams or have girls play as individuals. Assign or have girls choose an area such as health, family, recreation, school, home, work, industry. Then teams or individuals name at least five things that technology has created for use in that area.

Program Links

▲ *Girl Scout Badges and Signs*: Science in Action badge

Tips

▲ **Science and Technology Hunt:** Girls can do this handbook activity as a group or individually. As a group, they can hold a scavenger hunt or go on a group walk. As individuals, they can choose an example from the list and return to the next meeting with their observations.

Tips

▲ **Artist and Scientist:** The words listed to describe an object are best used when applied to something. For example, have the girls brainstorm descriptive terms for an object such as a ruler, an apple, or a hand. Note how difficult it is not to describe the object in terms of itself (e.g., a tool, a fruit, hand-shaped). A description of a standard ruler might be: "It is a three-dimensional rectangular object, measuring 6" x 1" x 1/8". It has lines that are marked off in equal distances from the end. It has numbers in ascending order marking every 1". It may be constructed of plastic or wood."

To do this activity, gather objects that girls might not easily identify.

Program Links

▲ *Girl Scout Badges and Signs*: Ecology badge; Science in the Worlds badge

Pendulums are used to keep time on many different kinds of clocks, but you can use a pendulum to create patterns.

You Will Need:

▲ A 6″ or 15 cm square of stiff construction paper

▲ Sand or salt

▲ String

▲ A thumbtack

▲ A large sheet of dark construction paper

▲ Scissors or a pin

▲ Chair or tabletop

▲ Hole puncher

▲ Glue

1. Fold the paper square in half to form a triangle, then again to form a smaller triangle. Open to form a cone. Tape sides to secure the cone.

2. Cut a small opening in the tip of the cone or pierce it with a pin. Punch holes in the longer tips of the paper cone and thread with string. Tie these ends to a longer string and suspend from a tabletop or chair.

3. Place construction paper under the cone. Fill the cone with salt or sand, holding a fingertip on the bottom opening. Swing the pendulum from the center and release it. (The design can be fixed by coating the construction paper ahead of time with a thin coat of white household glue.)

Try getting the pendulum to go straight back and forth and in spirals. What do you notice about the patterns?

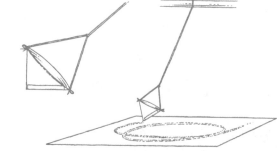

162

 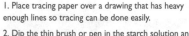

You can do an appearing act by using a chemical reaction to make an artistic design become visible. Sometimes, when chemicals react with each other, the result is a color change. Try this and have chemistry bring your work of art out for all to see.

You Will Need:

▲ White vellum tracing paper (available at art supply stores)

▲ A wide paintbrush

▲ An artist's thin paintbrush or flat nib pen

▲ Starch solution

▲ Iodine/alcohol solution

1. Place tracing paper over a drawing that has heavy enough lines so tracing can be done easily.

2. Dip the thin brush or pen in the starch solution and trace the drawing. If you are using a pen, be careful not to scratch the paper. Starch solution is colorless, so when it is dry, nothing will show on the paper.

3. Tape the corners of the paper to minimize curling. Dip the wide brush into the iodine/alcohol solution and, taking care not to rub, gently stroke over the tracing. Bluish-purplish lines will appear as the iodine chemically reacts with the starch.

Try some other activities using this chemical reaction: send a secret message, make a buried treasure map, put on a magic show for younger children.

Starch Solution: Mix 4 tablespoons (60 ml) of cornstarch in 1 cup (235 ml) of lukewarm water. Cooking water from potatoes or pasta may also be used.

Iodine/Alcohol Solution: Mix 1 tablespoon (15 ml) of tincture of iodine in 1 cup (235 ml) of rubbing alcohol. This solution will have a yellowish-brown color.

163

Tips

▲ **Pendulum Patterns:** This handbook activity could get sticky! Make sure you place newspaper beneath the pendulum. Dilute the liquid glue with water and set the finished products in a safe place to dry.

Note that the pattern formed by the pendulum is oval-shaped. The pattern will get smaller as friction slows the movement down. Unlike this pendulum, a clock pendulum is carefully balanced so it will swing in a straight line. In addition, a clock's pendulum is suspended in a way that offers very little friction. The springs and gears of the clock give the pendulum a small push to keep it swinging.

Supporting Activities

▲ Additional activities that explore the concept of pendulum motion can be set up easily. Help girls with the following activity:

1. Attach two objects of different weights to equal lengths of string.

2. Attach those strings to a string suspended between two chairs.

3. Have the girls hypothesize (guess) if the objects will take different lengths of time to swing ten gentle swings.

The girls may be surprised to discover that the objects take the same amount of time to swing even though the weights are different. Ask girls to then take two strings of different lengths and use the same object to time the swings. Have them find out whether the length of the string makes a difference. Did they guess correctly that the shorter string will swing faster with the same object?

Program Links

▲ *Girl Scout Badges and Signs*: Science in Action badge; Science Sleuth badge

Tips

▲ **Chemical Appearing Act:** Chemistry is the study of chemicals and how they can be combined into compounds or changed, through a chemical reaction, into a new substance. Chemical reactions happen all the time: silver jewelry tarnishes when exposed to air and coffee turns sweet when sugar is added.

The chemical reaction described in the badge activity combines a starch and iodine solution to create a reaction that can be seen. Girls can observe the same effect when lemon juice is used as the "secret ink." Using a paintbrush or cotton swab, girls can write a message or draw a picture with lemon juice. The message or drawing will become visible if the paper is placed in the sun or a warm oven for several minutes. Heat causes the chemical change to happen, changing the lemon juice to a substance that will absorb light, thus making it appear dark.

Compass Maker

Compasses work because the earth is like a giant magnet. When something is magnetized, it points to magnetic north. You can use that knowledge to make your own compass as the sailors did long ago. (See "Finding Your Way with a Compass," pages 181–182, to learn more about compasses.)

You Will Need:

▲ A strong magnet

▲ A needle (that will stick to the magnet)

▲ A cork big enough to lay the needle on

▲ A thumbtack

▲ A bowl of water

▲ A paper clip

▲ A real compass

▲ A dab of colored nail polish

1. Stroke the needle along the magnet one way until it acts like a magnet and attracts the paper clip.

2. Poke the thumbtack into the bottom of the cork to keep it from tipping over.

3. Lay the cork in the bowl of water so it floats in the middle. Lay the needle so it is flat on the cork.

4. Use a real compass to check which way your needle is pointing. Put a dab of nail polish on the end pointing north. Determine the cardinal points of your compass (North, South, East, West).

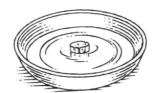

164

Environmental Observer

You don't always have to use the equipment of a scientist to decide whether a place is healthy or not for plants and animals to live (that includes you!). The Stream Health Checklist shown here tells you what to look for, smell, and touch to determine how healthy a stream is. Use the checklist to make an environmental report card for stream exploration, or develop your own list of checkpoints for an area you want to explore.

Stream Health Checklist

	Good	Fair	Poor
Variety of stream animals (fish, snails, insects, worms, and other living creatures). The greater the number of types, or species, the healthier the stream.			
Shade from overhanging vegetation.			
Stability (lack of erosion) of stream bank.			
Clearness of water.			
Turbidity of water (amount of stuff suspended in the water). Does water appear cloudy or clear?			
Smell of water.			
Signs of run-off from surrounding land.			
Amount of garbage along stream.			

Use your report card to encourage others to care for the stream in some way.

165

Handbook Page 164

Handbook Page 165

▲ **Compass Maker**: This activity will not work using a metal bowl, because the metal in the bowl will interfere with the direction the arrow points. Sailors used a compass made of magnetic iron, floating on straw or cork in water.

You might list questions for girls to answer when doing this activity, such as:

● What happens if you compare the direction of your handmade compass with that of a manufactured one?

● What happens if you turn the needle in a different direction?

● What happens if you hold a paper clip (steel) that has been magnetized near the compass needle?

Have the girls guess what might happen, then experiment to find out.

▲ *Girl Scout Badges and Signs*: Finding Your Way badge

▲ **Environmental Observer**: This activity asks girls to make observations and draw conclusions about what they observe. A stream biologist might use this method to judge the general health of a stream, environment, or ecosystem. She or he may then follow up with more sophisticated chemical tests to measure the amount of oxygen in the water or check for harmful chemicals or bacteria.

The stream health checklist is based upon indicators for a healthy environment that a scientist has been trained to observe. Explain to girls that it is very much like going to the doctor for a physical exam. If something is present that is not supposed to be, or something is not within a normal range (like blood pressure or temperature), the doctor will run tests or make a diagnosis based on her experience and knowledge.

Girls might want to check to see if there is a stream-monitoring network in their community, or have a scientist help them establish a "quality of life" checklist for another area. Some possible areas to focus on are: air, gardens, parks, and streets.

▲ *Girl Scout Badges and Signs*: Eco-Action badge; Ready for Tomorrow badge; Water Fun badge; Water Wonders badge

"Key" Maker

 Scientists need ways to sort, or classify, things so they can study them, describe them, and identify them again. A written or illustrated classification of things is called a key. Here's a way to develop your own simple key.

You Will Need:

▲ An assortment of things, such as different kinds of trees, leaves, shoes, things you write with, or even people

▲ Paper and a pencil

1. Gather all your samples.

2. Think of a way to divide your pile into two groups.

Then write one or two words to describe each group (for example, "leafy" and "needle").

3. Now divide each group into two more groups (for example, "hand-shaped," "oval," "short," "long").

4. Continue dividing and adding descriptions until each group contains only one thing.

5. Regather your things and start over. Create a new key with a new set of descriptions.

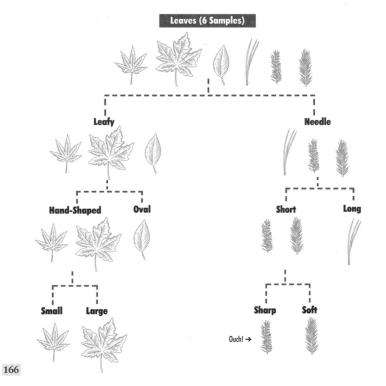

Leaves (6 Samples)

Leafy — Needle

Hand-Shaped — Oval   Short — Long

Small — Large   Sharp — Soft

Ouch! →

166

Kaleidoscope Creator

 You Will Need:

▲ A shiny picture postcard

▲ Tape

▲ Colored cellophane

▲ White tissue paper

▲ Scissors

1. Fold the postcard, with shiny side in, lengthwise into three equal sections. (Can you do it without a ruler?)

2. Tape the postcard (now a triangular tube) so the seam doesn't leak light.

3. Cut small pieces of colored cellophane.

4. Cut two pieces of white tissue paper 2" (5 cm) larger than the end of the tube.

5. Place the cut cellophane between the two pieces of tissue paper and tape around one end of the tube. You now have a kaleidoscope that relies on reflected light to create its special effects. Hold it up to the light. What do you see?

Using your kaleidoscope, find different reflections. Have a kaleidoscope party and ask others to bring different kinds of kaleidoscopes.

Science Challenge:

How do you make grass grow quickly using sunlight?

You Will Need:

•A sponge

•Water

•Grass seed

•A glass

•A saucer

Answer: Put some grass seed on a moist sponge, cover with a glass, and leave in the sunlight for several days. The glass acts as a greenhouse, producing heat and water in a contained environment.

167

▲ **"Key" Maker:** Suggest girls first construct a key using something simple, such as shoes or fruit, before tackling leaves, trees, or wildlife. When girls are ready for a more involved key, they can use pictures of animals, trees, or leaves, if they want to bring the outdoors indoors.

When first presenting this, the process of describing things is more important than naming things correctly in the key. Concentrate on classifying things based on what you see, measure, or feel. This can be very unsophisticated (large, small) or increasingly sophisticated (rounded tips, sharp tips).

Girls can work individually, in pairs, or in small groups to construct a key. Reclassifying the same group of objects to form a new key is an exercise in problem-solving and creativity.

Give the girls an opportunity to look at some real keys. Look for keys that give "either/or" choices or keys with very simple divisions. Your librarian can help you find resources that illustrate a simple key.

Program Links

▲ *Girl Scout Badges and Signs*: Plants and Animals badge; Science in the Worlds badge

Tips

▲ **Kaleidoscope Creator:** When gathering materials, instruct girls to find colorful, "busy" postcards. They need to be shiny to reflect light. Girls could also glue magazine pictures onto 5" x 7" index cards or use old picture postcards.

Although this project will not compete with a store-bought kaleidoscope, it will illustrate how reflected light can create visual effects. Manufactured kaleidoscopes rely on mirrors or shiny metal to reflect the light. They use stones, flakes of plastic, or even flowers to make patterns. Some kaleidoscopes are made to split images of things viewed outside the scope into patterns.

Supporting Activities

▲ Another way to explore light is to cover flashlights with different colored cellophanes. In a dark room, shine the flashlight on a white wall or ceiling. Blend primary colors to see what special effects can be created. Have the girls predict what they will see, then experiment to test the predictions.

Program Links

▲ *Girl Scout Badges and Signs*: Toymaker badge

Tips

▲ **Science Challenge:** Science challenges are meant to pose questions and give opportunities for scientific discovery. Each challenge illustrates a scientific principle that can be explored. Girls might set up a "control" on this experiment by preparing an identical sponge, without placing a glass over it. By controlling all the variables (or factors) except one, they can see what affected the growth. Another activity might be to assemble a terrarium to observe the greenhouse effect over time. Or you and the girls could visit a greenhouse.

Have you ever blown bubbles? Now is the time for some scientific bubble studies!

You Will Need:

To make a bubble solution:
▲ 1 cup (235 ml) of liquid dish soap

▲ 40-50 drops of glycerin (available at a drugstore)

▲ A 1-gallon plastic jug

▲ Enough water to fill up a 1-gallon jug

Mix ingredients in the plastic jug and let sit for 12 hours, if possible.

To study bubbles:
▲ Things to blow bubbles through such as drinking straws, plastic berry baskets, canning rings

▲ Rulers

▲ Smooth tabletops or plastic trays or pans

▲ Towels or rags

What Holds Bubbles Together?

Water molecules on the surface of water tend to stick together. This is called surface tension. When soap is added, it reduces the surface tension of water, allowing the bubbles to form. Bubbles pop when water evaporates out of the bubbles. Adding glycerin helps strengthen the bubbles by preventing the water from evaporating. If you want to touch a bubble without bursting it, wet your hand.

Bubbles are round when floating in the air because of air pressure. The air outside the bubble presses inward while the air trapped inside the bubble presses outward.

The colors you see when you look at a bubble are from light reflecting off the soapy coating on the water molecules. This soapy film is on the water molecules in layers, like paint in various thicknesses.

168

Make Bubbles and Bubble Domes

1. First, practice blowing bubbles. Dip berry baskets and other tools in the bubble solution. Blow air into the tool or move the tool through the air. Experiment with sizes and shapes.

2. Blow bubble domes (half-spheres) onto a tray or shallow pan by capturing bubble solution in a straw. Hold the straw just at the surface of the pan and blow gently. Carefully remove the straw.

Bubble Domes

Bubble Frame

Make a Bubble Frame

1. Cut two equal pieces of straw and run about 18" (46 cm) of string through the pieces of straw.

2. Knot the string.

3. Pull the knot into a straw.

4. Form a frame as shown, and lay the frame in the bubble solution (in a pan).

5. Lift it out carefully so you have a soap window across the frame. Make different frame sizes and shapes.

Look for rainbow colors in the frame and move the frame to form different shapes. Can you get another person to put a hand through your frame without bursting it? Make a super bubble by moving the frame slowly through the air. If you want to set your bubble free, pull the two straws together. This takes practice. Avoid popping the bubble in your face and eyes.

Watch your bubbles. Look for size, motion, and color. What happens when they touch?

169

▲ **Bubbleology (The Study of Bubbles!):** Have the girls list other words that end with "-ology" (meaning "the study of"). Explain that although bubbleology is not a recognized science, they can discover a lot of things about bubbles using the scientific method. Help girls understand the scientific method by having them do the following:

1. Pose a question you want to answer or a statement you want to explore. For example, "Can I make bubbles inside a bubble?"

2. Think about a possible answer to the question. This is an hypothesis (educated guess). For example, "If the first bubble is strong and a straw is gently inserted into it, another bubble can be blown."

3. Conduct an experiment to test the hypothesis. First get the needed materials: bubble solution, tray, and straw. Then develop a procedure. Figure out the steps and write them down so someone else can check your work. Be sure to control the variables. For example, maybe you need to experiment with bubble solution strength or the surfaces you blow on. Decide if altering any of the things will change the result of your experiment.

4. Analyze the results. Do the experiment more than once and keep records. Once might be a fluke. Maybe you can graph the results.

5. Draw a conclusion. Have you supported or failed to support your hypothesis? Decide how or why it happened. Write that down.

Using the scientific method may seem intimidating or boring at first, but many experiments can be fun, interesting, and help girls develop a positive attitude about science.

▲ **What Holds Bubbles Together?:** This sidebar is included to illustrate some basic scientific principles such as surface tension, air pressure, and light reflection.

Point out to girls that the rainbow of colors they see on a bubble is light reflected off the different layers. The thickness of the soap layers determines the color they see reflected. The unevenness of the layers gives the swirling effect. The thickest layers reflect red light, while the thinnest layers reflect violet light. This should help girls predict when a bubble is ready to burst!

▲ Bubble Challenges: Here are some questions for girls to explore while studying bubbles.

1. What is the average size of bubbles you have blown in your groups?

2. How many bubbles within bubbles within bubbles can you make?

3. What happens when two bubbles meet? Does this always happen?

4. Can you predict the "pop" time of your bubble by observing the color change on the top of your bubble?

▲ *Girl Scout Badges and Signs*: Science Sleuth badge; Water Wonders badge

Making Things Move

Technology has helped people improve the way they move themselves and things from place to place. Observe some simple movement principles in action with the following activities.

One-Pulley Lift

Pulleys can help you lift and move things more easily. A pulley is a wheel, and when you add a rope, it becomes a mover or a lifter. Real pulleys have grooves in the wheel to hold the rope.

You Will Need:

▲ 1 thread spool (wooden, if possible)

▲ A wire hanger or heavy-gauge wire

▲ A pole suspended between two chairs, or a hook on a door

▲ A small basket or bucket

▲ 10′ (3 meters) of string or cord

1. Bend the wire into a triangle or untwist the hanger to thread the spool as shown. Now you have a pulley.

2. Run the cord over the pulley suspended from the pole or hook.

3. Attach one end of the cord to a basket.

Is it easier to lift the basket with the pulley or without? Experiment with the length of cord needed to lift the load. How much cord do you need to raise the basket a foot off the ground?

170

Science Challenge: How do you make a book move across a bare floor using one finger? (Imagine the book is a big stone for a wall you are building.)

You Will Need:

▲ 1 big book

▲ 4 pencils

Answer: Lay the pencils in rows under the book and roll the book forward. Pick up the last pencil and place it in front of the book. This reduces friction between the book and the floor. Try rolling the book with one finger.

Science Challenge: How can you blow up a balloon without blowing into it?

You Will Need:

▲ Large-size plastic soda bottles (empty, with the cap removed)

▲ Balloons

▲ Dish or bowl with very hot water

Answer: Blow up the balloon and then let the air out. This will help stretch the balloon. Put the balloon over the top of the bottle. Now stand the bottle in the bowl of hot water. The heat from the water will warm the air inside the bottle and cause it to expand. What do you think will happen if you leave the open bottle in a refrigerator or a freezer before putting on the balloon and warming? Try it. Does this experiment show you anything about how hot air balloons work?

Learning About pH

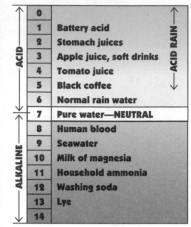

0		
1	Battery acid	
2	Stomach juices	ACID RAIN
3	Apple juice, soft drinks	
4	Tomato juice	
5	Black coffee	
6	Normal rain water	
7	Pure water—NEUTRAL	
8	Human blood	
9	Seawater	
10	Milk of magnesia	
11	Household ammonia	
12	Washing soda	
13	Lye	
14		

(ACID = levels above 7; ALKALINE = levels below 7)

Simplified pH scale

Scientists group chemicals that have common properties. pH describes how acid or how alkaline (base) a substance is. Acids are sour chemicals. Bases are the opposite. The pH of a chemical is measured by a special scale developed by scientists. The scale runs from 0 to 14, with the middle being 7 (or neutral), with 0 being the most acid, and with 14 being the most alkaline.

171

▲ **One Pulley Lift:** Pulleys and levers are some of the earliest examples of applied technology. Show girls some real pulleys as they make their own. A single pulley lifts things right beneath it. Pulleys can be combined with other pulleys or levers (such as cranes) to lift heavy things in different ways.

▲ **Science Challenge Badge Activity:** This challenge demonstrates a simple way to move a heavy object. This method of moving objects is one way early shipbuilders launched their ships and the way the building blocks for the Egyptian pyramids were moved from place to place.

Ask girls "What shape should the pencils be to reduce friction?" Girls can think of ways to compare different-shaped pencils and their effectiveness at moving objects. Have the girls look for examples of other ways that things are moved.

Program Links

▲ *Girl Scout Badges and Signs:* Science in Action badge

Tips

▲ **Learning About pH:** This activity will help girls understand acid rain, water quality, and chemical testing of water and soil. Plants and animals have a pH range within which they can survive in water or on land. Help girls understand the reasons for testing substances (to see if the water or soil is healthy, if it can support plants or animals, or if the acidity or alkalinity needs to be changed). pH-testing kits for soil can be purchased inexpensively at garden centers, while pH strips or litmus paper can be purchased at drug stores.

Girls may be intrigued when testing food and household materials for acidity and alkalinity. Therefore, warn girls to treat any unknown as a harmful substance when testing, and make certain that they do not touch or taste.

Program Links

▲ *Girl Scout Badges and Signs:* Eco-Action badge; Ecology badge; Ready for Tomorrow badge; Water Fun badge; Water Wonders badge

Radish pH Tester

 How do you test for pH? Set up a testing procedure to determine whether a substance is an acid or a base.

You Will Need:

- Radishes
- Tablespoons
- Water
- Small, clear glasses or plastic cups
- Knife
- Substances to test, such as milk, tomato juice, distilled water, vinegar, lemon juice, tap water, milk of magnesia, baking soda dissolved in water, chalk ground up in water

1. Scrape the skin from one radish into one glass of water. Scrape enough to turn the water a pinkish color. (Use your fingernail or the edge of a dull knife.) The pinkish water is the "tester."

2. Pour small amounts (about 2 tablespoons or 30 ml) of the tester into empty, clean glasses. Use as many glasses as you have substances.

3. Test for acid or base by adding a few drops of the liquid you want to test.

4. Here is what to look for:

Pink color changes to red = an acid

Pink color changes to bluish-green = a base

No color change = neutral

Once you know whether something is an acid or a base, try adding the opposite to see if the color changes again. You can also make a pH tester with red cabbage juice.

Instead of using radish juice to test pH, you can buy a specially treated paper, called litmus paper (narrow range), from a drugstore. Follow the directions on the package to test substances.

Acid and Base in Foods

Some foods contain acids. Lemon juice and vinegar both contain acids. They taste sour. But, many acids and bases are harmful to people. Bases have no strong taste in foods, and often feel slippery or soapy to the touch. Liquid bleach is a base.

Water and soil are tested for their pH. If a swimming pool is too acid, it will burn your eyes. If a pond is too acid, the fish will die. Something acid can be made less so by adding a base. Gardeners, fish biologists, and pool attendants often act as chemists when they test and change the pH of the soil or water by adding an acid or base.

Acid Rain

 Some parts of the country and the world have problems with acid rain. This is when rainwater has combined with chemicals in the air from car exhaust or factory smoke to form harmful acidic chemicals.

To see what acid rain will do to buildings, try this experiment, using chalk as your building stone. (Did you test the pH of chalk?)

You Will Need:

- 2 small bowls: 1 filled with water, 1 filled with vinegar or lemon juice
- 2 pieces of new chalk
- A ruler

1. Place the chalk in each of the bowls. What happens?

2. Leave the bowls for 12 hours. Are there still bubbles?

3. Take the chalk pieces out and compare them. What has happened? Why?

Can you find any buildings or stones (such as cemetery gravestones) affected by acid rain in your community?

Computers

Computers are like mechanical brains. People program computers or use already programmed software that tells the computer what to do.

 Ask someone to show you how a computer works. Find out the difference between computer hardware and software. Find out about the following computer hardware:

- Keyboard
- Mouse
- Printer
- Disk drive
- Monitor
- Desktop, laptop, and notebook computers

Use several different kinds of computer software. You might visit a computer store and ask for a demonstration.

Think Like a Computer

Write out all the steps for doing something simple, like eating, combing your hair, getting dressed, or fixing your favorite snack. Make a chart that shows the steps. Here's how:

1. Write questions in the pink diamonds.

2. Write information in the orange rectangles.

3. Write instructions in the green rectangles with the rounded corners.

4. Connect these different shapes with lines and arrows.

To get an idea of how this is done, follow "Steps in a Guessing Game" on the next page. Computer programmers call this type of diagram a flowchart.

Handbook Page 172

Handbook Page 173

▲ **Radish pH Tester:** Although a bit involved, this can be a lot of fun for girls because of the visible results. Other substances that can be used are cabbages, onions, beets, tea, or apple skins.

▲ **Acid Rain:** Acid rain is a worldwide problem, especially in countries that have unregulated factories. Automobile exhaust is a big contributor to this problem. Chemicals in exhaust gases react with chemicals in the air. This falls to earth when it rains. In some places scientists and wildlife biologists have reclaimed acidic lakes by dumping large quantities of lime into the water to change the pH.

A walk through a cemetery or a check of old outdoor statues will show some of the ravages of acid rain.

In the handbook activity, ask the girls to determine which material is acid and which material is base in this experiment.

Program Links

▲ *Earth Matters: A Challenge for Environmental Action* Contemporary Issues booklet

▲ *Girl Scout Badges and Signs*: Science Sleuth badge

Tips

▲ **Computers:** You will find that many girls are on their way to becoming "computer literate" through school and home use. Parents, a local school or college, the public library, or your council office may be able to recommend facilities where girls can work with computers.

"Think Like a Computer" is a flowchart that uses computer-like logic to arrive at a conclusion. Flowcharts are basic to writing computer programs. With programmed software, this skill is no longer necessary for most users, but it will help girls understand how a computer performs a function.

Program Links

▲ *Girl Scout Badges and Signs*: Dabbler badge in the World of Today and Tomorrow; Computer Fun badge; Math Whiz badge

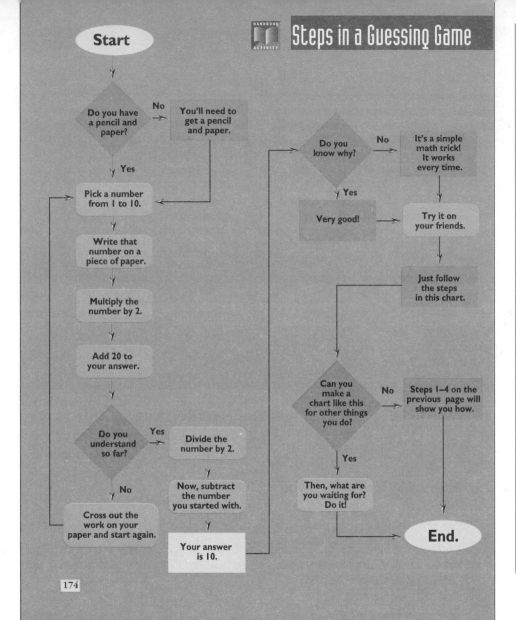

Steps in a Guessing Game

Start

Do you have a pencil and paper? — No → You'll need to get a pencil and paper.

Yes ↓

Pick a number from 1 to 10.

Write that number on a piece of paper.

Multiply the number by 2.

Add 20 to your answer.

Do you understand so far? — Yes → Divide the number by 2. ↓ Now, subtract the number you started with. ↓ Your answer is 10.

No ↓ Cross out the work on your paper and start again.

Do you know why? — No → It's a simple math trick! It works every time.

Yes ↓ Very good! → Try it on your friends.

Just follow the steps in this chart.

Can you make a chart like this for other things you do? — No → Steps 1–4 on the previous page will show you how.

Yes ↓ Then, what are you waiting for? Do it!

End.

Computer Talk

Did you know that you could talk to people, shop for clothes, or find information by using a computer? Here's how it works.

You Will Need:

• A computer

• A computer modem, a device that hooks the computer up to the telephone line

• Telecommunications computer software that lets your computer talk to other computers

How it is set up: The modem is connected between the computer and a telephone line. When you dial a computer network service with your modem in place, your computer connects to other computers, called servers. These computer servers have a lot more storage space than your own computer and they collect and store information. (Many computer servers speak to each other through Internet, a global network, or other commercial services. Some don't cost money, but many have a monthly fee for the amount of time used.)

What your options are: Once you are linked to a server, or are "on-line," you have a lot of options, just like going to a shopping mall. Within each option are further selections, just like in each store you visit. Here are some examples of what you might select:

E-Mail: You can send a message by E-mail (electronic mail) to someone in the same room or clear across the country. It takes 10 seconds for a message to go from the United States to Europe. You can link up to "bulletin boards" which contain messages sent by people interested in the same subjects.

Information files: There are many electronic filing cabinets that store information on every subject imaginable. You can search for something on cats or send in your own report on a rare plant you have found.

Services to make life easier: You can order pizza, shop for school clothes, or make airline reservations.

Games: You can hook up with others to play computer games.

What happens if you need help? Most of the computer servers will talk you through questions and problems. Some are more "user-friendly" than others. Many of the computer and software companies have "800" telephone numbers (there is no charge) you can call to get help.

 Note: Although you are cautioned not to speak to strangers in person, different rules seem to be at work on computer networks, where people "talk" to others they have never met. Beware of giving out your phone number, address, and any credit-card numbers on a computer network. Computers and software usually have special programs to prevent others from entering your computer through the network, or to prevent computer viruses from infecting your system.

Make up a play or game that demonstrates your understanding of computer networks. Investigate how they work and what they cost. If possible, access a computer network at home, school, library, or elsewhere and send a message on E-mail.

For more activities involving computers, see the Computer Fun badge in *Girl Scout Badges and Signs*.

174

175

Tips

▲ **Computer Talk:** Changes in the computer industry are happening so rapidly that information in a book like this can quickly become dated. The best place to discover new things about computers is by reading computer magazines or by visiting computer stores.

The badge activity is meant to help girls understand computer networks and give them hands-on experience. If you don't have access to a computer network, check with girls' parents or guardians, the library, workplaces in the community, or your council office.

If you go "on line" with the girls, discuss computer etiquette (What if everyone on-line reads what you contribute? How much time should you take if others are waiting to use it?) and safety (Should you give out your phone number or address?). You might even talk with another Girl Scout troop via computer! If words on a computer network seem foreign or unfamiliar, find a resource that lists computer abbreviations, acronyms, and new words.

Supporting Activities

▲ Suggest girls talk to someone whose job it is to communicate with people around the world. Girls can find out what kinds of technology are being used every day to communicate and get work done.

▲ Girls can learn about how new things are being made out of old. Some companies are recycling computer parts or ensuring that computers are constructed out of recyclable materials.

Program Links

▲ *Earth Matters: A Challenge for Environmental Action* Contemporary Issues booklet

▲ *Girl Scout Badges and Signs*: Computer Fun badge

▲ *Into the World of Today and Tomorrow: Leading Girls to Mathematics, Science, and Technology* Contemporary Issues booklet

REMINDER!

Create one job for each girl's family. In this way, you get the help you need and each family feels they are part of the troop or group. Large jobs, such as cookie captain, can be broken down into smaller jobs and shared by several families.

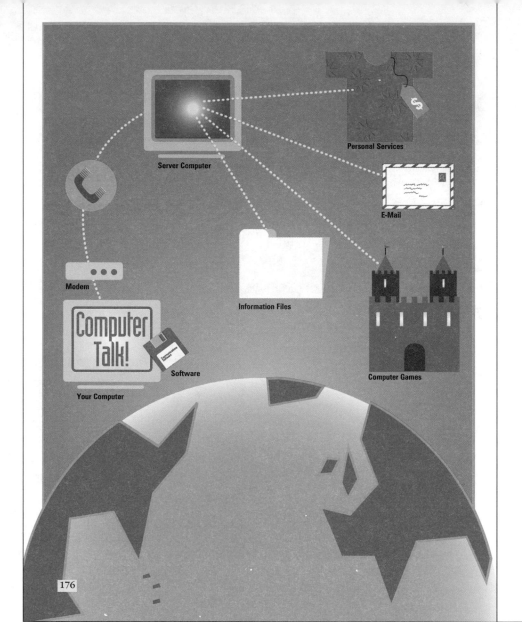

Handbook Page 176

Girl Scouts have always used the outdoors for activities. The 1912 Handbook for Girl Scouts encouraged girls "to meet out, follow open-air pursuits and to camp out in order to learn to appreciate nature to the fullest." Girls learned how to semaphore (use flags to signal the letters of the alphabet), stop runaway horses, shoot an arrow with a bow, and identify plants. They hiked, camped, and grew gardens for feeding themselves.

Today, open-air pursuits include playing outdoor sports, hiking, camping, biking, gardening, learning about nature, flying a kite, stargazing, snowshoeing, bird-watching, and other activities such as service projects. Add some of your favorite outdoor activities to this list.

Preparing for Outdoor Activities

Every time you prepare for an outdoor activity, remember to plan ahead, learn the skills you need, dress right, keep safe, and practice minimal impact in the outdoors.

Plan Ahead

Deciding where the outdoor activity or camping trip will take place is an important first step in planning outdoor activities. Your troop or group might want to brainstorm ideas to help choose a site and determine what you will do when you get there. (See pages 28–30 for the Travel Action Plan steps.)

Allow time to plan. One meeting is barely enough time to plan a hike; planning an overnight in a place you've never been to would require several meetings. Make telephone calls to find out about places. Get maps and brochures that tell you how far places are. Contact Chambers of Commerce or organizations to find out when places are open and what special programs are offered.

Handbook Page 177

Tips

▲ **Exploring the Outdoors:** Outdoor activities in Girl Scouting can open up a world of new experiences for girls. Familiar activities such as cooking, crafts, service projects, sports, or games present new challenges and different experiences when done outdoors.

Many outdoor activities do not require special training. Take girls to the playground, backyard, or neighborhood park. Whether walking in the city or camping out under the stars, girls should have the opportunity to experience their environment first-hand.

▲ **Preparing for Outdoor Activities:** Your most valuable resources are *Safety-Wise* and *Outdoor Education in Girl Scouting*, along with the *Junior Girl Scout Handbook*. Junior Girl Scout recognitions are written to allow for progression and exploration. Check with your local council for training offered in outdoor education and camping.

Libraries have wonderful resource books on nature appreciation and environmental education. You also can contact environmental groups or outdoor clubs for additional training, resources, or guided activities for children.

Tips

▲ **Planning Ahead/Planning a Camping Trip:** Even if you are just going out to play a game, check your site ahead of time. Are there bathrooms, drinking water, and nearby telephones? Are there potential hazards, such as traffic or a nearby stream?

When planning for an experience beyond the troop or group meeting, you or a parent should "dry run" the trip before taking the girls, if at all possible. Contact your council for suggestions and information about council-owned or recommended overnight sites.

Planning can be done as a group, in committees or patrols, or in teams. Encourage consensus in decision-making and avoid leader-generated "rules" unless safety is an issue. As a leader, you might suggest options from which girls can choose. As they become more experienced, girls should take greater initiative and responsibility for planning.

Competency training in outdoor skills is a must before planning trips with girls. You or a troop committee adult will need to attend council-required outdoor skills training before the girls plan and go on an overnight in the outdoors. Many councils have older girls who are trained to act as resource people for leaders and troops planning outdoor or camping activities.

While older girls cannot be left "in charge" of a group, they can help in the planning and teaching of skills.

Remember that *Safety-Wise* has specific guidelines for camping, cooking on camp stoves, traveling, backpacking, and advanced outdoor pursuits. Progression and planning are the keys to successful outdoor activities with girls.

Program Links

▲ *Girl Scout Badges and Signs*: Outdoor Cook badge; Outdoor Creativity badge; Outdoor Fun badge; Outdoor Fun in the City badge; Troop Camper badge

▲ *Outdoor Education in Girl Scouting*

Planning a Camping Trip

By the time you're ready to plan a camping trip, you will have had outdoor experiences close to home. Perhaps you've planned and enjoyed a hike or have had other outdoor experiences. Simple outdoor pursuits should come before camping.

When you're ready to plan a camping trip, the Troop Camper badge in *Girl Scout Badges and Signs* might be a good place to start. Another source of information is an adult from your council who is trained in camping and outdoor activities. Outdoor flag ceremonies, a Girl Scouts' Own, and special evening campfire programs can all be a part of your camping experience.

As you learn about camping, you may want to do more advanced camping, like pitching tents at resident camp, staying at a state park, or planning an overnight backpacking trip. You may want to become skilled at outdoor cooking, orienteering, canoeing, or other outdoor pursuits. Don't forget to explore the possibilities at your Girl Scout council's summer events or resident camp.

Camping "Prep" List

Use this list to plan an overnight camping trip. You might need a separate list for cooking and sleeping gear.

You Will Need:

- Adults to help you
- Parent/guardian permission slips
- Arrangements for the site (usually reservations are needed)
- Arrangements for transportation
- A schedule of activities
- Cooking equipment
- Menu and food
- Sleeping gear
- Kaper chart
- First-aid kit
- Personal items (proper clothing, personal hygiene items, any medications with directions for use, and day-pack items)
- Other resources (such as money, maps, compass, flashlight, or games)

Learning the Skills You Need

Decide which new skills you might need for your outdoor activity. Practice some of these before you set out. For example, learn how to read a map, use a compass, or follow trail markers. Learning how to dress for the outdoors is another skill you should learn.

Dressing for the Outdoors

"Be Prepared" is the best guide for choosing outdoor clothing. Always hope for the best with weather, but prepare for the worst.

178

Packing Your Day Pack

What do you put in your day pack? What would you carry in your day pack for a hike in the city? What about a hike in the woods? Write your items and see if they match the list that follows.

_____ _____

_____

_____

Basic day-pack contents:

- **A water bottle.** You need to replace water because you perspire, even on cold days. Use a plastic soda or water bottle.

- **A whistle.** Use this if you get lost or separated from the group. It saves energy and reduces stress in a scary situation.

- **A small mirror** for signaling if you get lost.

- **Rain gear.** This can be a poncho, or a windbreaker and rain pants. Be prepared!

- **A quarter** for emergency phone calls, along with emergency phone numbers.

- **Sunscreen and/or lip protection.** Use this to protect from sun and wind.

- **A pencil and paper.**

- **A map or transportation schedule** when traveling.

- **A portable snack,** such as a granola bar, an apple, a piece of hard candy, or "gorp," which can give you a quick surge of energy.

> RECIPE FOR GORP
> 1/2 cup roasted or boiled peanuts
> 1/2 cup sunflower seeds
> 1/2 cup raisins
> 1/2 cup chocolate chips
> 1/2 cup chopped dried fruit
> 1 cup unsugared dry cereal (not flakes)

Learning Camping Skills

The following are important camping skills.

- Making a fire
- Using a knife safely
- Making a bedroll
- Tying knots
- Doing dishes and disposing of waste
- Cooking on a gas stove outdoors

Read the section "Useful Skills for Outdoor Adventures" for instructions on some of these skills.

Keeping Safe

Safety is, of course, very important. So, with the help of your leader, review *Safety-Wise* checkpoints for the activity you are going to do. You also need to take responsibility for bringing permission slips signed by your parent or guardian and notifying your leader of any medical concerns you might have, like an allergy to bee stings. To help stay safe:

- Talk to someone who has visited or knows the outdoor place you plan to go. You might want to know whether or not there are bathrooms, clean drinking water, or a place to buy food or supplies, for example. You may have questions about the terrain (is the site hilly?) or animals (are there any to avoid?).

- Make sure you are physically fit. If you plan to hike or bicycle, get in shape so you can really enjoy it!

179

▲ **Camping Prep List:** As girls gain experience in the outdoors, they may want to plan an extended trip. Planning for an extended trip can foster teamwork and give girls a greater sense of responsibility. Help them focus on activities that are fun and possible to do at the chosen site.

▲ **Dressing for the Outdoors:** Stress the importance of dressing in layers and choosing clothing that "breathes." Clothes made of natural fibers, such as cotton and wool, are good choices. If girls are buying outdoor clothing, suggest they read clothing labels carefully to determine suitability.

Supporting Activities

▲ Your troop or group might do a "wicking" experiment with a strip of cotton material and a strip of wool material to illustrate which material is best to wear in snow or wet weather. Hang the material so one end of each strip is touching a glass of water. Observe what happens when capillary action takes over and water travels up the cotton fabric.

Tips

▲ **Packing Your Day Pack:** This section can help girls prepare for a day trip. Most girls have a day pack, but may not know what to carry for outdoor excursions. Note that some items are listed for emergency situations, such as getting lost.

If girls do not own a day pack, talk about what to look for in a hiker's day pack: good construction, lightweight material, water bottle pocket, padded shoulder pads, and, if possible, a waist belt to shift the weight off the shoulders. Have girls compare the advantages and disadvantages of using a larger "fanny pack."

Tips

▲ **Learning Camping Skills:** Provide ample time for girls to learn and practice skills before using them on a camping trip. Perhaps your council office can recommend books on skill-building, as well as resource people who can assist you at troop meetings. Remember that *Safety-Wise* is an essential tool when preparing to go camping.

Program Links

▲ *Outdoor Education in Girl Scouting*

▲ *Games for Girl Scouts*, Chapter Eight

Tips

▲ **Keeping Safe:** Make checking *Safety-Wise* a troop project. Girls need to understand that safety is planned, and that assessing an activity for hazards is part of that plan. Review with girls the bulleted items under this heading in the handbook before taking an outdoor trip.

Appendix Nine in *Safety and Risk Management in Girl Scouting* details water-purification methods including boiling, filtration, and chemical treatment. This resource is available in your council office.

(This section continues on the next page.)

❀ Learn about symptoms and first-aid treatment for emergencies in hot and cold temperatures (see pages 79–80).

❀ Only drink water that you know is from a safe source, like a city or county water supply. (Any water from lakes or streams must be purified before drinking to kill microscopic organisms that will make you sick.)

❀ Carry your own water and drink regularly to avoid getting dehydrated. This is especially important when you are working hard or when it is hot.

Look at the following list. How do these things impact the environment? Discuss what you would do instead if you practiced minimal-impact living skills. You might make a poster to illustrate your discussion.

- **Picking wildflowers**
- **Littering**
- **Dumping soapy water near a lake**
- **Not staying on the trail**
- **Leaving garbage**
- **Using non-recyclable drink containers**
- **Feeding wildlife**
- **Playing a loud radio**
- **Chopping down a tree**
- **Using a too-large campfire**
- **Rearranging nature**

❀ Always have a plan to follow if you should get lost. All girls must know what to do if they become separated from the group.

Practicing Minimal-Impact Skills

An unwritten motto of Girl Scouts has always been to leave a place the same way you found it, or in better condition. That is what minimal-impact living means. Everything you do in the outdoors affects the environment in some way. The air you breathe, the water you swim in, and the soil you walk on are all part of the environment, and together with plants and animals, make up the ecosystem you live in. Minimal-impact skills are actions you take to live with the environment. They can be practiced anywhere in the outdoors: while picnicking in the local park, backpacking in the mountains, or exploring a coral reef underwater.

Taking Care of the Ecosystem

Since you are a part of the ecosystem, think about conserving and using resources wisely. When you conserve, you keep something from being damaged or wasted. For example, you need to use water, but you can conserve it by taking short showers or turning the water off when you are brushing your teeth.

Here are some skills you might use while meeting out, moving out, exploring out,

cooking out, sleeping out, and camping out. Be sure your leader or another adult who has been trained by your Girl Scout council in outdoor skills helps you with activities that need special care, such as fire-making, using a camp stove, and handling the jackknife. If you go camping with your troop or group, you may learn other skills, such as pitching a tent, using a bow saw, or hiking with a backpack.

Finding Your Way with a Compass

A compass has a small, magnetized needle, inside the compass housing, that floats in air, water, or oil. The needle (red end) will always turn to point to magnetic north of the earth. When you know where north is, you can find any other direction.

The compass housing (see the compass on the next page) is marked with the 360 degrees of a circle. North, east, south, and west are the four main, or cardinal, points on the compass. If you look at the housing, or divide 360 into four, at what degree reading do you find each of the cardinal points? (Hint: North is at 0° or 360°.)

You need a compass, preferably similar to the one pictured on the next page, that has a transparent base for map reading.

Hold the compass in front of you at waist height, with the direction-of-travel arrow pointing straight ahead. To find north, turn the compass housing until north is on the direction-of-travel arrow. Now, slowly turn your body until the red arrow is pointing in the same direction as the direction-of-travel arrow. When this happens, you are facing north. Whenever you are facing north, the east is to your right, west is to your left, and south is behind you.

Five Ways You Can Help the Environment

1. Cut down on driving. Carpool with friends, use public transportation, ride your bike, walk.

2. Conserve water. Fix leaky faucets, install a water saver in your shower, use a timer for showers, use the washer or dishwasher only when full.

3. Recycle or reuse items whenever possible. Reuse shopping bags, buy recycled paper, participate in community recycling programs.

4. Help keep air clean. Don't smoke, don't burn trash, do plant trees.

5. Help prevent soil erosion. Stay on trails when hiking or walking.

6. Add your ideas to the list:

_____

_____

_____

For additional ways to help the environment, refer to the Contemporary Issues booklet *Earth Matters: A Challenge for Environmental Action.*

It is a good idea to check each girl's camping equipment prior to the camping trip. Be sensitive to those who do not have the necessary camping gear. Work with your service unit or council to borrow such things as sleeping bags, warm sweaters, and rain gear.

Girls should always use the buddy system. Let girls know that if one of them gets separated from the group, she should stay calm. If she cannot determine her location and walk to safety, she should conserve her energy and find shelter until help arrives. She should use her whistle or mirror to help signal if lost in the woods.

Part of a "lost" or emergency plan should be a parent phone tree. Designate a person to call who can then call several people, who in turn can call additional people. Changes in plans or emergency notifications can be handled in this manner.

Supporting Activities

▲ Try this role-playing activity with girls: two girls walk away from their campsite to get water and can't find their way back. Ask girls to act out the steps they should follow once they realize they are lost. See if the rest of the girls agree with their actions. If not, what actions would they take?

Tips

▲ **Practicing Minimal Impact Skills:** Minimal impact, the act of leaving the environment in the same condition or better, can be applied to any setting. Often, minimal impact is discussed in the context of camping but it can also refer to such things as precycling (purchasing groceries in bulk to reduce packaging) and recycling (buying and returning bottles and cans). Your council should have a copy of the video *From Backyard to Backcountry—Camping Lightly on the Land,* which can be used to illustrate how Junior Girl Scouts can learn progressive outdoor skills without harming the environment.

The de-emphasis of fire-building, lashing, and other high-impact camping skills in this handbook is intentional. Instead, skills and attitudes that emphasize minimal impact to the environment are stressed. When girls become adults, they are much more likely to tent or cabin-camp than build shelters, and use gas stoves rather than build campfires. As a leader, you can help girls develop the camping skills and knowledge they can use throughout their lives by introducing environmental and safety considerations.

Program Links

▲ *Girl Scout Badges and Signs*: Dabbler badge in the World of the Out-of-Doors; Eco-Action badge; Ecology badge; Troop Camper badge

Tips

▲ **Taking Care of the Ecosystem:** An ecosystem is "the interaction of living and non-living things to form a complex system." In other words, everything is connected and dependent upon one another. Help girls realize that their actions can make a difference. Help them also understand that they can make a bigger difference by working with others.

Program Links

▲ *Earth Matters: A Challenge for Environmental Action* Contemporary Issues booklet

▲ *Girl Scout Badges and Signs*: Eco-Action badge; Ecology badge; Ready for Tomorrow badge

(This section continues on the next page.)

To travel on a north line, look in the distance and follow the direction-of-travel arrow with your eyes. Look for a landmark, like a tree or a rock, in your line of sight. Walk to that object, then line up your red arrow with your direction-of-travel arrow, sight, and continue walking. Try that with other directions!

To travel back the way you came, subtract half of 360° (180°) from your degree reading on your direction-of-travel arrow. Then, set your direction arrow on that reading. Turn your body so that the red arrow lines up with the direction-of-travel arrow, and follow your sighting.

To make your own compass, see page 164.

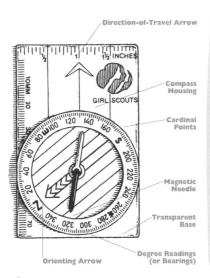

- Direction-of-Travel Arrow
- Compass Housing
- Cardinal Points
- Magnetic Needle
- Transparent Base
- Degree Readings (or Bearings)
- Orienting Arrow

A Zillion and One Ways to Take a Hike

Choose a theme hike from this list, or create your own, for your next outdoor exploration:

A trail-marker hike. Lay and follow trail markers (see *Outdoor Education in Girl Scouting* for complete directions).

An A-B-C hike. Find a plant or animal starting with each letter of the alphabet.

A throw-away hike. Pick up objects (like fall leaves and dried grasses) as you walk and arrange them on your hands to form a collage.

A spider-eye hike at night. Shine your flashlight beam parallel to the ground in grassy places and look for those red spider eyes.

A picture-story hike. Stop every _____ (yards, blocks, etc.) and frame a picture with your hands. Write a sentence about what you see. Then read all your sentences at the end of the hike.

A career hike. Keep track of how many careers you observe as you walk through an area with people working.

A food-chain hike. Build a food chain as you observe plants and animals that depend upon each other. Try for three to five links, then start over (for example: soil, grass, bug, sparrow, hawk).

A soundless hike. Hike a forest trail without making noise or talking.

A color-palette hike. Look for the primary and secondary colors as you hike.

A water-cycle hike. Look for parts of the water cycle as you hike: precipitation (rain, snow, fog); evaporation (sunlight, dried puddles); run-off (water moving on the ground, storm drains); bodies of water (lake, ocean); flowing water (streams, rivers).

A habitat hike. Look for different homes in the wild.

Math in nature hike. Find the following shapes while hiking: circle, square, hexagon, spiral, diamond, triangle, ellipse (oval).

Determining Your Pace

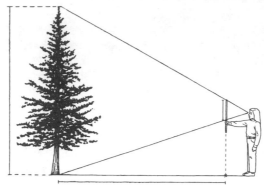

Pacing helps you measure distances as you walk. Once you know how to determine your pace, you can even measure the heights of trees! A pace is defined as two steps.

You Will Need:

- A 50' or 100' (15 or 30 meter) tape measure.

If you don't have a measuring tape, use string marked off in one-foot segments.

To determine your pace:

- Mark off 100' (30 meters) on a flat, straight surface.

- Walk the distance three times, each time writing down how many times your right foot hits the ground. Add up the three distances and divide by three. That number is the length of your pace.

____ + ____ + ____ = _____ total steps
÷ 3 = _____ (the length of your pace)

To estimate the height of an object using your pace (this works well with trees, flagpoles, or buildings):

- Hold one end of a stick or yardstick upright in your hand, with your arm outstretched in front of your body. The stick above your hand should be the same length as the distance from your outstretched fist to your eye.

- Walk back from the object (make sure you know where you are walking!) until the tip of the stick visually lines up with the top of the object and your thumb covers the bottom of the object.

- Mark the spot on the ground directly below the stick.

- Pace the distance from the mark to the object.

- Multiply the length of your pace times the number of paces you took to find out how high your object is.

Learn to judge distances using knowledge of pace and time. Walk a distance that you know to be one-half mile (1 km) at a comfortable pace. Time how long it takes you. Do this more than once and take an average. Use this knowledge to estimate how far you walk for an unknown distance.

Handbook Page 182

Handbook Page 183

▲ **Finding Your Way with a Compass:** The easiest kind of compass for girls to use is one with a clear plastic housing as shown on the handbook page. This is particularly true if girls are working with maps. If you or the girls need help using the compass, contact your council office for names of older girls who are skilled in compass reading, or others who are affiliated with local orienteering groups, science museums, or the military.

Supporting Activities

▲ Girls can use their compasses to locate the North Star in the constellation Ursa Minor (Little Dipper).

▲ To help girls become familiar with determining the four directions (north, south, east, west) in relation to the sun, pose the following questions:

● The sun rises in the east in the morning. If you stand with your left shoulder toward the sun in the morning, which direction are you facing? (South)

● The sun is in the west in the afternoon. If you stand with your left shoulder toward the sun, what direction are you facing? (North)

Program Links

▲ *Games for Girl Scouts*

▲ *Girl Scout Badges and Signs*: Finding Your Way badge

Tips

▲ **A Zillion and One Ways to Take a Hike:** Hiking can be a girl's first outdoor "awareness" experience. Stop along the way to explore your surroundings or listen to the wind through the trees. You and the girls can also hike to meet specific objectives, such as exercising, reaching a destination, or identifying things in nature. Girls can create first-aid kits to use outdoors, map their neighborhoods, or read nature books as part of their orientation to the outdoors.

Program Links

▲ *Girl Scout Badges and Signs*: Hiker badge; Outdoor Fun badge; Outdoor Fun in the City badge; Walking for Fitness badge

Tips

▲ **Determining Your Pace:** To do pacing and compass work together, find a flat area that will allow you to go in any direction at least 200 feet (60 meters). A park or playground works well, especially if it is surrounded by trees or buildings you can sight.

The trick to measuring the height of an object is to hold the stick so that it is the same length as the distance between your eye and the end of your outstretched hand. Grasp the stick firmly and hold it level with your eye. (You are actually doing a simple equation based on distance and triangular relationships.)

Reading a Map

Maps help you get from one place to another. Maps can help you figure out where you are if you are lost. They can also help estimate distances and tell you if you will be going up or downhill. Reading a map is an important skill to know, whether traveling in your family car, riding on a bus, or hiking in the woods. You can even read a weather map to see an approaching storm.

 Conduct a map symbol hunt. Find as many different kinds of maps as possible, including highway maps, bus maps, park maps, trail maps, topographic (elevation) maps, weather maps, world maps, etc. Look for symbols used on maps, placed in the map legend. Compare the distances represented in each map.

Map Symbols

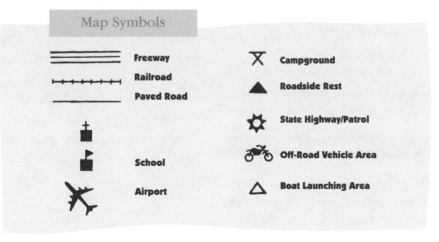

Freeway	Campground
Railroad	Roadside Rest
Paved Road	
	State Highway/Patrol
	Off-Road Vehicle Area
School	
Airport	Boat Launching Area

Tying Knots

Knots are used for tying packages or doing macramé. You need to know how to tie knots when you put up a tent. Learn basic knots. Then challenge yourself to learn the harder ones!

You Will Need:

• 2 pieces of clothesline or lightweight rope about 12-18" (30-46 cm) long.
• Bright-colored plastic tape

Tape ends of the rope with the plastic tape to keep them from fraying.

Knot	Use	Directions
Overhand	When only a simple knot is needed	
Square	To join two cords of the same thickness	
Half Hitch	To fasten a rope to a ring or tent stake	
Clove Hitch	To fasten one end of a rope to a tree or post	

Put together a bag full of string tied in knots for your troop or group to practice with or to help younger girls learn how to tie knots.

▲ **Reading a Map:** Gather an assortment of maps by borrowing some from the library or by having girls bring maps to the troop or group meeting. Girls can use a map to navigate around a shopping mall or the neighborhood. Or, girls can look at a map to find a place to hike (see the Hiker badge in *Girl Scout Badges and Signs*).

Orienteering is a challenging sport, recognized worldwide, in which a person or team uses a topographical map and a compass to navigate through a special cross-country course. Girls who become skilled at map and compass reading might want to investigate this sport.

Volksmarching is another leisure-time activity growing in popularity in the United States. It involves walking in the country or city using map-reading skills. Participants check in at points along the route.

▲ **Tying Knots:** When teaching knot tying, make the uses of knots relevant to girls. Tie a package, a scarf, or a rope to a boat. Consider completing a simple macramé project.

To facilitate learning, have girls practice with nylon rope or cotton clothesline cut in manageable lengths. Make sure the rope has no frayed ends. To prevent fraying with nylon or plastic ropes, burn the ends with a candle. Use caution around the open flame and melting rope, and do this outdoors.

Knot tying is also an activity to help strengthen girls' communication and teaching skills. Girls can instruct others in knot tying, and then discuss the skills involved. Girls might enjoy teaching knot tying to Brownie Girl Scouts.

Additional information on knot tying can be found in *Outdoor Education in Girl Scouting*.

▲ Besides the relay game described in the handbook (see next handbook page), girls might also have fun playing "Simon Says: Knots" in *Games for Girl Scouts*.

You Will Need:

- A 3' length (about 1 meter) of rope for each participant
- A list of knots everyone knows
- A leader

How to play: Every time "Simon says" to tie a certain knot, each girl must do it. If the command doesn't start with "Simon says," girls do nothing. A girl misses if she ties the knot incorrectly, ties the wrong knot, or ties one at the wrong time. After three misses, a girl is out.

▲ *Girl Scout Badges and Signs*: Outdoor Fun badge; Troop Camper badge

Knot	Use	Directions
Lark's Head	To loop cord around a ring	
Bowline	To make a loop that won't slip	
Tautline hitch	To make a loop that will slip	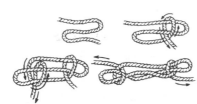
Sheetbend	To tie a thin cord to a thicker cord	
Sheepshank	To shorten a rope	

Decide which knot you would use for the following:

•Shortening a clothesline

•Tying a boat to a dock

•Anchoring a tent to a tent stake

•Tying a rope to a leather dog leash

Why not try a knot-tying relay game? Divide into teams. Each team gets a piece of cord or string. Each team member selects from a bag a piece of paper with the name of a knot written on it. The first person pulls out the name of a type of knot, ties it, and passes the cord and bag to the second person. The game continues until each team member has tied a knot correctly.

The jackknife is a tool often used when camping. Practice the following safety and care steps, then use your jackknife to slice an apple.

Opening the jackknife: Put your thumbnail in the slot of the blade. Keep your fingers away from the cutting edge. Pull the blade out all the way. Close the jackknife by doing the steps in reverse.

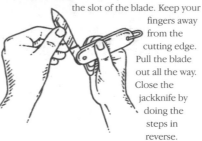

Cleaning the jackknife:
Always keep the jackknife clean and dry. To clean, hold the cloth at the back of the blade, away from the cutting edge. Wipe carefully across the whole blade. Oil the hinge with machine oil. Never clean the blade by rubbing it in dirt or sand. This dulls the blade and makes the knife hard to open and close.

Sharpening the jackknife: A sharp knife is safer and more useful than a dull one. Use a sharpening stone (called a Carborundum or whetstone) to sharpen your knife. Hold the stone in one hand and the open jackknife in the other. Keep fingers below the top of the stone.

Lay the flat side of the knife blade on the flat surface of the stone. Keep the knife blade almost flat, with the back edge of the blade slightly

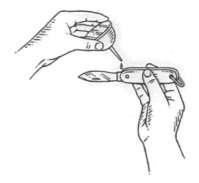

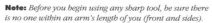

Note: *Before you begin using any sharp tool, be sure there is no one within an arm's length of you (front and sides).*

It's your responsibility to make sure you and others are safe while you use your knife.

Handbook Page 186

▲ **Using a Jackknife:** Knowing how to use a jackknife has been a traditional part of "being prepared." A jackknife can be a very useful tool for everyday life. You might ask girls to make a list of ways they might use a jackknife.

If girls are asked to bring jackknives to a troop or group meeting, make sure you discuss jackknife safety prior to the meeting. The jackknife should be seen as a tool, not a weapon. To avoid girls bringing in hunting knives or switchblades, show them what a jackknife looks like beforehand. Because not every girl will have access to a jackknife, include several in your own camping gear.

Have girls practice passing the knife opened and closed while sitting in a circle. Stress safety and care of the knife.

A girl will often try to cut upwards or cut the object while resting it on a part of her body, such as her lap or her leg. Neither one of these actions is safe.

Once it was common practice to gather and cut "green" sticks to make a campfire. Discuss with girls the environmental consequences of everyone cutting her own sticks. Challenge girls to come up with solutions that represent minimal-impact camping. For example, girls could purchase wire roasting sticks or use recycled wire hangers to reduce the need to cut wood.

Supporting Activities

▲ To practice using a jackknife, girls can make a simple firestarter "fuzz stick" using dry kindling. Instruct girls to hold the kindling and shave downwards in a circular pattern, leaving strips attached to the stick to create a bottle-brush effect. Girls can practice "knifecraft" skills with carrots, soap, soapstone, and balsa wood.

Program Links

▲ *Girl Scout Badges and Signs*: Outdoor Camper badge; Outdoor Cook badge; Troop Camper badge

▲ *Outdoor Education in Girl Scouting*

REMINDER!

Involve girls in using *Safety-Wise*. Girls should understand that activity checkpoints in *Safety-Wise* ensure that Girl Scout activities are safe. When planning activities, let one girl be responsible for finding the section pertaining to troop or group plans. If your troop or group is planning to do an activity not covered in the checkpoints, lead them through the section on activity considerations. Consulting *Safety-Wise* should be done as a matter of course and in partnership with girls.

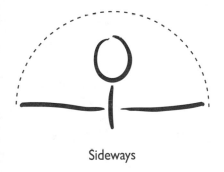

Sideways

Frontwards

Before you begin using any sharp tool, be sure there is no one within an arm's length of you (front and sides).

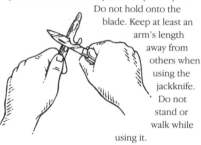

raised. Move the blade across the stone in a circular path several times. Turn the knife over and do the same motion again.

Passing the jackknife: Always close the jackknife before passing it to another person. If you are passing a knife that doesn't close, grasp the blade along the dull edge of the blade, holding the sharp side away from you, and pass the handle to the other person. This way you have control of the sharp edge. Always say "thank you" when you have received a knife. This signals that you now have control.

Using the jackknife: Hold the handle with your whole hand. Always cut away from you. Do not hold onto the blade. Keep at least an arm's length away from others when using the jackknife. Do not stand or walk while using it.

Using a Camp Stove

A two-burner gas stove is a great way to cook when camping. It is fast and saves firewood. Review "Portable Cook Stoves" in *Safety-Wise* before using your camp stove.

Before you camp:

•Read the directions for operating your particular stove before you travel.

•Know what kind of fuel your stove needs. Plan to take extra fuel.

•Gather all the equipment you will need for camp-stove cooking: pots, potholders or mitts, wooden matches, safety equipment (such as a trowel and loose earth or sand, baking soda, or a portable fire extinguisher), and a first-aid kit. Take a funnel if you are using gas fuel.

When Using Your Stove:

•Always have an adult present.

•Tie back your hair and do not wear loose clothing.

•Find a safe, level spot outdoors for your stove.

•Clear any debris away from around the stove, and do not use rocks to prop it up.

•Don't place the stove in a windy area. If the stove has a windscreen, put it in place to break the wind.

•Never use the stove in a tent or indoors. This is because it uses the oxygen you breathe and the fuel is dangerous, especially if spilled indoors. Stoves also can give off carbon monoxide, a gas that is harmful to people.

•Read the operating instructions again and light the stove according to the directions. Hold the match so the flame burns upwards.

•Adjust the flame for cooking. Blue flame is the hottest. You may want to soap the outside bottoms of your

pans before placing them over the flame so pot scrubbing is easier.

•Do not reach over the stove. When stirring, hold onto the pan with a mitt. On a small, single-burner stove, take the pot off the stove before stirring and then return it.

•Do not leave the stove unattended. If you run out of fuel, turn off the stove and let the stove cool. Refuel away from the stove and any heat source or flame. If fuel is spilled, let it evaporate and do not strike matches nearby. Never remove a fuel container from a stove without turning off the stove first.

•When you are finished cooking, let the stove cool before cleaning. Make sure that gas valves are all tightly turned off before packing.

One-Pot Meal

Try making this stew over a fire or a stove. You need one large pot. Serves four to six.

Vegetarian Chili

1 cup uncooked brown or white rice	1 tablespoon chili powder
1 6-oz. jar tomato paste	4 cups water
2 cubes low-salt chicken or vegetable bouillon	
2 12-oz. cans red kidney beans	
1 medium onion (chopped)	
3 stalks of celery (chopped)	
1 medium green or red pepper (seeded and chopped)	
1 tablespoon oil	
3 carrots (peeled or scrubbed and chopped)	

Sauté (fry) the onion and green pepper in the oil until soft. Add celery and carrots and sauté for 2-3 minutes. Add beans with liquid, chili powder, 4 cups of water, tomato paste, and bouillon cubes. Simmer (Heat on a low flame). Add rice. Cook until rice is done —20 minutes for white rice and 50 minutes for brown rice.

Checklist for Outdoor Cooking

Whether you are cooking in the backyard or backpacking with a portable stove, you will need:

• A cool, dry place to store food

• A safe place to build your fire or operate your stove

• A place to wash your hands

• A place to fix your food

• A place to eat

• A method for cleaning up

• A place to put garbage and items to be recycled

188

189

▲ **Using a Camp Stove:** It is very important that girls practice using the camp stove before their first trip. Start with something as simple as boiling water. Give each girl an opportunity to strike matches, and to start and shut off the stove. Supervise each girl carefully. Do not introduce the use of camp stoves to a group of girls without another adult present. Consult the *Safety-Wise* sections "Portable Cookstoves" and "Cooking, Food Preparation, and Cleaning."

Familiarize girls with the following safety tips:

1. Everyone who uses a camp stove should be trained in stove safety and the operation of the stove.

2. Camp stoves should be used only with adult supervision.

3. Establish the cooking area away from foot traffic (walkways, paths, etc.).

4. Don't overbalance the stove (e.g., a pot too large for the stove).

5. Let the stove cool before refueling.

If you do not have access to portable camp stoves, check with your council office. Parents may be able to help. If stoves are borrowed, inspect them yourself before girls operate them.

Girls this age may enjoy the challenge of solar oven construction and cooking, as outlined in the "Helps and Resources" section of *Girl Scout Badges and Signs*. More help can be found in *The Guide for Brownie Girl Scout Leaders*. Recipes for solar cooking can often be adapted from "slow cooker" or other cookbooks.

Program Links

▲ *Girl Scout Badges and Signs*: Outdoor Cook badge; Ready for Tomorrow badge; Troop Camper badge

Notes

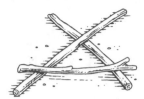

Girl Scouts learn how to make fires because it is a skill you can use when appropriate. In the United States, some cities and parks have banned fires because not enough wood is available, or there is a fire or pollution danger. Think about other ways to cook, or plan meals that don't require cooking!

Safety Tips for Making a Fire

Fire-making is a basic survival skill that provides heat for warmth and fuel for cooking. You may build a fire at camp with your troop or group or with your family at a campground. Always check fire-making rules of the area, and follow these safety tips:

• Keep a bucket of water and shovel (for stirring wet coals or placing dirt on the fire to smother it) on hand before building your fire.

• If you are building a fire in a fireplace, make sure the draft in the chimney is open and a screen is placed across the fireplace to prevent sparks from jumping out onto clothing or rugs. If building a fire indoors, observe proper safety rules.

• Tie back your hair and wear long pants.

• Do not start a fire during air-pollution alerts, high winds, or very dry conditions.

(For more about fire-making, see "Cooking Fires" in *Safety-Wise.*)

Before You Make a Fire

A fire needs fuel and air to burn. When making a fire you need three sizes of wood for a fire to last:

Tinder is small material that burns as soon as it is lit with a match. Tinder could be dry wood, dry leaves, or wood shavings.

Kindling is larger in diameter than tinder, thin enough to catch fire before the tinder burns out, and large enough to catch the fuel. Kindling should be dry enough to snap.

Fuel is larger wood that keeps a fire going. Fuel should be dry, seasoned wood found lying on the ground or in a woodpile.

When preparing to make a fire, use a fireplace or fire ring. If you need to prepare a fire ring, clear the area down to the soil, and avoid roots, dry materials, and overhanging branches. Have enough tinder, kindling, and fuel on hand so you do not have to leave your fire.

Building a Fire

1. Make a small triangle with three pieces of kindling, leaving an air space under the top bar of the triangle.

2. Lay a handful of tinder against the apex (top) of the triangle, leaving some air space. Lean tinder toward the center, upright. (You can use a combination of tinder and fire-starter at this point.)

3. Strike a wooden match close to the tinder and away from your body. Hold the match under the tinder at ground level so the flame burns upwards.

4. As the tinder catches, add additional tinder carefully, then begin placing kindling so it leans against the triangle above the flaming tinder. Continue adding kindling, building a cone shape.

5. Add fuel (large pieces of wood) to the fire so the kindling can catch it. Leave air spaces, and use only the amount of fuel you need.

Make the fire only as large as you need it. Conserve fuel and avoid smoke pollution.

190

191

Handbook Page 190

Handbook Page 191

▲ **Making a Fire:** Campfires and s'mores are a part of Girl Scout tradition. Today, conservation and other issues dictate the size of fires, as well as when it is appropriate to build them. However, fire-making is still an essential survival skill for keeping warm, cooking, and sterilizing. The simple act of boiling water can eliminate waterborne diseases worldwide.

When planning outdoor pursuits, discuss with girls when, where, and how to make fires. Girls should also learn about alternatives to fire-making, such as drying fruit in a food dryer or cooking in a solar oven. Determine whether to include an open fire by considering such things as wood shortages, environmental damage, safety, pollution, and park or forest regulations.

Acquaint girls with the following fire-making safety tips:

1. Check local fire rules and regulations. Is a fire permit required?

2. Make sure weather conditions are not too dry or windy.

3. Have a pail of water, a water hose, or sand nearby before lighting the fire.

4. Protect the environment. Try to build your fire in a previously used fire circle or in a fireplace. Keep your fire to a size that conserves fuel.

5. Roll up long sleeves and tie back hair when building or tending a fire.

Fire-building is a skill usually taught to leaders in basic outdoor training. *Safety-Wise* addresses the safety aspects and should be reviewed by you and the girls.

As girls become knowledgeable about outdoor activities, challenge them to learn new skills. Use the outdoors as a vehicle for adventure and discovery.

(This section continues on the next page.)

If you need a concentrated heat source (for boiling water, for example), continue making the cone shape and cook on the flame. You might also use a grate. As the fire burns down, it forms coals. This is the best heat to cook on.

When You Are Finished with a Fire:

1. Let the fire die down until only ashes are left.

2. With a long stick or shovel, stir the ashes, sprinkle them with water, then stir again. Continue until there is no gray ash and the fire bed is cool. Pouring water on a fire can cause steam and rock explosions.

3. Remove any signs that you were there, returning the site to the way you found it. If you've used a fireplace, leave it clean by removing the ashes.

Learn about other ways to cook, such as solar ovens, charcoal fires, or a camp stove.

Some Outdoor Cooking Tips

• One-pot meals are easiest to fix and clean up.

• Boiling water can be used to make a lot of things: gelatin, hot cocoa, soup, pasta, vegetables, instant meals.

• Dry foods, such as jerky, dried fruits, and rice keep without refrigeration.

• Meat and dairy products spoil the most quickly and need to be kept in a refrigerated place.

• Use plastic bags and reusable containers to carry food. Buy food in bulk and repackage for travel.

• Soap the outside of the pot when cooking on a fire. It's much easier to clean.

For more information on outdoor cooking, see *Outdoor Education in Girl Scouting*.

From sports to science to outdoor fun, you have a range of activities to try as a Junior Girl Scout. Sample some of the activities in this chapter and discover a lot about your interests, skills, and talents.

192

BRIDGING & RECOGNITIONS
CHAPTER 8

Junior Girl Scout Badges
page 194

Bridging to Cadette Girl Scouts
page 195

Activities to Earn the Sign of the World
page 204

Junior Girl Scout Leadership Pin
page 204

In this chapter, you will find information about earning Junior Girl Scout recognitions and bridging to Cadette Girl Scouts. All handbook badges can be found in this chapter and are listed under the badge name. You can also read about the bridging steps, requirements for earning the Sign of the World, and steps for earning the Junior Girl Scout Leadership pin.

193

Bridging and Recognitions

Supporting Activities

▲ The worldwide firewood shortage is an issue girls can learn about. What alternatives are available to people living in countries that do not have firewood or access to electricity? What happens when a country loses all its trees?

Program Links

▲ *Earth Matters: A Challenge for Environmental Action* Contemporary Issues booklet

▲ *Girl Scout Badges and Signs*: Outdoor Cook badge; Ready for Tomorrow badge; Troop Camper badge

▲ *Outdoor Education in Girl Scouting*

REMINDER!

Junior Girl Scout leaders develop their five senses: sense of humor, sense of fairness, sense of compassion, sense of respect, and sense of endurance!

Tips

▲ **Junior Girl Scout Recognitions:** Earning recognitions can be very rewarding. For many girls it is an opportunity to feel pride in accomplishment that is not dependent on school achievement. Don't structure activities so that everything is focused on earning recognitions.

Junior Girl Scouts can earn the following recognitions:

● White-backed badges from the *Junior Girl Scout Handbook*

● Green and tan background-color badges from *Girl Scout Badges and Signs*

● The Signs of the Rainbow, Satellite, and Sun from *Girl Scout Badges and Signs* and the Sign of the World from the *Junior Girl Scout Handbook*

● Junior Aide patch

● Bridge to Cadette Girl Scouts patch

● The Junior Girl Scout Leadership pin

● Religious recognitions

● Contemporary Issues booklet patches

Information on earning recognitions and the placement of insignia and recognitions on the uniform can be found in Chapter One of the handbook and in the introduction to *Girl Scout Badges and Signs*.

Junior Girl Scout Recognitions

Recognitions are badges, signs, and pins you earn as a Junior Girl Scout. They are symbols of your interests and accomplishments. Your *Junior Girl Scout Handbook* and the book *Girl Scout Badges and Signs* have activities to do to earn badges.

Junior Girl Scout Badges

You can find most Junior Girl Scout badges in *Girl Scout Badges and Signs*. This handbook has an additional 13 badges. *Girl Scout Badges and Signs* contains badges with green background colors and tan background colors. The green-backed badges are easier to do and take less time to finish. The badges with tan backgrounds take more planning and more time to complete. The beginning section of *Girl Scout Badges and Signs* has more information on these badges. Your *Junior Girl Scout Handbook* has badges with a white background and a dark blue border. Many badge activities are included in Chapters One to Seven of this handbook. But *all* handbook badges are included in this chapter. Look for the badge symbol. When you find one, you know that this activity is a badge requirement.

Signs and Other Recognitions

Besides badges, Junior Girl Scouts can earn signs such as the Sign of the World, Rainbow, Satellite, and Sun. Other recognitions you can earn as a Junior Girl Scout are: the Junior Girl Scout Leadership pin, the Junior Aide patch, the Bridge to Cadette Girl Scouts patch, religious recognitions, and patches you may get if you do activities from the Contemporary Issues booklets or go on special events sponsored by your Girl Scout council. (For more about insignia and recognitions, see Chapter One.)

The activities for the Sign of the World, which are included in this handbook, will help you learn more about yourself and your community. The requirements include badge activities. A badge activity can only be counted once in completing any of the signs. Signs should take you longer to earn than badges.

The Junior Aide Patch

You earn the Junior Aide patch when you work with Brownie Girl Scouts. The requirements for earning the Junior Aide patch are in *Girl Scout Badges and Signs*.

Bridging to Cadette Girl Scouts

Moving from one Girl Scout level to another is called bridging. You can begin to bridge to Cadette Girl Scouts in your last year as a Junior Girl Scout. As a Cadette Girl Scout, you can continue to enjoy camping, trips, and

many activities you enjoyed as a Junior Girl Scout, but Cadette Girl Scouts have more freedom, take on more responsibility, and enjoy new opportunities. As a Cadette Girl Scout, you could work on Fashion/Fitness/Makeup, Understanding Yourself and Others, Space Exploration, or Outdoor Survival interest project activities. You could go on national and international wider opportunities or learn to be a program aide or Counselor-in-Training. Cadette Girl Scouts have dug for dinosaur bones, climbed mountains, worked with children with special needs, helped build houses in Mexico, sailed on tall ships, and visited Pax Lodge in England and Sangam in India.

Cadette Girl Scouts have their own set of special recognitions, including the Cadette Girl Scout Leadership Award, the Cadette Girl Scout Challenge, and the Girl Scout Silver Award. There's room as a Cadette Girl Scout to explore your special interests and use your talents to create a Girl Scout experience that's right for you. When you are ready to take the following bridging steps, you can begin your path to Cadette Girl Scout adventures and earn your Bridge to Cadette Girl Scouts patch.

Step 1: Find out about Cadette Girl Scouting. Look through the *Cadette and Senior Girl Scout Handbook* and *Cadette and Senior Girl Scout Interest Projects*. Find three activities you would like to do.

Step 2: Do a Cadette Girl Scout activity. Do one of the three activities you chose in Step One.

Step 3: Do something with a Cadette Girl Scout. Visit a Cadette Girl Scout troop or group meeting or help with an activity that a Cadette Girl Scout has planned.

Step 4: Work on a service project with a Cadette Girl Scout. Find out about a service project a Cadette Girl Scout or a group or troop is doing and help out.

Step 5: Be a leader. Do something that builds leadership skills. You could do activity Number One in the Leadership interest project in *Cadette and Senior Girl Scout Interest Projects* or assist a leader with a troop or group of younger girls.

Step 6: Share what you learn about Cadette Girl Scouts with others. Talk to other Junior Girl Scouts or visit a Brownie or Daisy Girl Scout troop or group and teach a game or song you learned with Cadette Girl Scouts. Or, make a presentation of the special things about Cadette Girl Scouting.

Step 7: Help plan your bridging ceremony. Plan ways to make your ceremony special. Create or discover some special songs, poems, sayings, or decorations.

Step 8: Find out about opportunities and participate in a summer Girl Scout activity. What opportunities can you create?

194

195

▲ **Junior Girl Scout Badges:** Girls can find Junior Girl Scout badges in the handbook and in *Girl Scout Badges and Signs.* The handbook has 13 badges identified by dark blue borders and white backgrounds. Some handbook badge activities are scattered throughout the chapters to support the content, but all badge activities are found here in Chapter Eight. Chapter Two in Part I of this guide includes details about helping girls manage and complete badge activities. A sample recognition ceremony is also outlined in Chapter Two.

▲ **Signs and the Junior Aide Patch:** Junior Girl Scout signs and the Junior Aide patch are other kinds of recognitions girls at this age level can earn. See Chapter Two in Part I of this guide for more on helping girls earn signs and the Junior Aide patch.

▲ **Bridging to Cadette Girl Scouts:** Bridging activities are designed to help girls make the transition from one level of Girl Scouting to another. They also emphasize the continuity of the Girl Scout program and provide an opportunity for girls to work with older girls.

A bridging ceremony marks the culmination of these activities and celebrates girls' growth and achievements. See *Ceremonies in Girl Scouting* for bridging ceremony ideas.

Girls can begin to bridge to Cadette Girl Scouts in their last year as Junior Girl Scouts. Arrange to bring together as often as possible the girls who are bridging with Cadette Girl Scouts. Your Girl Scout council representative should be able to connect you with a Cadette Girl Scout troop or group.

You may want to schedule time during your troop or group meetings for girls bridging to report on their activities. Bridging activities should be fun for Junior Girl Scouts and fuel their enthusiasm about becoming Cadette Girl Scouts. Attention to their bridging efforts can mean a lot to girls who may be leaving the troop or group.

Notes

Arts and Media

Complete four activities.

 Please use extra care when doing art activities.

1. Do one of the music activities on page 151. Share what you learned with your troop or group.

2. Use the ideas on page 152 to create a drawing or painting.

OR Find out what a mural is. With your troop or group, develop an idea and work on a mural.

3. Do the printmaking activity on page 155.

4. Do the decoupage activity on page 153.

5. Read about sculpture on page 156. Make a sculpture of your choice.

OR Try making something using embroidery (see page 157), or find out about another kind of fabric art that interests you. Then, make something to show your troop or group.

6. Read about jewelry-making on pages 157–158 and try one of the activities.

7. Make a catch board (see page 159) following the woodwork instructions. (If you don't want to make a catch board choose another woodworking activity not included here.)

8. Create your own project combining art and music.

Careers

Complete five activities.

1. Think of women you admire. What characteristics do they have that you would like to have? Fill in "My Characteristics" chart on page 111.

2. Find out about community and school drug-prevention projects. Invite someone who works in one of these projects to come and speak to your troop or group.

3. Look at the list of health careers on page 96 and find out more about these jobs. Discover what education or training is required and what the average salaries are.

4. You can choose a career that involves personal care. A hairstylist cuts and styles hair. A dermatologist is a doctor who diagnoses and treats skin problems. Investigate other careers. Invite people who have careers in personal care to visit your Girl Scout troop or group.

5. Fashion designers can become very famous, but there are lots of other jobs in the fashion industry. Find out about careers in the fashion and cosmetics industries; for example, find out about clothing buyers, fashion consultants, personal shoppers, cosmetologists, hairstylists, textile designers, and salespersons. How can you find out about these careers? Maybe you can interview people who have these jobs or career-shadow them for a day.

6. Invite someone who works in the financial industry such as an accountant, bank officer, bank examiner, or personal finance manager to visit your troop or group and explain what she does.

7. Choose five activities from Chapter Seven and brainstorm a list of careers that could match those interests.

8. Look at the list of jobs on page 113. Why not look in the classified advertisements of a newspaper or phone the professional associations or some businesses and find out how much a person makes who has one of these jobs? Compare these salaries with some of the more traditional "female" jobs.

9. Find out about a career you might like to have. Find out about education, special training, and salary (beginning and after ten years). What clothes, tools, or equipment are used in this career? To what other careers does this career lead? If you and the other girls in your troop or group find out about different careers, what are some ways you could share or use this information?

Consumer Power

Complete four activities.

1. Get copies of two or more newspapers printed on the same day, choose one story that is printed in both and compare. Where does the story appear? the front page? later in the newspaper? in a different section? How long is the story? Is the information the same? What is the tone—the overall impression—of the story? positive, negative, neutral, anxious, upbeat?

2. Watch two or three news shows shown at the same time. Flip back and forth between the shows. Keep a log of what stories are reported, how much time is given to the story, who reports the story (the main newscaster or a reporter), and what differs in the report. Compare your log with other girls in your Girl Scout troop or group.

3. Do the television-viewing guidelines activity on page 119.

4. Do the smart music-video viewing guide activity on page 120.

5. Close your eyes for a moment. What advertisement pops into your head? Why do you remember it? How does this advertisement try to persuade you? In your troop or group, gather in small groups or in pairs and pick an advertisement or commercial to analyze (study carefully). Think of three different ways the advertisement is persuasive. Are there attractive people in the advertisement? Does the advertisement promise something new? What are some other messages the advertisement is sending? Pick one person in your group or pair to explain to the others what you discovered.

6. Do the food labels activity on page 96.

Discovering Technology

Complete six activities, including the two starred.

 Please use extra care when demonstrating some of the activities in number 6.

*1. Discover how often you rely on technology. Keep a log for a week listing how and when you use technology. Then do the "What Can You Live Without?" activity on page 160 with friends.

2. Discover "Pulley Power." Send a message or lift an object using pulleys. See page 170 for details.

3. Discover how technology is shaping the future. Find out about at least two of the following: voice recognition, virtual reality, lasers, tele-communications, robotics. If possible, use or view one of these technologies.

Tips

▲ **Arts and Media:** Arts and media activities cover a range of projects from music to sculpture to woodworking. Note that some of the activities require girls to exercise caution. Make sure the art supplies you are using are non-toxic. Most art materials are marked with warning labels or as non-toxic. Also remember to alert girls and their parents or guardians that art supplies and completed art projects should not fall into the hands of young children. For example, discuss with girls the danger a string of beads presents to a baby or young child.

Program Links

▲ *Girl Scout Badges and Signs:* Any of the badges in the World of the Arts; Outdoor Creativity badge

▲ *Junior Girl Scout Activity Book:* Chapter Seven

Tips

▲ **Careers:** Career badge activities will start girls thinking about career options. These activities range from helping girls focus on their abilities to gaining knowledge about specific fields. The activities also aim to expose girls to the range of jobs in a field. Often, girls of this age are attracted to the more glamorous or visible jobs since they haven't had exposure to other jobs in the field. If girls need career information, direct them to library reference materials. Many libraries have guidance and career information sections.

Program Links

▲ *Girl Scout Badges and Signs:* Business-Wise badge; Dabbler—The World of Today and Tomorrow badge; Making Decisions badge; Money Sense badge; Women Today badge

▲ *Junior Girl Scout Activity Book:* Chapter One

Tips

▲ **Consumer Power:** Consumer Power activities aim to strengthen girls' consumer skills. As girls grow, they will need to develop skills to evaluate quality, durability, and practicality of certain products. These activities challenge girls to think critically about how media, advertising, and packaging influence their buying decisions.

Program Links

▲ *Earth Matters: A Challenge for Environmental Action* Contemporary Issues booklet

▲ *Girl Scout Badges and Signs:* Communication Arts badge; Family Living Skills badge; Making Decisions badge

▲ *Junior Girl Scout Activity Book:* Chapter Three

Tips

▲ **Discovering Technology:** The activities in the Discovering Technology badge are designed to help girls see how technology and its application relate to everyday living. Activities also point to the role technology will play in the future. Have girls exercise caution with activity number six.

Program Links

▲ *Girl Scout Badges and Signs:* Any badges in the World of Today and Tomorrow; Communication Arts badge

▲ *Into the World of Today and Tomorrow: Leading Girls to Mathematics, Science, and Technology* Contemporary Issues booklet

▲ *Junior Girl Scout Activity Book:* Chapter Five

4. Discover how technology has changed the way things are done. Pick at least three careers and find out how technology is used in those professions. Has technology changed those jobs, or the way the jobs are performed? Share your findings with your troop or group by role-playing, participating in a panel discussion, or hosting a discussion by people in different professions.

*5. Discover computer networks. Make up a play or game that demonstrates your understanding of computer networks. Or, investigate how they work and what they cost. Or, access a computer network at home, school, library, or elsewhere and send a message on E-mail.

6. Discover a leisure-time activity that uses technology and share the activity or knowledge of the activity with your troop or group. For example, display photos or a videotape you have taken, sing karaoke, direct a remote-control boat or car, sew something on a sewing machine, use some exercise equipment with the help of an adult, or display greeting cards or a poster you have made from a computer graphics program.

7. Do the Science Challenge "How Do You Make a Book Move Across a Bare Floor Using One Finger?" on page 171.

Girls Are Great

Complete five activities.

1. Prepare a short skit using not only words but also pictures, symbols, and body language to deliver one of the following messages:
- What's special about being a girl?
- What's exciting about growing up?
- Your definition of beauty.

Perform your skit for other members of your troop or group and Daisy and Brownie Girl Scouts.

2. Interview women of different ages and backgrounds to find out what it was like when they were growing up. Talk to your grandmother, aunt, neighbor, older sister, teacher, mother, or Girl Scout leader. What challenges did they face when they were your age? What were their hopes and dreams? Collect their responses in a journal or on a tape recorder. What similar concerns do you have about growing up? What different concerns?

3. Make a list of some things girls seem to be expected to do. For example, your list might include play with dolls, cook meals, or babysit. Make a second list of things that boys seem to be expected to do such as play with trucks, cut the grass, and play basketball. Share your list with others and discuss how you feel about these things.

4. The definition of beauty has changed over the years. Visit your local library to find books or magazines that were published about 10 years ago, 20 years ago, 30 years ago, and so on. Page through the materials and lay some of the pictures you find next to pictures in current books and magazines. Make a list of the differences you find. Share your list with others.

5. Select one of your interests, talents, or hobbies and create a collage or poster that shows the contributions women have made in this area. Be sure to include women from different time periods and women who made important contributions but are not necessarily famous.

6. Complete the following statement: "I love being a girl because..." Ask some of your friends to do the same and then compare and discuss your lists. Were there any statements that caused disagreement?

7. Some mothers work outside the home and others do not. Talk to at least two women in each group to find out how they manage responsibilities. Think about some things you juggle in your own life like school, family, and friends. Did you learn anything from talking to the group of mothers that will help you manage your own responsibilities?

 Please use extra care when doing activities in numbers 1 and 10.

Complete five activities.

1. Choose three things from the "Maintaining Your Home" list on page 104. In your Girl Scout group or troop or with an adult, demonstrate that you know how to do them.

2. In your Girl Scout troop or group, discuss ways you could help each other manage time. Talk about times when you felt you had too little time to do the things you wanted to do. What could you have done differently?

3. Think of some activities that you can do alone or with friends rather than just "hang out." Look at Chapter Seven, which has lots of different activities, and choose three that look interesting. Try them, and introduce them to your friends.

4. Practice making emergency telephone calls in your troop or group or with an adult. Learn how to give the most important information quickly and how to follow the directions given to you. Look at page 81 for some practice situations. Try making up your own.

5. In your troop or group, discuss the stressful things that can happen to kids and teens. Discuss how to deal with stressful situations.

6. Look at some cigarette and alcohol advertisements. In your troop or group, discuss what messages are being sent and how you can make these ads more realistic.

7. In your troop or group, brainstorm some safety situations that fit into the categories of weather, water, personal safety, fire, and emergency preparedness. Role-play safe ways to act.

8. Create a game about safety using the safety information in Chapter Three. You could make a card game, board game, or a wide game (a game in which you move from station to station acting out or doing different activities).

9. Pick a sport. You could look at the sports on pages 148–150. Create a safety checklist, poster, or booklet for that sport.

10. Prepare a meal that uses foods from each of the categories in the food pyramid. Read the tips on page 95.

Leadership

Complete five activities, including the three that are starred.

1. List some leaders. Do the activity on page 133 and discuss what you find out with another person.

2. Interview someone you consider a leader in your community. Before you meet with her, make a list of questions to ask. Include a question about what she learned from her mistakes. Present what you learned from the interview to your troop or group.

Tips

▲ **Girls Are Great:** Girls Are Great activities help girls explore aspects of being female and are designed to help girls integrate a healthy sense of self. Some activities ask girls to examine their own values and interests in relation to girls and women of today and of the past. Consider suggesting girls link activities in this badge to yearly events, such as Women's History Month.

Program Links

▲ *Girl Scout Badges and Signs:* Becoming a Teen badge; My Self-Esteem badge; Women Today badge; Women's Stories badge

▲ *Girls Are Great: Growing Up Female* Contemporary Issues booklet

▲ *Junior Girl Scout Activity Book:* Chapter Two

Tips

▲ **Healthy Living:** Activities in this badge cover a range of healthy-living aspects. Through these activities girls can learn such skills as home repair, safety, and food preparation. Remind girls to use extra care when doing activities numbers one and ten.

Program Links

▲ *Developing Health and Fitness: Be Your Best!* Contemporary Issues booklet

▲ *Girl Scout Badges and Signs:* Exploring Healthy Eating badge; Health and Fitness badge; Hiker badge; Safety Sense badge; Sports badge; Sports Sampler badge; Walking for Fitness badge

▲ *Junior Girl Scout Activity Book:* Chapter Four

Tips

▲ **Leadership:** Leadership badge activities help empower girls to take on leadership roles. Girls can explore leadership styles, active citizenship, and characteristics of a leadership-in-action project. Earning the leadership badge is the Step Two requirement for the Junior Girl Scout Leadership pin.

Program Links

▲ *Girl Scout Badges and Signs:* Active Citizen badge; Junior Citizen badge

▲ *Junior Girl Scout Activity Book:* Chapter Eight

Notes

*3. Take on a leadership role for three months in your troop, school, or community. Be a leader for a sports team, an art project, a music group, or a computer network. Or, organize a neighborhood service club. Keep a journal of your time spent as a leader.

4. Learn about leadership styles by deciding which style matches each situation in the badge activity on the bottom right of page 135.

5. Discuss ways to avoid stereotypes and sexism when taking on a leadership role. Use the activity in the first column on page 135 as a guide.

6. Read the section on Sidshean O'Brien on page 138 and do the "It's Up to You" activity (see page 138).

*7. Use the chart on page 141 to examine problems in your community. Customize the chart for your school, neighborhood, or community by listing issues and actions that you might take.

*8. Read "Creating a Leadership Action Project" starting on page 142. Plan and carry out a leadership-in-action project to benefit your community.

Looking Your Best

Complete five activities.

 Please use extra care when doing activities in numbers 1, 4, 5, 6, 7, and 8.

1. Mend a piece of your own clothing or ask permission to mend a member of your family's clothing. See pages 101–102 for sewing tips.

2. Put on a fashion show with a theme. You might want to dress for different themes: Fashions for the Outdoors, Fashions for the Future, Fashions for Parties. What other themes can you create?

3. Have a hairstyle party. Try different hairstyles on each other. Look at the ideas on pages 88–89 or look through magazines, talk with older girls or adults, or dream up new hair creations! Remember not to share brushes, combs, and other hair appliances. If you can, take instant pictures or shoot a video of your new styles!

4. Do an aerobic activity at least three times a week, for at least 20 or 30 minutes, with a friend.

Plan on doing different types of activities, so you won't be bored. Walking is a very good exercise. You can play a favorite sport, too, as long as you are moving for at least 20 minutes. Some sports are more aerobic than others. Find out which are the most aerobic.

5. With the help of a trained adult, organize an exercise class for other girls your age. Demonstrate and teach activities that can be used to warm up, work out, and cool down.

6. Look through the sports and outdoor activities in Chapter Seven. Choose two and do them by yourself, with a friend, or with a group.

7. Plan a group health feast. Each person can prepare and bring one healthy food to share. Enjoy!

8. Create a troop or group recipe for a delicious, nutritious snack. Prepare your snack for meetings or trips. Or, create colorful wrappers or packages and sell your snack as a troop money-earning project.

9. Create a "Looking Your Best" booklet, poster, video, or collage that includes the most important tips girls your age need to look their best. Look through Chapter Two for some additional ideas on images of beauty.

10. Investigate what alcohol, drugs, and smoking do to your lungs, skin, and other parts of your body. Share what you learn with others.

Science Discovery

Complete six of the following activities, including the one that is starred.

 Please use extra care when doing activity numbers 3 and 4.

1. Discover surface tension by becoming a bubbleolgist. Do the activities on pages 168–171.

2. Discover how chemical changes can become art or secret writing. Do the chemical appearing act activity on page 163.

3. Discover more about pH by working with an adult to test water in a lake, river, or pool, or by testing soil pH. See page 172.

4. Discover some things about light and reflection by making the kaleidoscope on page 167.

5. Discover how the brain can be challenged or deceived by

learning about optical illusions. Look in books and magazines for puzzles, optical illusions, and after-image art. Try creating your own optical illusions or do the "Hidden Picture" activity on pages 154–155. Explain to your troop or group what you've learned about optical illusions.

6. Do the "Mathematical Moiré" activity on page 155.

7. Discover what's happening in science around you. Using a newspaper, telephone book, or magazine, go on a search for people, places, and things that are science related. As you make your list, you may want to create some categories. (Some examples might be: people—doctor, place—laboratory, things—microscope.) Share your list with others.

8. Share what you know about science discoveries with younger girls. You might use some of the science challenges in this book.

*9. Discover more about science by visiting a hands-on science museum in your area or by participating in a science-activity fair sponsored by your school, Girl Scout council, or service unit. What activities did you enjoy the most?

Talk!

Complete five activities.

1. Carry out a body-language study. See page 70 for more information.

2. Do the public service program activity on page 45.

3. To explore differences in values, try this activity with friends or family. Think about each statement and decide if you agree, disagree, or are not sure. Explain your feelings and listen carefully to what others say.

- Women in the military should have combat duty.
- Everyone should have the right to carry a gun.
- Watching violence on television encourages a person to act violently.
- Money brings happiness.

4. Pretend you are meeting someone for the first time. Think about who that person might be. Tell how you would introduce yourself to her. Talk about what you would say and how you would keep the friendship going. (See page 61.)

200

201

Handbook Page 200

Handbook Page 201

▲ **Looking Your Best:** Looking Your Best badge activities help girls learn about the value of healthy eating, exercise, and body care. Girls need to exercise caution with activities in numbers one, four, five, six, seven, and eight.

Program Links

▲ *Developing Health and Fitness: Be Your Best!* and *Tune In to Well-Being, Say No to Drugs: Substance Abuse* Contemporary Issues booklets

▲ *Girl Scout Badges and Signs:* Becoming a Teen badge; Exploring Healthy Eating badge; Jeweler badge; Sports badge; Sports Sampler badge; Walking for Fitness badge

▲ GSUSA video *Be Your Best!*

Tips

▲ **Science Discovery:** Science Discovery badge activities cover such scientific concepts as optical illusions, surface tension, and chemical change—all presented in the context of fun things to do and observe. Girls get to apply science and math principles when they work on earning this badge.

Program Links

▲ *Girl Scout Badges and Signs:* Any badges in the World of Today and Tomorrow; Communication Arts badge

▲ *Into the World of Today and Tomorrow: Leading Girls to Mathematics, Science, and Technology* and *Earth Matters: A Challenge for Environmental Action* Contemporary Issues booklets

▲ *Junior Girl Scout Activity Book:* Chapter Five

Tips

▲ **Talk!:** Through these activities, girls can explore different ways of communicating. Girls can learn about effective communication techniques and strengthen their own communication skills.

Program Links

▲ *Girl Scout Badges and Signs:* Across Generations badge; Creative Solutions badge; Healthy Relationships badge

▲ *Junior Girl Scout Activity Book:* Chapter Two

Notes

5. Read the situations on pages 72–74 and decide on the best way to respond. Make up your own situations or share a time when you had to choose how to respond.

6. Keeping a journal is a great way to learn about yourself, your values, and your feelings. For the next four weeks, write about what happens to you: a problem you had, a good time you had with a friend, something that upset or disappointed you. Then, reread your journal entries. What have you learned about yourself?

7. Think about a problem you experienced recently with a family member. Maybe you fought with your brother over which television show to watch or argued with your mother over cleaning your room. Review the conflict-resolution steps on page 57 and creative solutions on page 74. Use one of these tools to help work out a family problem.

Wider Opportunities

Complete five activities.

1. Create a brochure listing special places to visit in your community. Visit three or more different tourist attractions and historical sites with friends. Take notes and photos that you can use for your brochure.

2. Organize a travel conference. Each girl picks a state, city, or community she would like to visit and finds out as much as she can through books, magazines, television documentaries, travel agents, people from the area, and people who have traveled to the area. Share this information at the conference.

3. Invite a Cadette or Senior Girl Scout or someone from your Girl Scout council to talk to you and your friends about a wider opportunity. Find out which events and workshops you can attend as a Junior Girl Scout.

4. Learn about wider opportunities offered by

councils to Cadette and Senior Girl Scouts across the country. Ask your Girl Scout leader to bring her copy of *Wider Ops* to a troop meeting. Look through it and decide on three wider opportunities you would like to participate in. Make a list of the requirements, cost, location, and equipment you would need.

5. Find out what information is recorded in a passport. Create your own make-believe passport.

6. Page through *Wider Ops* and select an event that appeals to you. Then, figure out how to travel there by car. Collect road maps and chart out the best route. Estimate the number of miles you will travel.

7. Design a wider opportunity for a group of younger Girl Scouts. Work with other Junior Girl Scouts and Girl Scout leaders to investigate the kinds of wider opportunities younger girls would like and would be able to do. Then plan, research, and carry out an appropriate wider opportunity for a sister Daisy or Brownie Girl Scout troop. Make sure you involve Girl Scout leaders in the activity and that you have all the permissions you need.

You and Your Community

Complete five activities.

1. Create your own community forum on prejudice or another issue affecting your community.

2. Read about cliques on pages 65–66 and do the diary page activity on page 66.

3. Learn not to stereotype. Do the activity on page 126.

4. Survey your meeting place to see how accessible it is to all people. Then, choose a public building in your community and do a survey. Present your findings to your local government.

5. Interview senior citizens to explore the knowledge and history of senior citizens in your family and neighborhood. Create a list of questions about: the history of your community, the changing roles of women, the differences in children's lives from years past to today, or the impact of historical events on community members. Tape-record, write notes, or make a video of your interview. Make

sure to give a copy to the person you interviewed. Share this information with others.

6. Page through books and magazines or scan television programs to find stereotypes. (See pages 126–127 for examples.) Choose an example and show how you would break the stereotype.

7. Find out what services are available for people with disabilities or people in need in your community. Invite someone who works at one of these agencies or organizations to speak to your troop or group.

8. Try to discover all you can about contributions of groups different from your own to your community, county, or state. What did you discover?

Your Outdoor Surroundings

Complete five activities.

 Please use extra care when doing activity numbers 6, 7, and 8.

1. Visit an outdoor store or look through outdoor catalogs. Find out which synthetic and natural materials are best for different

kinds of weather. Investigate the kinds of equipment used in camping and traveling. Discuss if any of the items can be made or found in less expensive forms.

2. Find out about minimal impact on page 180. Discuss the list on that page with your family and friends before going on an outing.

3. Review the list under "Five Ways You Can Help the Environment" on page 181. Add to the list and then commit to doing at least two items. Express your commitment to help the environment by creating a poster or advertisement, for example, for your troop or group meeting.

4. Learn about classification keys on page 166. Use a simple plant key to identify trees at camp or in your community.

5. Be an artist and scientist in the outdoors. Do the "Artist and Scientist" activity on page 161.

6. Learn to use the camp stove and cook a one-pot meal. (See pages 188–189.)

7. Participate in an outdoor activity that can be enjoyed for a lifetime. Learn to ski, swim, golf, photograph nature, backpack, sketch outdoors, bird-watch, or do something else that people of all ages can do.

8. Take a hike! Pick one of the hikes listed on page 182 and plan to go on a hike with your Girl Scout troop or group or family members.

▲ **Wider Opportunities:** Wider Opportunities badge activities will help girls plan, organize, and gather information about trips. Girls can also learn about wider opportunities with nationwide participation which they can apply for as Cadette Girl Scouts.

Program Links

▲ *Girl Scout Badges and Signs:* Girl Scouting Around the World badge; Girl Scouting in the U.S.A. badge; On My Way badge; Traveler badge

▲ *Wider Ops* booklet

▲ **You and Your Community:** You and Your Community badge activities link Girl Scouts to the community in which they live. Activities focus on living with others and learning about groups other than one's own.

Program Links

▲ *Earth Matters: A Challenge for Environmental Action* Contemporary Issues booklet

▲ *Girl Scout Badges and Signs:* Active Citizen badge; Junior Citizen badge; Local Lore badge; My Community badge; The World in My Community badge

▲ *Junior Girl Scout Activity Book:* Chapters Three and Eight

▲ **Your Outdoor Surroundings:** Activities in this badge point girls towards outdoor pursuits. Girls can further their understanding of such concepts as preparation for outdoor living, minimal impact, and environmental conservation. Girls can also learn some outdoor skills through completion of these badge activities. Advise girls to use caution when doing activities in numbers six, seven, and eight.

Program Links

▲ *Earth Matters: A Challenge for Environmental Action* Contemporary Issues booklet

▲ *Girl Scout Badges and Signs:* Any badges in the World of the Out-of-Doors

▲ *Junior Girl Scout Activity Book:* Chapter Six

Notes

Sign of the World

By completing the activities in this sign, you will get to know yourself better, learn more about working with others, and gain skills in taking care of yourself and your environment.

1. Complete two badges from this handbook and one badge from the World of People in *Girl Scout Badges and Signs*.

2. Complete five activities from Chapter Two of this handbook.

3. Complete three activities from Chapter Five of this handbook.

4. Complete four activities from Chapter Three or Four of this handbook.

5. Read about leadership in Chapter Six. Plan and carry out a service project using the action plan outline on pages 142–144.

Junior Girl Scout Leadership Pin

The Junior Girl Scout Leadership pin requires you to participate in experiences that build leadership skills. As you progress through the steps, you will uncover the leader inside of you. The steps should be done in order.

STEP ONE

Read Chapter Six, Leadership in Action, in this book. Look at the Leadership Checklist on page 132 and circle the leadership qualities you feel you already have. Put a box around three qualities you need to develop. Talk to your Girl Scout leader, a parent or guardian, or other adult about ways you can develop these qualities.

What I learned about leadership after reading Chapter Six is:

_____

_____

_____

_____

STEP TWO

Earn the Leadership badge in this book. Describe for your Girl Scout troop or group or others the action project you completed.

Notes on my action project:

_____

_____

_____

_____

_____

STEP THREE

Earn *one* of the four Junior Girl Scout signs: the Sign of the World (described on page 204), the Sign of the Rainbow, the Sign of the Sun, or the Sign of the Satellite.

To earn the Sign of the _____,

I did these activities:

_____

_____

_____

_____

STEP FOUR

Complete a project that demonstrates your leadership skills. You can choose one of the following or develop your own with your Girl Scout leader's guidance.

1. Do a project that helps others. Investigate the services your community offers and volunteer your time. For example, you could volunteer at a food bank or soup kitchen, build some shelves for a homeless shelter, or repair used toys or make new ones to donate. You could tutor a person in math, reading, or another school subject, or coach a sport you play well.

2. Do a project that helps the environment. Ask your Girl Scout leader for the Contemporary Issues booklet *Earth Matters: A Challenge for Environmental Action* to get ideas for environmental action projects, or check with community groups that are working to protect the environment.

3. Do a project that helps people get along better. Read Chapter Five—Everyone Is Different. Then, plan a community forum to fight prejudice. Contact community groups working in this area and volunteer. Or, participate in a school project on mediation or conflict resolution. Or, see what your neighborhood needs and plan a community project.

4. Do a project that shows girls are great. For example, create a video or other display to foster positive attitudes about girls and women.

204

205

Handbook Page 204

Handbook Page 205

▲ **Sign of the World**: Junior Girl Scouts can earn four signs: Sign of the Rainbow, Sign of the Sun, Sign of the Satellite, and Sign of the World. The Sign of the World activities are included here. Activities for the other signs appear in *Girl Scout Badges and Signs.* The Sign of the World includes a service component and covers a variety of worlds of interest. Girls should complete the activities as they earn the Sign of the World. Girls may not substitute past activities to fulfill requirements for this sign.

▲ **Junior Girl Scout Leadership Pin:** Girls who earn the Junior Girl Scout Leadership pin are expected to demonstrate their leadership qualities by earning the Leadership badge, earning one of the signs, and doing a service project. The service project they do to earn the Junior Girl Scout Leadership pin may not be the same as the service project they complete for their Leadership badge or signs.

To earn this recognition girls may need adult help, but must take the primary leadership role in planning and executing all activities. See Chapter Two in Part I of this guide for information about helping girls select and earn their recognitions.

Junior Girl Scouts should be encouraged to work on other projects and recognitions prior to pursuing the Leadership pin. And, earning the Leadership pin should not become the sole focus of your troop or group's activities.

Although there are no strict rules about when a girl can earn her Leadership pin, it is recommended that she wait until her last year as a Junior Girl Scout to earn this recognition. If a girl first joins Girl Scouting in the fifth or sixth grade, and wants to work on the Junior Girl Scout Leadership pin, she will need to explore a variety of Girl Scout activities prior to pursuing this recognition.

On the Junior Girl Scout vest, the Junior Girl Scout Leadership pin will be worn on the right side above the proficiency badges and below the Brownie Girl Scout wings. On the Junior Girl Scout sash, the pin should be placed above the Junior Girl Scout signs and below the Brownie Girl Scout wings.

INDEX